Two Decades of Economic Reforms

Two Decades of Economic Reforms

Towards Faster, Sustainable and More Inclusive Growth

Editor

UMA KAPILA

ACADEMIC FOUNDATION

NEW DELHI

ACADEMIC FOUNDATION

First published in 2012
by

ACADEMIC FOUNDATION
4772-73 / 23 Bharat Ram Road, (23 Ansari Road),
Darya Ganj, New Delhi - 110 002 (India).
Phones : 23245001 / 02 / 03 / 04.
Fax : +91-11-23245005.
E-mail : books@academicfoundation.com
www.academicfoundation.com

Cataloging in Publication Data--DK
Courtesy: D.K. Agencies (P) Ltd. <docinfo@dkagencies.com>

Two decades of economic reforms : towards faster, sustainable and more inclusive growth / editor, Uma Kapila.
p. cm.
ISBN 13: 9788171889419
ISBN 10: 8171889417

1. India--Economic policy--1991- 2. Sustainable development--India. I. Kapila, Uma.

DDC 338.954 23

Typeset by Italics India, New Delhi.
Printed and bound in India.

Dedicated

With admiration and affection, to

DR MANMOHAN SINGH

The architect of India's economic reforms and a true scholar-statesman who has had the most decisive impact on the country in the last 20 years.

Contents

Editor/Contributors

Editor:

Uma Kapila .... *Reader (Rtd.) Department of Economics, Miranda House, University of Delhi; Presently: Senior Editor, Academic Foundation, New Delhi.*

Contributors:

Montek S. Ahluwalia ...... *Deputy Chairman, Planning Commission, New Delhi.*

Kaushik Basu .... *Chief Economic Advisor, Ministry of Finance, Government of India, New Delhi.*

K.C. Chakrabarty .... *Deputy Governor, Reserve Bank of India, Mumbai.*

Bibek Debroy .... *Professor, Centre for Policy Research, New Delhi.*

Subir Gokarn .... *Deputy Governor, Reserve Bank of India, Mumbai.*

Ashok Gulati .... *Chairman, Commission for Agricultural Costs and Prices (CACP), Ministry of Agriculture, Government of India, New Delhi.*

Vijay Kelkar .... *Chairman, India Development Foundation, New Delhi; Formerly: Chairman, Thirteenth Finance Commission.*

Deepak Mohanty .... *Executive Director, Reserve Bank of India, Mumbai.*

Pranab Mukherjee .... *Finance Minister, Ministry of Finance, Government of India, New Delhi.*

N.A. Mujumdar .... *Former Principal Advisor, Reserve Bank of India, Mumbai.*

Arvind Panagariya .... *Jagdish Bhagwati Professor of Indian Political Economy and Professor of Economics, Columbia University, New York.*

C. Rangarajan .... *Chairman, Economic Advisory Council to the Prime Minister, New Delhi; Formerly: Chairman, Twelfth Finance Commission; Ex-Member, Planning Commission, New Delhi.*

C.H. Hanumantha Rao .... *Honorary Professor, Centre for Economic and Social Studies (CESS), Hyderabad; Ex-Chairman, Institute of Economic Growth (IEG), Delhi and Ex-Member, Planning Commission.*

Manmohan Singh .... *Prime Minister of India, New Delhi.*

Anand Sinha .... *Deputy Governor, Reserve Bank of India, Mumbai.*

Duvvuri Subbarao .... *Governor, Reserve Bank of India, Mumbai.*

V.S. Vyas .... *Professor Emeritus and Member Economic Advisory Council to the Prime Minister, New Delhi.*

Preface

'India has travelled through a remarkable journey in the last two decades,' says C. Rangarajan (Chapter 3). The year 1991 is a landmark in the post-independent economic history of India when the country faced a severe economic crisis. The crisis was converted into an opportunity to affect some fundamental changes in the content and approach to economic policy. One year after the structural reforms, we brought out a publication on India's economic reforms entitled: *Recent Developments in Indian Economy with special reference to Structural Reforms* in 1992 followed by six-volume study entitled *Understanding India's Economic Reforms* in 1996. When India completed 10 years of economic reforms, we brought out the publication entitled *A Decade of Economic Reforms* in 2002. In all these volumes I was co-editor with my husband Raj Kapila. It was all his initiative. Now, when India has completed 20 years of economic reforms on July 24, 2011, I was reminded of our earlier publication *A Decade of Economic Reforms* and expressed my desire to work on *Two Decades of Economic Reforms*. This time I had to work alone due to indifferent health of Raj Kapila. However, I received his moral support and encouragement in abundance which kept me going, and hence this volume.

The publication includes contributions from eminent economists and policymakers. I am extremely grateful to Dr Manmohan Singh, Dr C. Rangarajan, Prof Kaushik Basu, Shri Pranab Mukherjee, Dr Ashok Gulati, Dr Bibek Debroy, Prof C.H. Hanumantha Rao, Dr Vijay Kelkar, Prof V.S. Vyas, Dr D. Subbarao, Dr Arvind Panagariya, Dr N.A. Mujumdar, Dr Subir Gokarn, Dr Deepak Mohanty, Dr K.C. Chakrabarty and Dr Anand Sinha whose contributions have made it possible. I owe a debt of gratitude to all of them.

It is indeed very heartening to note that in the earlier publication *A Decade of Economic Reforms*, we have had the privilege of having some common authors like Dr Manmohan Singh, Dr C. Rangarajan, Prof C.H. Hanumantha Rao, Prof V.S. Vyas, Dr Montek Singh Ahluwalia, Dr Vijay Kelkar and Dr Ashok Gulati in addition to several others. I would like to express my gratitude once again to all of them for their continued support and goodwill.

Last but certainly not the least, I wish to express my feelings of love and appreciation to my husband Raj Kapila who has been my inspiration and always stood by me in all my academic pursuits.

I must also acknowledge the tireless efforts of the staff of Academic Foundation for bringing out this volume in a record time.

— Uma Kapila

1 Two Decades of Economic Reforms

Towards Faster, Sustainable and More Inclusive Growth

Uma Kapila

Twenty Years ago, on July 27, 1991, India embarked on its new tryst with destiny when India's finance minister Manmohan Singh wound up his historic union budget speech with what Victor Hugo once said, 'No power on earth can stop an idea whose time has come. I suggest to this august House that the emergence of India as a major economic power in the world happens to be one such idea. Let the whole world hear it loud and clear, India is now wide awake. We shall prevail. We shall overcome'.

The finance minister Manmohan Singh and the Prime Minister P.V. Narasimha Rao believed that the real challenge before India was to ensure its 'emergence as a major economic power of the world'. Power in the modern world was based on the foundation of economic performance. Military power meant little if it was not backed by economic performance. The economic abilities of nations and governments have always been a force to reckon with. It is indeed a welcome initiative that the Ministry of Finance has come out with the Index of Government Economic Power (IGEP). The index has been created for 10 years (2000-2009) covering 112 economies. The IGEP endeavours to capture the ability of a government to project itself in the international sphere. There is also a normative content to this. Since the index shows the extent of charge a government has, it also can be used to determine how much say the government should have in multilateral fora. The index is composed of four variables: government revenues, foreign currency reserves, export of goods and services and human capital. These variables broadly capture a government's ability to raise resources, its creditworthiness and credibility in international financial markets, its influence on global economic activity, and its representational strength, that is how much of the global economy, including global manpower, it can claim to represent (*Economic Survey 2010-11*).

The 2009 results show that the top 10 ranks are occupied by: (1) the United States, (2) China, (3) Japan, (4) Germany, (5) India, (6) Russia, (7) Brazil, (8) France, (9) Italy and (10) the United Kingdom. In 2000, the top 10 places were held by: (1) the United States, (2) Japan, (3) China, (4) Germany, (5) France, (6) the United Kingdom, (7) Italy, (8) Republic of Korea, (9) Canada and (10) India. Among the top ranking economies some of the most dramatic rises in rank have been Brazil's ascent from 13th place in 2000 to 7th in 2009 and India's rise from 10th position in 2000 to 5th in 2009. Japan was replaced by China in the second spot in 2004. The United Kingdom went down from 6th place in 2000 to 10th in 2008 and continued there in 2009. Canada fell from 9th in 2000 to 15th in 2008.

On an analysis of the countries holding the 4th, 9th and 10th positions in 2000 (namely, Germany, Canada and India), India moves from an index value just below Canada in 2000 to one very close to Germany by 2009.

Interestingly, there is a strong positive correlation between the growth in economic power (percentage change in index value between 2000 and 2009) and the change in GDP across the post-crisis period (that is between 2009 and 2010) indicating a link between growth in economic power as measured by the index and the ability to recover from the crisis (*Economic Survey 2010-11*).

Improved economic performance has dramatically altered global perceptions of India's potential. An early recognition of this was a Goldman Sachs report of November 2002, which included India, with Brazil, Russia and China in a new BRIC group of emerging market countries which was predicted to overtake the G-8 in terms of total GDP by 2035. Continued strong performance in the decade of the 2000s and resilience in the face of a global slowdown, has reinforced this positive assessment. The general perception today is that India may now be on the path of sustained high growth based on high rates of domestic savings, high quality of entrepreneurial and managerial skills, and the cumulative effect of economic reforms on productivity (Montek S. Ahluwalia, Chapter 8).

In his K.R. Narayanan Oration (Kelkar, 2004) boldly titled 'India: On the Growth Turnpike'. Vijay Kelkar was clearly among the first to appreciate the breadth and depth of the reforms. The shift to double-digit or even higher growth Kelkar had predicted has so far not come true but something very close to it has happened. India clocked the steady annual growth of 8.5 per cent for six years beginning in 2003-04 and ending in 2008-09. Even during the crisis year of 2008-09, the country could achieve 6.7 per cent growth and recovered in the second quarter of 2009-10 to 7.9 per cent. (Arvind Panagariya, Chapter 4).

The Development Strategy

The development strategy initiated in India in the early post-independence years was focussed on four key elements: (i) an emphasis on the development of basic and heavy industries, (ii) a system of centralised investment planning, (iii) an overarching role for the public sector and (iv) national self-reliance via import-substitution coupled with 'export pessimism'. While there is a tendency now-a-days to underplay the achievements of this 'Nehruvian' development strategy, it cannot be denied that this strategy laid the basis for a modern industrial economy, and kept the macroeconomy on a moderate inflation path in spite of several droughts, international oil price shocks, and at least three major military conflagrations (Nachane, 2011). However, in the late 1960s, the system was stretched in several directions, resulting in a highly bureaucratic and over-regulated economy. Some of the undesirable consequences of this Licence Permit Raj were: (i) a high-cost domestic industry protected from foreign competition via tariffs and quotas, (ii) artificially low nominal interest rates (financial repression) combined with high inflation resulting in extremely low (often negative) real interest rates, in turn contributing to the adoption of undue capital-intensive techniques in manufacturing and (iii) fiscal dominance over monetary policy, leading to a tendency towards fiscal profligacy (Nachane, 2011).

The initial hesitant steps in the direction of liberalisation were taken in the 1980s but the reforms story really begins with the balance of payments crisis of 1991, which forced the country to approach the IMF for assistance. Partly in response to the urging of the IMF and partly owing to the general disillusionment with existing policies that inevitably accompanies a crisis, the government made a distinct historical break with the past and launched an ambitious reforms programme spanning several areas. The crisis was converted into an opportunity to effect some fundamental changes in the content and approach to economic policy, says C. Rangarajan (Chapter 3). Considering that several comprehensive accounts of the reforms measures abound in the literature, we do not go into a detailed recounting of all the measures. Some of the papers, Deepak Mohanty (Chapter 2) and C. Rangarajan (Chapter 3) included in this volume provide a crisp and an uptodate account of the reform measures taken since 1991 relating to industry, infrastructure, external sector, fiscal reforms and financial sector reforms.

Reforms and Growth

The core premise of the reform process initiated in 1991 was that greater competition, both internal and external would help accelerate economic growth. The entire spectrum of reforms, from the abolition of industrial licensing to the sharp reduction in trade barriers and the termination of allocative controls on finance, were intended to simultaneously introduce competitive forces into the economy, while freeing up the choices that producers had in terms of what, where and how to produce. These choices, in turn, could be supported by a financial system that was allowed to make its own risk-return calculations. Although some essential requirements of a truly competitive market economy, notably the elimination of exit barriers, were not introduced with the same degree of enthusiasm, the reforms that were done turned out to have a powerful impact, says Subir Gokarn (Chapter 6).

Judged by many of the externally visible signs, the Indian reforms story has been a remarkable success (Nachane, 2011). As Table 1.1 shows after a long period of stagnation in the years following independence, growth rates shifted into high gear sometime during the 1980s and in the last decade accelerated sharply, reaching undreamt heights (Table 1.2). This growth resurgence has enabled India to move up in the world per capita (PPP-corrected) GDP rankings from 93 (out of a total of 109 countries) in the mid-1970s to 58 by 2004 (Basu and Maertens, 2007). On several other macroeconomic indicators, the country has been doing equally well. Investment as a proportion of GDP, for example, rose from about 10 per cent in the 1950s to about 23 per cent in the early 1980s and is now close to 36 per cent (Rangarajan, Chapter 3). Similarly, India today qualifies as an 'open economy' with exports (as a percentage of GDP) amounting to nearly 20 per cent, as compared to less than 5 per cent in the mid-1960s. And finally on the forex front, we have transited from a perennially shortage situation to one that can only be described as an 'embarrassment of riches' (Nachane, 2011). Inflation, always a serious concern in the Indian context, was sharply reined in, in the late 1990s, and even though it has once again shown signs of strong revival in the last year, it is not clear as to what extent it poses a serious threat to the overall success story. All these trends seem to have generated a great deal of optimism about India's future.

Table 1.1

Growth Rates in India over Successive Plan Periods (1951–2010-11)

Plan Period		*Annual Growth Rate of GDP (Factor Cost) %*	*Average Annual Gross Domestic Capital Formation (as % of GDP at Factor Cost)*
I.	1951-1956	3.6	10.3
II.	1956-1961	4.2	15.4
III.	1961-1966	2.8	15.6
IV.	1969-1974	3.3	17
V.	1974-1979	4.8	20.2
VI.	1980-1985	5.6	21.9
VII.	1985-1990	6.0	25.2
VIII.	1992-1997	6.7	25.4
IX.	1997-2002	5.5	25.9
X.	2002-2007	7.6	27.51
	2005-06	9.5	34.2
	2006-07*	9.6	35.9
	2007-08*	9.3	38.0
	2008-09*	6.8	35.4
	2009-10*	8.0	36.1
	2010-11*	8.6	35.8 (QE)

Source: Basu and Maertens (2007); * Ahluwalia (Chapter 8).

Table 1.2

Growth Rates (%) for Select Countries in Asia, 1981-2008

Country	*1981-1990*	*1991-1997*	*1998-2003*	*2004-2008*
India	5.6 (5.4)	5.3 (5.7	5.7 (5.5)	8.1 (8.3)
China (Mainland)	8.9 (8.8)	10.3 (10.2)	8.0 (7.8)	10.7 (10.5)
China (Hong Kong)	6.3 (6.2)	5.5 (5.3)	2.2 (2.4)	6.1 (6.6)
Singapore	6.9 (7.5)	8.4 (8.2)	2.7 (2.2)	6.5 (7.5)
Bangladesh	3.9 (4.0)	4.5 (4.5)	5.0 (5.0)	6.1 (6.1)
Indonesia	5.3 (5.4)	6.7 (6.8)	4.0 (3.9)	5.6 (5.6)
Korea	8.3 (8.3)	6.7 (6.8)	3.9 (5.4)	4.1 (3.9)
Malaysia	5.8 (6.2)	8.8 (9.0)	2.7 (3.4)	5.6 (5.7)
Thailand	7.6 (7.3)	6.5 (7.6)	4.7 (4.9)	4.6 (4.8)
Pakistan	6.0 (6.0)	4.1 (4.2)	3.5 (3.3)	6.4 (6.3)
Sri Lanka	4.2 (4.3)	5.1 (5.1)	3.8 (4.6)	6.3 (6.3)

Source: International Financial Statistics, IMF.

Note: The figures in brackets represent the winsorized growth rates (i.e., calculated by omitting the highest and lowest observations over each sub-period).

Narrating India's growth story (Chapter 5), RBI Governor D. Subbarao remarks, for a nation that once believed that the Hindu rate of growth was its destiny, the average annual growth performance of 9 per cent in the five-year period (2003-2008) was certainly a cause for celebration. However, the India growth story was thrown off track by the global financial crisis which engulfed virtually every country in the world. Although we recovered from the crisis sooner than other countries, but the growth rate is yet to reach the pre-crisis level. A number of questions are being asked. Is our growth story faltering? Has India's potential growth rate declined because of the crisis? Are the growth drivers that worked our way still intact? When will we reach double digit growth, and what indeed should be done to achieve that? To quote Subbarao, 'my simple and single answer to all of the above questions is that the India growth story is still credible. If the East Asians are the tigers, and China the dragon, India is commonly "the elephant"—a strong animal with enormous potential but given to a lumbering pace. For a world that once believed that an elephant does not have any animal spirit, our march up the high growth trajectory proved that an elephant too can dance. But the elephant dance got interrupted by the "zoo party" of the global financial crisis, and to get it back on course, we need to rejig the dance.' For India to regain its growth momentum and indeed accelerate it further, we need to address several challenges and according to Subbarao there are 10 most important challenges that we need to address to move up the growth ladder (Subbarao, Chapter 5).

According to C. Rangarajan (Chapter 3), the broad macroeconomic parameters relating to savings and investment are conducive to achieving a growth rate of 8 to 9 per cent in a sustained way. This, however, is the potential and to achieve it we must also take actions to remove constraints that may come in the way like taming inflation, reducing current account deficit around the manageable level of 2.5 per cent of GDP and fiscal consolidation.

Practically all the papers on economic reforms have looked into the impact of reforms on growth and how do we ensure faster and sustained growth in the future.

Sustainable and More Inclusive Growth

As very rightly remarked by Prime Minister Dr Manmohan Singh, 'of course, growth has never been our sole objective. Our aim has always been inclusive growth, by which we mean growth which ensures a broad spread of benefits to all sections of our population, particularly the scheduled castes, the scheduled tribes, the other backward castes and other marginalised groups and also protects the environment. A criticism often advanced is that while we have delivered high growth, we have not done nearly as well on inclusiveness. I believe there is some truth in this criticism, in the sense that we should have done better. However, it is not true to say that progress on this front has not been significant.' (Chapter 9)

According to Montek Singh Ahluwalia (Chapter 8), it is more difficult to assess performance on inclusiveness than on growth for certain reasons aptly discussed and a summary of what has been achieved on this front is well documented in the chapter.

An important aspect of our performance which is relevant for inclusiveness is agricultural growth, which had decelerated to an average 2.2 per cent per year in the Tenth Plan and is likely to clock 3.5 per cent in the Eleventh Five Year Plan. Chapters 14 and 15 are devoted to this most important subject. V.S. Vyas has looked into the challenge of transforming

Indian agriculture providing a vision of dynamic agriculture. 'A strong agriculture sector is necessary for our food and nutritional security and for the welfare and well-being of our population that is still engaged in farming. Indeed without providing livelihood security to the farmers we can not achieve the goal of inclusive growth in its true sense' (Manmohan Singh, 2012).

Indian agriculture is facing a serious crisis, evident in falling share of agriculture in GDP with little decline in the workforce depending on agriculture; progressive diminution of agriculture holdings and impoverishment of large majority of farmers who can not make two ends meet with their agriculture income, says V.S. Vyas (Chapter 14). We have to relate policies, programmes and delivery systems to the reality of a small farm dominated agrarian structure on the one hand, and changing demand pattern for agricultural produce on the other. Then alone we will be able to face the challenge of transforming a stagnant and impoverishing agriculture to a just, efficient and dynamic sector.

First green revolution was initiated and sustained by medium and large farmers. With appropriate supportive actions, the next revolution can be ushered in by the small farmers. And that will be the just and sustainable transformation.

Ashok Gulati also echos the same sentiments, 'But one thing needs to be made clear to our policymakers: unless the agri-sector takes off to a four per cent plus growth trajectory, the chances of reducing poverty in any significant manner and within a short timeframe will remain dim, no matter how many freebies are doled out. The approach paper to the coming Twelfth Five Year Plan (2012-2017) itself recognises that a one per cent growth emanating from the agriculture sector would be at least two to three times more effective in reducing poverty than the same growth coming from non-agriculture sectors' (Chapter 15).

Economic Sustainability of Reforms

We now look to a longer-term perspective on the sustainability of the general strategy of development adopted in the post-reforms period, which has been based on the cardinal principles of marketisation, export orientation, domestic and external financial liberalisation, and a host of industrial policies aimed at encouraging large foreign and domestic investments in manufacturing, services and infrastructure.

Perhaps the biggest revolution in the independent India has been the rise of the Great Indian Middle Class, a process that accelerated dramatically after Dr Manmohan Singh ushered in economic reforms two decades ago. This middle class, in turn, is leading its own set of revolutions in different fields. Even in the economic field, the rise of the middle class has meant that for the first time since independence, India is getting a market (for products such as mobile phones) that is big enough to allow companies that are truly global in scale to operate. Hence, the rise of the Indian multinational.

Though the rich obviously have a higher propensity to consume, the larger number of the middle class means it is far greater in significance when it comes to economic clout. Nearly 49 per cent of all cars are owned by the middle class, compared with just 7 per cent by the rich. Similarly, 53 per cent of all air conditioners are owned by middle-class homes. Nearly 46 per cent of all credit cards are to be found in middle-class households. Given this, and the way the middle class is likely to rise, its growing clout is hardly surprising. 'The rise of a growing middle class not only represents an important welfare gain, but also an important social development, with potentially large positive effects in terms of expectations, values and a rising demand for better and more accountable government' (Ahluwalia, Chapter 8).

Global macroeconomic imbalances are at the heart of destabilising sustainable economic growth at the international level. All imbalances are not bad as some of them reflect multi-paced growth, different savings-investment behaviour and productivity levels across economies. Such differences may not be destabilising per se. At the same time, some imbalances reflect structural inefficiencies usually created by policy distortions relating to the external sector, trade, capital flows and exchange rate policies, financial markets, tax and subsidy regimes, which have to be addressed.

The reform of the International monetary system is high on the agenda of the G-20 and various issues including capital flows management, financial safety nets, measuring global liquidity, composition of the SDR basket are currently under discussion (Pranab Mukherjee, Chapter 13).

Regarding the issue of economic sustainability one has to examine the sources of economic growth and the sectoral composition of this growth. In particular, it is necessary to discuss the oft-posed question as to whether services-led growth can be sustainable. Special sectoral problems in the agricultural and manufacturing sectors can also impinge significantly on the issue of sustainability. Financial sector reforms, their pace and design also crucially impinges on the overall issue of long-term price and financial stability. Finally, external sector imbalances can seriously threaten economic and political stability.

Sources of Economic Growth

Most studies seem to explain the high growth momentum via the twin factors of: (i) a shift in resources towards the services sector and (ii) the relatively faster total factor productivity (TFP) growth in services as compared to manufacturing and agriculture (Nachane, 2011).

Services Sector

One of the most remarkable features of India's recent growth experience relates to the spectacular showing by its services sector. During the last decade and a half (1995-96 to 2009-10), this sector has recorded an average annual rate of growth of 7.55 per cent much in excess of those recorded in the agricultural sector (2.6%) and the industrial sector (5.6%). Today, the share of the services sector in India's GDP is around 64 per cent with much of this increase being at the expense of the agriculture sector's share. There is diverse opinion on the long term prospects of service-led growth. The criticism against service-led growth focuses on three special aspects of services growth: (i) its dependence on growth in the other sectors especially manufacturing; (ii) its low employment potential and (iii) its concentration in a few selected sub-sectors (construction, hotels and restaurants, communication, finance, insurance, real estate and business services) RBI report finds substantial forward linkages of the services sector with the rest of the economy, though the backward linkages are weak for agriculture and only moderate for the industrial sector. The strong forward linkages reflect the crucial dependence of sustained growth in the services sector on the rest of the economy especially manufacturing. OECD (2010) however holds a contrary view that it is manufacturing activity that flows to countries with adequate services infrastructure.

Agricultural Sector

That high growth rates of overall GDP, such as witnessed in the last decade, can only be secured by a robust agricultural sector, has been recognised by successive Indian governments since Independence. In recent years, a 4 per cent growth rate target for agriculture has been repeatedly affirmed but could not be achieved in all Plan documents since the Ninth Plan.

By now, it is almost certain that the agri-GDP growth for this ongoing Eleventh Five Year Plan (2007-2012) will remain around 3.2 per cent, way below the targetted growth rate of 4 per cent per annum. This is not the first time that the achievement will be short of the target by a full 20 per cent; in the last five year plan (2002-2007), the situation was even worse when the actual agri-GDP growth was only 2.4 per cent against a target of 4 per cent, and almost similar to the performance (2.5%) in the plan even before that (1997-2002). This repeated failure to achieve a modest target of 4 per cent, plan after plan, speaks volumes of the hollowness in our policy making process, which either does not understand what drives growth in agriculture, or does not know how to design policies that can work towards attaining that target, or does not have the political will to do so (Gulati, Chapter 15).

Industrial Sector

Industrial liberalisation in India has proceeded via two routes *viz.*, deregulation (relaxation of licensing and investment restrictions) and disinvestment in public sector enterprises (PSEs), that is, selling of government stakes usually between 1 to 49 per cent. In the pre-reform period, 18 industries were reserved exclusively for the public sector, which has now been brought down to two namely atomic energy and railways. At present only five industries are under licensing mainly on account of environment, health, safety and strategic considerations. Similarly, the list of 800 items reserved exclusively for the small-scale sector has been progressively pruned to 20 currently (Mohanty, Chapter 2). Two of the cardinal points of industrial policy in the pre-reforms era had been the Monopolies and Restrictive Trade Practices (MRTP) Act 1969 (which subjected investment by large industrial houses to several restrictive provisions) and the Foreign Exchange Regulation Act (FERA) 1973 (which imposed strict limits on foreign exchange transactions on the current as well as capital account). Both now stand replaced by much more liberal versions *viz.*, the Competition Act 2002 and the Foreign Exchange Management Act (FEMA) 1999. Further, several liberalisation measures for attracting foreign direct investment (FDI) were introduced in the wake of the reforms in 1991, while foreign portfolio investment (FPI) was also selectively liberalised from 1995-96 onwards.

There has been a great deal of discussion in recent years regarding the long-term structural constraints on manufacturing growth. While there is a near unanimity about the constraints posed by transport and power supply bottlenecks, the role of other factors is not clear. One issue in particular, which is extremely contentious, is the role of labour market reforms.

Public *versus* Private Ownership

The interesting and important question that we should all be asking ourselves is: what should the portfolio composition of the government be? What assets should be held by the state? We need to think about this question, and once we have a consensus and clarity about what the portfolio composition ought to be, we should embark on a set of adjustments that take us to a different, and hopefully better, asset composition (Vijay Kelkar, Chapter 16).

Infrastructure

In a comprehensive sense, infrastructure includes both physical and social infrastructure. Physical infrastructure is being viewed as a critical binding constraint on growth and hence a determinant of economic sustainability, while social infrastructure, an equally important long-term determinant of economic and social sustainability.

Physical Infrastructure

The Indian (physical) infrastructure sector suffers from a huge backlog, in part inherited from the pre-reform years, when the typical approach *vis-à-vis* infrastructure was a bottleneck approach, that is, one in which specific bottlenecks were identified and sought to be removed as and when they started cutting into the growth process. What was essentially missing was a forward looking approach in which infrastructure was built up ahead of projected demand. The strategy of the current government (especially since 2004) is that of forward looking approach to the infrastructure sector.

The task on the physical infrastructure front is daunting, to say the least (Bibek Debroy, Chapter 10). At a modest estimate, if the Indian growth rate is to be maintained around the targetted rate of 9 per cent, then the investment in physical infrastructure will have to be stepped up from its modest level of 5 per cent of GDP (as obtains now) to a figure comparable to that of China, which currently invests about 9 per cent of its GDP in infrastructure. The Deepak Parekh Committee Report (Ministry of Finance, 2007), estimated an investment of US $320 billion (at 2005-06) prices for maintaining growth rates around a high of 9 per cent or so. The Committee stresses the public-private partnership (PPP) model as the most suitable for generation of funds on this scale, with a major role assigned to foreign institutional investors (FIIs).

Compared to other developing countries, India has been slow to urbanise, but the pace of urbanisation is expected to accelerate over the next two decades. The 2011 Census also shows an increase in the urban population from 27.8 per cent in 2001 to 31.2 per cent in 2011, and it is likely to exceed 40.0 per cent by 2030. This would generate a heavy demand for better quality infrastructure in urban areas, especially water, sewerage, public transport and low cost housing. Since it takes time to create urban infrastructure, it is necessary to have a sufficiently long-term focus on urban planning in the Twelfth Plan.

The Twelfth Plan must continue the thrust on accelerating the pace of investment in infrastructure, as this is critical for sustaining and accelerating growth. Public investment in infrastructure will have to bear a large part of the infrastructure needs in backward and remote areas to improve connectivity and expand the much needed public services. Since resource constraints will continue to limit public investment in infrastructure in other areas, PPP-based development needs to be encouraged wherever feasible. It is necessary to review the factors which may be constraining private investment, and take steps to rectify them. PPP, with appropriate regulation and concern for equity, should also be encouraged in the social sectors, such as health and education. Several State Governments are already taking steps in this direction (Planning Commission, 2011).

However, there is one aspect of infrastructure, which can be termed as an Indian success story *viz.*, the telecom sector. This sector is almost playing the role of what some of the neo-Schumpeterian growth theories call a general purpose technology (GPT) (Nachane, 2011).

For coming decades, water, environment and urban infrastructure are going to be the key binding constraints on India's growth ambition. To remove these binding constraints, we will require large investments to accelerate the country's march towards high quality growth. Disinvestment and privatisation policy has now assumed strategic importance in our country. The portfolio composition of the state is not something that should remain static at all times. (Kelkar, Chapter 16).

Financial Sector Reforms and Macroeconomic Stability

In India, financial liberalisation has proceeded apace with considerable impetus since the 1990s and the financial sector roadmap has been extensively redrawn. Financial liberalisation was viewed as an integral component of overall liberalisation, in the twin beliefs that: (i) liberalisation in the real sector could not proceed satisfactorily in the absence of financial liberalisation and (ii) financial liberalisation was an 'enabling condition' of faster economic growth, as it increases competition, transfer of know-how, and transparency. However, it is becoming increasingly clear that financial liberalisation is at best a double-edged weapon. On the one hand, there does seem to exist a positive association between financial liberalisation, savings (domestic plus foreign) investment and growth (though the causal nexus seems to run both ways). On the other hand, financial liberalisation poses several problems for monetary and fiscal policy and increases the vulnerability of developing economies to banking and currency crises.

Chapter 18 (D. Subbarao) and Chapter 19 (Anand Sinha) discuss monetary policy dilemmas and reforms in the banking sector respectively.

External Sector Liberalisation

One of the key pillars of reforms has been the extensive liberalisation of international trade and investment. As a result of these measures, India's share in world exports of goods and services rose from about 1 per cent in 1990 to about 4 per cent in 2007, with the share of exports in GDP rising from 19 per cent to 49 over the same period. But apart from the rapid rise in exports (as well as imports), there has also been a marked rise in trade diversification. However, from a long-term point of view certain constraints are becoming evident. First, the stagnation in the WTO Doha Round has meant that certain measures considered very crucial from the developing world point of view, such as the special safeguard measures in agriculture, are not making headway. Second, in the aftermath of the recent global crisis there has been a strong revival of protectionist sentiments in the developed world (in spite of the impressive rhetoric to the contrary at the successive G-20 Summits). Finally, in the Indian context the absence of a strong trade facilitating infrastructure is increasingly emerging as a binding constraint (Nachane, 2011).

Issues of Social Sustainability

If growth is not broad-based, if it has little impact on poverty, and if the benefits of growth are increasingly cornered by a very small section of the population, the consequent social tensions and political instability will inevitably frustrate the growth process. This brings us to the second dimension of sustainability *viz.*, social sustainability. For economic growth to be socially sustainable concrete results need to be evident in terms of poverty reduction as well as moderation of interpersonal and interregional inequality. Poverty and inequality are distinct but highly interconnected phenomena, whose incidence is an outcome of the general growth strategy adopted and its implications for wage levels and unemployment, as well as the specific policy interventions for prompting social infrastructure and financial inclusion.

Progress in Reducing Poverty

Reducing poverty is a key element in our inclusive growth strategy. There has been considerable dispute in this country in estimating the people below the poverty line. There is no consensus yet on what constitutes the poverty line. According to the methodology adopted by the Planning Commission until recently, the number of people below poverty line in 1993-94 was 36.0 per cent. According to the same methodology, it came down to 27.5 per cent in 2004-05. However, the Tendulkar Committee by adopting a slightly different methodology came to the conclusion that the overall poverty ratio was 45.3 per cent in 1993-94 and 37.2 per cent in 2004-05. While the Tendulkar Committee estimates are higher than the earlier estimates, both methodologies show that the reduction in the poverty ratio was in the range of 8 to 8.5 per cent. While growth has contributed to reducing the poverty ratio, it has to be acknowledged that the absolute level of poverty is still high. Truly we have miles to go before eliminating poverty. We need to ensure that the growth process is such as to include every section of the economy. We must maintain, nevertheless, a high growth rate which will alone enable the government to raise the resources to meet the various socioeconomic obligations.

The Eleventh Plan had set a more ambitious target of achieving a decline in poverty ratio of two percentage points per year. While the actual performance in this regard was below this target, it was better than it was in the earlier decade. A summary assessment is that the pace of poverty reduction has accelerated, though it may still be short of the target. Nevertheless, it is heartening to note that looking ahead; India is well poised to meet the Millennium Development Goal (MDG) target of 50 per cent reduction of poverty between 1990 and 2015 (Planning Commission, 2011).

One critical parameter to examine the degree of inclusiveness is to see what has happened to the real farm wages in the rural areas. The largest numbers of poor, primarily landless workers, are in rural areas and the majority of them still rely on farm work for their livelihood. It is comforting to see that during the period 2007-2010 (calendar years), the average real wage rates increased by 16.0 per cent at the all-India level. The growth was the fastest in Andhra Pradesh (42%) and Orissa (33%). Even in states like Bihar and Uttar Pradesh, real farm wages went up by 19 and 20 per cent respectively, over the three-year period (Planning Commission, 2011).

Employment and Livelihood

For growth to be inclusive it must create adequate livelihood opportunities and add to decent employment commensurate with the expectations of a growing labour force. India's young age structure offers a potential demographic dividend for growth, but this potential will be realised only if the extent and quality of education and skill development among new entrants to the workforce is greatly enhanced. One of the most remarkable things brought out by the 66th Round of NSSO survey on Employment (2009-10) is that the number of young people in education, and therefore, out of the workforce, has increased dramatically causing a drop in the labour participation rate. The total number of young working-age (15-24) people who continued in educational institutions doubled from about 30 million in 2004-05 to over 60 million in 2009-10 (Planning Commission, 2011).

The survey also shows that between 2004-05 and 2009-10, the overall labour force expanded by only 11.7 million. This was considerably lower than comparable periods earlier, and can be attributed to the much larger retention of youth in education, and also because of lower labour force participation among working-age women. Over the same period, 18 million job opportunities were created on current daily status basis. Thus, in absolute terms, unemployment came down by 6.3 million; and the unemployment rate which had increased from 6.06 per cent in 1993-94 to 7.31 per cent in 1999-2000 and further to 8.28 per cent in 2004-05, came down to 6.60 in 2009-10 (Planning Commission, 2011).

There is an influential strand of thinking (Panagariya, 2008) that locates the source of the employment problem in India in the labour market rigidities and the various legislations effected in the past to safeguard workers' interests (such as the Minimum Wages Act, Contract Labour Act, Industrial Disputes Act, etc.). It is argued that such safeguards (which typically apply for enterprises above a threshold scale and mainly in the organised sector) act as a disincentive for exploiting scale economies. Further by pushing up labour costs they discourage the use of labour-intensive techniques.

A laudable policy initiative to meet the unemployment problem headlong has been the introduction of the Mahatma Gandhi National Rural Employment Guarantee Scheme (MGNREGS for short) in February 2006. This ambitious scheme is addressed to guaranteeing a minimum of 100 days of wage employment every year to all rural households on asset creation projects. In spite of several shortcomings which have emerged in the operationalisation of the scheme, overall the initiative merits praise for making a significant dent in the rural underemployment problem.

Inequality and Interregional Disparities

One important feature of growth which is relevant for inclusiveness is balanced regional development.

As India has moved on to the growth turnpike, accelerated growth has reached every single state. On the poverty front, all states have seen the rate of poverty decline between 1993-94 and 2004-05 largely representing the post-reform period (Panagariya, Chapter 4).

An important aspect of this impressive growth story is the phenomenal growth some of the poorest states have experienced in recent years. Three of the bottom six states among the larger states have grown 8 per cent or more annually during 2003-04 to 2008-09. Rajasthan and Orissa have grown 9.4 per cent each and Bihar 8.4 per cent. Likewise, all three of the newest states, which were carved out of three of the poorest four larger states have grown at rates exceeding 9 per cent. (Panagariya, Chapter 4).

According to Rangarajan (Chapter 3), comparing the periods of 1993-1994 to 1999-2000 and 1999-2000 to 2008-09, there is a strong evidence of 'catching up' by the lower income states. The median growth rate increased one-and-a-half times between the two periods, increasing from 3.9 per cent in the earlier period to 5.7 per cent in the latter period. States with lower per capita GSDP like Assam, Orissa, Uttar Pradesh and Bihar have made significant gains in growth rates in the latter period. Notwithstanding these gains, convergence was subdued because some of the higher income states like Gujarat, Kerala and Haryana also posted high growth rates. In other words, what the recent data indicate is that while most of the lower income states have shown stronger growth rates, several of the higher income states have also shown an increase in the recent period.

According to C.H. Hanumantha Rao (Chapter 11), sociopolitical factors play a decisive role in determining the rate of growth of an economy, regional disparities in growth, and how the benefits from growth are distributed between different social and income groups. This works through their impact on the mobilisation of resources and their allocation to different sectors and schemes as well as on the effectiveness with which the schemes formulated are implemented.

Rising income inequalities, dispossession, loss of traditional livelihoods, inadequate measures for compensation, rehabilitation and resettlement, and emerging social tensions forced both India and China to attempt a course correction in their policies, surprisingly around the same period, in the formulation of their respective Eleventh Five Year Plans. India's Eleventh Plan (2007-2012) promised 'Faster and Inclusive Growth' through 'reforms with human face', and China's Eleventh Plan (2006-2010) came out with the objective of 'Building Harmonious Society' by 'putting people first'. Unlike in India where the multi-party system with a parliamentary democracy can force a change in the policy framework relatively quickly in response to the emerging unrest, the delayed response to the discontent in China could well be attributed to its political system which assigns a pre-eminent place to a single party.

The emergence of inequalities is often a consequence of high growth owing to the differential comparative advantages experienced by different regions arising from geographical and other locational factors, and to the interpersonal differences in access to education, skills and resources. An analysis of income inequalities in China concludes that the 'most important factors explaining overall inequality are differential returns to schooling and sector of employment...investing in people, in particular improving education service in lagging areas to poor people are important for sustainable growth and equitable distribution in the long-run' (Luo and Zhu, 2008). Neglect of the development of education and skills in the lagging regions and sectors and among the poor is traceable to the biases in decision-making regarding the allocation of resources and other measures. The sensitivity and resilience of the prevailing political system to take timely corrective measures could make a big difference to the degree of inequalities and mass deprivation.

The basic goal has to be the political and economic empowerment of the disadvantaged sections whether by caste, religion, gender or regions. A two-pronged strategy to address the problem is called for: first, 'social and economic empowerment' of the excluded groups by improving ownership of capital assets like land and business, and education and skills; and second, providing 'equal opportunity' for them through legal safeguards, reservations and similar measures in public as well as private sectors, and by ensuring adequate participation in governance at various levels through broadening and deepening of the working of our democracy by effectively extending it to the grassroots. Achieving equity through such measures will not only restore self-esteem and confidence among the socio-economically disadvantaged sections, but also improve the overall efficiency of the economic system and ensure the sustainability of growth momentum by tapping the vast underutilised human potential (Thorat and Newman, 2009) (Rao, Chapter 11).

Social Infrastructure

The crucial importance of social infrastructure in determining the social sustainability of the reforms momentum is now universally recognised. The two most important dimensions to social infrastructure are education and health.

Education

The Eleventh Plan had articulated the need for expanding educational facilities and improving quality of education, as key instruments for achieving faster and inclusive growth. There has been notable success in expanding capacity, but the challenge of improved quality still persists.

In particular, the passage of the Right of Children to Free and Compulsory Education Act 2009 is widely regarded as a landmark achievement. A major achievement is that most children are now in school. The ASER 2010 report shows that for the age group 6–14 years in all of rural India, the per centage of children who are not enrolled in school has dropped from 6.6 per cent in 2005 to 3.5 per cent in 2010. The proportion of girls in the age group 11–14 years who were out of school has also declined from 11.2 per cent in 2005 to 5.9 per cent in 2010. However, the absolute numbers of children who are out of school remains large. While this needs to be reduced, it is not unreasonable to state that access is now more or less universalised. We now confront the greater challenge of improving the quality of school education.

The problems ailing the education sector are not located in resource allocation alone, though resources to this sector have always been some kind of a residual and subordinate charge on both the Central and state governments' expenditure commitments. The total expenditure on education as a proportion of GDP which has in recent years been about 3.5 per cent of GDP is only slightly more than half the norm (6 per cent of GDP) suggested by the Kothari Commission nearly half a century ago.

Health

The situation on the other major dimension of social infrastructure *viz.*, health is even more dismal.

The Eleventh Plan had drawn attention to the fact that India's health outcome indicators continue to be weaker than they should be, at our level of development. The Plan had therefore expressed the necessity of allocating additional resources to health and laid down monitorable targets for parameters relating to Infant mortality rate (IMR), maternal mortality rate (MMR), institutionalised delivery, extent of full immunisation, etc. Data on these parameters, available for the first three years of the Eleventh Plan, show some improvement. The IMR fell from 57.0 per cent in 2006 to 50.0 per cent in 2009. The percentage of deliveries in institutions increased from 54.0 per cent in 2006 to 73 per cent in 2009, while the MMR came down by 32 points to 212 (2007-09). These are marked improvements but their rate of decline is lower than what is needed for achieving the desired targets.

In the Eleventh Plan, the total public expenditure on health in India by Centre and the states was less than 1.0 per cent of GDP and it needs to be increased substantially.

Environmental Sustainability

The third dimension of sustainability (ecological) is critically dependent on whether sufficient attention is paid in the development process to long-term issues such as energy, environment, and natural resources. In India, energy has already emerged as a significant bottleneck to the official targets of a high and inclusive growth. The successful overcoming of this bottleneck would require massive investments in both the energy as well as the transport sectors. An important fallout of global climate change is the likelihood of increasing recurrence of natural disasters whose severity is often aggravated by corruption and other governance failures.

Governance and Corruption

According to Rangarajan one issue that is critically important cutting across all sectors is governance. That good governance is at the very heart of economic growth and poverty reduction, and even political legitimacy, is now part of conventional wisdom (Chapter 3).

Apart from these issues, there is a wider set of issues related to the reforms process such as corruption, the degree of 'autonomy' of domestic policy, the freedom of the press from vested interests, and the quality of public opinion and sociopolitical unrest. While it has not been possible to cover these issues in this volume, the subject of corruption has been taken up in some papers.

We got Independence in 1947, economic independence in 1991 and in 2011 people have realised that if you want both political and economic independence, you also need a corruption-free state.

Kaushik Basu puts forward a new idea for the control of one kind of corruption namely bribery, in India: 'in describing this as "new", I am aware that as a research idea it is sufficiently obvious not to be thought of as novel. It constitutes a standard exercise of backward-induction reasoning in two-period games. Yet, in the world of policymaking this kind of analysis is new—this became more evident by the angry reaction to the original version that I made available on the web—and I am convinced that this kind of "law and economics" analysis needs to be used in conjunction with civil society activism, if we really want to control corruption and do so in ways that are morally acceptable.' (Basu, Chapter 12).

I feel tempted to quote Basu again 'if we want to really get at corruption, what we need to build up are values of honesty and integrity in society. In the language of the *Arthashastra,* we have to wean fish off water. This has received so little attention and even to make such an argument sounds like moral claptrap because mainstream economics has taught us that human beings are endlessly self-seeking. In truth, they are not. Honesty, pro-social preferences and a sense of right and wrong constitute a part of the human psyche (Hauser, 2006), even though we can create societies where such traits are barely visible. It is possible to go further and argue that we cannot have an efficient market economy unless human beings are endowed with a minimal amount of integrity and pro-sociality. Because of the propensity of economics to ignore these traits, these are under-researched areas. But if we want to substantially cut down the incidence of corruption, such as bribery, and want an efficient and vibrant economy, alongside getting our laws and economic policies right, we need to work on building up appropriate social and cultural traits, which provide the foundations for such an economy.'

Conclusion

In conclusion, one may say that the reforms strategy, which seemed to be on a gradual track in the early years of the reforms process (1991-1996), was suddenly shifted into high gear around 1996 with a distinct thrust in favour of large-scale industry and foreign investment. Since 2005, however, the government seems to be seriously concerned with the 'human face' aspects of the reforms and has initiated a number of laudable initiatives (Mujumdar, Chapter 7). But clearly far more needs to be done on this front. To quote Prime Minister Dr Manmohan Singh 'Our biggest challenge today remains that of banishing poverty, ignorance and disease. As I look ahead I see five key challenges facing the nation: challenge of (i) livelihood security (ii) economic security (iii) energy security (iv) ecological security and (v) national security. In addressing each of these five challenges we must work together as a nation, while working with like-minded nations around the world' (Chapter 20).

'A new wave of democracy demanding the empowerment of ordinary people is sweeping the world and India stands tall as a functioning democracy. We are a nation of over a billion people, plural, secular, democratic—with all the great religions of the world freely practiced here, with so many languages and cuisines, so many castes and communities—living together in an open society. This is an achievement for which every Indian can be proud.'

'The world acknowledges this achievement. I do believe that the world wants India to succeed because India offers hope. The world is watching India with great interest. The world has a stake in India's success because a peaceful prosperous democratic India is a stabilising force in the world. Let us show the world that democratic India is capable of building a prosperous, inclusive, secular and plural nation on the path of sustainable growth (Manmohan Singh, Chapter 9).

References

Acharya, Shankar and Rakesh Mohan (eds.) (2010). *India's Economy Performance and Challenges*. New Delhi: Oxford University Press.

Basu, Kaushik (ed.) (2004). *India's Emerging Economy: Performance and Prospects in the 1990s and Beyond*. New Delhi: Oxford University Press.

Basu, K. and A. Maertens (2007). "The Pattern and Causes of Economic Growth in India", *Oxford Review of Economic Policy* 23(2): 143-67.

Government of India (2011). *Economic Survey 2010-11.*

Kapila, Raj and Uma Kapila (2002). *A Decade of Economic Reforms in India: The Past, The Present and the Future*. New Delhi: Academic Foundation.

Kapila, Uma (ed.) (2011). *Indian Economy Since Independence*, 22nd Edition. New Delhi: Academic Foundation.

Kochhar, Sameer and Ramachandran (2010). *Building from the Bottom*. New Delhi: Academic Foundation.

Mujumdar, N.A. (2011). *India's New Development Agenda: Building a Value-based Society*. New Delhi: Academic Foundation.

Nachane, D.M. (2011). *India Development Report 2011*. Indira Gandhi Institute of Development Research. Mumbai: Oxford University Press.

OECD (2011). *OECD Economic Survey of India*, June. New Delhi: Academic Foundation.

Panagariya, Arvind (2008). *India the Emerging Giant*. New Delhi: Oxford University Press.

Planning Commission (2011). *Approach to the Twelfth Five Year Plan*.

Reserve Bank of India (2010). *Annual Report 2010.*

Singh, Manmohan (2012). *PM's Speech of the Workshop on Agriculture* at Rashtrapati Bhawan, February 15.

2 Indian Economy

Progress and Prospects

Deepak Mohanty

India is home to 1.21 billion people, which is about 17.4 per cent of the global population. However, it accounts for only 2.4 per cent of world GDP in US dollar terms and 5.5 per cent in purchasing power parity (ppp) terms. Hence, there exists a huge potential for catch up. The global welfare too is linked to progress in India as reflected in the keen global interest in India. But, India seems to inspire and disappoint at the same time. This is reflected in various comments on the Indian economy. Yasheng Huang and Tarun Khanna in their much debated article in July 2003 issue of Foreign Policy had observed: '"Can India Surpass China?". This is no longer a silly question.' The July 23rd 2011 issue of The Economist observed, 'Twenty years ago they said the yardstick against which India should be measured was its potential. On that measure, there is much to do.'

As a fledgling democracy, India's economic experiment of planned development was held out as an example to many aspiring low-income countries in the 1950s. While some countries raced ahead in the development process, India lagged behind. This is evident from the fact that it took 40 long years from 1950-51 for India's real per capita GDP to double by 1990-91. But, 1991-92 was a defining moment in India's modern economic history as a severe balance of payments (BoP) crisis prompted far reaching economic reforms, unlocking its growth potential. As a result, in only 15 years, India's per capita income doubled again by 2006-07. If the current pace of growth is maintained, India's per capita income could further double by 2017-18, in 10 years time. While acceleration in India's recent economic growth is noteworthy, maintaining the pace, no doubt, will be challenging.

The assistance provided by Dhritidyuti Bose and Abhiman Das is acknowledged.

Against this background, I propose to highlight the key policy reforms since 1991-92, review the economic progress made so far and then conclude with some reflections on policy challenges in the way forward.

Policy Reforms Post-1991

Macroeconomic crisis of 1991 marked a turning point in India's economic history for two reasons. First, fiscal deficit-driven external payment crisis with a dip in foreign exchange reserves to below US $1 billion in July 1991 drew a crisis resolution strategy to restore macroeconomic stability. Sharp correction in fiscal deficit-GDP ratio and reduced monetisation of deficits contributed towards restoring macroeconomic balance by the mid-1990s. The reduced dependence of fisc on monetisation enabled the Reserve Bank of India to reduce its statutory pre-emption of funds from banks, thereby freeing resources for the private sector. Second, simultaneously efforts were made towards wide ranging structural reforms encompassing areas of trade, exchange rate management, industry, public finance and the financial sector.

An abiding objective in respect of industrial policy measures since then has been to create a competitive environment to improve productivity and efficiency. New industrial policy fostered competition by abolishing monopoly restrictions, terminating the phased manufacturing programmes, freeing foreign direct investment (FDI) and import of foreign technology and de-reservation of sectors hitherto reserved for the public sector. These measures created a favourable environment for industry to upgrade its technology and build up its capacity through imports in order to cater to growing domestic and external demand.

At present, only five industries are under licensing, mainly on account of environmental, health, safety and strategic considerations. Only two industries are reserved for the public sector, *viz.*, atomic energy and railway transport. Reservation of industrial products for the small-scale sector is still a lingering issue. However, the definition of small-scale industry (SSI) has been changed to facilitate modernisation and now only 20 items are reserved for manufacturing in the small-scale sector. FDI up to 100 per cent is allowed under the automatic route in most sectors, with a few exceptions.

The infrastructure sector has been thrown open to the private sector. Considering the large requirements of funds for infrastructure, 100 per cent FDI has been allowed in all infrastructure sectors. There are extended tax holidays to enterprises engaged in the business of development, operation, and maintenance of infrastructure facilities. The emphasis has been on public-private partnership (PPP) as one of the preferred modes for infrastructure project implementation.

Comprehensive fiscal reforms covered tax reforms, restructuring of public sector undertakings and improving fiscal-monetary coordination before eventually carrying these reforms forward under rule-based fiscal consolidation path from 2004-05, which was interrupted by the global financial crisis in 2008-09. Reduction in customs duties over the years reflected India's commitment towards converging towards the ASEAN levels over the medium term.

The monetary policy framework and the associated operating procedures of monetary policy in India have evolved over time with the changes in the underlying macroeconomic structure and development of financial markets. A landmark development was the abolition of the system of automatic monetisation of fiscal deficit from April 1997, which provided instrument independence to the Reserve Bank of India in the conduct of monetary policy. This, combined with the introduction of auctioning system in the government securities, enabled the Reserve Bank to switch from direct to indirect instruments of monetary control.

With the opening up of the economy and deregulation of the financial sector, the stability of money demand function became suspect. The Reserve Bank, therefore, switched from a monetary targetting framework, adopted in the mid-1980s, to a multiple indicator approach. Under this approach, various indicators such as rates of return in different markets, movements in currency, credit, fiscal position, trade, capital flows, inflation rate, exchange rate, refinancing and transactions in foreign exchange—available on a high frequency basis—are juxtaposed with output data for drawing policy perspectives. This approach continued to evolve and is presently in its augmented version, wherein forward looking indicators drawn from the Reserve Bank's industrial outlook survey, capacity utilisation survey, professional forecasters' survey and inflation expectations survey are used for macroeconomic assessment. The operating procedure of monetary policy also underwent a change with the overnight interest rate emerging as the operating target of monetary policy.

In the financial sector, the objective was to provide operational flexibility and functional autonomy to banks and other financial institutions so that they could allocate resources more efficiently. Some of the important initiatives in the financial sector were: reduction in statutory pre-emptions so as to release greater funds for commercial lending, interest rate deregulation to enable price discovery, allowing new private sector banks to create a more competitive environment, dilution of government holding in public sector banks and institution of prudential norms such as capital adequacy, income recognition, asset classification, provisioning and exposure norms to strengthen the health of the banking system besides improving transparency and disclosure standards.

The development of financial markets has been regarded as a critical prerequisite for improving the operational effectiveness of the transmission of monetary policy. During the first phase of financial sector reforms, various structural rigidities were eased, so as to increase participation in financial markets as well as develop and strengthen interlinkages amongst market segments, and foster competition. The focus of various reform measures in financial market was on ensuring adequate liquidity in various segments of the market spectrum, and developing the regulatory, legal, institutional and technological infrastructure for orderly functioning of market activity. In the second phase of reforms, more sophisticated financial instruments were introduced. Further, issues relating to the stability of financial markets received priority in the policy agenda.

The key objective of the external sector reforms was to move to a more open trade regime by correcting for the implicit anti-export bias. Moreover, there was a greater recognition of the need to view trade policies, exchange rate policies and industrial policies in an integrated manner. In pursuance of this, the administered exchange rate regime gave way to a flexible market-determined system. The exchange rate has since been guided by underlying demand and supply conditions and the broad principles of careful monitoring and management of exchange rates with flexibility, without a fixed or preannounced target or band.

The trade policy reforms comprised withdrawal of the quantitative restrictions on exports and imports, phasing out of the system of import licensing and lowering the level and dispersion of nominal tariffs so as to bring them on par with the East Asian economies. The peak customs tariff rate was progressively brought down from 150 per cent in 1991-92 to 10 per cent by 2008-09. The liberalisation of restrictions on various external transactions led to current account convertibility under Article VIII of the Articles of Agreement of the IMF in 1994.

With respect to capital account liberalisation, India embarked on a gradual and well-sequenced opening up of the capital account. The active capital account management framework was based on a preference for non-debt creating capital inflows like FDI and foreign portfolio investment. The capital account is virtually free for non-residents and resident corporates with some restrictions on financial institutions and higher restrictions on resident individuals.

Economic Progress Post-1991

The initiation of economic reforms in the 1990s saw India gradually breaking free of the low growth trap which was euphemistically called the 'Hindu growth rate' of 3.5 per cent per annum. Real GDP growth averaged 5.7 per cent per annum in the 1990s, which accelerated further to 7.3 per cent per annum in 2000s. A feature of the growth acceleration during the period was that while the growth rate of industry and services increased, that of agriculture fell. This was because there was no notable technological breakthrough after the 'green revolution' of the mid-1960s which saw sharp increase in yields of cereal production particularly in northern part of India. By the 1990s, the momentum of 'green revolution' had died down. Consequently, the yield increases in the 2000s were much lower than those experienced even in the 1990s.

Notably, the decade of the 2000s encompassed the inflexion point in the growth trajectory with an annual average GDP growth of about 9 per cent for the five-year period: 2004-2008. Growth in all the sub-sectors of the economy, including agriculture, accelerated during this period. However, this growth process was interrupted by the global financial crisis. Subsequently, the average growth slowed down to 7.8 per cent during 2009-2011 with a noticeable slowdown in both agriculture and industry.

The growth dynamics altered the structure of the Indian economy with a decline in the share of agriculture from 28.4 per cent in the 1990s to about 15 per cent in 2009-2011. There was corresponding gain in the share of services, including construction, from 52 per cent to 65 per cent during the same period. What is, however, of concern is that the share of industry has remained unchanged at around 20 per cent of GDP. This suggests that India's growth acceleration during the last two decades has been dominated by the services sector. The pace of average annual industrial growth had nevertheless picked up from 5.7 per cent during the 1990s to 9 per cent during 2004-2008 before being interrupted by the global financial crisis (Table 2.1).

Table 2.1

Real Economy

Item	*1991-2000*	*2001-2010*	*2004-2008*	*2009-2011*
1	*2*	*3*	*4*	*5*
	(Percentage change)			
1. Overall real GDP	5.7	7.3	8.9	7.8
1.1 Agriculture	3.2	2.4	5.0	2.3
1.2 Industry	5.7	7.3	9.0	6.7
1.2.1 Manufacturing	5.6	8.0	10.0	7.1
1.3 Services	7.1	9.0	10.1	9.5
2. Demand-side aggregates				
2.1 Private final consumption expenditure	4.8	6.4	7.4	7.9
2.2 Government final consumption expenditure	6.3	5.8	5.6	10.6
2.3 Gross fixed capital formation	7.2	10.2	15.7	5.8
	(Per cent)			
3. Share in GDP				
3.1 Agriculture	28.4	19.4	18.9	14.9
3.2 Industry	20.1	20.0	20.1	20.1
3.3 Services	51.5	60.6	61.1	65.0

While the share of industry in GDP remained stagnant, there was noteworthy structural transformation in manufacturing over the period. As a process of restructuring, while the gross value added in organised manufacturing increased by 8 per cent per annum at current prices, employment fell by 1.5 per cent per annum during 1995-2003. Subsequently, during 2004-2009, gross value added growth accelerated to 20 per cent per annum at current prices; but significantly, employment also increased by 7.5 per cent per annum.

With work participation rate of 39.2 per cent, India had a workforce of 400 million in 2009-10. Of this, 53 per cent was in agriculture and the rest 47 per cent in non-agricultural activity. While the bulk of the employment is in agriculture despite its shrinking share, the noteworthy feature of the employment structure has been that for the first time the absolute workforce in agriculture declined in the latter half of the 2000s (Table 2.2). The overall unemployment rate in the economy also declined from 8.3 per cent in 2004-05 to 6.6 per cent in 2009-10.

Table 2.2

Labour Force

(In million)

Usual Status	*1993-94*	*1999-2000*	*2004-05*	*2009-10*
1	*2*	*3*	*4*	*5*
1. Agriculture	210.7	225.4	238.8	212.6
1.1 Self-employed	126.6	130.2	153.2	127.9
1.2 Regular wage/salaried employee	2.9	3.2	2.6	1.9
1.3 Casual labour	81.2	91.9	83.0	82.9
2. Non-agriculture	115.8	140.0	169.5	187.4
2.1 Self-employed	52.1	62.8	79.0	76.0
2.2 Regular wage/salaried employee	40.2	47.9	55.6	60.5
2.3 Casual labour	23.4	29.3	34.8	50.9
Total	326.5	365.4	408.2	400.0

Not surprisingly, the growth acceleration was accompanied by a sharp pickup in the rate of growth of gross fixed capital formation which had more than doubled from an annual average of 7.2 per cent in the 1990s to 15.7 per cent in the high growth phase of 2004-2008. It, however, has dropped significantly in the post-crisis period to 5.8 per cent (Table 2.1).

The structure of Indian economy also underwent a change during this period in terms of openness. The stereotypical view that India is a closed economy has not been borne out by the openness of Indian economy which was increasing rapidly. Exports and imports of goods and services have more than doubled from 23 per cent of GDP in the 1990s to 50 per cent in the recent period of 2009-2011. If the trade flows are considered alongside capital flows, the rise in openness (measured as current receipts and payments plus capital receipts and payments) was more dramatic from 42 per cent of GDP in the 1990s to 107 per cent in the recent period (Table 2.3) Empirical evidence suggests that with increasing openness of the Indian economy, the trade and industrial cycles were getting more synchronised with the global business cycle.

Table 2.3

Openness Indicators

(As per cent to GDP)

	Item	*1991-2000*	*2001-2010*	*2004-2008*	*2009-2011*
	1	*2*	*3*	*4*	*5*
1.	Exports plus imports of goods & services	22.9	39.2	40.8	49.8
2.	Current receipts & payments plus capital receipts & payments	41.9	78.7	83.5	106.5

The high growth phase of 2004-2008 was accompanied by sharp increase in exports and imports as well as capital inflows. Net capital inflows as percentage of GDP more than doubled from 2.2 per cent in the 1990s to 4.6 per cent of GDP during 2004-2008. Subsequently, growth rates in both trade and capital inflows moderated following the global financial crisis. The openness of the Indian economy has been accompanied by improvement in India's external position as the debt to GDP ratio fell from about 29 per cent in the 1990s to 19 per cent in the recent period. The debt service ratio has also declined from 25 per cent to under 5 per cent during the period (Table 2.4).

The openness in the capital account has resulted in two-way movement in capital with a sharp pickup in India's outward FDI since the mid-2000s (Table 2.5). Uptrend in outward FDI mainly reflected the large overseas acquisition deals of Indian corporates to gain market share and reap economies of scale amidst progressive liberalisation of the external payments regime.

Table 2.4

External Sector

Item	*1991-2000*	*2001-2010*	*2004-2008*	*2009-2011*
1	*2*	*3*	*4*	*5*
1. Balance of payments				
1.1 Merchandise exports (% change)*	8.6	17.7	25.4	15.8
1.2 Merchandise imports (% change)*	9.6	19.5	32.3	14.6
1.3 Trade balance/GDP (%)	-2.8	-5.3	-5.4	-8.6
1.4 Invisible balance/GDP (%)	1.6	4.8	5.1	6.1
1.5 Current account balance/GDP (%)	-1.3	-0.5	-0.3	-2.6
1.6 Net capital flows/GDP(%)	2.2	3.4	4.6	2.7
1.7 FDI to India (US $ billion)	1.6	16.3	15.3	31.4
1.8 Reserve changes (BoP basis) (US $ billion) [(increase (-)/decrease (+)]	-3.3	-22.9	-40.3	-2.1
2. External debt indicators				
2.1 Debt-GDP ratio (%)	29.0	19.0	17.7	18.6
2.2 Debt service ratio (%)	24.9	8.8	8.3	4.7

Note: * : Based on DGCI&S data.

Table 2.5

Foreign Direct Investment

(US $ billion)

Year	*Inward*	*Outward*	*Net FDI to India*	*Outward/ Inward (%)*
1	*2*	*3*	*4*	*5*
2000-01	4.0	0.8	3.3	18.8
2001-02	6.1	1.4	4.7	22.7
2002-03	5.0	1.8	3.2	36.1
2003-04	4.3	1.9	2.4	44.7
2004-05	6.0	2.3	3.7	38.0
2005-06	8.9	5.9	3.0	65.9
2006-07	22.7	15.0	7.7	66.2
2007-08	34.7	18.8	15.9	54.2
2008-09	37.7	17.9	19.8	47.4
2009-10	33.1	14.4	18.8	43.3
2010-11	23.4	16.2	7.1	69.4

Source: Reserve Bank of India.

Gradual improvements were also observed in the fiscal position with fiscal deficit moderating sharply during the high growth phase of 2004-2008, which also coincided with a period of switch-over to a rule-based fiscal consolidation process. In fact, the high growth phase of 2004-2008 saw a primary surplus for the Centre enhancing debt sustainability. The deficit indicators, however, have deteriorated in the recent period following crisis induced fiscal expansion (Table 2.6).

Table 2.6

Government Finances

(As per cent to GDP)

Item	*1991-2000*	*2001-2010*	*2004-2008*	*2009-2011*
1	*2*	*3*	*4*	*5*
1. Central government finances				
1.1 Tax revenue	6.8	7.2	7.6	7.4
1.2 Revenue deficit	3.0	3.4	2.3	4.4
1.3 Fiscal deficit	5.9	4.8	3.6	5.8
1.4 Primary deficit	1.6	0.8	-0.2	2.6
2. State finances				
2.1 Gross fiscal deficit	3.1	3.1	2.7	2.6
2.2 Outstanding liabilities	22.3	29.3	30.1	24.8
3. Combined government finances				
3.1 Revenue deficit	4.2	4.4	2.7	4.5
3.2 Fiscal deficit	7.7	7.8	6.3	8.5
3.3 Primary deficit	2.7	2.2	0.7	3.7
3.4 Outstanding liabilities	63.2	75.1	76.5	68.5

The average saving rate also showed a substantial increase from 23 per cent of GDP in the 1990s to about 31 per cent in the 2000s with a peak saving rate of over 33 per cent achieved during the high growth phase of 2004-2008. Fiscal consolidation helped in lifting the overall saving rate as public sector saving rose significantly. The efficiency of capital utilisation also improved as the incremental capital output ratio (ICOR) declined to 3.7 during the high growth phase of 2004-2008 from 5 in the 1990s. Subsequently, however, capital efficiency has declined in the post-crisis period (Table 2.7).

Table 2.7

Saving and Investment

Item	*1991-2000*	*2001-2010*	*2004-2008*	*2009-2011*
1	*2*	*3*	*4*	*5*
(As a ratio to GDP at current market prices)				
1. Gross domestic savings	23.0	30.7	33.4	33.0
1.1 Household saving	17.7	23.1	23.4	23.6
1.1.1 Financial assets	9.9	11.0	11.3	11.3
1.1.2 Physical assets	7.8	12.1	12.1	12.4
1.2. Private corporate sector	3.8	6.3	7.2	8.0
1.3. Public sector	1.5	1.3	2.9	1.3
2. Gross domestic capital formation	24.4	31.2	34.3	35.5
3. ICOR*	5.0	4.4	3.7	4.9

Note: *: Ratio of real investment rate and real GDP growth.

The high growth was achieved in an environment of price stability as headline wholesale price index (WPI) inflation dropped to an annual average of 5.5 per cent in the 2000s from 8.1 per cent in the 1990s. There was also similar drop in consumer price inflation. Subsequently, however, in the post-crisis period the inflation trend has reversed with the headline WPI inflation averaging over 7 per cent and the consumer price inflation crossing double digits during 2009-2011. The uptick in food price inflation was particularly sharp during 2009-2011 (Table 2.8).

Table 2.8

Inflation

Item	*1991-2000*	*2001-2010*	*2004-2008*	*2009-2011*
1	*2*	*3*	*4*	*5*
(Annual average percentage change)				
1. Wholesale price index	8.1	5.4	5.5	7.1
1.1 Food articles	10.2	5.8	5.2	13.3
1.2 Fuel group	10.6	8.9	7.3	7.2
1.3 Non-food manufactured products	6.8	4.0	5.0	4.0
2. CPI- industrial workers	9.5	5.9	5.0	10.6
2.1 CPI- industrial workers food	9.8	6.2	5.5	12.5

During this period, financial deepening of the Indian economy has also increased: broad money (M3) to GDP ratio rose from an average of 50 per cent in the 1990s to 85 per cent in the recent period of 2009-2011. Credit penetration, measured as credit to GDP ratio, also increased from 21 per cent of GDP to about 50 per cent during this period. The high growth phase of 2004-2008 was accompanied by acceleration in growth of bank credit to the private sector to about 27 per cent per annum from about 15 per cent in the 1990s. However, during the high growth phase of 2004-2008, the average increase in M3 remained contained which aided price stability. This was made possible due to deceleration in banks' investment in government securities to about 13 per cent per annum during 2004-2008 from 21 per cent in the 1990s. Fiscal consolidation opened up the space for private credit expansion without exerting much additional pressure on monetary expansion (Table 2.9).

Table 2.9

Money and Credit

Item	*1991-2000*	*2001-2010*	*2004-2008*	*2009-2011*
1	*2*	*3*	*4*	*5*
(Percentage change)				
1. Narrow money (M1)	15.6	16.0	19.6	12.3
2. Broad money (M3)	17.2	17.5	18.6	17.4
3. Non-food bank credit	15.4	22.4	26.7	18.7
4. Investment in government securities	20.9	17.7	13.3	16.2
(Per cent)				
5. Credit-GDP ratio	20.6	37.7	39.5	49.7
6. Broad money-GDP ratio	49.9	73.6	74.3	84.6

Policy Challenges

The draft approach paper for the Twelfth Five Year Plan (2012-2017) released in August 2011 targets an annual GDP growth rate of 9 per cent. This is challenging but not unattainable. Why? Because India has already achieved an average growth rate of about 9 per cent during 2004-2008 which was interrupted by the global financial crisis. Subsequently, average growth has dropped by about one percentage point to 7.8 per cent during 2009-2011. In 2011-12, the terminal year of the Eleventh Plan, growth is expected to be about 8 per cent. Hence, growth will have to be raised by an additional percentage point per annum which is challenging because it will require a conducive global environment and policy reforms at home. While there are several tasks to be addressed, I will focus on six key issues.

First, India will have to raise agricultural productivity and diversify agriculture to feed its own population. The food entitlement has increased with the public employment guarantee programme (MGNREGA) which guarantees for 100 days of employment to one member of each family in the rural areas. This has also given better bargaining power to labour and consequently the overall wage rates have gone up raising the demand for food. While the country currently has sufficient food grains stocks, it is not yet self-sufficient in pulses and oilseeds. Further, demand for protein-based products like meat, egg, milk and fish as well as fruits and vegetables has increased substantially with rise in income. The demand-supply mismatches in the case of these items have resulted in rise in their prices. There is, therefore, a need for another technological breakthrough to give fresh impetus to agriculture. At the same time, greater emphasis will have to be placed in the management of supply chain with investment in rural infrastructure. The annual growth in agriculture has to be raised to at least 4 per cent from the current trend growth rate of around 3 per cent.

Second, the fact that 53 per cent of overall workforce is still engaged in the agricultural sector—whose share of GDP has shrunk considerably—is worrisome. A substantial part of this labour force will have to be ejected from agriculture not only to improve the productivity in agriculture but also in the overall economy. It is unconceivable that they can all be absorbed gainfully in the services sector. Hence, industrial employment will have to expand, so also the relative contribution of industry. This needs a focussed attention as we have seen that the share of industry in the overall GDP has stagnated over the last two decades. In this direction, the Government has taken up a major policy initiative to create National Manufacturing and Investment Zones (NMIZs) to increase the sectoral share of manufacturing in GDP to 25 per cent by 2022 and double the current employment level in the sector. Good physical infrastructure, a progressive exit policy, structures to support clean and green technologies, appropriate investment incentives, and business-friendly approval mechanisms will be the cornerstones of this new initiative.

Third, to support industrialisation and increased economic activity, there is a need to step up investment in infrastructure. The assessment of the Planning Commission suggests an investment of 45 trillion (US $1 trillion) over the Twelfth Plan (2012-2017). Given the large requirement of long-term funds, financing infrastructure would be a big challenge. Besides budgetary support, the bulk of the funds has emanated from banks. However, channelling domestic and foreign financial savings of this scale into infrastructure will require developing the domestic private corporate debt market. Apart from the need for substantial financial outlays for infrastructure, there are several non-financing constraints: particularly land acquisition delays need to be addressed to avoid time and cost overruns.

Fourth, there is a need for the Government to revert to its rule-based pre-crisis fiscal consolidation path without compromising on the quality of fiscal correction. This is necessary to obviate the risk of twin deficits and to raise the overall saving rate. This will require further reform in the tax structure to ensure revenue buoyancy and greater focus on quality of expenditure with an emphasis on reduction of subsidy. In this regard, major reforms in the pipeline are the introduction of an integrated Goods and Services Tax (GST) by the Centre and the states to reduce cascading effect and improve tax compliance and operationalisation of a Direct Taxes Code (DTC), to improve allocative efficiency and equity of the direct taxes.

Fifth, credit markets have, historically, played a crucial role in sustaining growth through efficient intermediation of funds between savers and investors. Although India has a well-diversified financial system, and several measures for financial inclusion have been taken in the recent past, credit penetration continues to be relatively low in comparison with several other developed and emerging market economies. The extent of financial exclusion is staggering with around 61 per cent of population having a deposit account and only 10 per cent of population having a credit account. The Reserve Bank has embarked on a plan of making available basic banking services to all habitations of population of over 2,000 by 2012 through a combination of brick and mortar branches and a system of business correspondents (BCs). Accelerated economic growth will depend on access to formal finance by the bulk of the population and greater credit penetration.

Sixth, empirical evidence suggests that the threshold level of inflation is in the range of 4-6 per cent. Hence, without bringing inflation down from the current level it will be difficult to sustain a high level of growth. This will require greater monetary-fiscal coordination and alleviation of supply constraints, particularly in agriculture.

Conclusion

Envisioning India's emergence as a major economic power in the world, Dr Manmohan Singh in his Union Budget 1991-92 speech that launched wide ranging economic reforms had quoted Victor Hugo's saying, 'no power on earth can stop an idea whose time has come'. Ever since, there has been no looking back as India launched wide ranging structural reforms and has made significant economic progress over the past two decades. India's industrial environment has become more competitive and open, infrastructural gaps have been sought to be bridged through public-private initiatives with both domestic and foreign sources of funding, current account has become fully convertible while capital account is virtually free for non-residents. The policy environment has become more enabling with rule-based commitment on fiscal policy and considerable instrument independence for operation of monetary policy. As statutory pre-emptions were reduced and interest rates were deregulated, banks gained operational autonomy for commercial lending. As a result, India's per capita income, which had taken four decades to double by 1991, doubled thereafter in 15 years and is likely to double again in 10 years by 2017-18. If India could maintain the current pace of growth it will lift millions out of poverty and enrich the global economy. While India has come a long way, maintaining the current pace would itself be challenging and require continued reform efforts.

Speech delivered at the Harvard Business School, Boston, 27th September 2011.

3 The Indian Economy

Current Concerns and Future Prospects

C. Rangarajan

India has travelled through a remarkable journey in the last two decades. The growth rate of the economy has been steadily increasing except, of course, in the current year. In the Ninth Plan, the annual growth rate was 5.5 per cent. It rose to 7.5 per cent in the Tenth Plan, and to 8.2 per cent in the first four years of the Eleventh Plan. Without doubt, India has moved to a higher trajectory of economic growth.

There are, however, many challenges on the way forward. First, we must sustain a high growth rate of 8 to 9 per cent over the next two decades. This is necessary to raise the living standards of our population substantially. Second, growth must lead to reduction of poverty. The process of growth must be broad-based to include all segments of society. Third, we must expand employment opportunities and improve productivity in all sectors of the economy. Fourth, we must narrow economic disparities across and within the states. And, finally, we must improve on social indicators. Thus, the agenda for achieving growth with equity is formidable.

The year 1991 is a landmark in the post-independent economic history of India. The country faced a severe economic crisis, triggered in part by a serious balance of payments situation. The crisis was converted into an opportunity to effect some fundamental changes in the content and approach to economic policy.

Trends in Growth

That the content of process of our economic reforms are on the right track is indicated by the performance of the economy since the launch of reforms. India's economic growth in the first three decades after

Independence was low. The annual growth rate of the economy was around 3.5 per cent. With population growing almost at 2 per cent, the per capita income grew at only 1.5 per cent. Subsequently, there was some pickup in the 1980s when the average annual growth rate was 5-7 per cent. (Table 3.1). However, the economy collapsed in 1991-92 when the growth rate fell to 1.6 per cent and the country ran into severe balance of payments and fiscal problems. There were also severe year to year fluctuations. In the post-reform period beginning 1992-93, the economy has grown at an average rate of 6.9 per cent per annum, a significant improvement over the pre-reform period.

Coming to the more recent period, economic growth in the six-year period beginning 2005-06 despite the crisis affected year of 2008-09, was at an average of 8.6 per cent. This clearly represented an acceleration in the pace of growth. Per capita GDP grew at an average of 7.0 per cent in these six years.

Under the severe impact of the global crisis, the Indian economy registered a growth of 6.8 per cent in 2008-09 after having registered a growth rate exceeding 9 per cent for these consecutive years. By any standard, the Indian economy was able to protect itself reasonably well in the turbulent conditions of the financial crisis.

The growth rate picked up soon and the economy achieved a growth rate of 8 per cent in 2009-10, despite a severe drought. During that year, industries grew at 8 per cent and services at 10.1 per cent.

Thc growth ratc increased further to 8.5 per cent in 2010-11. There was a substantial jump in agricultural production. The monsoon was good and, therefore, the agricultural GDP grew at 6.6 per cent. The manufacturing sector grew by 8.3 per cent and the services sector at 9.4 per cent.

Initially the growth rate in 2011-12 was forecast by the Economic Advisory Council to be 8.2 per cent. However, subsequent events have shown that this may not be attainable. The monsoon has been good and we should expect to see agriculture grow reasonably well. The expected growth rate of 3.5 per cent in agriculture will be on top of a strong growth of 6.6 per cent in the previous year. It is in the case of industry a slackness has been noticed. The growth rate of index of industrial production in July,

Table 3.1

Growth in GDP at Factor Cost and its Components at 2004-05 Prices

(Per cent per annum)

	Agriculture, Forestry & Fishing	*Mining & Quarrying*	*Manufacturing*	*Construction*	*Electricity, Gas, and Water Supply*	*Trade, Hotels, Storage, Transport and Communications*	*Finance, Insurance, Real Estate & Business Services*	*Community, Social and Personal Services*	*GDP at Factor Cost*
1980-81	12.9	12.2	0.2	13.2	5.7	5.7	1.9	4.1	7.5
1981-82	4.6	13.7	8.2	5.5	9.5	6.2	8.1	2.1	5.7
1982-83	-0.3	11.9	3.3	-7.0	6.6	5.4	9.5	7.7	2.9
1983-84	10.1	2.9	10.2	5.4	6.9	5.1	9.8	3.7	7.8
1984-85	1.6	1.2	4.2	3.5	10.8	4.8	7.5	6.9	4.0
1985-86	0.3	5.5	3.2	5.7	7.9	7.9	9.8	5.7	4.3
1986-87	-0.4	12.2	5.5	2.4	10.3	6.0	10.5	7.5	4.5
1987-88	-1.6	3.8	5.6	5.7	7.8	5.3	7.3	7.2	3.7
1988-89	15.6	16.2	8.5	7.0	9.7	5.8	9.8	6.0	10.1
1989-90	1.2	7.6	8.8	7.0	9.7	7.4	12.4	7.9	6.3
1990-91	4.0	10.5	4.8	11.8	6.7	5.1	6.2	4.4	5.4
1991-92	-2.0	3.4	-2.4	2.1	9.7	2.6	10.8	2.6	1.6
1992-93	6.7	0.9	3.1	3.5	6.9	5.6	5.4	6.0	5.3
1993-94	3.3	1.4	8.6	0.6	7.5	6.9	11.2	4.5	5.7
1994-95	4.7	9.3	10.8	5.4	9.4	9.9	3.9	2.3	6.4
1995-96	-0.7	5.9	15.5	6.0	6.8	13.2	8.1	7.3	7.4
1996-97	9.9	0.6	9.5	1.9	5.4	8.1	6.2	8.1	7.8
1997-98	-2.6	9.8	0.1	10.5	7.7	7.5	11.7	8.3	4.5
1998-99	6.3	2.8	3.1	6.3	7.0	7.6	7.8	9.7	6.6
1999-00	2.7	3.2	3.2	8.4	5.5	8.2	9.2	11.5	6.5
2000-01	-0.2	2.4	7.7	6.2	2.1	7.3	4.1	4.7	4.4
2001-02	6.3	1.8	2.5	4.0	1.7	9.2	7.3	4.1	5.7
2002-03	-7.2	8.8	6.8	7.9	4.7	9.4	8.0	3.9	4.0
2003-04	10.0	3.1	6.6	12.0	4.8	12.0	5.6	5.4	8.4
2004-05	0.05	8.2	8.7	16.1	7.9	10.7	8.7	6.8	7.6
2005-06	5.1	1.3	10.1	12.8	7.1	12.2	12.7	7.0	9.5
2006-07	4.2	7.5	14.3	10.3	9.3	11.6	14.0	2.9	9.6
2007-08	5.8	3.7	10.3	10.7	8.3	11.0	11.9	6.9	9.3
2008-09	-0.1	1.3	4.2	5.4	4.9	7.5	12.5	12.7	6.8
2009-10	0.4	6.9	8.8	7.0	6.4	9.7	9.2	11.8	8.0
2010-11	6.6	5.8	8.3	8.1	5.7	10.3	9.9	7.0	8.5

Note: For years prior to 2004-05, the 1999-2000 base series is taken backwards based on splicing.

Source: National Income Accounts, CSO.

August, and September 2011 have been below 5 per cent. In October, there was a decline by 5.1 per cent. This trend was reversed in November when the growth rate was positive of 5.9 per cent. While growth may pick up in the coming months, the overall growth rate in industry will be well below the initial expectations. The world economic situation is also not very encouraging. Under these circumstances, the growth rate during the current year may be between 7 per cent and 7.25 per cent.

2012-13 may turn out to be better than 2011-12 for three reasons. First, inflation may settle down at a lower level and this can lead to easing of interest rates. Second, output and capacity-creation targets in the crucial infrastructure sectors such as coal, power and roads may be fulfilled. Third, there would be greater clarity on issues relating to land acquisition and environment. The external situation may, however, show no improvement. For the three reasons mentioned above, one can expect the growth rate in 2012-13 to be an improvement over the current fiscal.

Distribution of Income

Before going into the issue of the medium-term trends, let me turn to the issue of distribution of income. While growth is important, it is necessary to remember that it is not the only dimension for measuring performance or achievement. It is equally important to know who benefits from growth. There has been considerable dispute in this country in estimating the people below the poverty line. There is no consensus yet on what constitutes the poverty line. According to the methodology adopted by the Planning Commission until recently, the number of people below poverty line in 1993-94 was 36.0 per cent. According to the same methodology, it came down to 27.5 per cent in 2004-05. However, the Tendulkar Committee by adopting a slightly different methodology came to the conclusion that the overall poverty ratio was 45.3 per cent in 1993-94 and 37.2 per cent in 2004-05. While the Tendulkar Committee estimates are higher than the earlier estimates, both methodologies show that the reduction in the poverty ratio was in the range of 8 to 8.5 per cent. While growth has contributed to reducing the poverty ratio, it has to be acknowledged that the absolute level of poverty is still high. Truly we have miles to go before eliminating poverty. We need to ensure that the growth process is such as to include every section of the economy. We must maintain, nevertheless, a high growth rate which will alone enable the government to raise the resources to meet the various socioeconomic obligations.

One aspect of the growth process is balanced regional development. It is normally expected that with economic development, the per capita income of the states will show a tendency to converge. Comparing the two periods of 1993-94 to 1999-2000 and 1999-2000 to 2008-09, data do not show a convergence. However, there is a strong evidence of 'catching up' by the lower income states. The median growth rate increased one-and-a-half times between the two periods, increasing from 3.9 per cent in the earlier period to 5.7 per cent in the latter period. States with lower per capita GSDP like Assam, Orissa, Uttar Pradesh and Bihar have made significant gains in growth rates in the latter period. Notwithstanding these gains, convergence was subdued because some of the higher income states like Gujarat, Kerala and Haryana also posted high growth rates. In other words, what the recent data indicate is that while most of the lower income states have shown stronger growth rates, several of the higher income states have also shown an increase in the recent period.

Potential Rate of Growth

In the light of India's economic performance in recent years, a frequently asked question is whether India has the potential to grow at 9 per cent in a sustained way. In 2006-07, India's domestic savings rate exceeded 34 per cent and the investment rate was close to 36 per cent. These rates further improved in 2007-08. Since then, these rates have come down. However, the rates already achieved indicate the potential that exists. Even with an incremental of capital-output ratio of 4, the investments rate achieved should enable the Indian economy to grow at 9 per cent. Thus, the broad macroeconomic parameters relating to savings and investment are conducive to achieving a growth rate of 8 to 9 per cent in a sustained way. This, however, is the potential and to achieve it we must also take actions to remove constraints that may come in the way. In this context, I would like to highlight three macroeconomic concerns and two sectoral constraints.

Macroeconomic Concerns

Inflation

The first and foremost, we must tame inflation. We have had two years of high inflation (Figure 3.1). In 2009-10, the economy was badly affected because of the deficient monsoon. Food grain production declined by 17 million tonnes. The decline in the production of rice alone was 11 million tonnes. As a consequence, inflation was triggered by the increase in food grain prices. Food inflation stood at as high as 21 per cent in February 2010. Overall inflation as measured by the wholesale price index (WPI) touched the peak of 10.9 per cent in April 2010. It was expected that inflation would moderate through 2010-11. It in fact started happening till November 2010. However, prices started rising after that. As of March 2011, year on year inflation had touched 10.0 per cent. While the food price inflation of 2009-10 was triggered by the rise in food grain prices, in 2010-11 it was triggered by the rise in the prices of vegetables, fruits and eggs, meat and fish. The increase in vegetable prices has been significant. The late rains had a severe impact on the supply of some vegetables including onion. Inflation in vegetables rose to 34 per cent in December 2010 and 67 per cent in January 2011. Normally, vegetable prices show a seasonal decline during winter months. During 2010-11, prices of raw cotton rose on an average by 43 per cent. The persistence of food inflation led to the spread of inflation to other sectors. Inflation in manufactures rose from 5.35 per cent in March 2010 to 7.4 per cent in March 2011. In 2010-11, the weighted contribution of the manufacturing sector to total inflation was 41.8 per cent.

Inflation continues to remain an area of concern in the current fiscal. Until November 2011 the headline inflation had remained above 9 per cent. However, there was a break in December 2011, when the headline inflation came down to 7.4 per cent. This was due primarily to the decline in food inflation.

According to the weekly data, food inflation had turned negative in the third week of December 2011 and it continues to be so in the first week of January 2012. This declining trend in food inflation may continue through January and February 2012. Perhaps, the headline inflation will come below 7 per cent by March 2012. We, however, have to bear in mind that

Figure 3.1

Monthly Inflation 2009-2011

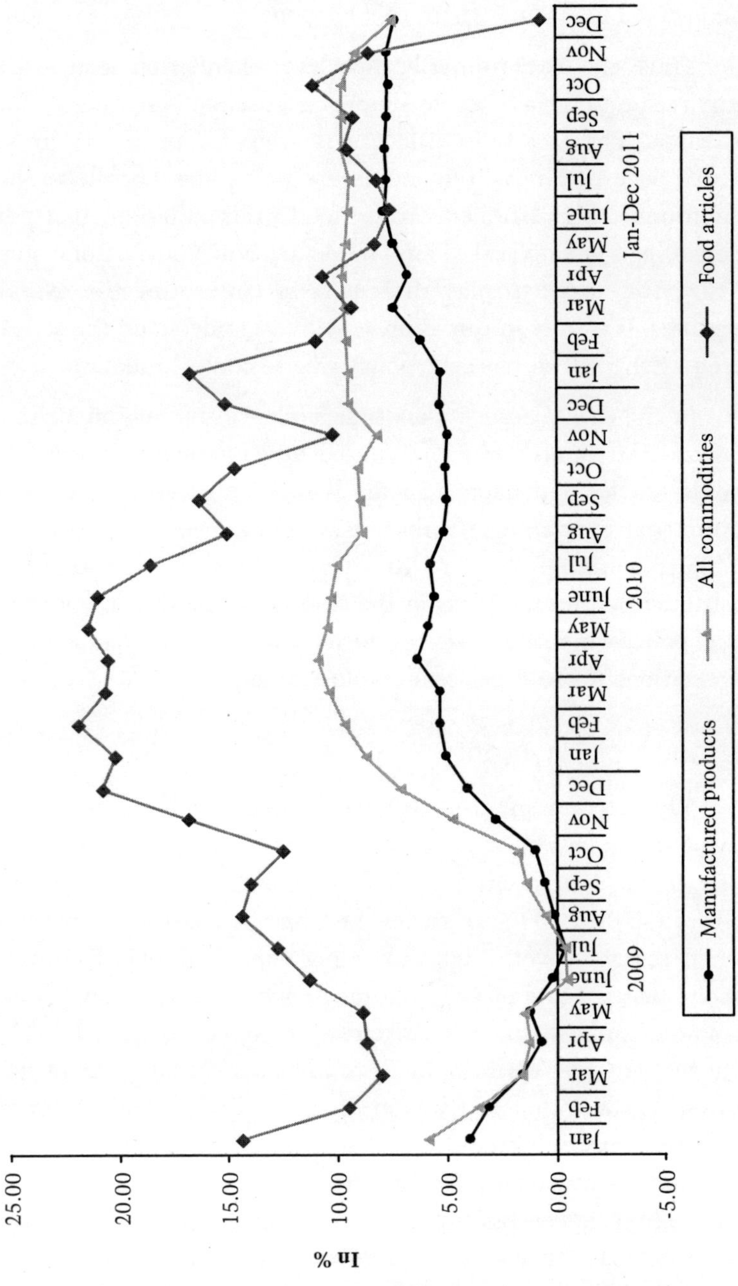

the rationalisation process in the pricing of petroleum products is still to be completed and, as and when, this happens, it will impact overall inflation.

Thus, the extraordinarily high level of inflation seen in the last two years is due to certain severe supply constraints, particularly of agricultural products. The fact that inflation is triggered primarily by supply-side shocks does not mean that monetary policy has no role to play in such conditions. As mentioned earlier, food price inflation, if it persists long enough, gets generalised. Thus, monetary policy and at one step removed, fiscal policy have to play their part in containing the overall demand pressures. It is only in this context one can understand the series of actions taken by the RBI to raise the policy rate to control inflation.

In the early decades after Independence, the argument that inflation was endemic in economic growth led to very steep increases in prices. We should not let that happen in the years of high growth. We must remain committed to maintain inflation at a low level. High growth does not warrant a higher level of inflation. We must use all of our policy instruments—interventions in the food grains market, monetary policy and fiscal policy—to bring down the current inflation and re-anchor inflationary expectations to the 5 per cent comfort zone.

Balance of Payments

The second macroeconomic concern relates to the balance of payments. India's current account deficit remained low till 2008-09. Since then, it has started climbing and the current account deficit was 2.8 per cent of GDP in 2009-10. In the first half of 2010-11, the current account deficit remained very high at 3.7 per cent of the GDP. However, in the second half, exports picked up strongly while import growth was weaker. It is now estimated that the current account deficit for 2010-11 is 2.6 per cent of the GDP. We have had no problems till last year in financing the current account deficit. Even in 2010-11, capital flows were adequate to cover the current account deficit and add to the reserves $15 billion. The current account deficit (CAD) in the current year may turn out to be higher than last year. Besides, in the current year, capital flows have not been adequate. It is this mismatch between CAD and capital flows that has put pressure on the rupee. Efforts must be made to keep the current account deficit around the manageable level of 2.5 per cent of GDP. This is desirable to impart much needed stability on the external payment front and to reduce the risk the domestic economy runs from volatility in international financial markets. Over the next decade, we must work towards achieving a balance in the current account.

Fiscal Deficit

The third macro-economic concern is fiscal consolidation which is a necessary prerequisite for sustained growth. In the wake of the international financial crisis, India like many other countries adopted an expansionary fiscal policy in order to stimulate demand. As a consequence, the fiscal deficit of the Government of India which was coming down, started rising. In 2008-09, the fiscal deficit was 6 per cent of GDP. It rose to 6.4 per cent in the next year. Unlike other countries in the advanced world, where there is a continuing debate regarding when to terminate the expansionary fiscal policies, we in India have taken a decision to initiate the process of fiscal consolidation. In 2010-11, the fiscal deficit came down to 4.7 per cent of GDP and it is projected to fall to 4.6 per cent in the current year. Perhaps this is difficult to achieve. To gain credibility, it is important that fiscal deficit remains close to this level. Over the medium term, we should draw up an appropriate roadmap to reach the FRBM target of 3 per cent of GDP. We must focus particularly on reducing the overall level of subsidies as a proportion of GDP.

Sectoral Constraints

In the medium term, the two sectors which pose a major challenge are the farm economy and the power sector. The first of these, farm economy is primarily constrained by the relatively low levels of yield in major cereal crops and pulses as compared to other Asian economies especially China. We have large science and technology establishments for agricultural research. But the results in terms of productivity gains leave much to be desired. Thus, necessary steps must be taken to revitalise the traditional crop agriculture which is vital to food security and farm income. Equally, as shifts in demand occur reflecting changes in income and taste, agricultural production must also respond to them. The last two years have clearly shown how a decline in agricultural production can cause serious distortions in the economy. It is, therefore, imperative that we aim at GDP originating from agriculture and allied activities growing at 4 per cent per annum.

The second challenge for the country is the shortage of physical infrastructure of which the single most important item is electricity. Shortage of electric power leads not only to direct production losses but also results in inefficiency in a broad range of areas impacting profitability and competitiveness. Recent data clearly indicate a shortfall in achieving the targets for capacity creation during the Eleventh Plan. This is despite the fact that the achievement in capacity creation in the first four years of the Eleventh Plan is higher than that in the first four years of the Tenth Plan. Government is the largest player in production, transmission and distribution of power and a high order of Government intervention in capacity creation and other supportive components of electricity business is crucial to sustaining a high growth rate of 9 per cent. A more aggressive path of capacity creation must start immediately. Constraints such as the availability of coal, land acquisition and environmental issues need to be tackled so that the desired growth in capacity expansion can be achieved.

Good Governance

Besides the sectoral constraints, one issue that is critically important cutting across all sectors is governance. That good governance is at the very heart of economic growth and poverty reduction, and even political legitimacy, is now part of conventional wisdom.

What is good governance? As per textbook definition, good governance is the manner in which the authority of the state is exercised in the management of a country's economic and social resources for maximising welfare. In the ultimate analysis, it is the quality of governance that separates success and failure in economic development. Across countries, application of the same policies in roughly similar contexts has produced dramatically different results. In our own country, we have seen vast differences across states in development outcomes from out of the same mix of development policies. These differences across countries as well as across regions within countries, even as they adopt similar policy packages, arise because of differences in governance. Indeed research shows that per capita incomes and the quality of governance are strongly correlated indicating a virtuous circle in which good governance results in economic development. Good governance needs at all levels administrative systems that are efficient, effective and accountable.

Good governance is essential for ensuring that we get the full benefits of the various policy interventions. We need ideas. We need capacity to turn those ideas into policies and programmes. And we need boldness and a sense of purpose to implement those policies and programmes. Ideas, policies and execution form the triad of good governance and therefore of rapid growth.

Need for High Growth

As mentioned earlier, with the investment rate touching 36 per cent of the GDP, the economy should be able to grow at 9.0 per cent. Pushing the economy beyond that will run into problems. First of all, it will be difficult to achieve the required investment rate, second, pushing the economy beyond its capacity would result in strong inflationary pressures re-emerging. The deficit in the current account of the balance of payments will also widen. It is, therefore, prudent to aim at a growth rate of 9 per cent.

Some people raise a question whether it is necessary at all to grow at this rate. Growth is an important factor in generating employment and reducing poverty. Obviously, the composition of growth is equally important. As I mentioned earlier, particular focus on agriculture is extremely important. Growth in agriculture is necessary not only from the point of view of ensuring food security but also in making a dent on poverty. Nevertheless, overall growth is an important factor while examining the progress in terms of living standards. With population growth rate coming down, a strong growth will mean a substantial growth in the per capita income. If we grow at 9 per cent per annum, India's per capita GDP will increase from the current level of $1,600 to $8,000-10,000 by 2025. Then we will become part of the middle income group of countries. Without a strong growth, we will not be able to provide employment to the growing number of young people who will join the labour force. Analysis of the preliminary NSSO data for 2009-10 suggests that, compared to 2004-05, there has been a reduction of about 3-4 percentage points in the poverty ratio. Continued strong growth will help to accelerate the declining trend in poverty ratio. In the recent period, we have launched a number of schemes aimed at broadening the base of growth. These include employment guarantee scheme, universalisation of education, expansion of rural health and food security. All these programmes have made a substantial demand on public expenditure. This has been made possible only because of the strong growth that we have seen in recent years. Growth has facilitated raising more resources by the Government.

Development has many dimensions. It has to be inclusive; it must be poverty reducing and it must be environment-friendly. We need to incorporate all these elements in the growth process. However, at our present stage of development, we cannot afford to sacrifice growth. It is key to improving the living standards of our people. A strong and balanced growth will enable the economy to achieve multiple goals including lowering inflation. Equity and growth should not be posed as opposing considerations. They must be weaved together to produce a coherent pattern of development. Therein lies economic statesmanship.

In recent years, India's integration with the rest of the world has deepened as evidenced by the fact that exports and imports taken together as a percentage of GDP have increased from 20 per cent in 1998-99 to 41 per cent in 2008-09. The two-way capital and current flows increased from 44 per cent of GDP in 1998-99 to 112 per cent in 2008-09. As India's integration with the rest of the world grows, it will be increasingly affected by what happens externally. For example, India's high growth in the period 2005-2008 was greatly facilitated by the prosperity of the advanced economies. Similarly, in 2008-09, the international financial crisis resulted in the slowing down of India's economic growth. In the current year, one can see again the impact of international situation on the Indian economy. While the slowing down of India's growth in the current year cannot be attributed solely to external factors, some segments of India's economy have been directly influenced by the external factors. The balance of payments situation has turned worse and the rupee was affected because of the reduced capital flows. If the European situation worsens, it may adversely affect our growth as well. The current world situation is not thus hospitable for achieving a high growth. Since India's growth is largely propelled by domestic demand, we must on our own steam be able to grow at 8 per cent. If the world situation improves, we should be able to achieve the goal of 9 per cent sooner.

Foundation Day Lecture delivered at the Associated Chambers of Commerce and Industry of India, January 31, 2012, New Delhi.

4 India on the Growth Turnpike

No State Left Behind

Arvind Panagariya[1]

Vijay Kelkar is that rare policy economist who can see economic policy reforms necessary to promote growth and poverty alleviation before anyone else, effectively communicate the rationale behind them to policymakers and wider public and sometimes even successfully implement them himself. In a paper published in 1999 (Kelkar, 1999), Vijay spelt out the entire gamut of reforms necessary to place the economy on a higher growth path. While the then National Democratic Alliance (NDA) government implemented many of these reforms, many others remain on the current agenda of most reform-minded economists.[2]

In this remarkably succinct four-page article, published in the *Economic and Political Weekly*, Vijay even called for 'innovative measures

1. Work on this paper has been supported by Columbia University's Program on Indian Economic Policies, funded by a generous grant from the John Templeton Foundation. The opinions expressed in the paper are those of the author and do not necessarily reflect the views of the John Templeton Foundation. Grateful thanks are due to R.C. Mody for pointing out an important error in an earlier draft of the paper.

2. In the paper, Kelkar (1999) emphasised the need for the 'parliament to adopt the Fiscal Responsibility Act,' 'simultaneous action both at the center and the states to increase user charges particularly of electricity, water, transport, etc,' 'privatisation of non-strategic public sector enterprises including banking sector,' promotion of 'transparency and good governance,' 'an independent monetary authority by giving greater independence to the Reserve Bank of India,' 'strengthening of independent regulatory agencies such as SEBI, TRAI, CERC, etc., and treating their independence at par with that of the judiciary,' 'reduction of both short-term and long-term real interest rates,' 'competition in product markets and the services sector by allowing free entry and freer international trade,' 'flexibility in labour markets, reform of 'laws of bankruptcy and corporate control' and 'financial markets,' 'innovative measures for creating a social safety net, such as the employment guarantee schemes of Maharashtra,' replacing product-based subsidies including food subsidies by 'food stamps and education vouchers for meeting the needs of the socially disadvantaged and weaker sections of society' ('government can be a financier but need not be a producer of such services') and taking the reforms 'to the level of the states'.

for creating a social safety net, such as the employment guarantee schemes of Maharashtra' that the United Progressive Alliance (UPA) went on to introduce years later under the title of the 'National Rural Employment Guarantee Scheme'. In the paper, Vijay also pointed out that India needed to replace product-based subsidies including those on food by 'food stamps and education vouchers' that find overwhelming support among economists today but unfortunately, meet resistance from politicians who instinctively go for more opaque instruments.

Kelkar (1999) also understood and emphasised before most others the connection between reforms and the demographic pattern in the Indian context. But rather than mindlessly claim the inevitability of accelerated growth just because India now had a younger labour force that was getting younger by the day, as many commentators erroneously do, he powerfully cited this phenomenon as the reason for the urgency of reforms. Putting his background in physics to good use, he argued (Kelkar, 1999: 2329):

> The reason for emphasising urgency [of reforms] is the unique state of our demographic transition. In the next couple of decades India will have the once-in-a-lifetime chance of having a population structure where the share of the working population will be the largest. After these decades, the process of aging will catch up and the vigor of the working population will decline. When a satellite is put into orbit, it requires high velocity to ensure exit from the earth's gravitational force, similarly, if our economy is to exit from the gravitational pull of poverty, it requires an exit velocity of double-digit growth rate over the next two decades.

Vijay also has an uncanny ability to predict big economic changes before other analysts, even when the latter are armed with large-scale forecasting models. While I like to claim the credit for being the first to predict India's shift to 5 to 7 per cent growth path in a paper (Panagariya, 1994) cautiously titled 'India: A New Tiger on the Block?' in view of the fragility of reform process at the time, Vijay was perhaps the first to predict the shift to the current near-double-digit growth path in his K.R. Narayanan Oration (Kelkar, 2004) boldly titled 'India: On the Growth Turnpike'. He was clearly among the first to appreciate the breadth and depth of the reforms Prime Ministers Rajiv Gandhi, Narasimha Rao and Atal Bihari Vajpayee had by then cumulatively put in place. To underline the point, it is worthwhile to recall the concluding paragraph of his oration in its entirety:

> Now, I would like to sum up. Thanks to painstaking policy reforms initiated over the last two decades by successive Governments, I believe that India is at the threshold of "a golden age of growth", with India's democratic framework being a key growth fundamental. It seems to me that, over time, India has paid the 'fixed costs' of democracy in terms of the creation of institutional infrastructure, traditions and conventions. Further, India's democratic system has also internalised what Prime Minister Vajpayee calls *Coalition Dharma*, showing that coalitions can provide stable government and push economic reforms. This means that in the future, the economy can reap the dividends from the resultant systemic stability. Thus, India—riding the wave of growth fundamentals such as demographic transition, human capital accumulation, improved incentive structures, diffusion of new technologies such as IT, total factor productivity accelerators through 'network industries', and an improved security environment—will be growing at growth rates which can be above 10 per cent per annum i.e. double digit growth rates. There is an ineffable sense of joy for me personally, and professionally, to see India embark on this growth odyssey, a journey that I call "India: On the growth turnpike".

The shift to double-digit or even higher growth Vijay had predicted has so far not come true but something very close to it has happened. India clocked the steady annual average growth of 8.5 per cent for six years beginning in 2003-04 and ending in 2008-09. Even during the crisis year of 2008-09, the country pulled off an impressive 6.7 per cent growth and recovered in the second quarter of 2009-10—the latest quarter for which we have the data—to 7.9 per cent. The country is almost certain to perform even better in the forthcoming years.

Against the backdrop of these developments, I recently asked Vijay whether in his view India could transition to growth rates of 10 per cent or higher, even recognising the reluctance of the UPA to carry forward the reform agenda. His answer was an emphatic yes. The reason, according to him, is the momentum and energy he has witnessed in almost every one of India's states that he visited as the Chairman, Thirteenth Finance Commission as a mandatory part of the Commission's consultation process.

This then is the long-winded background to the present paper. The paper honours Vijay by undertaking a detailed investigation of growth in various states of India in recent years to throw light on his hypothesis of India's impending transition to double-digit growth. My conclusion, in a nutshell, is that data support Vijay's observation during his state visits in one important respect: growth momentum has reached almost all states in India. Since 2003-04, the year in which the national shift to 8 to 9 per cent took place, virtually every state has grown faster than in any of the previous periods for which data are available. Nearly all of them have also crossed the 6 per cent threshold of growth. If we combine this shift with the hypothesis Jagdish Bhagwati and I offered in our *Wall Street Journal* article (Bhagwati and Panagariya, 2004) that increased prospects of change turn the electorate more demanding and therefore create a more favourable environment for growth-enhancing reforms, especially at the level of the state, a sound basis for Vijay's optimism is established.

The remainder of the paper is divided into four sections. In the first section, I identify large and small states and union territories and examine the growth experience in 18 larger states representing 93 per cent of India's population. I show that every single one of these states has seen its growth accelerate during 2003-04 to 2008-09 relative to all prior periods no matter how we define these periods. In the second section, I consider the impact on poverty in these same states. I show that between 1993-94 and 2004-2005, which can be largely identified as the post-reform period, poverty fell in every one of these states. In the third, I repeat this analysis for the smaller states and UTs accounting for the remaining 7 per cent of the country's population. The smaller states include the three newest states carved out of Madhya Pradesh, Bihar and Uttar Pradesh in November 2000, six tiny states created out of Assam beginning with Nagaland in 1963, Sikkim and Goa. I demonstrate that the same broad pattern found in the larger states applies to smaller states. With rare exceptions, growth has significantly accelerated in all smaller states and UTs during 2003-2009 and poverty has declined uniformly between 1993-94 and 2004-05. Indeed, data exhibit such an impressive decline in poverty in the six states carved out of Assam that I feel forced to speculate whether this may not have resulted from sampling and non-sampling errors. In the final section, I conclude the paper.

Growth: No State Left Behind

Any state-level analysis must begin with the qualification that the quality of the data for states is not as good as that for the country as a whole.[3] The Central Statistical Organisation (CSO), which compiles the data, specifically warns at the bottom of each table that the data are not strictly comparable across states and union territories (UTs) due to differences in 'methodology of compilation'. There are also bound to be differences in the underlying prices at which output is valued in different states. Additionally, we encounter difficulties in comparison over time since the CSO provides data for different periods using different base years. Nevertheless, these data being the only ones available and surely of much better quality than those available for most developing countries, there is ample justification for inferring some broad trends from them.

I begin with a broad perspective on the Indian states and UTs from the economic standpoint. Table 4.1 reports the net state domestic product (NSDP) in all 28 states (except Nagaland) and four UTs (Andaman & Nicobar Islands, Chandigarh, Delhi and Puducherry) in the descending order in the year 2006-07.[4] While data for many states and UTs are available for years 2007-08 and 2008-09, 2006-07 is the latest year for which they are available for all states except Nagaland and for the four UTs.

The key observation from Table 4.1 is that once we get past Jammu and Kashmir, the remaining states and UTs are tiny from the national perspective. Of the 31 states and UTs listed, the last 10 produced output worth less than 100 billion rupees or $2 billion. Going by the information available for 2005-06, Nagaland also falls below these thresholds. This leaves only 20 states and Delhi with NSDP exceeding 100 billion rupees. Whereas it is important to analyse the smaller entities—eight states and three UTs—from the standpoint of welfare of their respective citizens, at least in an accounting sense, economic outcomes in them have very limited consequences for the country as a whole. This conclusion calls for focussing at least the initial analysis on the 20 larger states and Delhi. Out

3. Although formally the Central Statistical Organisation (CSO) is the source of the state-level data, the latter are actually compiled by respective states. CSO simply reproduces the data it receives from the states.

4. The remaining UTs—Dadra and Nagar Haveli, Daman and Diu and Lakshadweep—are tiny and not considered in this paper.

Table 4.1

Net State Domestic Product (NSDP) at Factor Cost in 2006-07 at 1999-2000 Prices in Descending Order of Magnitude

State	*NSDP in 2006-07 (Billion Rupees at 1999-2000 Prices)*	*NSDP in 2006-07 ($Billion)**
Maharashtra	3276.0	72.3
Uttar Pradesh	2100.4	46.4
West Bengal	1865.7	41.2
Andhra Pradesh	1854.6	41.0
Tamil Nadu	1853.1	40.9
Gujarat	1499.3	33.1
Karnataka	1300.2	28.7
Rajasthan	1036.2	22.9
Kerala	1004.3	22.2
Delhi	893.1	19.7
Haryana	879.4	19.4
Madhya Pradesh	864.3	19.1
Punjab	810.6	17.9
Bihar	748.3	16.5
Orissa	607.5	13.4
Assam	437.8	9.7
Jharkhand	421.4	9.3
Chhattisgarh	361.8	8.0
Uttarakhand	206.4	4.6
Himachal Pradesh	193.1	4.3
Jammu & Kashmir	185.6	4.1
Goa	85.0	1.9
Chandigarh	79.9	1.8
Tripura	78.9	1.7
Meghalaya	48.0	1.1
Puducherry	41.6	0.9
Manipur	38.7	0.9
Arunachal Pradesh	23.7	0.5
Mizoram	19.7	0.4
Andaman & Nicobar Islands	13.2	0.3
Sikkim	13.0	0.3
Total	22840.5	504.4

Note: * The conversion into US dollars is done at the average financial year exchange rate of rupees 45.2849 per dollar reported in Table 149 in RBI (2009).

Source: State related tables in RBI (2009).

of this smaller group, three states—Chhattisgarh, Jharkhand and Uttarakhand—were created only recently in November 2000. Therefore, our initial focus is on 17 states and Delhi, which together accounted for 93 per cent of the population as per 2001 Census. We will return to the small states and UTs and the recently created states later.

Before I turn to the growth experience of the restricted set of states and Delhi, however, it is useful to examine the pattern of per capita NSDP across all 28 states and four UTs. The latest year for which we have NSDP data for all states and UTs is 2006-07. For most but not all states and UTs, it is also available for the following two years. Therefore, in Table 4.2, I report per capita NSDP for years 2005-06, 2006-07 and 2007-08 at 1999-2000 prices for all states and UTs when available. The states and UTs are now ranked from the highest to lowest per capita NSDP in the year 2005-2006. There are occasional shifts in the rankings between two adjacent entities during 2006-07 and 2007-08 but not drastic movements.

Three points regarding per capita NSDP may be gleaned from Table 4.2. First, Chandigarh, Goa and Delhi in that order exhibit per capita income levels that are exceptionally high relative to all other states and UTs. Chandigarh is the capital of both Punjab and Haryana—two of the most prosperous states—and Delhi of India. Goa is the smallest state by area and attracts tourists from around the world. Given these special circumstances of the top three, substantively speaking, Haryana and Maharashtra in that order are the richest states. Even in these cases, the closeness of Haryana to Delhi and the presence of Mumbai in Maharashtra play a crucial role. Second, based on 2005-06 data, strictly speaking, only 43 per cent of the population enjoys income above the countrywide average. Andhra Pradesh is the last state to qualify as having income above India-wide average. If we take a slightly more relaxed attitude, however, and count Sikkim, Uttarakhand and West Bengal as more or less having income equal to the countrywide average, the proportion of population enjoying the national per capita income rises to 51.8 per cent. Finally, Madhya Pradesh, Uttar Pradesh and Bihar, accounting for 30.1 per cent of India's population, remain the three poorest states of India. Per capita incomes in these states at 1999-2000 prices remained below 15,000 rupees in 2007-08. In considering the growth experience below, special attention will have to be paid to these and other states at the low end of per capita income spectrum.

Table 4.2

Per Capita NSDP at Factor Cost in Descending Order of Per Capita NSDP in 2005-06

State/Union Territory	*Per Capita NSDP (Rupees Per Year at 1999-2000 Prices)*			*Share in Population (2001 Census)*
	2005-06	*2006-07*	*2007-08*	
Chandigarh	66134	70361	75480	0.09
Goa	52201	56021	60232	0.13
Delhi	48885	54821	60189	1.35
Puducherry	36397	38488	40931	0.09
Haryana	32975	37314	39796	2.06
Maharashtra	28683	30982	33302	9.42
Andaman & Nicobar Islands	28637	31009	–	0.03
Punjab	28487	30041	31439	2.37
Himachal Pradesh	27443	28639	30586	0.59
Kerala	27220	30044	32961	3.1
Tamil Nadu	25558	28320	29445	6.07
Gujarat	25487	27027	–	4.93
Karnataka	21913	22952	25226	5.14
Tripura	21524	22987	–	0.31
Andhra Pradesh	21334	22835	25044	7.41
Sikkim	20777	22167	23761	0.05
Uttarakhand	20355	22178	–	0.83
West Bengal	20212	21753	23229	7.79
Mizoram	18616	19220	19750	0.09
Meghalaya	18501	19292	20094	0.23
Nagaland	18318	–	–	0.19
Arunachal Pradesh	18081	20087	20570	0.11
Jammu & Kashmir	16086	16817	17590	0.99
Rajasthan	15541	16460	17334	5.49
Chhattisgarh	14694	15660	16740	2.03
Manipur	14559	15047	15270	0.21
Assam	14419	15152	15857	2.59
Orissa	13957	15528	16149	3.58
Jharkhand	12950	14252	15303	2.62
Madhya Pradesh	12567	12881	13299	5.87
Uttar Pradesh	10758	11334	11939	16.16
Bihar	6719	8167	8703	8.07
All-India	20868	22580	24295	100

Source: Tables related to macro and state-level data in RBI (2009).

I finally turn to the growth experience of the 17 largest states and Delhi. For expositional convenience, in the rest of the paper, I will refer to Delhi as a state as well. Given that this UT has its own Chief Minister and cabinet to look after most aspects of its local administration, this is not altogether without justification. Table 4.3 reports the average annual growth rates of NSDP for selected periods between 1981-82 and 2008-09 for the 18 states. Based on the sharpness of differences in the national growth rates, I have divided the post-1980 period into two parts in my book *India: The Emerging Giant* (Panagariya, 2008: Chapter 1): 1981-82 to 1987-1988 and 1988-89 and beyond. Given the smaller number of years exhibiting 8 to 9 per cent growth rate at the time I wrote the book, I also hypothesised the emergence of a second break in the growth rate in the year 2003-04. This hypothesis is now a reality requiring a division of post-1980 period into 1981-82 to 1987-88, 1988-89 to 2002-03 and 2003-04 to 2008-09.[5] Accordingly, in the first three columns with numbers in Table 4.3, I report the average annual growth rates during these periods labelled 1981-1988, 1988-2003 and 2003-2009, respectively. For those who like to think of 1991-92, the year in which systematic reforms at the national level began, as defining the dividing line, I also report the average growth rates for periods 1981-82 to 1991-92 and 1992-93 to 2002-03 in the last two columns of Table 4.3, respectively. The states are listed in the declining order of per capita NSDP in the year 2005-06.

Several points emerge from the growth rates in Table 4.3. First and most strikingly, for every single state in the table, growth rate during 2003-2009 exceeded that in every preceding period, however defined. Growth momentum has now penetrated all large states, which together account for 93 per cent of the total population as per 2001 Census. Second and related, with the exception of Jammu and Kashmir and Assam, both of which have been subject to insurgencies, every single large state and Delhi have grown 6 per cent or faster during the last six financial years. Even Jammu and Kashmir and Assam are not far behind, respectively growing 5.7 and 5.5

5. The CSO does not provide a single series of the NSDP at the state level. Instead, the NSDP data for 1980-81 to 1993-94 are provided at 1980-81 prices, those for 1993-94 to 1999-2000 at 1993-94 prices and those for 1999-2000 to 2008-09 at 1999-2000 prices. I use these data to first compute the annual growth rate for each year and then, treating the resulting growth rates as a single series, compute the average annual growth rates shown in Table 4.3.

Table 4.3

Annual Average Growth Rates of NSDP at Factor Cost with States Listed in the Descending Order of Per Capita NSDP at Factor Cost in 2005-06

Year	*1981-1988*	*1988-2003*	*2003-2009*	*1981-1992*	*1992-2003*	*1981-2009*
Delhi	7.7	7.8	11.2*	7.9	7.6	8.4
Haryana	4.6	6.6	10.0	5.9	6.1	6.8
Maharashtra	4.2	6.7	8.9*	6.3	5.4	6.5
Punjab	5.5	4.2	6.1	5.3	3.8	4.9
Himachal Pradesh	3.3	6.5	7.5*	4.6	6.6	5.9
Kerala	1.3	6.1	9.4*	3.5	5.8	5.5
Tamil Nadu	4.8	5.5	8.6	5.4	5.1	6.0
Gujarat	2.8	7.8	10.3#	7.0	5.3	6.8
Karnataka	5.1	6.0	7.7	5.5	6.0	6.1
Andhra Pradesh	5.2	6.2	8.6*	5.7	6.0	6.4
West Bengal	4.2	5.9	6.9*	4.4	6.5	5.7
Jammu & Kashmir	0.9	4.7	5.7*	2.9	4.3	3.9
Rajasthan	4.1	6.7	9.4	7.6	3.8	6.6
Assam	4.1	3.0	5.5	3.9	2.6	3.8
Orissa	2.7	3.9	9.4	3.4	3.7	4.8
Madhya Pradesh	3.6	4.3	6.0*	4.1	4.1	4.5
Uttar Pradesh	4.1	3.7	6.1	4.3	3.2	4.3
Bihar	4.3	4.2	8.4	3.3	5.4	5.1

Note: * This growth rate is based on the average of growth rates from 2003-04 to 2007-08 since the NSDP for this state for 2008-09 is still not reported.

This growth rate is based on the average of growth rates from 2003-04 to 2006-07 since the NSDP for this state for 2007-08 and 2008-09 are still not reported.

Source: Author's calculations using state-level data in RBI (2009).

per cent annually during this period. In comparison, only one state (Delhi) during 1981-1988 and nine states during 1988-2003 grew at rates of 6 per cent or higher. Third, some of the poorest states have shown some of the highest growth rates during 2003-2009. Rajasthan, Orissa and Bihar, all of them among bottom six states (respectively ranking 13th, 15th and 18th), grew at annual rates of 9.4, 9.4 and 8.4 per cent, respectively. Growth rates in Orissa and Rajasthan exceed those in all states except Delhi, Gujarat and Haryana. Finally, the bottom six states, which account for 41.8 per cent of the population as per 2001 Census, have together grown at the annual average rate of 7.1 per cent during 2003-2009.[6] This rate is in contrast to 3.8 per cent during 1981-1988 and 4.0 per cent during 1988-2003. A major breakthrough for the bottom two-fifths of India seems clearly to be in the making.

As a footnote, I may state that in my book, published two years ago, I had already noted the signs of a turnaround in the bottom six states in Table 4.3. The evidence emerging in the recent years more firmly establishes that trend. In a key paragraph in the book (Panagariya, 2008: 164), I had stated,

> According to Table 8.2, among the six bottom states, only Assam saw a clear decline in its growth rate in Phase IV [1988-2004] over Phase III [1981-88]. Among the remaining five, Rajasthan, Madhya Pradesh and Orissa saw a clear and significant rise in the growth rates of per-capita net domestic product in Phase IV. Bihar saw a sharp decline from 2.1 per cent during Phase III to –0.3 per cent during 1988-94 but recovered to 2.8 per cent during the longer phase of 1994-04. Uttar Pradesh had the opposite fate: its growth rate rose from 1.7 per cent in Phase III to 2.2 per cent during 1988-94 but fell to 1.2 per cent during 1994-04.

Poverty: Progress Everywhere

Development economists have seen growth not as an objective in itself but as an instrument of poverty alleviation. It is therefore important to ask if rising incomes have been translating into reduced poverty. Here it is important to remind at the outset that while rapid growth is likely to speed up poverty alleviation, even slow growth is expected to eventually eradicate poverty. While low per capita incomes in the states such as Bihar, Uttar Pradesh and Madhya Pradesh are likely to be associated with higher poverty levels, rising income levels even in these states are likely to be associated with reduced poverty.

Table 4.4 reports the proportion of the population below the official poverty line in the 18 largest states in 1983, 1993-94 and 2004-05. Two clear observations follow from the data. First, poverty declined or remained unchanged in every single state shown in Table 4.4 in the post-reform

---

6. Because the NSDP for Madhya Pradesh for 2008-09 is not available, the underlying six-state growth rate for this last year is computed on the basis of the remaining five states only.

decade of 1993-94 to 2004-05. Growth during this period has been inclusive across the board. Poverty also declined in most states between 1983 and 1993-94 but there are four exceptions: Haryana, Himachal Pradesh, Jammu and Kashmir and Assam. The rise in Assam and Jammu and Kashmir was one percentage point or less but larger in Haryana and Himachal Pradesh. If we consider the entire period from 1983 to 2004-05, poverty declined in every single state.

Table 4.4

Poverty Ratios with States Listed in the Descending Order of Per Capita NSDP in 2005-06

States/UT	*1983*	*1993-94*	*2004-05*
Delhi	26.2	14.7	14.7
Haryana	21.4	25.1	14
Maharashtra	43.4	36.9	30.7
Punjab	16.2	11.8	8.4
Himachal Pradesh	16.4	28.4	10
Kerala	40.4	25.4	15
Tamil Nadu	51.7	35.0	22.5
Gujarat	32.8	24.2	16.8
Karnataka	38.2	33.2	25
Andhra Pradesh	28.9	22.2	15.8
West Bengal	54.9	35.7	24.7
Jammu & Kashmir	24.2	25.2	5.4
Rajasthan	34.5	27.4	22.1
Assam	40.5	40.9	19.7
Orissa	65.3	48.6	46.4
Madhya Pradesh	49.8	42.5	38.3
Uttar Pradesh	47.1	40.9	32.8
Bihar	62.2	55.0	41.4
All-India	44.5	36.0	27.5

Source: Adapted from Table 18 posted on the Planning Commission website accessed on January 10, 2010.

The second observation flowing from Table 4.4 is that while one can hardly expect the ranking according to poverty rates to match that according to per capita income, there is broad correspondence between the two. High per capita income states, listed in the upper half of Table 4.4, exhibit lower poverty levels on the average than lower per capita income states, listed in the lower half of the table. Madhya Pradesh, Uttar Pradesh and Bihar are the bottom three states by per capita income and they have the highest poverty ratios. Delhi, Haryana, Punjab, Himachal Pradesh and Kerala are among the states with highest per capita incomes and lowest poverty ratios. Maharashtra, Tamil Nadu and Karnataka are the three exceptions that show high poverty ratios despite their relatively high per capita incomes. Precise reasons why this is the case requires closer investigation.

Before I conclude the discussion, it is useful to check the relationship of per capita incomes to another possible, even if, crude indicator of poverty: the number of telephones per hundred individuals or teledensity. Even if the absolute level of this indicator does not reflect poverty since it has been almost surely rising much faster than poverty is declining over time, it may still give us some idea of relative magnitudes of poverty across states. It may be hypothesised that most people want to own a telephone but are unable to do so unless they reach a minimum level of income. If this hypothesis is correct, in a phase when the cost of owning a telephone is rapidly declining, teledensity will achieve higher levels in states with lower poverty ratios than those with higher poverty ratios.

Table 4.5 reports teledensity for the 18 largest states with the states continuing to be listed in the declining order of per capita NSDP in 2005-2006. The pattern turns out to be remarkably consistent with the above hypothesis. In broad terms, states in the upper half of the table show higher teledensity than those in the lower half. Setting aside the anomalous case of Assam, which is richer than Orissa, Madhya Pradesh and Uttar Pradesh but has a slightly lower teledensity than them, the bottom four states by per capita income also exhibit the lowest teledensity and highest poverty ratios.

Smaller and Newer States and Union Territories

Let me now briefly turn to the remaining 14 smaller and newer states and UTs that I have excluded from the discussion up to this point. At 7 per cent, these states and UTs represent only a tiny proportion of Indian population. Nevertheless, given the large absolute size of the country, their inhabitants currently number approximately 80 million. Of the 14 entities to be discussed in this section, 11 enjoy statehood and three are UTs. The states in this group were conferred statehood at different times, the earliest one being Nagaland in 1963 and the latest ones Chhattisgarh, Jharkhand and Uttarakhand in 2000. The three UTs are Andaman and Nicobar Islands, Chandigarh and Puducherry. I first consider the three largest states among the group of 11 to be covered in this section: Jharkhand, Chhattisgarh and Uttarakhand. These are also the newest states.

Table 4.5

Teledensity (Number of Phones Per 100 People) as of March 31, 2009 with States Listed in Descending Order of Per Capita NSDP in 2005-06

State	*Telephones Per 100 Individuals*
Delhi	140.18
Haryana	43.67
Maharashtra	50.95
Punjab	58.25
Himachal Pradesh	55.80
Kerala	58.48
Tamil Nadu	59.92
Gujarat	45.16
Karnataka	45.21
Andhra Pradesh	39.59
West Bengal	33.60
J&K	32.76
Rajasthan	37.15
Assam	20.65
Orissa	23.30
Madhya Pradesh	23.79
Uttar Pradesh	24.28
Bihar	17.78
National average	36.98

Source: Telecom Regulatory Authority of India (2009).

Three Newest States

Jharkhand, Chhattisgarh and Uttarakhand were created out of Bihar, Madhya Pradesh and Uttar Pradesh, respectively, in November 2000. As per 2001 Census, the three states together accounted for 5.48 per cent of the country's population. This means the remaining states and UTs account for just 1.5 per cent of the country's population.

One way to judge the performance of these new states is to compare them to respective mother states. This is partially done in Table 4.6, which provides per capita incomes of the new states, their respective mother states and how the former stack up relative to the latter in years 1999-2000 and 2005-06 to 2008-09.[7] Uttarakhand began at a per capita income level 1.4 times that of Uttar Pradesh in 1999-2000. By 2006-07, the latest year for which the necessary information is available, it had raced off to per capita income twice that of its mother state. Chhattisgarh began at per capita income nine-tenths that of Madhya Pradesh but steadily bridged the gap and achieved an impressive 30 per cent lead over the latter by 2007-08. Finally, Jharkhand began at per capita income twice that of Bihar and has lost ground relative to it since its creation. It rebounded in 2008-09 in relative terms but not enough to recover its original 1999-2000 lead. Based on press accounts, it is almost certain that during the years under consideration, Uttarakhand and Chhattisgarh were led by administrations superior to the respective mother states while in the case of Jharkhand, the opposite was true.

Next compare the relative growth rates of NSDP and poverty ratios for the three newest states and their respective mother states shown in Table 4.7. Three observations follow from this table. First, the three newest states have fully shared in the rapid growth during 2003-2009, each of them growing faster than 9 per cent per year. These rates exceed the growth rates in the prior period by wide margins. Second, all three states have grown faster than their respective mother states during 2003-2009. Finally, the poverty ratio in each of the three newest states remains extraordinarily high. In two cases (Uttarakhand and Chhattisgarh), the poverty ratio is higher than the corresponding mother state. But since we do not have the poverty data in a prior period, we cannot judge the performance of the newest states relative to the mother states in poverty alleviation. It is possible that they were born with larger poverty ratios.

---

7. Even though the states were actually created in November 2000, the CSO is able to compute and report the data for them beginning in 1993-94, presumably because it has data at the level of the districts.

Table 4.6

Three Newest States: Real and Relative Per Capita NSDP

State/Union Territory	Per Capita NSDP (Rupees Per Year)					Share in Population (2001 Census)
	1999-2000	2005-06	2006-07	2007-08	2008-09	
Uttarakhand (2000)	13516	20355	22178	N.A.	N.A.	0.83
Chhattisgarh (2000)	11629	14694	15660	16740	17684	2.03
Jharkhand (2000)	13260	12950	14252	15303	16294	2.62
Uttar Pradesh	9749	10758	11334	11939	12481	16.16
Madhya Pradesh	12384	12567	12881	13299	N.A.	5.87
Bihar	5786	6719	8167	8703	9586	8.07
Uttarakhand/ Uttar Pradesh	1.4	1.9	2.0	N.A.	N.A.	N.A.
Chhattisgarh/ Madhya Pradesh	0.9	1.2	1.2	1.3	N.A.	N.A.
Jharkhand/Bihar	2.0	1.6	1.6	1.8	1.7	N.A.

Note: N.A. stands for 'not available'.

Source: RBI (2009) and the author's calculations.

Table 4.7

Three Newest States: Growth and Poverty

State	Growth Rate of NSDP		Poverty Ratio
	1994-2003	2003-2009	2004-05
Uttarakhand	4.8	9.4*	39.6
Chhattisgarh	2.0	9.1	40.9
Jharkhand	3.7	9.3	40.3
Uttar Pradesh	3.3	6.1	32.8
Madhya Pradesh	3.4	6.0^	38.3
Bihar	5.7	8.4	41.4

Note: * Based on data until 2006-07 only.
^ Based on data until 2007-08 only.

Source: Growth rates are calculated by the author using NSDP figures in the tables in RBI (2009) and poverty figures are from the Planning Commission website.

Smaller Northeastern States, Sikkim, Goa and UTs

I finally turn to the remaining eight states and three UTs accounting for 1.53 per cent of the country's population as per the 2001 Census. Of the former, six—Arunachal Pradesh, Manipur, Meghalaya, Mizoram,

Nagaland and Tripura—have been carved out of Assam at various times beginning with Nagaland in 1963 and account for 1.14 per cent of India's population. Goa was turned from a UT to state in 1987 and Sikkim was turned from an autonomous region within the Indian Union to a state in 1975. As already noted, the three smaller UTs are: Chandigarh, Andaman and Nicobar Islands and Puducherry.

Table 4.8 reports per capita incomes of the eight states and three UTs in three recent years. I first list the six states carved out of Assam followed by Sikkim and Goa and then the three UTs in alphabetical order. In each case, the name of the state is followed by the year in which it was created. The differences between Goa and the three UTs on the one hand and the remaining states on the other are stark. The former group enjoys per capita incomes well above the national average while the latter systematically falls below it. Indeed, Chandigarh and Goa in that order have the highest per

Table 4.8

Per Capita NSDP at 1999-2000 Prices in Smaller States and UTs

State*/Union Territory	Per Capita NSDP (Rupees Per Year)					Share in Population (2001 Census)
	1999-2000	2005-06	2006-07	2007-08	2008-09	
Arunachal Pradesh (1987)	13990	18081	20087	20570		0.11
Manipur (1972)	11549	14559	15047	15270		0.21
Meghalaya (1972)	14355	18501	19292	20094		0.23
Mizoram (1986)	16443	18616	19220	19750	20483	0.09
Nagaland (1963)	13819	18318	—	—		0.19
Tripura (1972)	14119	21524	22987	—		0.31
Sikkim (1975)	14890	20777	22167	23761		0.05
Goa (1987)	42296	52201	56021	60232		0.13
Andaman & Nicobar Islands	24005	28637	31009	—		0.03
Chandigarh	44502	66134	70361	75480		0.09
Puducherry	30865	36397	38488	40931		0.09
All-India	15881	20868	22580	24295	25494	100

Note: * Year next to a state's name indicates the time of conferral of statehood.

Source: RBI (2009).

capita NSDP in the country (followed by Delhi). It is quite clear that a long history of insurgencies and conflicts in various tribal regions of Assam have led to a division of the original state into ever-smaller states without delivering significant income gains.

In Table 4.9, I report the growth rates as well as poverty ratios for the eight smallest states and three UTs. The pattern we have observed for larger states continues to reproduce itself here as well. With rare exceptions, growth rates during 2003-2008 are significantly higher than in the prior period. The only anomalous case is that of Puducherry, which experienced a large 11.9 per cent decline in its NSDP in 2004-05 leading to an overall low growth of 3.1 per cent during 2003-2008. Poverty rates spring something of a surprise. In all six states carved out of Assam and Sikkim, poverty rates have been cut in half or less between 1993-94 and 2004-05. Whether this change is real or the outcome of some statistical quirk needs to be investigated.

Table 4.9

Smaller States and UTs: Growth and Poverty

State/UT*	*Annual Growth in NSDP*		*Poverty Ratio*		
	1994-2003	*2003-2008*	*1983*	*1993-94*	*2004-05*
Arunachal Pradesh (1987)	3.9	6.9	40.9	39.4	17.6
Manipur (1972)	3.7	6.5	37.0	33.8	17.3
Meghalaya (1972)	6.7	6.1	38.8	37.9	18.5
Mizoram (1986)	6.6	4.0	36.0	25.7	12.6
Nagaland (1963)	7.3	7.5^	39.3	37.9	19.0
Tripura (1972)	8.2	8.0^	40.0	39.0	18.9
Sikkim (1975)	6.3	8.3	39.7	41.4	20.1
Goa (1987)	6.7	10.2	18.9	14.9	13.8
Andaman & Nicobar Islands	4.1	8.8^	52.1	34.5	22.6
Chandigarh	10.0	11.5	23.8	11.4	7.1
Puducherry	13.5	3.1	50.1	37.4	22.4

Note: * Year next to a state's name indicates the time of conferral of statehood.

^ Excludes year 2007-08.

Source: Per capita incomes and population from tables in the RBI Handbook, 2009. The year of statehood is from official websites of various states.

Conclusions

Perhaps the single most important and robust conclusion to come out of the detailed exercise undertaken in this paper is that as India has moved on to the growth turnpike, accelerated growth has reached every single state. On the poverty front, all states have seen the rate of poverty decline between 1993-94 and 2004-05 largely representing the post-reform period. Of course, poverty rates from 2004-05 do not reflect the full effect of the accelerated growth since this phenomenon had just set in prior to the 2004-05 survey.

An important aspect of this impressive growth story is the phenomenal growth some of the poorest states have experienced in recent years. Three of the bottom six states among the larger states have grown 8 per cent or more annually during 2003-04 to 2008-09. Rajasthan and Orissa have grown 9.4 per cent each and Bihar 8.4 per cent. Likewise, all three of the newest states, which were carved out of three of the poorest four larger states have grown at rates exceeding 9 per cent. In concluding this extraordinary story, I can justifiably join Vijay Kelkar in expressing 'personal and professional joy' in seeing India not only push ahead full-speed on the growth turnpike but also carry all its parts—big and small and rich and poor—with it.

References

Bhagwati, Jagdish and Arvind Panagariya (2004). "Great Expectations", *Wall Street Journal*, May 24.

Kelkar, Vijay (1999). "India's Emerging Economic Challenges", *Economic and Political Weekly* 34(33): 2326-29, August 14-20.

———. (2004). "India: On the Growth Turnpike", *Narayanan Oration*, Australian National University, April.

Panagariya, Arvind (1994). "India: A new Tiger on the Block?", *Journal of International Affairs* 48(1): 193-221, Summer.

———. (2008). *India: The Emerging Giant*. New York: Oxford University Press.

Reserve Bank of India (RBI). (2009). *Handbook of Statistics on Indian Economy*. Available at *http://www.rbi.org.in/home.aspx*

Telecom Regulatory Authority of India (TRAI) (2009). *The Indian Telecom Services Performance Indicators April-June 2009*. New Delhi, India, October 1.

Kochhar, Sameer (ed.) (2010). *India on Growth Turnpike (Essays in Honour of Vijay Kelkar)*. New Delhi: Academic Foundation.

5 Rejigging the Elephant Dance

Duvvuri Subbarao

India Growth Story

India clocked average annual growth of 9 per cent in the five-year period from 2003-2008. For a nation that once believed that the Hindu rate of growth was its destiny, this remarkable growth performance was cause for celebration. It was also a trigger for setting off an aspiration for double digit growth.

The India growth story was thrown off track by the global financial crisis which engulfed virtually every country in the world. We recovered from the crisis sooner than other countries, but the growth rate is yet to reach the pre-crisis level. There is widespread anxiety that we may have got derailed from the high growth trajectory, and a number of questions are being asked. Is our growth story faltering? Has India's potential growth rate declined because of the crisis? Are the growth drivers that worked our way during 2003-2008 still intact? When will we reach double digit growth, and what indeed should we be doing to achieve that?

Elephants too Dance

My simple and single answer to all of the above questions is that the India growth story is still credible. If the East Asians are the tigers, and China the dragon, India is commonly 'the elephant'—a strong animal with enormous potential but given to a lumbering pace. For a world that once believed that an elephant does not have any animal spirit, our march upto the high growth trajectory proved that an elephant too can dance. But the elephant dance got interrupted by the 'zoo party' of the global financial crisis, and to get it back on course, we need to 'rejig' the dance.

So, for India to regain its growth momentum and indeed accelerate it further, we need to address several challenges. What I propose to do is to outline what in my view are the 10 most important challenges that we need to address to move up the growth ladder.

First Challenge: Raising Agricultural Production and Productivity

The first challenge is stepping up agriculture production and productivity. We have, of course, come a long way from the chronic food shortages of the early years of independence; and even as population increased, we have been able to maintain food self-sufficiency, thanks to investment in irrigation, improved farming practices and better technologies. But in recent years, there has been growing concern about erosion at the margin of food self-sufficiency. The supply-demand gap in the food sector is, in part, a problem of success—a consequence of a shift in dietary habits from cereal to protein-based foods reflecting rising incomes, especially rural incomes. Regardless, our quest for inclusive growth will be jeopardised if we are not able to address the root causes of structural food inflation.

Some analysts argue that agriculture cannot be a concern from an overall growth perspective because it accounts for only about 15 per cent of GDP, and that the share will further decline as the economy matures. This argument is flawed. Even as its share may be small and declining, agriculture still accommodates 53 per cent of the labour force. Besides, agriculture has very vital supply-demand linkages with other sectors of the economy. Raising agricultural production and productivity is, therefore, important for containing price pressures, raising rural incomes and making growth more inclusive.

There are several initiatives necessary to launch the second green revolution—larger public investment, greater input efficiency, soil conservation, improved farming practices, developing resilience to rainfall variations and climate change effects, to name just a few. And to build forward and backward linkages, there is need to invest in rural infrastructure and the supply chain. We also need to be mindful that land and water costs will only increase over time; and inclusive growth will push up wages thereby putting upward pressure on inflation. In a context of rising costs, improving productivity becomes imperative to balance the needs of producers for higher prices and the demand of consumers for low prices.

Second Challenge: Expanding Employment

The second major challenge to making growth inclusive is to expand employment opportunities. Even as more people than ever before are in work, there is a sense of crisis about jobs. That is not surprising because unemployment is the most significant cause of economic pain in a poor country.

Unemployment may be one of our biggest problems, but analysing the problem is a challenge not the least because there are no reliable statistics. There is an enormous amount of unemployment and underemployment in the rural sector but the size and nature of the problem are unclear. Millions of people are locked in low productivity jobs in the unorganised industry and service sectors. India's high end IT service sector may be dazzling the world but, contrary to popular perception, it employs no more than three million. So, the problem of jobs is that a lot of people are out of work, and where they have work to do, they are performing below their potential.

The recent National Sample Survey Organisation (NSSO) data suggest that both unemployment rate and employment growth declined during the period 2004/05 to 2009/10. This is intriguing, but has been explained as a result of a large number of young people pursuing education resulting in fewer job seekers. This means only a temporary respite, as once out of school, these people will add to the labour force. There will be other pressures too. As agricultural productivity goes up, it will release millions of surplus labour who will have to be found jobs outside the farm sector. Also, more women will join the labour force and add to the demand for jobs. Putting all these trends together, various estimates suggest that India's labour force will increase by 250-300 million in the next 20 years.

Finding productive jobs for such huge numbers is a big challenge, and clearly the answer lies in stepping up growth, and importantly, stepping up the employment intensity of growth. Where are the jobs going to come from? To examine that, it will be interesting to look at the relative shares of different sectors of the economy in GDP and in jobs. Table 5.1 shows the figures for 2009/10.

Table 5.1

Sectoral Shares of GDP and Employment 2009/10

(Percentages)

	Share of GDP	*Share of Employment*
Agriculture	15	53
Industry	20	12
Services	65	35

The above numbers clearly underscore the need to move people out of low productivity jobs in agriculture to industry and services. A portion of the surplus labour in agriculture could be absorbed in non-farm allied activities. There will be opportunities also in the construction sector which is growing, but a major expansion of job opportunities in the service sector will not be possible without skill improvement. That will inevitably take time. So, much of the burden of job creation falls on the manufacturing sector.

For a long time, it was believed that India defied the textbook development paradigm by leapfrogging directly from agriculture to services, skipping the manufacturing sector. Our experience clearly demonstrates that such a 'leapfrog' cannot be sustained. We have to heed the textbook and look to manufacturing for expanding employment.

The recently unveiled National Manufacturing Policy aims at raising the share of manufacturing in GDP from 16 per cent to 25 per cent and generating additional employment of 100 million by 2022. To exploit the full job potential of this emphasis on manufacturing, we need to liberalise our labour laws and employment regulations so that perverse incentives to push labour into the unorganised sector are eliminated.

My discussion of the challenge of job creation will be incomplete if I do not address the issue of 'demographic dividend'. The demographic dividend argument, which has gained increasing currency in recent years, goes as follows. Demographics are in India's favour because the working age population is growing faster than the overall population. This expanding working age population will earn, and will save, thereby contributing to higher savings and higher investment, which will lead to higher growth. Aren't we carrying this 'demography is destiny' argument too far? There is nothing inevitable about the demographic dividend. Demographic dividend will flow if, and only if, we are able to find jobs for the growing labour force.

To summarise, the second challenge to sustaining India's growth momentum is to expand employment opportunities and improve labour productivity.

Third Challenge: Raising Productivity

Job expansion is one side of the challenge to inclusive growth. The other side is enhancing productivity. Historical evidence clearly demonstrates a quantum jump in productivity as labour moves from the agriculture to the secondary and tertiary sectors. Back of the envelope calculations show that at the current stage of our economic development, as a worker moves from agriculture to other sectors, his/her productivity increases by nearly a factor of five.

Productivity improvement entails better managing factors of production as well as factor productivity. In terms of factors of production, managing surplus labour in the farm sector, raising the rate of domestic savings, attracting stable foreign savings, sustainable use of natural resources and managing the demand on land from key growth sectors will be important.

Improving factor productivity hinges critically on raising the skill endowment of the labour force. The skills gap is no longer just a handicap; it is turning out to be a crisis. For example, we want to scale up steel production to 120 MT, and that requires millions of skilled people. Yet finding even a crane operator is oftentimes a challenge. Even as demand for skills increases, the supply-side response is lagging far behind. India churns out 350,000 engineers every year, but barely a quarter of them are employable. We have 7,000 Industrial Training Institutes (ITIs), but their curriculums are woefully outdated.

There is an incentive issue in skill training. Skill development is a quintessentially merit good where the societal cost-benefit calculus is higher than the individual cost-benefit calculation. The private sector will be reluctant to invest in skills since workers can migrate with their skills. This was the understanding that prompted the Government to launch the ambitious National Skill Development Programme as a public-private partnership (PPP) initiative to train 500 million people by 2022. Several states are also allowing vocational training institutions to be set up as PPP initiatives as well as not-for-profit societies.

To conclude, we need to focus a lot more on improving productivity across a broad range of areas in order to raise the growth rate as well as the quality of growth.

Fourth Challenge: Managing Urbanisation

Historically, there has been a strong correlation between urbanisation and economic growth across countries and across time with the causation possibly running both ways. Empirical studies show that middle income countries reach about 50 per cent urbanisation and high income countries typically have 70-80 per cent urbanisation. China's rapid growth over the last two decades, for example, ran concurrently with an increase in urbanisation rate from 32 per cent in 1997 to 50 per cent in 2010, consistent with its low middle income status. In India, we are behind on urbanisation. In the 20 years since the start of reforms, the proportion of urban population increased from 26 per cent in 1991 to just about 31 per cent in 2011.

Accelerating growth, therefore, presents two tasks from the urbanisation perspective. First, the rate of urbanisation has to pick up pace so as to move people up the productivity ladder, and second, we have to manage the pressures of urbanisation proactively.

The costs of unplanned urbanisation are already very visible in terms of the huge strains on infrastructure and sanitation, pressure on utilities and inadequate and low quality social service provision. Our cities are clearly unprepared for the influx of migrants on the scale that it is occurring and the result is slums and squatter settlements. Unplanned urbanisation has also entailed other problems ranging from crime, law and order, pollution, congestion and environmental degradation.

Expanding urban infrastructure demands huge resources. Isher Judge Ahluwalia and others have estimated that investment requirements for urban infrastructure over the 20-year period (2012-2031) would be about Rs 40 trillion which translates to an annual average investment of about $100 per capita. Mobilising resources of this order is obviously a big challenge and will call for more effective taxation, efficient project planning and implementation, innovative urban governance and much greater sensitivity to embracing the migrants into the urban ecology.

Fifth Challenge: Bridging the Infrastructure Deficit

It is widely acknowledged that infrastructure deficit is by far one of the most binding constraints to accelerating growth. Even so, our efforts to bridge the deficit have fallen way short of the task. The Eleventh Five Year Plan projected investment in infrastructure of $500 billion but the final expenditure is likely to fall well short of that. The Twelfth Plan doubles the projected investment over the five-year period (2012-2017) to $1 trillion which means that annual investment in infrastructure has to increase from the current level of 6 per cent of GDP to over 10 per cent.

Given its fiscal compulsions, the Government will clearly not be able to mobilise resources of this order. The Twelfth Plan projections call for 50 per cent of the projected investment to come from the private sector and much of the project implementation to happen in the PPP mode.

Infrastructure investment, therefore, poses three sub-challenges: mobilising the necessary resources, reforming regulations and contractual arrangements and efficient project planning and execution.

Let me make a comment here on the Reserve Bank's efforts to support infrastructure financing. Infrastructure requires long-term finance, and it should ideally be funded by long-term sources like insurance and pension funds. Since these markets in India are still not deep enough, the burden of financing infrastructure is falling on banks. Banks cannot expand lending for infrastructure beyond a point because of exposure risks. In financing infrastructure, banks also face an asset-liability mismatch problem since their liabilities are largely short-term whereas infrastructure funding is typically long-term.

In order to support infrastructure financing by banks, the Reserve Bank has relaxed regulatory norms to the extent prudential limits would permit. These include higher exposure norms in respect of single borrowers and borrower groups, permitting banks to invest in infrastructure debt funds (IDFs) and to enter into take-out financing arrangements, relaxing regulations governing bank guarantees for infrastructure financing and for financing promoters equity, and creating a separate category of non-banking financial companies (NBFCs) specialising in infrastructure finance (infrastructure finance companies).

Development of the corporate bond market will go a long way in augmenting infrastructure financing. Both the Government and the Reserve Bank have taken a number of initiatives to develop the corporate bond market and some further initiatives are in the pipeline. Even as these measures to ease the supply side of the corporate bond market are important, it is also the case that the corporate bond market remains demand-constrained suggesting that we need to address the issue from that perspective as well.

Sixth Challenge: Improving Social Sector Outcomes

India's human development indicators are distressing. As per the UNDP's Human Development Index (HDI) 2011, we rank 134 out of 187 countries, clearly in the bottom third of the league of nations. Even as education and health outcomes have improved over the years, on many indicators such as life expectancy at birth, educational attainment and nutrition levels, we rank well below average.

Historical evidence shows that economic development and social development are strongly correlated with the causation possibly running both ways. In recent years, the Government has stepped up expenditure on education, health and nutrition, revamped social sector programmes and tried to improve the delivery systems.

Among the many lacunae of our social sector programmes is that we continue to emphasise outputs and not outcomes. For improving service delivery, we need to spend more on the twin merit goods of primary education and basic health. But we also need to spend more efficiently, because better education and health are a function not just of the quantum of expenditure but also of the quality of that expenditure.

Let me illustrate this by an example. The Centre and the states in India today spend a total of 4 per cent of GDP on education. The goal is to raise this ratio to 6 per cent of GDP. That is necessary but not sufficient. Note that countries in our neighbourhood—China and Sri Lanka - spend less than 4 per cent of their respective GDPs on education. Yet they have literacy levels in the range of 90+ per cent as compared to our 74 per cent. The same goes for the health sector too. So, what matters is not just the quantum of expenditure, but also the quality of expenditure as measured by outcomes. Just to illustrate, according to a 2010 report by Pratham, an NGO focussed on education, only 17 per cent of children in classes 1 to 8 in rural areas have the ability to read a word and only 40 per cent are able to recognise numbers.

Seventh Challenge: Promoting Financial Inclusion

Why is financial inclusion important? It is important because it is a necessary condition for sustaining equitable growth. There are few, if any, instances of an economy transiting from an agrarian system to a post-industrial modern society without broad-based financial inclusion. As people having comfortable access to financial services, we all know from personal experience that economic opportunity is strongly intertwined with financial access. Such access is especially powerful for the poor as it provides them opportunities to build savings, make investments and avail credit. Importantly, access to financial services also helps the poor insure themselves against income shocks and equips them to meet emergencies such as illness, death in the family or loss of employment. Needless to add, financial inclusion protects the poor from the clutches of the usurious moneylenders.

Apart from helping the poor at the micro level, financial inclusion delivers benefits at the macro level too. By transferring money directly to the bank accounts of the beneficiaries, the Government can minimise the leakage in its affirmative action programmes. Financial inclusion gives access to banks of a large pool of low cost and stable funds which will aid their asset-liability management. Financial inclusion is, therefore, a win-win proposition for the poor, for the banks, for the governments at the Centre and the states and for the national economy.

Yet the extent of financial exclusion is staggering. Out of the 600,000 habitations in the country, less than 30,000 have a commercial bank branch. Just about 40 per cent of the population across the country have bank accounts, and this ratio is much lower in the northeast of the country. The proportion of people having any kind of life insurance cover is as low as 10 per cent and proportion having non-life insurance is an abysmally low at 0.6 per cent.

These statistics, distressing as they are, do not convey the true extent of financial exclusion. Even where bank accounts are claimed to have been opened, verification has often shown that these accounts are dormant. Few conduct any banking transactions and even fewer receive any credit. Millions of people across the country are thereby denied the opportunity to harness their earning capacity and entrepreneurial talent, and are condemned to marginalisation and poverty.

Over the last four years, the Reserve Bank has launched several initiatives to deepen financial inclusion. Our goal is not just that poor households must have a bank account, but that the account must be effectively used by them for savings, remittances and for credit. Our most ambitious initiative has been the 'business correspondent' model or branchless banking which helps reach banking services to remote villages at a low overhead cost.

By far the biggest factor inhibiting financial inclusion is that banks continue to see it as an obligation and not an opportunity. If banks take a slightly longer-term view, they will, I am sure, change their perception. Remember that illustration they give in business strategy courses. A business executive of a shoe company was sent to a large developing country to assess the market potential there. What he saw was millions of people going without shoes. He came back and reported to the management that there was no business potential there because no one wears shoes. A few months later, a strategist of a rival company went and saw the same picture. He came back and reported to his management that there is tremendous business potential in that country because of the number of shoes they can sell. Ultimately, it is a question of mindset. And such a change in mindset is what is necessary to make financial inclusion meaningful.

Eighth Challenge: Managing Globalisation

Globalisation, as measured by the movement of ideas, people, goods, services and capital across borders has undoubtedly been one of the defining features of the last 25 years. For countries that believed that geography is destiny, globalisation has opened up incredible opportunities, but also exposed them to ruthless challenges. If the 'Great Moderation' in the years before the crisis—steady growth in advanced economies and accelerating growth in emerging economies, and low and stable inflation all around the world—was an indication of the positive side of globalisation, the devastating toll of the global financial crisis was its negative side.

India too is integrating with the world, more extensively, more deeply, and faster than we tend to acknowledge. India's remarkable growth acceleration in the period 2003-2008 is a demonstration of the positive side of globalisation. We benefitted from steady growth and stability around the world. But on the flip side, the fact that we were affected by the crisis, no doubt by less than other countries, is an illustration of the negative side of globalisation. There was dismay, if not despair, that we were affected by the global financial crisis of 2008. This is because our expectations were shaped by the Asian crisis a decade ago where we came out relatively unscathed. The reason we got hit by the 2008 crisis is that between the Asian crisis of the late 1990s and the global financial crisis of 2008, India's integration with the world has deepened as evidenced by the numbers in Table 5.2.

Table 5.2

India's Deepening Global Integration

	As Percentage of GDP	
	1998-99	*2008-09*
(Export+import)/GDP	20	41
Two way (capital+current flows)/GDP	44	112

As may be seen, India's two-way trade flows doubled in the 10-year period (1998-2008), but the two-way current and capital flows increased by more than two and a half times evidencing that India's trade integration with the world got deeper, but that its financial integration got even deeper.

Globalisation as an economic force is here to stay. It is too potent a force to be comprehensively reversed, although there may be some short-term blips. As Nayan Chanda says in his book, *Bound Together: How Traders, Preachers, Adventurers and Warriors Shaped Globalisation*, globalisation was, is, and will always be inevitable. No revolution in human history has been totally benign. So it is the case with globalisation. It comes with benefits and costs.

The challenge for us, as indeed for every country in the world, will be to minimise the costs and maximise the benefits of globalisation. As India further embraces globalisation, there are many things we should be doing to optimise the cost-benefit calculus. I will cite just two examples to illustrate the point.

From the macro perspective, we need to manage the 'impossible trinity'. According to the 'impossible trinity' theory, a country cannot simultaneously have a fixed exchange rate, an open capital account and independent monetary policy. Most advanced economies give up on the fixed exchange rate to gain policy leverage on the other two parameters. Emerging economies typically eschew corner solutions in favour of middle solutions. For example, in India, our capital account is partly open, we let the exchange rate float and intervene only for the purpose of managing excess volatility and disruptions to macroeconomic stability, and operate our monetary policy-taking into account the impact of external developments on our domestic situation. Our challenge will be to continue to manage this impossible trinity even as we gradually open up our economy further.

Another dimension of the globalisation challenge that I want to illustrate is 'innovation'. Innovation has always been, and will always be, the well-spring of growth, but its importance increases in a knowledge economy. History has shown that as an economy grows, first incomes and then wages rise, and it then loses competitiveness in labour intensive industries forcing it to seek new sources of growth through innovation. Or else, it gets locked into what has now come to be called the 'middle income trap'. For example, in India we enjoyed a comparative advantage in the IT industry because of our superior technical manpower and knowledge of English. But that advantage is now threatened as other countries are fast catching up. In order to continue to benefit from globalisation, we need to move up the value chain and the only way that can happen is through innovation.

To summarise, given that globalisation is inevitable, and India will further embrace globalisation, we need to harness it to our advantage so that it aids both the quantum and quality of our growth.

Ninth Challenge: Providing a Stable and Predictable Macroeconomic Environment

That a stable and predictable macroeconomic environment is a necessary condition for growth is too obvious to need any reiteration. It is only in such an environment that both savers and investors can make informed decisions so that savings translate efficiently into productive investment. Every country that has got into a crisis in the last 25 years tells a story of excess—an excess carried to an unsustainable level and then an implosion. Fast growth gained through an excess can be an allure because the signs of instability brewing in the underbelly are oftentimes not visible in real time. But when the implosion inevitably happens, the losses by way of lost growth and welfare can be monumental.

I want to emphasise the importance of a stable macroeconomic environment by referring to two of our biggest tasks. The first is reduction of fiscal deficits both at the Centre and in the states to stabilise the debt-GDP ratios at sustainable levels. The harm that fiscal irresponsibility can cause is evident from both our own experience and that of other countries. In charting a roadmap for fiscal consolidation, we also need to be mindful of the quality of fiscal adjustment—which is to weed out unproductive expenditure and protect, if not enhance, growth-promoting expenditure.

The second task is to bring inflation down first to 5 per cent, and then even lower, consistent with India's broader integration into the global economy. A high inflation scenario makes both savers and investors uncertain. The current inflation we are experiencing is a consequence of both supply shocks and demand pressures. The Reserve Bank's monetary tightening has been aimed at restraining demand and anchoring inflation expectations. This has to be supplemented by supply-side responses to raise the potential output of the economy.

Tenth Challenge: Good Governance

I have so far highlighted nine challenges to accelerating our growth. Identifying these challenges and drawing up plans to address them is the relatively easy part. What is infinitely more difficult is the translation of those policies into action. That brings me to the final item on my list—the challenge of providing good governance.

That good governance is at the very heart of economic growth and poverty reduction, and even political legitimacy, is one of the undisputed lessons of development experience from around the world over the last 60 years.

In the ultimate analysis, it is the quality of governance that separates success and failure in economic development. Across countries, application of the same policies in roughly similar contexts has produced dramatically different results. In our own country, we have seen vast differences across states in development outcomes from out of the same mix of development policies. These differences across countries as well as across regions within countries, even as they adopt similar policy packages, arise because of differences in governance. Indeed research shows that per capita incomes and the quality of governance are strongly correlated indicating a virtuous circle in which good governance results in economic development.

Rejig the Elephant Dance

Let me now conclude. I have highlighted 10 challenges that we need to address in order to accelerate output growth with focus on the quality of growth. I must admit that this list is by no means exhaustive, and individual lists can vary both in content and emphasis. I hope my list would, at the least, serve as a reference point for thinking through.

As people we are understandably eager for our economy to sprint like a tiger rather than amble like an elephant. Yet few animals have an elephant's stamina. And elephants do not always amble; they dance too. And when elephants start dancing, they can go on for a long long time. But while dancing, an elephant can go off course occasionally. That calls for rejigging the dance.

Haksar Memorial Lecture delivered at the Centre for Research in Rural and Industrial Development, Chandigarh, November 25, 2011.

6 Growth, Resilience and Reform

Reflections on Post-Crisis Policy Challenges

Subir Gokarn

Introduction

The last 20 years have undoubtedly been a period of dramatic change for the Indian economy. Significantly, much of that change has come about because of the adoption of a policy framework, which was founded essentially on the proposition that the late Mr Shroff attached great value to the prominent role of private enterprise in the development process. Of course, as we observe the 20th anniversary of what was clearly a big-bang reform initiative, we can afford to take a more objective and nuanced look back over the period to see how the entire process of change impacted the economy. To put it very broadly, reforms hugely expanded the opportunities for economic activity. This resulted in more rapid growth, to which higher productivity contributed significantly.

However, it also brought with it increased risks, particularly with respect to the increased exposure to the global economy that the reform process generated. These risks occasionally manifested themselves during the past 20 years. The Asian crisis of 1997-98 and the impact of the US recession of 2001 on the Indian IT sector in 2001 are two illustrative examples. But, none of these episodes came anywhere close to the magnitude of the impact that the financial crisis of 2008 had on either the global or the Indian economy.

Globally, the debate on policy and regulation has been significantly affected by that crisis. Across a number of domains, the emphasis has

Inputs from Bhupal Singh are gratefully acknowledged.

shifted from the opportunities created by the spread of market forces and free enterprise to the risks that they have introduced into the system. Unbridled enthusiasm about the virtues of the market has given way to, at best, nervousness and at worst, disdain and contempt. Like all such debates, however, the eventual outcome, on which long-term policy thinking and action will be based, will be somewhere in the middle. The relationship between effectively functioning market forces and economic performance cannot be ignored, certainly in an economy in India's state of development. Sustaining rapid growth is something that market forces have contributed to and that remains an imperative.

Equally, the vulnerabilities caused by the greater integration and exposure of domestic markets to the global economy, which was one of the significant outcomes of the development strategy initiated in 1991, cannot be wished away. If economic performance is not to be held hostage by global turbulence, certain safeguards have to be built into the strategy. The productivity and efficiency gains that emerge from domestic competition and global exposure have to be balanced with safety and stability concerns that might require the imposition of certain boundaries on these forces. The crisis of 2008 has highlighted the need for maintaining a balance between efficiency and stability. Too much emphasis on the former can cause severe problems, as we saw in 2008. Given the degree of global integration, these can spread very quickly around the world. On the other hand, excessive concerns with safety can dilute the benefits that accrue from effectively functioning market forces, both domestically and globally.

The central proposition that I want to put forward in this lecture is that the balance between efficiency and stability must be built into the development strategy. Reforms that engender competition, both internal and external, and thereby contribute to greater efficiency and more rapid growth must be complemented with safeguards that address the risks that these forces generate. I will argue that achievement of this balance contributed to both the sharp acceleration in growth that the Indian economy experienced in the five years preceding the crisis and the resilience that it demonstrated in the face of the crisis. I will then go on to talk about some policy challenges in the broad context of this balance between efficiency and stability.

An Organising Framework

It is meaningful to analyse the performance of the Indian economy over the past decade or so in terms of the simple framework displayed in Figure 6.1. The 2x2 matrix shows four scenarios emerging from favourable and unfavourable global and domestic conditions. It is quite easy to classify the period from 2003 to 2010 into two of the boxes. The first five years of this period, i.e., the years preceding the crisis, clearly fall into the top right-hand box, reflecting favourable conditions both globally and domestically. From a growth perspective, this was a dream run for the Indian economy, which averaged 8.9 per cent per year over those five years. To illustrate the power of this rate of growth, GDP would increase by over 50 per cent during a five-year run at this rate and double in about eight and a half years. Many sectors in the economy have experienced the impact that this can have on the demand for their products and services.

Figure 6.1

Growth Scenarios

Global conditions	Favourable	??	2003-2008 (8.9%)
	Unfavourable	2008-2010 (7.4%)	2010+
		Unfavourable	Favourable
		Domestic conditions	

From both economic policy and business strategy perspectives, this period provides a benchmark for future performance. However, the framework should inject a dose of reality into those expectations. It highlights the fact that this rate of growth was achieved in a clearly favourable global environment, which may not be a characteristic of the next few years!

Getting back to the framework, the crisis period, 2008-2010, clearly falls into the bottom left-hand box, reflecting unfavourable global and domestic conditions. The financial crisis, of which the tipping point was perhaps the collapse of Lehman Brothers in September 2008, was the most vivid feature of the hostile global environment, but there were several other threats that also manifested themselves in that period. Food inflation soared around the world in the first half of 2008, as did oil prices. Both these trends reinforced the inherent inflationary pressures that were being felt domestically as a result of the sustained high growth. In these circumstances, the monetary policy stance had to be firmly anti-inflationary, culminating in the repo rate reaching its highest ever level of 9 per cent in July 2008. The combination of global turbulence and domestic demand compression would have undoubtedly caused growth to fall, which it did. However, what may have come as a surprise is that it did not fall by very much. The economy grew by 6.8 per cent in 2008-09 and by a relatively robust 8 per cent in 2009-10, at a time when much of the global economy was still very sluggish. This was clearly a sign of resilience in the face of a very severe shock, which, I want to re-emphasise, emanated from unfavourable conditions, both globally and domestically.

I will now go on to talk about the relationship between the reform process and growth on the one hand and between boundaries and resilience on the other.

Reforms and Growth

The core premise of the reform process initiated in 1991 was that greater competition, both internal and external would help accelerate economic growth. The entire spectrum of reforms, from the abolition of industrial licensing to the sharp reduction in trade barriers and the termination of allocative controls on finance, were intended to simultaneously introduce competitive forces into the economy, while freeing up the choices that producers had in terms of what, where and how to produce. These choices, in turn, could be supported by a financial system that was allowed to make its own risk-return calculations. Although some essential requirements of a truly competitive market economy, notably the elimination of exit barriers, were not introduced with the same degree of enthusiasm, the reforms that were done turned out to have a powerful impact.

Of course, it did not happen all at once. As the line in Figure 6.2 indicates, the early growth dividends from the 1991 reforms were somewhat short-lived. Growth accelerated to cross the seven per cent threshold during the three years from 1994 to 1997, but slumped back to a rather tepid five per cent for the five years following. This performance legitimately raised questions about the merits of the entire reform process; if the growth dividend was going to be this small, was it worth all the institutional disruption and political challenges that it entailed? As it turned out, the acceleration in growth that took place from 2003 onwards quelled that particular debate.

Looking back over that period, a reasonable interpretation of events is that the reform process took long time to fall into place. Trade reform, for example, manifested in a two-stage transition, first from quantitative restrictions on imports to tariffs and then the lowering of tariff rates to internationally comparable levels. Similarly, financial sector reforms did not fall into place all at once; they unfolded slowly, across domestic banks, market mechanisms and liberalisation of the capital account. The exchange rate regime went through some intermediate steps before current account convertibility was achieved. While industrial licensing for domestic investors was eliminated early on in the process, the policy regime for foreign direct investment also unfolded slowly, contributing to uncertainty about the evolving competitive environment. In a nutshell, this was an evolutionary rather than a revolutionary process. Its full impact, therefore, would only manifest when all of the different forces at work reached a critical threshold—the tipping point.

This evidently arrived in 2003, when the growth rate accelerated sharply to over eight per cent in 2003-04 and, with the exception of a slight dip in the following year, stayed well above that mark for a five-year period, which was represented in the top right-hand box in the scenario matrix.

The bars in Figure 6.2 display a pattern, which, to my mind, is a critical driver of the growth acceleration. The higher set represents the investment-GDP ratio, which clearly accelerated from the 25-30 per cent range before 2003 to over 35 per cent during the high-growth period. An important contributor to this though by no means the only one, was precisely the tipping point; the evolution of reforms in different domains had more or less come to an end, resulting in a significant reduction in uncertainty about the domestic investment environment. A stable environment clearly encouraged investment activity, which was further buoyed by emerging optimism about the huge potential that the domestic market offered. Accelerating investment provided a double bonus; it created new capacity, while speeding up the assimilation of new technology. As a result, more was produced with higher productivity.

Figure 6.2

Virtuous Cycles:Rising Investment, Falling Deficits

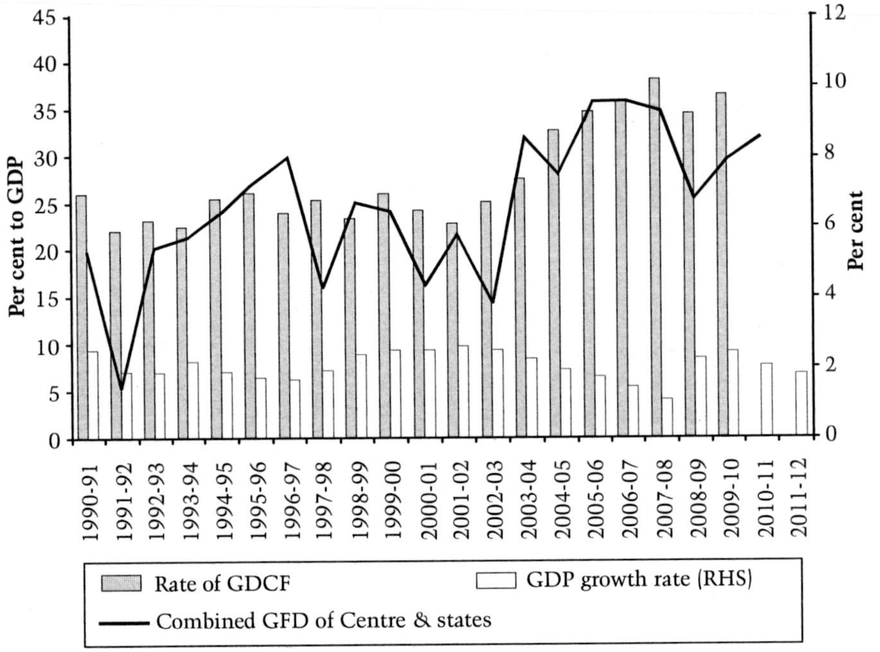

Source: GoI.

The lower set of bars also represents a development of enormous significance. The government committed to a fiscal consolidation process through the Fiscal Responsibility and Budget Management Act in 2003. Notwithstanding the transition in the regime in 2004, the consolidation path was adhered to. Very significantly, this was not a commitment of the Central government alone; the states contributed as well. The combined Centre and state fiscal deficit-GDP ratio steadily declined from 2003-04, bottoming out at about four per cent in 2007-08, the last year before the crisis hit.

We should not underestimate the role of this very dramatic expenditure switch between investment and government spending. Keep in mind the fact that the investment-GDP ratio includes public investment, while the fiscal deficit largely comprises a revenue deficit, i.e., what the government borrows in order to meet its operating (as opposed to capital) expenditure. Cutting consumption, while raising investment is a textbook formula for accelerating growth. Its validity was amply demonstrated in the Indian high-growth period of 2003-2008. And, this switch was achieved by two reform drivers. First, the set of industrial, trade and financial sector reforms, which, once stabilised, greatly enhanced the attractiveness of investment. Second, government finances were brought under control, in effect, freeing up resources for investment.

Having seen the virtues of the reform process in terms of their eventual impact on growth, let us now take a look at the risks that they introduced into the system. Competition is, of course, an inherently risky process and the failure of individual businesses in an intensely competitive environment is only to be expected. But, in the domestic context, this is hardly a disruptive force, since there are also successful outcomes. In other words, there is no systemic risk that emerges from a more competitive domestic environment in most circumstances. However, it is a somewhat different matter when it comes to global exposure. The greater is the degree of integration between the domestic and global economies, the larger are both the opportunities and threats that come with integration. I will focus on two of the risk factors.

The first one is the risk stemming from the degree of global integration. As Figure 6.3 indicates, the Indian economy became significantly more globally integrated. The bars in the figure reflect the gross volumes of activity on the different dimensions depicted. The trade bar represents the sum total of exports and imports, the current account bar the sum total of receipts and payments on that account and so on. On every dimension, the Indian economy has become significantly more globally integrated over the past 20 years, which is an outcome of reforms in both current and capital account transactions as well as very strong performance on both goods and services exports. Significantly, at the time of the crisis, the aggregate of all balance of payments transactions was more than GDP.

Figure 6.3

Increasing Global Integration

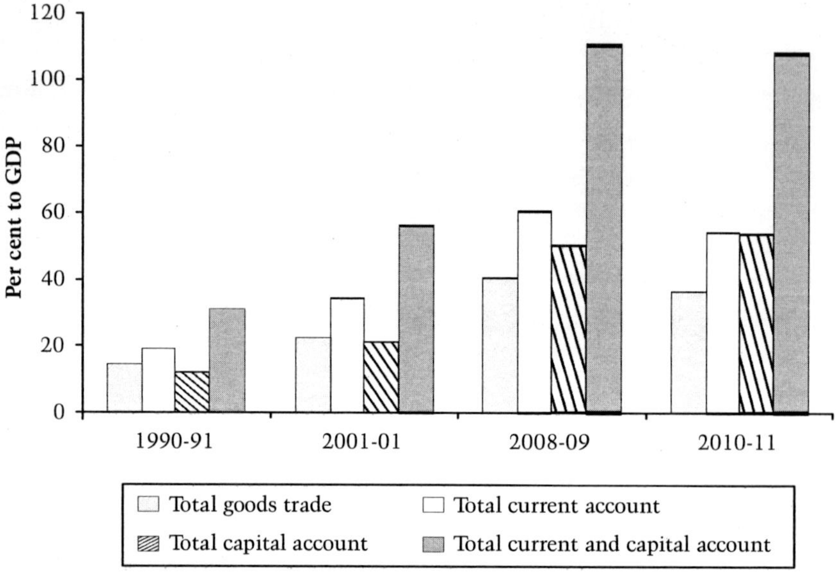

This is precisely where risk considerations come in. When the crisis hit, across the emerging market economies (EMEs), including India, capital flowed out in large quantities, exerting enormous pressure on exchange rates and domestic liquidity conditions. These channels of transmission highlighted the vulnerability that global integration created for these economies, which were otherwise relatively healthy. Fortunately for them, they had the capacity to respond with appropriate policy measures. I will address this issue in the Indian context a little later in the lecture.

The second risk factor that we need to pay attention to is the economy's dependence on imported energy. Although this is a structural condition, which would have an influence on domestic conditions under any circumstances, the fact is that the rapid growth of the economy did contribute to an overall increase in energy consumption and energy intensity, which made the economy more vulnerable to global energy price shocks. Figure 6.4 provides an indication of this vulnerability from the inflation perspective. The white segment of the bar represents the contribution of energy prices overall to headline inflation. Although energy prices are certainly not the only driver of inflation in India, the pattern suggests that, over the past decade, high energy prices have typically been concomitant with high inflation.

Figure 6.4

Contributors to Inflation

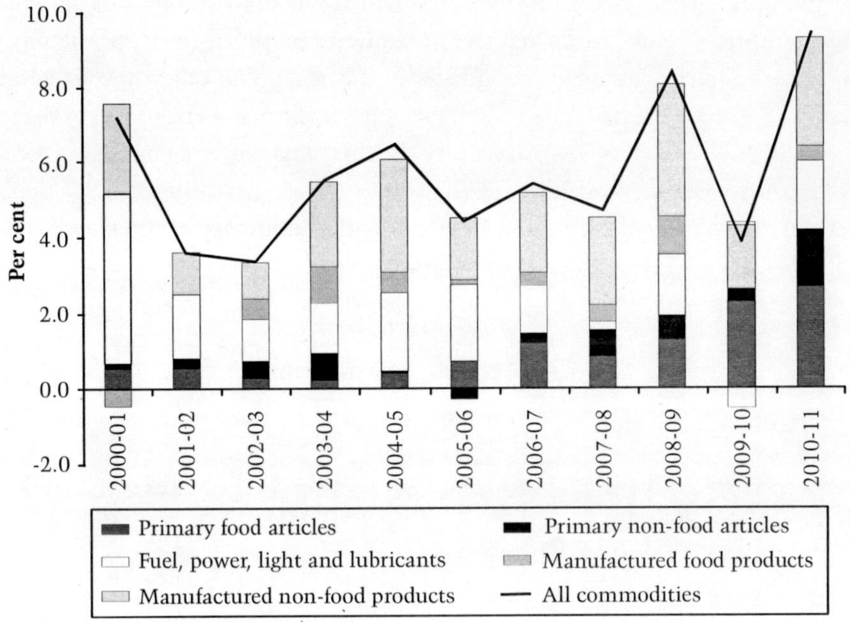

Boundaries and Resilience

As it turned out, the adverse growth impact of the crisis was relatively short-lived. Growth dropped below 7 per cent in 2008-09, the year in which the crisis precipitated, but recovered to 8 per cent in the subsequent year. Although the numbers varied across countries, this was a broader characteristic of EMEs. It was striking to see that the impact of the crisis on the growth performance of developed economies was both large and persistent, while being relatively small and transitory for the EMEs. Clearly, there were some common features that EMEs shared, which contributed to this resilience, but that is too broad a subject to be addressed here. I will confine myself to the possible sources of resilience in the Indian context.

To my mind, four factors are important. First, notwithstanding the very large increase in global linkages, the fact is that the Indian economy remains primarily driven by domestic factors. From the demand side, as Figure 6.5 indicates, the relatively large share of private consumption spending has been a contributory factor to the overall stability of demand. Consumption tends to be relatively resilient in the face of, particularly, transitory shocks, because individuals and households take time to adjust their spending patterns. It is only when the shock turns out to be persistent that patterns will change significantly. In this sense, it is a stabilising force, giving other sources of demand that can be quickly influenced by policy actions, time to respond to and help mitigate the impact of the shock.

Figure 6.5

Stable Private Consumption

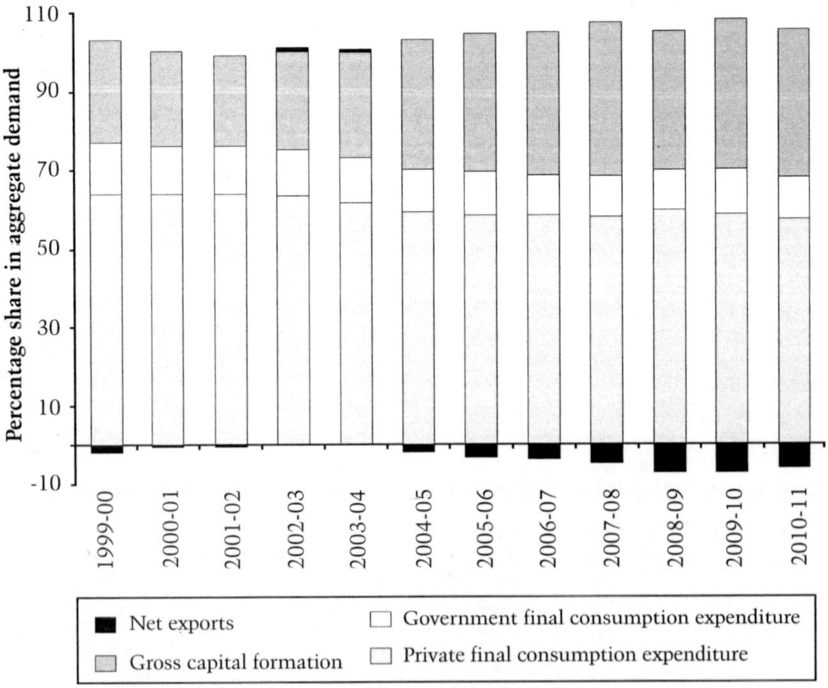

Second, the capacity to launch a strong policy response was in place when the crisis hit. On the monetary front, the tight, anti-inflationary stance that preceded the crisis had taken policy rates and the cash reserve ratio to relatively high levels. As the crisis precipitated, it had a dramatic impact on commodity, particularly energy, prices, which then helped inflation move rapidly down, along with other drivers. This, in turn, provided the basis for a quick and large reversal in the monetary stance. As Figure 6.6 shows, both policy rates and the cash reserve ratio were significantly reduced over a relatively short period of time.

I earlier referred to the risks that increased global integration brought with it. One of the most significant adverse impacts of the crisis on the Indian economy was caused by rapid capital outflows in the immediate aftermath of the collapse of Lehman Brothers. Even for businesses whose fundamentals remained intact, the massive constriction of liquidity could easily have been life-threatening, with a prolonged liquidity shortage escalating into a solvency problem. The massive amount of liquidity that

Figure 6.6

Monetary Policy Responses

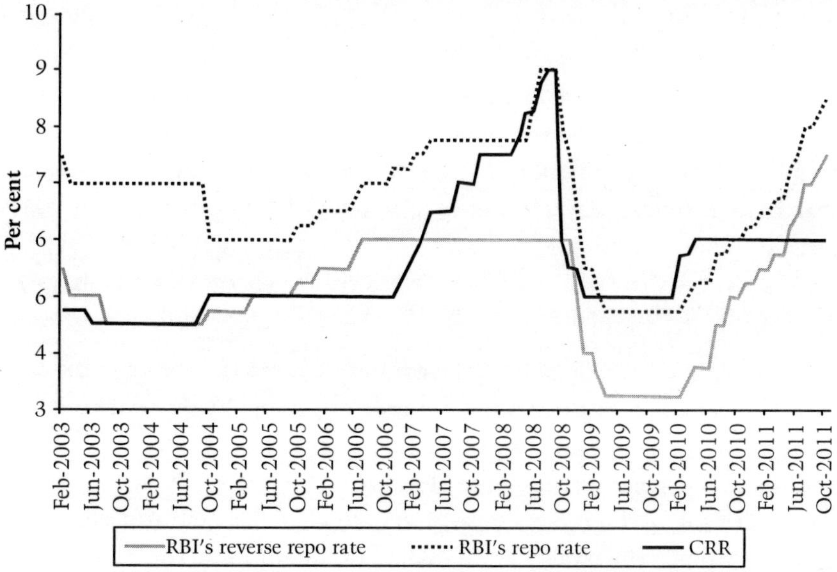

the reversal of the monetary policy stance infused into the system helped to avert that possibility.

Fiscal policy also contributed, as was displayed in Figure 6.2. As indicated earlier, the process of fiscal consolidation that preceded the crisis had put government finances in relatively good shape. In doing so, it had created the capacity to respond to a slowdown in private demand, particularly investment, by quickly ramping up public spending. Of course, the risk inherent in this kind of policy response is that the increased fiscal commitments persist beyond the time they are required. This is a major issue of debate globally. Some countries have attempted to exit from crisis-induced fiscal commitments while private demand is still soft, while others have made more lasting commitments, which, on the back of resilient private demand, have contributed to rising inflationary pressures. Be that as it may, it is important to recognise the fact that fiscal space and the willingness to use it was an important reason for resilience.

However, beyond these two contemporaneous sources of resilience, I would like to suggest two structural reasons for why the Indian economy was resilient to the shock. These are what I would describe as 'boundaries'. The first of these is the nature of bank portfolios. Figure 6.7 shows the balance sheet composition of the Indian banking system. The relatively large and stable proportion of loans is an important contributor to resilience. Both in India and across EMEs in general, the balance sheets of banks typically comprised a larger share of loans relative to investments. The latter, being subject to mark-to-market requirements, are vulnerable to sharp downward movements in asset prices. The former also carry balance sheet risks through provisioning requirements for non-performing assets, but in economies that are growing reasonably fast, these are probably less onerous than vulnerabilities to asset prices, which move very sharply in times of market turbulence.

Balance sheet adjustments played a critical role in the impairment of financial systems in developed economies, by sharply reducing their capacity to provide finance. In turn, this probably contributed to both the magnitude and persistence of the slowdown in growth. By contrast, while EMEs were hit by liquidity constraints, which I referred to earlier in the Indian context, the stability of balance sheets as a result of a more 'traditional' structure helped to preserve the systems' capacity to provide

Slide 6.7

Banks' Balance Sheet Composition

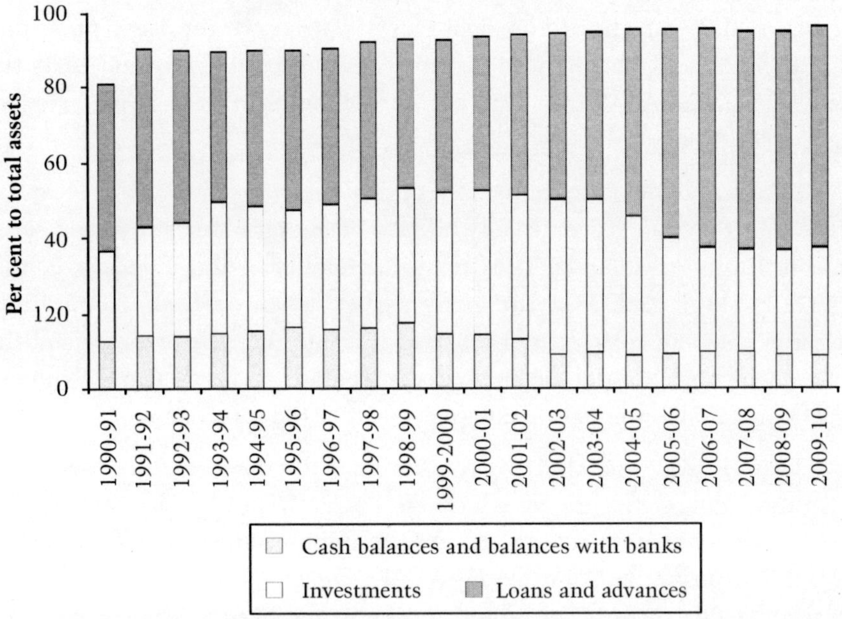

Source: World Bank Online and RBI.

finance. Liquidity infusions quickly transmitted through to businesses and helped prevent the escalation from liquidity to solvency problems.

The second structural factor in the Indian context, in my view, is the capital account management framework. Before the crisis, capital controls were generally seen as a hindrance to smooth global integration and a source of inefficiency. The perspective has changed somewhat, with an emerging view that some kinds of capital controls may provide temporary relief from the instability being transmitted from global shocks through high volatility in capital flows. This is still an evolving global debate, but the Indian experience perhaps makes some contributions to it.

Broadly speaking, the Indian approach to capital controls is based on a preference ordering. There are virtually no limits on foreign direct investment, apart from some sector-specific restrictions, which are not directly motivated by macroeconomic considerations. This channel is seen as being growth and productivity enhancing. There are virtually no limits on foreign portfolio investment into equities. In this channel, both market risks and exchange rate risks are fully borne by the foreign investor. However, there are limits on debt flows. These are the least preferred, essentially because the domestic borrower is obliged to repay and bears the exchange rate risk. Within this category, long-term debt is preferred to short-term debt.

External debt obligations can put enormous strain on the capital account if they are redeemed in the face of a global shock. Putting some kind of limits on them reduces the vulnerability of the economy to this strain. Looking back over the crisis period, when outflows from equity investments were so large, it is easy to imagine that the pressure and the consequent impact on domestic markets would have been far more intense if debt obligations were also being redeemed at the same time.

I would describe the restrictions on debt inflows with respect to quantum, tenure and pricing which are currently in place as 'strategic' in nature. They are motivated by the need to impose some limits on the risks of global exposure and not by day-to-day considerations of exchange rate volatility. Consequently, the rupee moves in response to daily supply and demand patterns against the backdrop of these strategic restrictions. In turn, these restrictions can be lowered in response to strategic considerations, such as the increasing demand for foreign funds for infrastructure investment, which has been done over the past year. But, to return to the issue of resilience in the face of the crisis of 2008, it could be argued that the preference ordering reflected in the capital account management framework helped to minimise the severity of the impact on the domestic economy.

Policy Challenges

Let me repeat the basic argument I am advancing. Reforms were a critical contributor to the acceleration of growth in the Indian economy. However, the reform strategy, as productive as it was, brought with it some risks. Recognition of these risks and the response to them in terms of some boundaries helped the economy to be resilient in the face of a very severe shock. The essential message from this argument is that the combination of growth and resilience comes from a reform process that balances expansion of opportunities with mitigation of risks—efficiency with stability.

With this in mind, let me return to the organising framework that I began the lecture with. The recent past has been categorised into two of the boxes. Let us look at the future in terms of the other two. Of these, the top left-hand box appears at this point in time to be irrelevant. It is difficult to foresee a situation for some time to come in which the Indian economy will be beset by problems while the rest of the world is doing relatively well. That leaves the bottom right-hand box, in which the Indian economy is experiencing favourable conditions, while the rest of the world is not.

The unfavourable global conditions postulated in this scenario are certainly a realistic assumption. The question then is: how do we ensure that the domestic economy moves into the favourable zone? This is essentially where the policy challenge lies. Drawing on the reform-growth-resilience triangle, what are the policy priorities, which will help the economy to sustain growth while keeping risks in check?

This opens up a wide canvas, but I will confine myself to issues I have covered in this lecture, viewing them from the growth-resilience perspective. First, let me return to the issue of inflation, which I raised in the context of vulnerability to global forces in the form of rising energy prices. This clearly calls for an integrated energy strategy, with the objective of both conserving overall use of energy and shifting the balance to domestic resources, preferably renewable ones.

However, from a somewhat broader perspective, the continuing vulnerability to inflationary shocks from energy can also be mitigated by addressing other sources of inflation, over which there is a greater degree of control for domestic policy. In this context, I would like to emphasise the very real threat from food inflation. A growing demand-supply imbalance in some major food items—protein sources, vegetables and fruits—is helping entrench food inflation. Figure 6.8 shows clear signs of an escalating trend. This raises the average rate of inflation, making the system even more vulnerable to external energy shocks or, for that matter, any other source of inflation.

Slide 6.8

Food Inflation: Proteins and Others

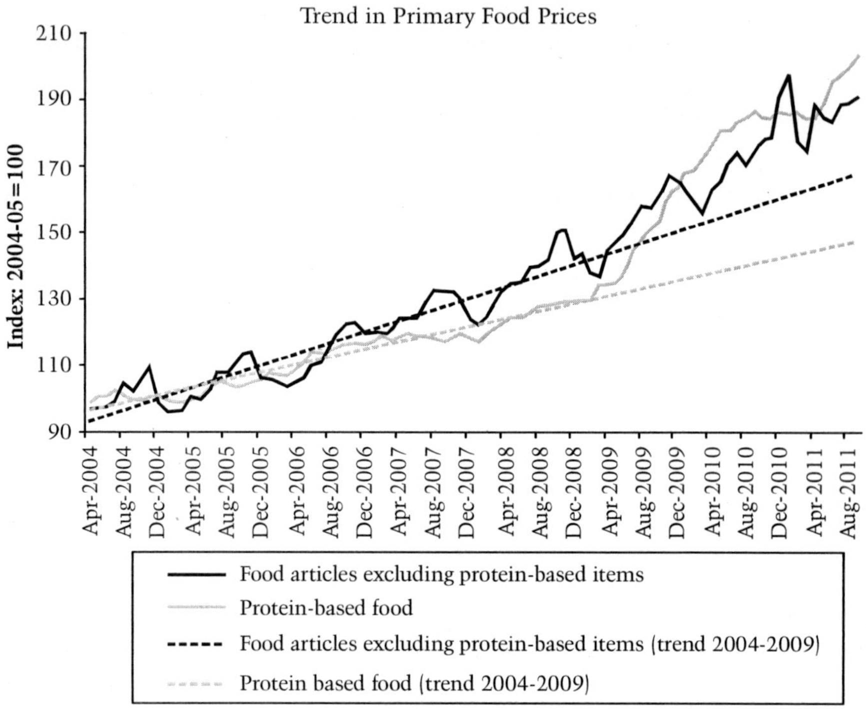

There are some direct growth-resilience implications of this pattern. It is a historical given that people diversify their diets as they become more affluent. One key common characteristic of long-term development is that the food economy has accommodated this by more efficient supply (either through production or trade) of the foods that people want more of. If this does not happen, households tend to spend more money on food and less on other things, which acts as a damper on the growth of demand for non-food products. As was suggested earlier, aggregate private consumption expenditure can be a stabilising force; the more diversified it is, the more it can contribute to stability. But, macroeconomic implications apart, from a development and welfare perspective, it is a matter of concern that increased access to better nutrition is hindered by rising food prices. Rapidly expanding supply is really the only solution to this problem.

Second, continuing with the theme of diversification as away to promote growth with resilience, the sectoral composition of GDP and employment suggest key policy priorities. Figure 6.9 displays a striking contrast between the drivers of GDP growth and the pattern of employment. While agriculture has been steadily shrinking in terms of its share of GDP, its share in employment remains both dominant and relatively static. In effect, a constant proportion of the labour force is generating a declining share of output. On the other hand, industry, which is expected to be a natural absorber of workers from agriculture, providing them more productive and better paying jobs, has not just about maintained its share in both GDP and employment. It has clearly not played the role of an engine of either growth or employment.

Figure 6.9

Different Speed of Transition

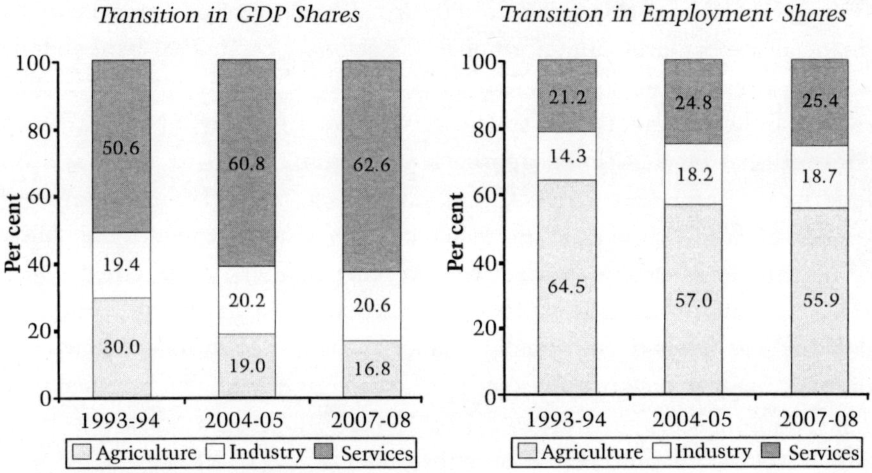

Source: CSO and *Economic Survey*, Government of India.

High dependence on services for GDP growth and on agriculture for employment is clearly a source of vulnerability. Balancing out the share of GDP with the share of the labour force does not necessarily have to be one-for-one; however, the shares should be moving with some rough correspondence to provide stability to the growth process.

What needs to be done to facilitate rapid growth in industry is well known. Infrastructure is a key requirement. Labour regulations need to be streamlined. Workers need to be appropriately skilled. Taxes need to be streamlined. This is a long and familiar agenda on which, there are many welcome signs of progress—the New Manufacturing Policy, the Goods and Services Tax, the National Skill Development Corporation, amidst others, are all initiatives that provide a foundation for the sector to emerge as an engine of growth and employment. But, all these various dimensions need to reach certain thresholds together before their full benefits will be realised. Earlier, I discussed about the cumulative impact of a variety of reforms causing a sudden and massive acceleration in growth—the tipping point. We must learn from that experience the lesson that the more various reform initiatives are synchronised, the quicker that tipping point will arrive. Time is not a luxury we can count on in this context.

Third, growth with stability requires strong support from a financial system that can also grow with stability. The post-crisis perspective on financial sector development emphasises strongly capitalised banks along with restrictions on deployment of funds, with a view to maintaining robust balance sheets. In India as well as in many EMEs, a more conventional or traditional approach to banking, with its emphasis on lending as opposed to investment, appears to have been a source of resilience. At the same time, too much conservatism may reduce the ability of the financial system to meet the evolving financial requirements of a rapidly growing economy. In this context, a strategy for financial development needs to continually balance the ability to introduce new ways of financing new opportunities with the means to measure and mitigate the risks that these opportunities bring. It really is a tightrope walk, from which it is very easy to fall off on either side!

Finally, with respect to capital account management, the key lesson from the experience of the crisis is that a combination of strategic capital controls and a floating currency can provide an effective buffer against global financial turbulence. The controls described earlier impose some limits on the vulnerability of the domestic economy to external shocks. Within these boundaries, a floating exchange rate acts as a shock absorber. It eliminates the burden on policymakers to either absorb surplus inflows, with potentially inflationary consequences, or accommodate outflows, with potentially adverse implications for credibility.

Concluding Remarks

I would like to conclude by re-emphasising three key messages from the paper. First, reforms, which balanced growth opportunities with risk mitigation contributed to both the Indian economy's growth performance before the crisis of 2008 and its resilience to the crisis. Second, the future performance of the Indian economy depends even more heavily on reinforcing domestic drivers of growth and stability in a generally unfavourable global environment. Third, drawing on lessons from past experience, speed, synchronisation and the balance between exploiting opportunities and managing risk, will maximise the dividends from any reform strategy.

The 45th A.D. Shroff Memorial Lecture delivered at Indian Merchants' Chamber, Mumbai, 2nd November, 2011.

7

India's Development Drama (1991-2011)

From Milton Friedman to Mahatma Gandhi

N.A. Mujumdar

Introduction

Admittedly, India's growth story is impressive with GDP growth recording an annual average growth of 8.5 per cent during the five years—2003 to 2008. Even during the year 2009-10 of global meltdown, India managed to post a growth of 7.2 per cent. In the medium term it is reasonable to expect the economy to resume its robust growth path of around 9 per cent. This is indeed beyond all expectations for an economy which was supposed to be condemned to a Hindu rate of growth of 3 per cent.

In the euphoria of sustained high growth we generally tend to overlook the mistakes committed by our policymakers during this period of liberalisation. The period of the so-called economic reforms—a period of liberalisation of the Indian economy from 1991 to 2004, I would submit, was the most retrogressive phase in the history of India's economic development. We may not have our own Reagonomics or Thatcherism to bury but our policymakers during this period were soaked in the market theology of the IMF/World Bank. The focus was on liberalisation, market-led growth, fiscal correction, promotion of private and foreign investment, development of the capital market, and generally creating of an environment of consumerism. More basic issues of development were overlooked which led to neglect of agriculture, disdain for subsidies, whether food subsidy or credit subsidy, and more disturbingly disregard for the elementary principles of food security.

A word about the theme of my paper.[1] I have chosen to focus on India's economic development during the last two decades i.e., 1991-2011 with a purpose. I have divided the period into two distinct phases: the first from 1991-2004, a period of liberalisation and economic reforms, which I have called the Milton Friedman phase. Intoxicated with the philosophy of market-led growth of the IMF/World Bank, our policymakers went about ruthlessly seeking higher growth rate, with all its adverse effects on development issues. The second phase (2004-2011), which I have called the Mahatma Gandhi phase is a period when Indian policymakers began to rediscover, as it were, Mahatma Gandhi's development philosophy. Community-centred development holds the key to policy pursued during this phase when policymakers are even dreaming of a sort of food utopia. The second phase represents a dramatic departure from the policies pursued in the first phase. Thus, there is an element of drama in our approach to development. This dramatic change has to be judged against the global financial and economic crisis of 2008 which has dramatically changed the institutional and policymaking landscape. This crisis in a way reflected the loss of faith in the capitalist system led by unbridled market forces. This takes us well beyond growth models to the realm of economic philosophy of development. We must grow up from the conventional growth models trapped in the market theology to resonate to the larger concerns of holistic development including promotion of broad-based decentralised growth which alone could facilitate access by the poor to employment, food, nutrition and health, and quality education and to putting in place safety nets to reduce the vulnerability of the poor. The proposed Food Security Act reflects the crux of new agenda of development. If the conventional development economics is a failed God, are we now re-writing the script of development economics? We have to judge the Indian development experience in the broader context of disillusionment with development economics as a discipline. The frontiers of development

---

1. This theme and sub-themes have been developed over the years. For any further documentation and evidence in support of the statements made here, the reader is invited to refer to my following books. *Financial Sector Reforms and India's Economic Development*, two volumes (2002); *Economic Reforms Sans Development* (2004); *Inclusive Growth, Development Perspectives in Indian Economy* (2007); *India's New Development Agenda: Building a Value-based Society* (2011). All these books are published by Academic Foundation, New Delhi.

economics are expanding further. The 'commitment deficit' of our policy-makers and development administration, as we will spell out shortly, is impairing the outcome of our development efforts. The recent mass outbursts against widespread corruption raises another related issue of national character. Do these developments reinforce the imperative need to build a value-based and compassionate society? We should ponder over.

I

Milton Friedman Phase: 1991-2004

During this phase, the growth culture itself seems to have gone through a fundamental change with reformers repeating parrot like phrases borrowed from the IMF/World Bank vocabulary. 'There is no free lunch', perhaps meaning that the poor must fend for themselves. Despite graduating to the league of fast growing economies of the world, India continues to be the abode of the largest number of underfed and under-nourished people in the world. FAO estimates show that the number of undernourished people in India has risen from 206 million in 1990-1992 to 230.5 million in 2003-2005, a rise of some 24 million. The Human Development Index of UNDP (2009) ranks India as the 134th out of 182 countries of the world. The HDI is based on three indicators, namely, GDP per capita, life expectancy at birth, and education as measured by adult literacy rate and gross enrollment ratio. India is thus still in the Medium Human Development category with even countries like China, Sri Lanka and Indonesia having higher ranking.

A community-centred analysis thus exposes clearly the darker side of the development policy pursued during this period. While there is enough literature on the harm inflicted on the economy by the centrally planned economic phase—the so-called Licence Permit Raj—little attention has been paid to the negative impact of the pursuit of unbridled market theology during the 1991-2004 phase. Economic historians need to pay greater attention to this aspect.

What is ironical was that this approach to development came to be adopted at a period when the American capitalist model collapsed in 2008. Market fundamentalism embodied in the neoliberalism based on the notion that markets are self-correcting, allocate resources efficiently and serve the public interest well has collapsed. The so-called 'Washington Consensus' in favour of privatisation and liberalisation now stands stripped of its sanctimonious robe. It has now become clear that unbridled market forces are not self-correcting, regulation and direction of some sort is needed. This state has a critical role to play in the management of the economy.

I would be content with citing the following five concrete instances to substantiate how the mindless pursuit of market theology during the phase de-emphasised development: food grains management, watershed development as part of the broader theme: home-grown green revolution, inequitable interest rate structure, the microfinance mess and fiscal inequity. At some point of time in the economic history of a nation, there arise occasions when somebody has to speak the truth like the innocent boy who spoke out about the emperor's clothes. As one who is engaged in the study of India's economic development for the last five decades, and now with one foot in the grave, as it were, I thought I am qualified to do the job and hence I have set out to do it not so much in anger as in agony, agony because Indian economic development has some elements of a Greek tragedy as illustrated with some episodes.

India is a pioneer in development planning having launched its First Five Year Plan in 1951. After six decades of development planning, alas, we are still preoccupied with measuring poverty. Three officially sponsored reports proposing new method for identification of the poor and for the measurement and eradication of poverty have been brought out in 2009. Dr Shylendra who has done an excellent critical review of these reports comes to the conclusion that, 'we are no wiser than before about poverty and ways of tackling it'.[2] He asserts that under the current political economy 'there seems to be no escape from the prevailing muddle over understanding poverty and the trap of reformism laid by the neoliberal framework in our efforts to banish poverty'. What a travesty of development planning!

2. Shylendra, H.Y. (2010). "The New Methods of Poverty Assessment and Reduction: The Muddle and the Trap of Neoliberalism", *Working Paper*, Institute of Rural Management, Anand, December.

Reverting to development, Avinash Dixit asks: 'what feature or features of policies are important for good economic outcomes regard-less of what kind of government makes those policies? Here much of the literature does find one point of agreement: credibility of commitments is vital'.[3] During this phase of India's development, it is the commitment deficit which stands out as a villain of the tragedy.

Let us now take up the five concrete cases.

Food Grains Management Policy

The most disturbing policy during this phase was that India chose to export a huge quantity of 27 million tonnes of rice and wheat during the three consecutive years 2001-02 to 2003-04. This was the result of two regressive measures taken earlier; first, the Government introduced in 1997 targetting the public distribution system (PDS) in the form of targetted public distribution system (TPDS). This narrow targetting of the PDS based on absolute income poverty excluded a large part of the nutritionally vulnerable population from PDS due to the continuous raising of the issue price of food grains—inspired by the objective of cutting the size of food subsidies. The concessionally priced food grains became increasingly inaccessible to the poor. The inevitable consequence was the mounting food stocks with the Food Corporation of India (FCI). At one time, the stocks reached a peak of 60 million tonnes. No wonder our policymakers sought the soft option in exports for tackling the so-called 'surplus food grains' problem. This was nothing short of development atrocity when viewed against the background of India being the abode of the largest number of underfed and undernourished persons in the world, as mentioned earlier.

The irony was compounded further: while the policymakers' ostensible objective was to reduce subsidies for domestic consumption of food grains, the same policymakers did not have any qualms about subsidising exports of food grains! If Mahatma Gandhi were alive perhaps, one could speculate there would have been a *satyagraha* against such mindless pursuit of flawed food grains management policy.

---

3. Dixit, Avinash (2006). "Evaluating Recipes for Development Success", *World Bank Policy Research Paper* 3859, March.

Bhikhu Parekh has admirably encapsulated the poverty profile, as sketched by the Mahatma, in the following paragraph:

> ...Second, poverty dehumanises human beings, wastes the potential and deprives their lives of all sense of meaning and purpose. It is one of the worst violence that human beings can commit against other human beings. It is as bad as killing, and even worse for the fact that it is silent, slow and invisible, arouses no anger and is outside the purview of anyone's direct responsibility. As long as even one person is starved, is malnourished or lacks decent housing, the social order stands indicted lacking legitimacy. Basic human needs have the first claim on Society's resources, and it is an obligation to arrange its economic affairs in a manner that the needs of all members are met.[4]

In my Introduction to a book on agriculture, I wrote in 2006:

'It was tragic enough for a predominantly agricultural economy not to be able to produce in the 1960s adequate quantities of food grains to meet the domestic consumption requirements of the population: it is perhaps a greater systemic tragedy today that even when we are able to produce adequate quantities of food grains we are unable to ensure that food grains so produced do reach the needy'.[5]

Hunger and poverty are an affront to a civilised society and subsidies are a characteristic of a civilised society. One begins to wonder whether we are dismissing poverty or reduction of poverty as mere phrases of a dialectic process, denying thereby its moral urgency of addressing the task.

Ironically, the pendulum seems to have swung to the other extreme. Today, the National Food Security Bill, 2011 seeks to create a sort of 'food utopia' by seeking to ensure 'home delivery', as it were, of a specified quantum, of subsidised food grains to the bulk of the population. We will discuss it presently.

Home-Grown Green Revolution: Watershed Development

It has become fashionable to harp on the theme that a second green revolution can alone ensure food security in the current scenario. The first

---

4. Sharma, Anand (ed.) (2007). *Gandhian Way: Peace, Non-violence, and Empowerment*. New Delhi: Academic Foundation.
5. Mujumdar, N.A. and Uma Kapila (2007). *Indian Agriculture in the New Millennium*. New Delhi: Academic Foundation.

green revolution was achieved through a genetic breakthrough in seed technology, a technology which was accessible to all. Today the circumstances are different. I would submit there are more mundane and less glamorous alternatives to attain food and nutrition security, perhaps not wholly but substantially. One does not have to 'import' farm technology, as we did in 1960s.

Future agricultural growth will have to be necessarily water-centric and what better alternative there could be than watershed development, which I regard as the mother of all water management modes. Watershed development projects, both micro and macro, hold out great promise for future agricultural growth: the potential area to be covered is huge, with about 60 per cent of the area under crops being rainfed: capital investment is modest, the projects are labour intensive and do not require much technical know-how. By its very nature, growth under watershed development is 'inclusive'.

Yet, why despite all the sound and fury, we have not made any appreciable progress? For instance, the Macro Management of Agriculture (MMA) assistance during 2010-11 has been used to treat a mere 3 lakh hectares of land under the National Water Development Programme for Rainfed Areas (NWDPRA).

In fact watershed development programmes have a fairly long history. It was in 1986 that the NWDPRA was introduced in 99 districts in 16 states. But, what has happened in the subsequent quarter century? The Government of India issued in 2008 'The Common Guidelines for Watershed Development Projects'—the first set of guidelines that apply to watershed development projects across three Government of India ministries—Ministry of Rural Development, Ministry of Agriculture and Ministry of Environment and Forests. Trust the bureaucracy of mystify, sometimes with a little help from academicians, a perfectly simple and workable growth tool! We have had scholarly discourses on watershed development like the Parthasarathy Committee Report. There is enough of sound and fury. But where are the results? Even in a progressive state like Maharashtra, the proportion of area covered by micro watershed development to the total eligible area is not significant.

It is necessary to demystify the whole approach to watershed development. Considering the humble animal—watershed development—the punditry and complexity of the 'Guidelines' mentioned above is astounding. In contrast, look at the success stories of individual initiatives. In Maharashtra, Anna Hazare's Ralegan Siddhi project has now become a part of folklore of watershed movement. A more recent case is that of Hiware Bazar, a drought prone poverty-stricken village about 100 kilometres from Pune. The efforts of one man Popatrao Baguji Pawar have converted this village into a model village (*adarsh gaon*). The International Groundwater Association has given to this village the International Groundwater Management Award. Neither Hazare nor Pawar could have read and appreciated the erudition and comprehensiveness of the 'Guidelines', referred to above. Yet they were able to evolve their own region and location-specific models and emerge as the new Schumpeterian heroes of agricultural growth and rural development. There may be similar leaders in Gujarat, Rajasthan and elsewhere. It may be useful to produce the growth profiles of these successful stories so that we may be able to replicate them, on a large scale.

The mid-term appraisals of Plans of relevant states should have contained a separate section on the progress of watershed development projects. Alas! This is not so. All this shows a sort of 'commitment deficit' on the part of policymakers and the development administration.

Take another instance of our policymakers' high profile initiatives—the India-US collaboration on agricultural technology. The 'Joint Statement of Prime Minister Manmohan Singh and President Barack Obama' issued on 8 November, 2010, at end of the latter's visit to India mentions the decision 'to work together to develop, test, and replicate transformative technologies to extend food security, as part of the Evergreen Revolution'. The Prime Minister has lauded the US's role in launching India's first green revolution, transforming Indian agricultural production and has welcomed US collaboration in spurring a 'second green revolution' (see Economic and Political Weekly, December 11, 2010). We must remember that much of the inventions of high-yielding varieties of seeds that launched India's first green revolution took place under the auspices of publicly-funded research institutions. But today the intellectual property rights of the genetically modified (GM) seeds are held by the Monsantos,

DuPonts and Dows. These are purely agribusiness corporations aiming at maximising their profits. They are not freely accessible to all farmers.

One does not have to look to the US to increase the level of yields of our crops even at the current level of technology and farm management practices. The gap between the yields in our agriculture research centres at the state level and the actual farm level is quite wide: for example, in the case of wheat it is 84 per cent for Madhya Pradesh; for rice over 100 per cent in Assam, Bihar, Chhattisgarh and Uttar Pradesh; for soyabean 185 per cent in Karnataka and for sugarcane it is 167 per cent in Madhya Pradesh. Hence, if we can bridge these yield gaps, we can increase production by 50 per cent. Over the years, unfortunately, we have de-emphasised the role of agricultural extension services—which played a critical role in facilitating the first green revolution and today the services have become practically dysfunctional. Of course, we must rejuvenate these services. Given the poor state of government extension services, we could induce public sector banks (PSBs) to extend their help. In the past, performance of PSBs in this area was excellent. We may renew such efforts.[6]

We could have a time-bound programme of development of watershed projects, covering the bulk of the eligible area in the country in the next two or three years. Perhaps the Mahatma Gandhi National Rural Employment Guarantee Scheme (MGNREGS) could in the relevant regions be made to focus on these projects. Such concerted action pursued with dogged determination could yield good results.

Inequitable Interest Rate Regime

These who pontificate on why the concessional lending rates do not help the poor, further expose their innocence of the realities of the present interest rate structure. Financial sector and banking sector reforms implemented in the 1990s resulted in the emergence of an inequitable interest rate structure, a structure designed to pamper the private corporate sector, and which is biased against agricultural and the small borrower generally. For instance, a small farmer was made to pay an interest rate of

6. Khan, H.R. (2010). "Issues and Challenges in Indian Agriculture Bankers Perspectives", *RBI Bulletin*, October.

12 per cent at a time when highly rated corporate entity could raise money from banks at 6 per cent. This paradoxical situation was the result of mindless implementation of Basle norms and adoption without adaptation of concepts like 'risks' as understood in the developed world. As I have discussed elsewhere, this concept of 'risks' should be made to stand on its head.[7] When some of us raised this question of inequitable interest rate structure in the early 1990s, Reserve Bank of India (RBI) ignored the protest. Wisdom finally dawned on RBI in 2005-06 when its *Report on Currency and Finance* 2005-06 provided valuable insights into the structure of interest rates. The bulk of bank lending has been taking place at sub-benchmark prime lending rate (sub-BPLR). For instance, the share of sub-BPLR lending increased to 82 per cent by March 2007. While higher credit rated corporates are getting credit at sub-BPLR rates, agriculture and small industry and other small borrowers are generally charged BPLR, or in some cases, above BPLR rates. To quote the RBI Report: 'to compensate for such sub-BPLR lending, other segments are charged higher rates of interest, thus leading to cross subsidisation of the economically well-off borrowers by the economically poor borrowers'.[8] This is indeed disturbing especially when the objective of both the inclusive growth in the real sector as envisaged in the Eleventh Plan and financial inclusion is to promote growth with equity. Although this inequitable situation was modified to some extent by the Government providing interest rate subvention since 2008-09 to ensure that farmers get short-term crop loan upto Rs 3 lakh at 7 per cent, the basic issue remains. Interestingly enough, none of the reformers of financial sector has identified the problem. It is to the credit to Reserve Bank of India (RBI) that they brought out the problem in the open and appointed a Working Group in April 2008 to look into the issue.

The Working Group on Benchmark Prime Lending Rate submitted its Report on October 2009. As a result of the Group's recommendation, the banking system switched over from BPLR to the base rate system with effect from July 1, 2010. The base rates set by major banks are in the range of 7.25 per cent to 8 per cent. In retrospect we can see how the previous

7. *Risk Philosophy: An Enquiry into Risk and Uncertainties in Indian Agriculture*. Monograph prepared for NABARD.

8. *Report on Currency and Finance, 2005-06*. Mumbai: Reserve Bank of India. p.159.

interest rate regime 'exploited' the small borrowers, including small farmers, by changing say, 12 per cent. While the corporate sector is quite vocal in seeking a low interest rate regime for itself on the pretext that high interests would adversely affect growth, our policymakers were insensitive to the unmerited interest rate burden inflicted on the silent small borrowers. It took two decades for the RBI to correct the distortion in the interest rate structure.

The Microfinance Mess

The recent crisis witnessed by the microfinance sector provides yet another concrete evidence of how RBI has become insensitive to the problems of the small borrower. It seems RBI has yet to recover from the hangover of the market-obssessed reform phobia. I have provided an in-depth analyses of these developments elsewhere[9] and here I will be content with highlighting the main issues. It is not a case of RBI's benign neglect. RBI became a co-conspirator in the metamorphosis of MFIs into glorified moneylenders charging usurious interest rates of 30 to 40 per cent. RBI's blessings came in the form of public sector support to the sector. Such support was extended from public sector banks (PSBs), NABARD and SIDBI. Even after the crisis, RBI's Malegam Committee has 'sanctified' a 26 per cent interest rate for MFIs. This is most unfortunate because historically RBI has the image of a guardian-angel of small farmers or small borrowers generally.

More recent revelations of for-profit microfinance institutions (MFIs) have exposed how these institutions are exploiting the situation in the name of financial inclusion. In addition to the usurious lending rates of 30 to 40 per cent, the managing directors of some of the biggest MFIs were paid obscenely high remuneration packages of say Rs 4 crore to Rs 8 crore—the level higher than that of managing director of HDFC Bank. There was also no transparency in the mutual benefit trusts (MBTs)—shareholding vehicle for MFIs (Economic Times investigations). Perhaps, the last nail in the coffin of these for-profit MFIs was hit by the recent statement of Dr Y.V. Reddy, former Governor, Reserve Bank of India (RBI),

---

9. Mujumdar, N.A. (2011). "Macro Economic Policy Mix and Micro Finance Institutions", N.A. Mujumdar and M.G. Shirahatti (eds.), *Rethinking on Micro Finance*. Mumbai: Himalaya Publishing House.

that for-profit MFIs were worse than moneylenders. Moneylender lends out of his own money whereas MFIs were actually borrowing money from depositors and banks and onlending the money. So, 'MFI is essentially a leveraged moneylender' (*Economic Times*, 23 November, 2010). He went on further to add that many finance experts believed, but did not have the courage to admit publicly, that microfinance is India's subprime: 'ultimately, it is something like subprime lending'. The studied silence of experts has cost the economy a great deal. In retrospect, the Government of Andhra Pradesh deserves to be congratulated on its ordinance issued in 2010 which spelt out clearly the malpractices of such MFIs: 'whereas these SHGs are being exploited by private Micro Finance Institutions (MFIs) through usurious interest rates and coercive means of recovery resulting in their impoverishment and in some cases leading to suicides...' This triggered a crisis which almost paralysed for-profit MFIs, with banks reluctant to lend, 'repayments dwindling and depositors tending to withdraw their money'. It is this shock therapy which led to subsequent soul-searching on the part of those MFIs, the promoters of which were fattening themselves on the sweat of the poor borrowers. The Microfinance Institutions Network (MFIN), a grouping of for-profit microlenders, has now set up a committee to look into these deficiencies. In fact, the clout of these MFI seems to be so strong that in spite of all that has been now exposed, some influential papers plead: 'don't kill microfinance'. The short answer to such pleas is: 'we do not want to kill these MFIs; but we certainly want to prevent them from killing their poor borrowers'.

No doubt, the for-profit MFIs represent the predatory face of financial capitalism. But this was compounded by the institutional support which was extended to these MFIs. Such support came from Reserve Bank of India (RBI), public sector banks (PSBs), NABARD and SIDBI. For instance, during 2008-09, banks extended loans worth Rs 3,700 crore. Now, why should PSBs extend loans to MFIs at something like 12 per cent, when they were fully aware that these funds would be onlend by MFIs at 25 to 30 per cent? The answer is that such loans by PSBs to MFIs were treated as priority sector lending. So this had the blessings of RBI. Similarly, some equity or quasi-equity support came from SIDBI and NABARD, of course, at concessional rates. RBI could have stipulated that PSBs should lend only to 'not-for-profit category' of MFIs. PSBs could have also stipulated, on their part, that the onlending rate of beneficiary MFIs should not 'exceed say 17 or 18 per cent'. This was not done. This systemic support perhaps also lent some respectability to for-profit MFIs. Thus, public sector financial resources were used to perpetuate usurious lending practices of MFIs.

In all humility, we may ask Dr Reddy: it is one thing to say that RBI had no statutory powers to regulate MFIs; but was it obliged to support for-profit MFIs? RBI could have stipulated that PSBs should lend only to not-for-profit MFIs, fixing a ceiling on their onlending rates. This support made the system, in a manner of speaking, a co-conspirator in this business of exploiting poor rural borrowers. Public funds were allowed to generate private profits. RBI has not covered itself in glory in this episode.

The sordid story does not end here. Because of high returns, some may even say, with obscenely high returns, stemming from exorbitant lending rates, for-profit MFIs have become attractive investment destinations for private equity and venture capitalists. The recent success of initial public offering (IPO) of SKS Microfinance Ltd. is a case in point. It attracted high profile investors like billionaire George Soros, venture capitalist Vinod Khosla and Infosys Founder Narayana Murthy. Alluding to this transformation of the humble animal microfinance, Muhammad Yunus, the father of microfinance movement said: 'it is a complete detour and nothing but a quitting of microfinance mission'. The original micro finance concept of helping the poor via small loans at reasonable rates of interest has been abdicated (*Economic Times*, 13 December, 2010). Is it a case of Shylocks masquerading as microfinance institutions? One wonders.

Basically, lending to the rural poor at 30 or 40 per cent defies all economic logic. Our small rural borrowers are not Schumpeterian mini-heroes, who can make the project or activity for financing what they have borrowed, financially viable. In fact, by inflating interest cost, we are building *ab initio* non-viability into the project. Secondly, the engagement of for-profit MFIs with borrowers has been shallow based on 'touch and move' business models shorn of any development content. 'The average loans per client in both MFIs and SHGs have been low, between Rs 3500 and Rs 5000. The duration of the loan is short, typically one year or less. The small loan and the short duration do not enable most borrowers to do much except to ease liquidity problems'. (*Microfinance India: State of the*

Sector Report, 2008). It was M.L. Darling who wrote long ago that the Indian peasant is born in debt, lives in debt and dies in debt, thanks to the moneylender. Are we trying to promote the Darling syndrome?

It should be underlined that the policymakers' indifference to exorbitant rural lending rates is in sharp contrast to their concern for corporate sector. Whenever RBI even contemplates raising of repo rates by say 0.25 per cent, the corporate lobby is up in arms, 'don't raise lending rates, it will hurt growth.' More often than not, RBI yields to the corporate sector plea.

Whatever RBI's Malegam Committee has recommended, covers some ground towards reforming the for-profit MFIs. But it seems to have missed the central point. The public sector support to for-profit MFIs should be withdrawn forthwith. After all, why did PSBs begin to extend their support to such MFIs? Because these MFIs provided 'an easy escape route' to their responsibility regarding meeting the priority sector credit target of 40 per cent. In doing so, we have landed ourselves into a greater mess. Then there was this façade of financial inclusion. This empirical experience has demonstrated that under such circumstances it is better not to have borrowed at all, at prohibitive costs, than borrowed and lost. It is better to remain 'excluded' than 'included'.

Where do we go from here? Indian policymakers must be reminded that India, unlike many other countries like Bangladesh, for example, has a healthy home-grown segment of microfinance. Public sector banks (PSBs), restructured regional rural banks (RRBs) rejuvenated cooperative credit system, NABARD's self-help groups (SHGs)-bank linkage programme (SBLP), which has emerged as a major channel of microfinance. Then there is the Post Office, which is already functioning as a semi-bank, with its 1.55 lakh branches and some 16 crore customers. This has great potential, given appropriate policy support, to emerge as a low-cost microfinance channel. The point is that these public or semi-public sector segments have successfully blended profitability criteria with social banking. Of course, 'not-for-profit' MFIs are indeed welcome to join the stream. Our policy-makers could do well to refocus their energies on further developing this segment, rather than trying to reform rogue MFIs. In the business of financial inclusion, there is enough pace for not-for-profit MFIs but not for rogue MFIs.

Fiscal Inequity

The Indian fiscal system is distinguished by the fact that dividends received by individuals are totally exempt from income tax without any limit. Similarly, there are exemptions without limit, from long-term capital gains from the stock market. Thus persons receiving thousands of crores of rupees of dividend income are totally free from income tax, while those earning modest incomes from professions are taxed at high rates. These exemptions are sought to justified on the ground that they foster the development of equity market. The ostensible rationale is that since corporate have already paid the tax, taxing dividend income of individuals would be tantamount to double taxation. This is a specious argument. In the idiom of public finance, corporate and individuals are distinct entities and hence they ought to be taxed separately. Dr S.S. Tarapore, former Deputy Governor of RBI, has correctly argued that unlimited exemptions of dividend income are incongruous with distributive justice and are nothing short of fiscal atrocity.

Contrast this with the recent proposition by Warren Buffett, the billionaire investor and founder of Berkshire Hathaway that the richest should be taxed heavily: 'tax us more'. Supporting this move 'France's 16 richest persons have pressed for more taxes. Where are our pretensions to the socialistic pattern of society?

II

Development Economics: The God that Failed

Before we move on to the discussion of the next stage of India's economic development: 2004-2011, it may be useful to raise some broader questions. Has the process of disillusionment with development economics already started? Let us take a quick look at the more recent developments.

The Commission on Growth and Development sponsored by among others the World Bank, submitted its Report in June 2008.[10] The Commission's main recommendations stem from an investigations into

10. Commission on Growth and Development (2008). *The Growth Report: Strategies for Sustained Growth and Inclousive Development*. Washington D.C.: World Bank.

the empirical experiences of 13 countries, which recorded an average annual GDP growth of 7 per cent for 25 years or longer, since 1950. These countries were Botswana, Brazil, China, Hong Kong, Indonesia, Japan, the Republic of Korea, Malaysia, Malta, Oman, Singapore, Taiwan and Thailand. The Commission adds that two other countries—India and Vietnam—were on their way to joining this group.

These success stories demonstrate that fast and sustained growth is possible. At this pace of expansion, an economy almost doubles its size every decade. The Commission rejects the view that these are 'economic miracles'. The Commission believes that there are perfectly rational explanations for these success stories. Distilling the empirical experience of these 13 countries, the Commission comes up with five essential ingredients for faster and sustained growth: (i) these countries fully exploited the world economy; (ii) they maintained macroeconomic stability; (iii) they mustered high rates of saving and investment; (iv) they let markets allocate resources and (v) they had committed, credible and capable governments.

So far so good. Can these ingredients help us to draw up blue prints for growth and development of other poor countries? 'But it is hard to know how to replicate these characteristics', the Report reveals!

This is the tragedy of development economics. The Commission admits that there is no generic formula for growth. 'Each country has specific characteristics and historical experiences that must be reflected in its growth story'. Indian policymakers in the post 1990s phase were, as we have seen, soaked in the market theology of the IMF and the World Bank and tried to mimic the American capitalist model. This was reflected more prominently in financial sector reforms and in their obsession with privatisation. The Commission itself is cautious that 'governments in these high growth economies were not free market "purists"'. We have thus come a long way from conventional development models.

At this stage it may be appropriate to recall the famous observation of the Noble Laureate Robert Solow: how often all the discussions of the sources of growth and development seem to end in a blaze of sociology, which also explains the stubbornly large residuals in all growth accounting models. He used his theoretical progress. 'The technological change residual' so-called because it is part of the growth that cannot be explained by identifiable factors such as capital accumulation or labour force growth. We have today moved well beyond Solow: the five essential ingredients of the growth receipe identified by the Growth Commission demonstrate that it is inappropriate to call other factors—other than the conventional factors like saving rate, capital-output ratio and the rate of growth of labour force—as 'residual'. Bereft of these five elements, growth accounting models would be reduced to barren econometric exercises. That is how perhaps development economics failed many countries. Our basic approach to development was perhaps flawed.

The disillusionment with development economics was not only in terms of theoretical constructs but also with development policy. When Robert McNamara launched a crusade for poverty eradication as the main goal of the World Bank, the World Bank began to articulate its development vision through its World Development Reports (WDRs). No wonder many policymakers in developing economies, particularly those that borrowed from the IMF and the World Bank, looked with awe and admiration at the WDRs hoping to derive some policy guidelines and the World Bank perhaps honestly believed that the WDR could provide some policy inputs. A critical look at these Reports which began to be published since 1978 has been taken by Shahid Yusuf, on the eve of 30th Anniversary of WDRs, in 2009.[11] This assessment finds that WDRs were mainly a summaries of inside and outside academic research, and they offered no meaningful development policy guidance.

Dr Khatkhate[12] concludes his brilliant review of Shahid Yusuf's monograph on WDRs in the following words:

> ...It is now clear after reading this essay that the WDR far from illuminating development issues and contributing to the science of policy making is more like, to use a resonating phrase of Nandan Nilekani, a Niagara Falls of well-worn ideas and Sahara of new exciting ones.

Is this another episode of the emperor's clothes parable? One wonders.

---

11. Yusuf, Shahid *et al.* (2009). *Development Economics through the Decades. A Critical Look at 30 Years of the World Development.* Washington, D.C.: World Bank.

12. "Reprise of the Canons of Development Economics", *Economic and Political Weekly*, November 11, 2009, p. 31.

III

Mahatma Gandhi Phase: 2004-2011

Rediscovering the Mahatma

The year 2005, may be said to mark a dramatic departure from the market-centred development policy or what I have broadly categorised as the Milton Friedman phase. This is when Indian policymakers began to rediscover, as it were, Mahatma Gandhi, escaping from the trap of market fundamentalism embodied in neoliberalism. Maintaining a sustainable growth of 8 per cent for five years was, in itself, a significant achievement. But this was not enough. Inclusive growth has to be sought. It is here that India's growth story ceases to be a mere growth story: it transfigurates itself into a development drama, with community-centred development as its central theme. This takes us well beyond growth models—a failed God—to the realm of philosophy of development: it urges us to grow up from the conventional growth economics trapped in market theology to resonate to the larger concerns of holistic development including promoting of broad-based, decentralised growth which alone could facilitate access by the poor to employment, food, nutrition and health and quality education; and putting in place appropriate safety nets to reduce the vulnerability of the poor, and above all to build a value-based compassionate society. Do we need to rewrite the script of development economies?

The ambitious Bharat Nirman programme launched in 2005 with a massive investment of Rs 1.74 lakh crore involved a time-bound programme of rural infrastructure development focussing on six subjects: roads, drinking water, irrigation, housing, electricity and telephones. In a way, this symbolises the beginning of the rediscovery of Mahatma's philosophy of rural development. This was subsequently supplemented by other flagship schemes for education and health, Sarva Shiksha Abhiyan (SSA) for education, mid-day meal scheme providing cooked meals to school children, Integrated Child Development Services (ICDS) to promote nutritional supplement to children upto the age of six years. The mid-day meal programme covers some 15 crore children.

The Mahatma Gandhi National Rural Employment Guarantee Act (NREGA), 2005, is the best thing that could have happened to the rural poor. This guarantees 100 days of employment in a year to every rural household. Today, about five crore rural households benefit from this programme. The Budget speech for 2009 summed up the new approach to development '...The UPA Government has gone for a paradigm shift for making the development process more inclusive. It involves creating entitlement barced by legal guarantee to provide basic amenities and opportunities for livelihood to vulnerable sections. *Aam Admi* is now the focus of all our programmes and schemes'. Are we recapturing the rhythm of our old growth song with which we launched our development in 1951?

The process of discovery of the Mahatma did not stop here. The pendulum seem to have swung to the other extreme. We have become ambitious to 'feed' the bulk of the population at subsidised prices. Contrast this with the Milton Friedman phase when our policymakers keen on abolishing food subsidy exported 'surplus' food grains. Secondly, the 'commitment deficit' which hampers our development endeavours warrants that we go beyond the textbook development economics to development philosophy designed to build a value-based society. Let us discuss these two aspects.

A Sort of Food Utopia

The culmination of these efforts is the proposed National Food Security Bill. At present a sense of supreme complacency and total disregard for ground realities seem to characterise the approach of the authors of the National Food Security Bill (see the Document of February 21, 2011) and Food Minister K.V. Thomas. Between themselves they seem to have created a sort of 'food utopia'. The basic approach of home delivery, as it were, of a specified quantum of subsidised food grains—doorstep delivery of PDS grains is the wording in the draft Bill—is flawed. We know that many poor households do not use the public delivery system (PDS) even when they have the necessary entitlement. Even subsidised food grains is far more important than mere legal entitlement. We therefore have to adopt a holistic approach to ensure food security.

Basically, the National Advisory Council (NAC) recommends a much higher coverage of the population to subsidised food. Individual food entitlements proposed by NAC are: priority category 7 kgs per month and general category 5 kgs per month. It recommends a larger coverage of 72 per cent of the total population in the first phase: and 78 per cent in the final phase. In the first phase, NAC estimates a total PDS requirement of 49.4 million tonnes. If we add non-PDS food grains requirements for schemes like the mid-day meals and ICDS, total requirement works out to some 58 million tonnes. The NAC feels that procurement of some 60 to 65 million tonnes of food grains annually 'should not be difficult'. In 2009-10 for instance, procurement of rice and wheat was around 54 million tonnes. The subsidy implication of NAC proposals are that the total subsidy would jump from the present level of Rs 56,700 crore to Rs 71,837 crore.

Apart from financial implications, such larger procurement and distribution of rice and wheat poses problems of logistic disaster. As it is, PDS is in a tottering condition. How does one go about increasing production and strengthening PDS? Here NAC's Explanatory Note merely lists a bunch of good intentions. There is no agenda for action. For instance, 'there is a large potential for higher food grain production. India has vast untapped production reservoir in most farming systems, even with the currently available technologies'.

Regarding storage of food grains—in the light of the recent criticism of insensitivity of FCI to wastage of food grains through inappropriate storage—the NAC merely states: 'urgent efforts are needed to expand, improve and modernise storage of food grains in the country...' NAC also advocates 'urgent reform of PDS'.

Where do these homilies lead us? Recent researchers have provided concrete evidence of corruption in the PDS. Estimates of diversion of grains from PDS include leakages due to corruption, transport losses and losses due to spoilage. Reetika Khera[13] has shown that the situation has deteriorated between 1990-2000 and 2007-08. At the beginning of the period, 24 per cent of the grain was diverted. In 2004-05, 54 per cent of the grains was diverted. At the end of 2007-08, 44 per cent of the grain was diverted. Although there are interstate differentials, this was the picture at the all-India level. There were seven major states whose performance was

13. Khera, Reetika (2011). "Trends in Diversion of Grain from the Public Distribution System", *Economic and Political Weekly*, May 21-27.

excellent, in the sense of negligible diversion. We can not therefore label the PDS as 'dysfunctional'. One thing is quite clear. Unless this deficiency is rectified, it would not be too prudent to entrust PDS with greater responsibilities.

In the face of such evidence, Food Minister is complacent about the FCI. In a recent interview to a financial paper, he said: 'but the key thing is that the machinery has to be equipped. Compared to earlier periods, the recruitment to FCI has risen by 10 per cent. We have modernised FCI godowns through computerisation. Sitting in my office, I know the quantity, quality and distribution of grain from each godown. We have put CCTV cameras to watch operations' (*Economic Times*, June 1, 2011). If the picture is so rosy, one may ask: why did the Supreme Court ask the Government of India to distribute the grains free of cost to the poor, instead of allowing it to rot in the open storage of FCI? It is to the credit of NDTV, that they showed a couple of godowns of FCI where the grain was allowed to rot exposed to rain, or rats were eating away grains from one such godown. The point is that much needs to be done to improve the storage of grains in the godowns of the FCI. Entrusting PDS with greater responsibilities before raising food grains production and before streamlining FCI storage system is like putting the horse before the cart. Thus, the basic approach of NAC to food security is flawed. Providing food security does not mean that Government should produce and deliver a stipulated quantity of food grains at subsidised prices to targetted households, as the NAC proposals seem to suggest. The magnitudes involved in such operations are so forbidding that it may result in logistic disaster. What is required is creating an environment which enables households to purchase food grains through employment generation, moderating open market prices of rice and wheat, and by streamlining marketing arrangements of some items like fruits and vegetables. If public sector banks can use business correspondent (BC) model there is no reason why FCI can not use private trade to reach targetted households. Private and public sector participation should be an essential ingredient of a well-designed food security model. Protecting the vulnerable sections of the population through say mid-day meals or child nutrition programmes would, of course, continue to be the exclusive responsibility of public sector institutions.

Building a Value-based and Compassionate Society

This brief critical review of India's development drama over the last two decades brings us back to the larger concerns of society. Basically, we have seen that building development models or conducting econometric exercises is not the best way to generate practical policy prescriptions. Country-specific issues need to be addressed. The key to success of development in a particular country lies in the answer to the question: What ails development? In India we have seen that 'commitment deficit' haunts many of our development endeavours. It is here that development economics spreads its arms into the broader area of development philosophy. As Ricupero Rubans puts it: 'we should never forget the economy is not something that is beyond our control. The market has to be our servant, not our master. The economy is not like the planetary system or the genetic code; something that is given once and for all and which one cannot alter; it is a product of culture, it is a product of human choices; of choice of values. That is why we have to choose the right values and put competition exactly in the balance with other values and decide what are the higher values for us. We have to particularly provide people with tangible reasons to hope for the future'.[14] This takes back to the Mahatma.

Mahatma Gandhi had distilled the core of Indian philosophy from our ancient scriptures and evolved his own philosophy. In addition to basic needs of the common man being the first charge on the society's resources, he had another important ingredient: the concept of trusteeship. We should hold our wealth as trustees and not as exclusive owners, so that this wealth is available for sharing by others who need it most. Dr Swaminathan would like to add intellectual property rights as well to the concept of wealth.

From times immemorial, Indian philosophy has maintained that the all-round development of a society is best achieved through betterment of individuals which no doubt includes economic well-being but extends well beyond it. Social conscience must be inculcated among individuals through education at all stages and also professional training. All individuals must be sensitised, at their young age itself, to abject poverty, the squalor, disease, ignorance and illiteracy that surround us. They must begin to

---

14. Quoted by Dr Y.V. Reddy (2010). *Life After Global Financial Crisis*. India International Centre. Occasional Publication 14, New Delhi.

think in terms of what is our *dharma* or duty towards alleviating some of the infirmities that affect our less fortunate fellow human beings. Some Asian countries, recently, have introduced in school textbooks lessons on corruption. But that is a narrow and negative concept. More positively, we must aim at building a holistic concept of the right conduct.

One of the ancient scriptures of India The *Brihadaranyaka Upanishad* enjoins us that our life must be guided by the following three D's—*Damya*, that is control yourself, *Datta*, that is give to others and *Dayadhwam*, that is be compassionate. Thus, we must practice self-control, charity and compassion. Collectively, these three characteristics constitute 'development conscience'.[15] Building up such conscience among all sections of the population would go a long way towards evolving a compassionate society—an ideal which the Mahatma sought to achieve. We must add this ingredient to our development approaches.

---

15. Mujumdar, N.A. (2007). "The Development Conscience Factor", in *Inclusive Growth*.

Presidential Address at the 71st Annual Conference of the Indian Society of Agricultural Economics organised by the University of Agricultural Sciences, Dharwad (Karnataka), November 3, 2011.

8 Prospects and Policy Challenges in the Twelfth Plan

Montek S. Ahluwalia

The year 2011-12 is the last year of the Eleventh Plan and this is therefore an appropriate time to review what has been achieved with a view to identify weaknesses in the strategy that need to be corrected, and also identify new challenges that may require new initiatives. This paper is presented in the hope of spurring a broader discussion on these issues. Section I provides an overview of performance against the stated objectives of the Eleventh Plan. Section II provides a macro-level assessment of the prospects of improving growth performance in the Twelfth Plan. Section III identifies some key policy challenges that need to be addressed.

Review of Recent Performance

The Eleventh Plan aimed at delivering faster and more inclusive growth and it is logical to assess performance against this dual objective. Growth and inclusiveness were presented as coequal objectives in recognition of the fact that GDP growth can never be an end in itself. However, faster growth, especially of a particular type, accompanied by economic and social support programmes, which are themselves made more feasible by high growth and buoyant revenues, can bring about an improvement in incomes and living standards for the bulk of the population, which is the end objective.

India's Growth Performance

There is no doubt that the economy has done very well on the growth front, and this is best appreciated when viewed in a long-term perspective. For two decades in the 1960s and 1970s, India's GDP growth rate averaged only 3.5 per cent per year at a time when other developing countries were growing much faster. The 1980s saw the beginning of a reorientation of policies to achieve higher growth and indeed growth accelerated to 5.6 per cent in that decade. A much broader effort at 'systemic reform' was initiated in 1991, based on a wider play of market forces, gradual liberalisation of the financial sector, and opening of the economy to world trade and capital flows. The growth rate of the economy accelerated significantly in the first half of the 1990s, but then slowed down in the second half, averaging 5.7 per cent over the decade as a whole, which was not very different from that in the 1980s.[1]

India's performance improved significantly in the first decade of the 2000s, spurred by favourable global conditions and the cumulative effect of the systemic reforms initiated in 1991. The Tenth Plan (2002-03 to 2006-2007) had targetted a growth rate of 8 per cent and achieved an average growth rate of 7.8 per cent. The Eleventh Plan (2007-08 to 2011-12) aimed at 9 per cent growth and as shown in Table 8.1, the economy achieved 9.3 per cent growth in the first year, but this momentum was interrupted by the global financial crisis of 2008 when GDP growth dropped to 6.8 per cent for the year 2008-09. However, thanks to contra-cyclical stimulus measures, the economy recovered quickly to record 8 per cent and 8.6 per cent growth, respectively, in the next two years. Growth in 2011-12 was initially projected at 9 per cent in the Central government budget but is likely to be lower at around 8.5 per cent. Even so, the average for the Eleventh Plan would be 8.2 per cent, a remarkable performance considering that this period saw the greatest economic crisis the world has faced since the Great Depression.

Improved economic performance has dramatically altered global perceptions of India's potential. An early recognition of this was a Goldman Sachs report of November 2002, which included India, with Brazil, Russia and China in a new BRIC group of emerging market countries which was predicted to overtake the G-8 in terms of total GDP

1. This led some scholars—notably Rodrik and Subramaniam (2004)—to argue that the strategy of giving freer play to market forces and opening the economy to world trade and capital flows, was perhaps not as important as was made out by proponents of the reforms. I have argued against this interpretation in Ahluwalia (2009).

by 2035.[2] Continued strong performance in the decade of the 2000s and resilience in the face of a global slowdown, has reinforced this positive assessment. The general perception today is that India may now be on the path of sustained high growth based on high rates of domestic savings, high quality of entrepreneurial and managerial skills, and the cumulative effect of economic reforms on productivity. Similar transitions have been achieved by the other Asian countries such as Japan, Korea, Taiwan, and most recently China, and it is felt that India may also now be in the same position. How far this forecast is reasonable, and the many constraints that have to be overcome to realise this potential, are discussed in Sections II and III.

Table 8.1

Macroeconomic Balance

	2005-06	*2006-07*	*2007-08*	*2008-09*	*2009-10*	*2010-11*
1. Rate of growth of GDP	9.5	9.6	9.3	6.8	8.0	8.6
2. Rate of inflation % (average over previous year)						
• WPI	4.4	6.5	4.8	8.0	3.6	8.2
• GDP deflator	4.2	6.4	5.8	6.7	7.5	9.6
• CPI (IW)	4.4	6.7	6.2	9.1	12.4	10.0
3. Fiscal deficit (% GDP)						
• Centre	3.97	3.32	2.55	6.04	6.39	5.1
• States	2.33	1.82	1.49	2.40	3.00	2.62
• Combined	6.30	5.14	4.04	8.44	9.39	7.72
4 Current account deficit (% GDP)	-1.2	-1.0	-1.3	-2.3	-2.8	2.5*
5. Foreign direct investment inflows ($ billion)	8.96	22.83	34.84	35.18	37.18	24.0
6. Foreign portfolio investment inflows ($ billion)	12.49	7.00	27.27	-13.86	32.38	35.0*

Note: * Advance Estimates.

2. The report was largely based on the notion of convergence which holds that countries at lower per capita income have low capital per person endowments and are therefore likely to have much higher marginal product of capital which will ensure a flow of capital to these countries and faster growth than richer countries.

Performance on Inclusiveness

It is more difficult to assess performance on inclusiveness than on growth for three reasons. First, inclusiveness is a multidimensional concept and progress therefore needs to be assessed in many different dimensions. Second, the data relating to various aspects of inclusiveness become available only after a considerable lag, and information for the Eleventh Plan period is often not available. Third, most policies aimed at inclusiveness have an impact only over a relatively long term, and this means that even when policies are moving in the right direction, the results may only be evident much later. For example, steps taken to improve education for the poor will improve their earning ability in future, but this impact will only be reflected in actual income earning much later.

Multidimensionality of Inclusion

The multidimensional nature of inclusiveness is best illustrated by listing some of the many dimensions that are relevant. The extent of reduction in the percentage of the population below the poverty line is clearly a very important indicator of progress. However, many families that are above the poverty line in terms of per capita consumption may lack access to basic services such as education, health, clean drinking water and sanitation. Inclusiveness must obviously include progress in delivery of these essential services. Inclusiveness must also extend to addressing concerns about inequality. It is sometimes argued that inequality should not matter as long as the poor are getting better off and it is probably true that a rapid rate of improvement in incomes for the poor may make them willing to accept some increase in inequality. However, large increases in inequality, accompanying only modest improvements in the levels of living of the poor, are unlikely to be acceptable. Inequality in this context relates not only to the distribution of income or consumption across individuals, but also inequality across states, and in some cases, even across regions within states.

Inclusiveness in the Indian context also requires a special focus on particular social groups such as the scheduled castes (SCs) and scheduled tribes (STs), and also the minorities. Since these groups are concentrated in the lower ranges of the income distribution, it may be thought that an effective strategy for reducing poverty or inequality addresses the concerns of these groups. However, if inclusiveness is defined as bringing these groups at par with the rest of the population, it has to address the issue of achieving a fair representation for these groups along the entire income distribution. This is conceptually very different from reduction in overall poverty or inequality, in the sense that it can be achieved leaving the incidence of poverty and the level of inequality unchanged.

The Eleventh Plan explicitly recognised the multidimensional nature of inclusiveness by enumerating 27 monitorable targets of which GDP growth was only one. The others focussed on different aspects of inclusion such as growth in agriculture, reduction in poverty, growth of employment opportunities, etc. One consequence of multidimensionality is that the extent of progress in different dimensions will vary. For example, it is perfectly possible for poverty to decline while inequality increases. Similarly, inequality among households in the country as a whole may decrease, or remain unchanged, while inequality across states increases. Any overall assessment of progress on inclusiveness will have to be based on a composite view of all these developments.

Subject to these caveats, a summary of what has been achieved in the Eleventh Plan is attempted below.

Reduction in Poverty

Table 8.2 summarises the change in poverty between 1993-94 and 2004-05, which is the latest year for which official data are available. The table reports the earlier estimates, based on the Lakdawala Committee method, and also the new poverty estimates based on the recommendations of the Tendulkar Committee. The poverty estimates of the Tendulkar Committee are higher, but both estimates show a decline in the percentage of the population in poverty in the pre-Eleventh Plan period. However the pace of reduction is very modest, about 0.85 percentage points per year using the Lakdawala estimates and slightly lower at 0.81 percentage points per year using the Tendulkar estimates.[3]

3. The Tendulkar Committee was appointed by the Planning Commission in 2009 to make recommendations on whether the poverty lines and the method of indexation being used by the Planning Commission following the methodology recommended by the Lakdawala Committee needed modification. The Tendulkar Committee concluded that the urban poverty lines were broadly appropriate but rural poverty line for each

contd...

The Eleventh Plan had set a more ambitious target of reducing poverty by 2 percentage points per year. Abhijit Sen (2010) has estimated that poverty declined sharply from 37 per cent in 2004-05 to 29 per cent in 2007-08, which is much more than 2 percentage points per year. However, 2007-08 was a 'thin sample' round and is therefore not used for computing official estimates of poverty. The next large sample round is the 66th Round for 2009-10 and the Planning Commission will compute poverty from this round once the unit level data become available.

Some indication of what the 2009-10 data will reveal can be had from the estimates made by C. Ravi of the Centre for Economic and Social Studies, Hyderabad working with group data for 2009-10. His results, also reported in Table 8.2, show that poverty in 2009-10 was 32 per cent, an increase over the 2007-08 level, possibly reflecting the recession and the severe drought in 2009. At 32 per cent, poverty between 2004-05 and 2009-10 declined at the rate of 1 percentage point per year, better than in the previous period, but well below the Eleventh Plan target. Fortunately, recognising that the 2009 poverty estimate may be distorted because of the drought, the National Sample Survey Organisation (NSSO) has decided to conduct a second large sample survey in 2011-12. It is only when estimates from this survey become available will we be able to get reliable estimates of the rate of poverty reduction actually achieved in the Eleventh Plan period.

It is interesting to note that the performance in reducing poverty between 2004-05 and 2009-10 varies considerably across states. The four southern states (Andhra Pradesh, Tamil Nadu, Kerala and to lesser extent Karnataka) all report impressive reduction in poverty, as do Maharashtra, Orissa, Madhya Pradesh and Himachal Pradesh. There is no improvement in Uttar Pradesh and Bihar, very little improvement in West Bengal and an actual deterioration in Assam. Punjab and Haryana had relatively lower poverty rates to begin with, but do not seem to have improved their

...contd...

state needed to be modified to make the rural poverty line more comparable with the urban poverty line. The result of the change in methodology is that the urban poverty numbers are more or less unchanged but the rural poverty line has been raised and the proportion of the population below it has also increased. The Tendulkar Committee specifically warned that for intertemporal comparisons the same method must be used for both observations.

position. How far these differences reflect differences in the pace and nature of growth in each state, and how far they reflect differences in the implementation of anti-poverty schemes, is a subject that needs further investigation based on the final official estimates of poverty obtained from unit level data.

Table 8.2

Percentage of Population Below Poverty Line

States	*Lakdawala Methodology*		*Tendulkar Methodology*		*Tentative Estimates*[1]
	1993-94	*2004-05*	*1993-94*	*2004-05*	*2009-10*
Andhra Pradesh	22.2	15.8	44.6	29.9	20.0
Assam	40.9	19.7	51.8	34.4	39.2
Bihar	55.0	41.4	60.5	54.4	54.8
Gujarat	24.2	16.8	37.8	31.8	26.6
Haryana	25.1	14.0	35.9	24.1	23.8
Himachal Pradesh	28.4	10.0	34.6	22.9	11.7
Jammu and Kashmir	25.2	5.4	26.3	13.2	12.8
Karnataka	33.2	25.0	49.5	33.4	26.5
Kerala	25.4	15.0	31.3	19.7	11.3
Madhya Pradesh	42.5	38.3	44.6	48.6	40.5
Maharashtra	36.9	30.7	47.9	38.1	26.4
Orissa	48.6	46.4	59.1	57.2	46.4
Punjab	11.8	8.4	22.4	20.9	19.3
Rajasthan	27.4	22.1	38.3	34.4	29.4
Tamil Nadu	35.0	22.5	44.6	28.9	18.3
Uttar Pradesh	40.9	32.8	48.4	40.9	40.5
West Bengal	35.7	24.7	39.4	34.3	32.5
All-India	36.0	27.5	45.3	37.2	32.2

Note: 1 Estimates for 2009-10 have been made by C. Ravi of the Centre for Economic and Social Studies, Hyderabad based on group data from the 2009-10 NSSO Survey and using the Tendulkar Committee poverty line for 2004-05 adjusting for using the CPIAL for rural areas and the CPIIW for urban areas. These estimates are an approximation of what can be expected when the Tendulkar methodology is applied to the unit-level data as will be done by the Planning Commission when the unit-level data become available.

Accelerating Agricultural Growth

Since half the population derives the bulk of their income from agriculture, and this sector had decelerated to about 2 per cent growth per year in the decade preceding the Eleventh Plan, the Plan had targetted 4 per cent growth in agriculture as one of the 27 monitorable targets relevant for inclusiveness. Performance thus far suggests that we are unlikely to exceed 3 per cent per year. The reversal of the earlier decline is a welcome development, but the Twelfth Plan must aim at a better agricultural performance if poverty is to be reduced at a faster rate.

Access to Basic Services

Tables 8.3 and 8.4 demonstrate that poverty in terms of lack of access to basic services is larger than the 37 per cent estimated to be below the poverty line in 2004-05 according to the Tendulkar Committee. The proportion of children suffering from severe malnutrition was 40 per cent in 2005-06, of children not fully vaccinated in 2005 was 45.5 per cent and of women not benefitting from safe delivery in 2005 was 41 per cent. Turning to education services, the proportion of children that dropped out of elementary school by Class VIII in 2007-08 was 43 per cent.

The extent of deprivation is clearly substantial and is made more dramatic by the fact that in some of these areas India lags behind other developing countries in similar or even more difficult circumstances.[4] On the positive side however, Tables 8.3 and 8.4 also show clear improvement in these indicators over a 10-year period. This is evident even in the lower income states of Bihar, Madhya Pradesh, Rajasthan, Uttar Pradesh and Orissa. There are, however, some interesting differences. Whereas the infant mortality rate (IMR) has declined in all these states, the data on vaccination shows only modest improvement from the very low levels in these states except for Bihar where the jump in the full vaccination rate is very substantial, though from an abysmally low level to a level that is still very low.

Access to education is particularly important for inclusiveness because it increases income opportunities in future, and it is therefore interesting to consider how much progress is being made. As shown in Table 8.4, the net enrollment rate in primary schools had increased from 71 per cent in 1997-1998 to 96 per cent in 2007-08 and further improvement has taken place since then. The dropout rates by the end of elementary school (Class VIII)

4. For example, India's IMR of 50 is higher than of our neighbour Bangladesh, which has an IMR of 41. Vaccination rates in Bangladesh are also much higher.

Table 8.3

Progress over Time in Select Health Indicators

	Maternal Mortality Rate		*Infant Mortality Rate*		*Full Vaccination*		*Safe Delivery*		*Child Malnutrition-Underweight*	
	*1999-2001**	*2004-06**	*2001**	*2009**	*2005@*	*2009@*	*2005@*	*2009@*	*1992-93$*	*2005-06$*
All-India	327	254	66	50	54.5	61.0	58.9	76.2	47.9	40.4
Andhra Pradesh	220	154	66	49	72.3	68.0	77.8	95.6	42.9	29.8
Assam	398	480	74	61	25.8	59.1	40.3	65.5	44.1	35.8
Bihar	400	312	62	52	19.0	49.0	25.5	53.2	58.7	55.0
Gujarat	202	160	60	48	63.1	56.6	74.8	85.2	42.7	41.3
Haryana	176	186	66	51	57.2	71.1	53.1	69.3	31.0	38.2
Karnataka	266	213	58	41	86.9	78.0	74.6	88.4	46.4	33.2
Kerala	149	95	11	12	82.1	81.5	99.4	99.9	22.1	21.2
Madhya Pradesh	407	335	86	67	38.9	42.9	42.7	82.9	57.4	57.9
Maharashtra	169	130	45	31	58.9	78.6	75.5	85.5	47.3	32.5
Orissa	424	303	91	65	53.2	59.5	52.7	79.1	50.0	39.4
Punjab	177	192	52	38	83.5	83.6	71.6	66.7	39.9	23.6
Rajasthan	501	388	80	59	49.9	53.8	45.4	75.8	41.8	36.9
Tamil Nadu	167	111	49	28	79.6	77.3	92.7	98.6	40.7	25.9
Uttar Pradesh	539	440	83	63	33.8	40.9	34.4	64.2	52.7	41.5
West Bengal	218	141	51	33	54.4	64.9	54.6	72.6	53.2	37.6

Note: @ Coverage Evaluation Survey, UNICEF. $ National Family Health Survey (NFHS).

Source :* Various SRS Bulletins, Office of the Registrar General, GoI (MHA).

had also fallen from 56 per cent to 43 per cent. However, since it is children from poorer households who are likely to have the highest dropout rates, they remain significantly disadvantaged relative to the rest of the population in terms of completion of elementary schooling. The problem is clearly more severe in some states. The dropout rate in Bihar, Orissa, Madhya Pradesh and Rajasthan has declined only marginally, and ranges between 60 per cent and 70 per cent. In Assam, it has actually increased. Uttar Pradesh however has recorded a very substantial improvement.

Table 8.4

Progress over Time in Select Education Indicators

	Net Enrollment Ratio in Classes I-V (Primary Education)		*Dropout Rates Classes I-VIII (Elementary)*		*Literacy Rate Population Age 7 Years and Above*	
	*1997-98**	*2007-08**	*1997-98**	*2007-08**	*2001$*	*2011$*
All-India	71.1	95.9	56.1	43.0	64.8	74.0
Andhra Pradesh	68.6	78.8	73.4	48.7	60.5	67.7
Assam	98.4	88.8	69.1	73.5	63.3	73.2
Bihar	75.9	99.5	77.1	70.7	47.0	63.8
Gujarat	86.4	86.3	60.3	48.2	69.1	79.3
Haryana	73.4	65.0	30.8	6.5	67.9	76.6
Karnataka	88.6	98.6	56.4	33.9	66.6.	75.6
Kerala	71.5	68.0	-0.8	0.0	90.9	93.9
Madhya Pradesh	88.1	94.2	48.3	46.1	63.7	70.6
Maharashtra	84.4	84.9	39.9	30.5	76.9	82.9
Orissa	69.7	92.7	66.4	61.3	63.1	73.5
Punjab	70.6	53.0	28.4	26.0	69.7	76.7
Rajasthan	71.6	85.2	64.0	62.3	60.4	67.1
Tamil Nadu	84.6	97.8	30.0	9.1	73.5	80.3
Uttar Pradesh	46.8	90.4	52.6	28.6	56.3	69.7
West Bengal	55.6	84.1	72.2	63.9	68.6	77.1

Source: $ Office of the Registrar General, GoI (Ministry of Home Affairs).
* Ministry of Human Resource Development, GoI.

The real problem is that improved access in terms of enrollment and even retention in school does not necessarily mean comparable access to education across income classes adjusted for quality. The quality of education in private schools is widely perceived to be higher than in government schools, and since children from lower income groups go predominantly to government schools which are free, opportunities may be less equal than they seem. The latest Annual Status of Education Report (2010) shows that 36 per cent of the children in Class III-V in rural areas cannot read texts meant for Class I, and 41 per cent cannot perform simple arithmetic exercises meant for Class I.[5] What is particularly worrisome is that these surveys show only a small improvement between 2007 and 2010, too small to be of any comfort. Poor quality of education reflects well-known problems relating to the difficulty in recruiting qualified teachers and equally important, the difficulty in enforcing accountability among teachers once recruited. These are major challenges that need to be addressed in the Twelfth Plan.

Gap between SC/ST and the Rest

Another test of inclusiveness is whether the gap between the SCs and STs, and the rest of the population is being reduced. Thorat (2010) has documented (Table 8.5) that the percentage of the SC and ST population in poverty (using the old Lakdawala poverty estimates) is much higher than for the population as a whole and this is also true for the Muslim minority. However, the incidence of poverty in all these groups is falling and the reduction in the percentage in poverty for the SCs and the Muslims is roughly comparable to that for the population as a whole. The STs however have benefitted less than the others; they not only have the highest percentage in poverty, but also the smallest reduction over time. This is possibly because they are geographically much more concentrated in backward areas than the SCs, who therefore have greater access to expanding opportunities emerging from economic change.[6]

---

5. The proposition that quality of education in private schools is better than in government schools is widely believed but not easy to establish statistically because if the kind of parents who are likely to encourage their children to study prefer to send them to private schools, then private schools will do better. It is therefore necessary to make comparisons after controlling for this. Studies conducted by ASER have attempted to do this and they found that private schools remain better after controlling for the parental factors but the difference is reduced.

6. See Kapur *et al.* (2010).

Table 8.5

Poverty by Castes and Other Sub-Groups
(Percentage of the Population in Poverty Using Lakdawala Method)

	1983	*1993-94*	*2004-05*
All	46.5	37.2	28.0
Scheduled castes	59.0	48.6	37.1
Scheduled tribes	63.9	50.6	44.7
All Hindus	47.0	36.8	28.0
Muslims	51.2	45.2	33.0
Other minorities	30.2	26.8	17.9

Source: Sukhadeo Thorat (2010). "How Socially Inclusive Has Growth Been?", Presidential Address at the 93rd Annual Conference of the Indian Economic Association.

Inequality in Consumption

Rising inequality has been an issue in many industrialised countries and also emerging market countries such as China. Inequality is normally discussed in terms of inequality of incomes, but since there are no official data on the distribution of household incomes in India, trends in inequality can only be measured on the basis of inequality in the distribution of consumption. Available data summarised in Table 8.6 show that there was a modest increase in inequality in urban areas, though no similar trend can be discerned in rural areas. More importantly, the Gini coefficients are fairly low, much lower than reported for other fast growing economies

Table 8.6

Measures of Consumption Inequality, India
(1973-74 to 2004-05)

	1983	*1987-88*	*1993-94*	*2004-05*	*2009-10*
Gini coefficient of distribution of consumption					
Rural	0.30	0.30	0.28	0.30	0.28
Urban	0.30	0.35	0.34	0.37	0.37
Rural-urban ratio of mean consumption					
Current prices	0.69	0.52	0.61	0.52	0.52
Constant prices	0.65	0.69	0.61	0.58	0.59

including China. The data also reveal some increase in rural-urban differences. The ratio of rural to urban consumption has fallen over time, both in current and constant prices, but the decline is gentle suggesting only a mild worsening in the rural-urban differential. This trend was also evident in the pre-reforms period and does not seem to have accelerated.

Inequality across States

One of the concerns about economic reforms was that the richer states would benefit while the poorer states might become poorer. It was feared this might happen because the reduced role of the public sector and the elimination of industrial licensing as a means of controlling location decisions by the private sector would dilute the ability to the direct investment to the less developed states. Table 8.7 presents the available data on growth of gross state domestic product (GSDP) across states in three successive decades and brings out several interesting features. The notion that the richer states are growing richer while the poor are growing poorer is simply not borne out by the data. Punjab was the richest of the major states until a few years ago but it has grown more slowly than average and has fallen behind Haryana, Gujarat and Maharashtra.

It is true that the poorer states, notably the so-called BIMARU states, Bihar, Madhya Pradesh, Rajasthan and Uttar Pradesh slowed down in the 1990s compared to the 1980s. However, they accelerated after 2000-01 and, except in the case of Rajasthan, the growth rates in the 2000s have actually been higher than in the 1980s. Bhalla (2011) has shown that the extent of acceleration in growth in the post-reform period is negatively correlated with the level of per capita GSDP, i.e., the poorer states have actually experienced a greater increase in growth, which is consistent with what one would expect under conditional convergence.

One way of testing whether differential growth in the states has led to an increase in overall interstate inequality is to construct a Gini coefficient for interstate inequality. Figure 8.1 shows the movement over time of such a Gini coefficient. Interstate inequality increased in the initial stages of the reforms in the 1990s, but this process did not continue in the decade of the 2000s. Interstate inequality today is higher than it was before the reforms but it has stabilised as the growth process has become less uneven.

Table 8.7

Growth Rate of Major Indian States

State	Growth in GSDP (% Per Annum)		
	1981-82 to 1990-91	1991-92 to 2000-01	2001-02 to 2009-10
Andhra Pradesh	6.4	5.6	7.6
Assam	4.2	2.5	5.2
Bihar	4.9	3.9	7.0
Chhattisgarh	na	na	9.4
Haryana	6.6	5.1	9.0
Gujarat	5.9	6.3	10.2
Jharkhand	na	na	7.1
Karnataka	5.2	6.9	7.0
Kerala	3.7	5.6	8.0
Madhya Pradesh	5.2	4.2	5.9
Maharashtra	6.1	6.1	9.3
Orissa	3.3	4.2	9.0
Punjab	5.3	4.7	6.1
Rajasthan	8.1	4.9	6.9
Tamil Nadu	5.7	6.3	7.4
Uttar Pradesh	5.1	3.6	5.8
West Bengal	4.4	6.5	6.7
All-India (National Accounts)	5.4	5.6	7.6

Note: Growth rates are averages for the periods indicated. The growth rate for 1981-82 is the growth rate over 1980 81.

Source: Central Statistical Organisation, Ministry of Statistics and Programme Implementation.

A new aspect of regional inequality that has gained political visibility in recent years relates to inequality within states. Fast growing states such as Maharashtra, Gujarat, Andhra Pradesh and Karnataka, all have significant areas that are perceived to be lagging behind and the differential is often attributed to neglect by the state governments. Since data on GSDP or on poverty are not available at the district level, it is difficult to judge whether concerns expressed on this count reflect a situation where the extent of inequality within states has actually deteriorated, or whether awareness and expectations have increased to a level that makes the pre-existing situation unacceptable. The Central government has recognised the problem and has devised geographically targetted interventions, such as the Backward Regions Grant Fund, which now also includes a special programme for tribal districts, to deal with this problem.

Figure 8.1

Trends in Interstate Inequality

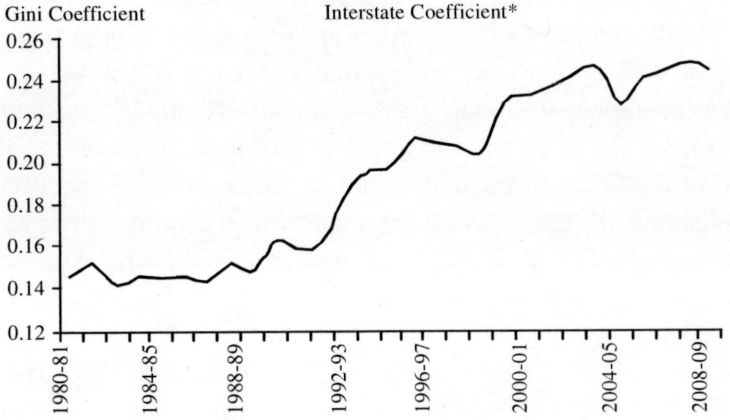

Note: * The Gini coefficient is calculated assuming that all individuals within each state have gross income equal to per capita GSDP. This method ignores the inequality arising out of the unequal distribution within each state, and focusses only on inequality arising from interstate differences in per capita GSDP.

There are other dimensions of inclusiveness which are relevant but have not been discussed for want of space. Gender inequality is the most important dimension which has not been discussed explicitly, mainly because the facts are indisputable, but which does need to be acknowledged. The decline in the sex-ratio in the age group 0-6 observed in the 2011 Census is a truly alarming warning call in this context as it signals a continuing social bias which must be countered.

To summarise, the picture of performance on inclusiveness is clearly mixed. Both the extent of poverty and the lack of access to essential services remain serious problems. However on the positive side, there is steady improvement in many areas and if the rate of improvement observed in the period for which data are available has continued—and there is every reason to think it would have—the current situation may be significantly better than what the latest data suggest. Nevertheless, it cannot be denied that we have seen slower progress in ensuring inclusion than on accelerating growth and this contrast feeds the public perception that rapid growth has only led to a concentration of income and wealth at the upper end.

The perception of concentration of wealth and widening disparities is sharpened by the tendency of the media, including especially the electronic media which now has very wide reach, to publicise success at the top end, including the conspicuous consumption with which it is often associated, while simultaneously focussing attention on the depth of poverty at the other end. Both extremes are understandably viewed as newsworthy, but in focussing disproportionately on them, the steady improvement in living standards of the very substantial population in the middle, and the associated rise of a growing middle class receives much less attention than it should. And yet this not only represents an important welfare gain, but also an important social development, with potentially large positive effects in terms of expectations, values and a rising demand for better and more accountable government.

Inflation and Macro Balance

A weak spot of recent economic performance, which is relevant for both growth and inclusiveness, is the buildup of inflationary pressure over the past three years. A modest rate of inflation is tolerable, and may even be necessary to accommodate relative price changes that have become unavoidable. However inflation beyond this tolerable level—usually put at 5 per cent to 6 per cent by the government and 4 per cent to 5 per cent by the Reserve Bank of India (RBI)—is regressive and also distortionary, damaging both inclusion and growth. Inflation has been well above this level in the past two years and while India is not the only emerging market country experiencing this problem—the resurgence of inflation is a concern in most emerging markets—the rate of inflation in India has been higher than in most other countries.

Table 8.1 presents alternative measures of inflation since 2005-06. The GDP deflator is perhaps the best measure of overall inflation and the average inflation rate on this measure has averaged about 7.4 per cent in the first four years of the Eleventh Plan whereas it averaged at 5.3 per cent in the Tenth Plan. High rates of inflation in food prices, especially vegetables, fruits, milk, eggs, etc., have been a matter of special concern, and this is reflected in double digit rates of inflation as measured by the consumer price index (CPI) in the past two years. Inflationary pressure in India has been variously attributed to: (a) the rise in global prices of crude oil, food grains and metals, (b) domestic supply constraints in the food economy other than food grains and (c) overheating caused by the fiscal expansion initiated in response to the global crisis. All these factors have probably been at work, but whatever the specific factors that triggered the inflationary upsurge, once inflation becomes broad-based—and that seems to be happening—it becomes a macroeconomic phenomenon, and must be tackled through a suitable combination of fiscal and monetary policy combined with efforts to remove specific supply constraints which are identifiable.

Monetary policy is the traditional instrument for dealing with overall inflation, and it has been tightened gradually, but it can be effective only if it is supported by appropriate fiscal policy. As shown in Table 8.1, fiscal stimulus policies led to the fiscal deficit of the Centre and the states taken together increasing from 4 per cent of GDP in 2007-08 to 9.4 per cent in 2009-10. While the stimulus succeeded in countering the effects of the recession, it has clearly raised the fiscal deficit to an unsustainable level. A process of correction was initiated in 2010 and the combined fiscal deficit was reduced from 9 per cent in 2009-10 to 7.7 per cent in 2010-11. These policies will need to be pursued further to bring the fiscal deficit back to pre-crisis levels. We return to this issue in Section 3.

Growth Prospects for the Twelfth Plan

This section presents a macro-level assessment of the prospects for rapid growth in India. In making such an assessment, it is important to avoid the complacent view that since growth has been accelerating it will continue to remain high, as long as the policies which generated this growth in the past continue. This approach is overly simplistic because there are examples of countries that grew rapidly for a while and then slowed down.[7] This can happen for two reasons. First, the economy may

7. Brazil, for example, grew at an average rate of 9 per cent for 20 years in the 1960s and 1970s, and then collapsed to an average of 2 per cent growth for the 1980s and 1990s. It has done better in the current decade, but even then, the average growth rate has been a little over 3 per cent per year. The Southeast Asian high performers of yesteryear have also found it difficult to get back to the high growth they experienced before 1997.

come up against new internal constraints, themselves often emerging from structural changes produced by rapid growth. Continuing the old policies without addressing these constraints is not enough in these circumstances. Second, the external environment may have changed, necessitating a different approach. We look first at demand-side constraints on achieving higher growth and then at supply-side constraints in the context of likely changes in both internal and external circumstances.

Demand-side Constraints on Growth

The most important demand-side constraint on future growth arises from the change in the global environment in the post-crisis period, whereby the industrialised countries are expected to grow more slowly. The pace at which exports can increase to the US and Europe will therefore be lower. It is often pointed out that although India has become a more open economy in the post-reform period. It is still less dependent on export demand than other emerging market countries, and its growth prospects should therefore be less affected.[8] Nevertheless, it is relevant to ask how India can actually expect to grow faster in an environment in which export demand will be weaker.

One part of the answer is that even if export demand from industrialised countries is weaker, many emerging market countries are projected to grow more rapidly, and our export performance could be improved by targetting the faster growing markets. It is sometimes argued that India is much more dependent on domestic demand and in this context domestic consumption can be a strong driver of growth in India. This particular argument ignores the fact that since savings ratios are projected to increase—and indeed this is often listed as one of India's strong fundamentals—consumption is not expected to grow faster than GDP. The real solution to the demand deficiency resulting from slower growth of exports lies in ensuring higher levels of domestic investment, particularly investment in infrastructure. Poor infrastructure is a critical weakness in India and an expanded investment programme in this area will not only bolster demand in the short run, it will also increase

8. The IT sector is perhaps an exception to this generalisation since it has been highly dependent upon markets in industrialised countries. However, given the competitiveness of the sector, the impact may not be very large.

competitiveness and thereby boost the supply-side of growth in the medium run.

Higher levels of investment in an environment where export growth may be subdued may lead to a widening of the deficit in the balance of payments and this strategy therefore depends critically upon our ability to finance the higher deficit. Traditionally, we have viewed current account deficits of around 2 per cent of GDP as comfortable. As shown in Table 8.1, the current account deficit in 2010-11 was already around 2.5 per cent of GDP. An aggressive effort to push investment could take the current account deficit to say around 3 per cent of GDP for some years. The key issue therefore is whether a deficit of this order can be financed through long-term capital flows, including especially FDI. It can be argued that India has only recently begun to attract global capital and given the size of the economy, and its perceived high growth potential, it will remain an attractive investment destination as long as policy towards investment in general and FDI in particular is seen to be supportive and the macroeconomic environment is judged to be sound.

This positive assessment needs to be qualified by noting that the external environment is vulnerable to growing concern about the fiscal situation in some industrialised countries. Worries about fiscal unsustainability, especially in the US, could lead to higher long-term interest rates globally and also greater volatility in capital flows to emerging markets. However, India's relative attractiveness as an investment destination could offset this effect if the policy environment is viewed as macroeconomically sound and investor-friendly. Some of the relevant issues are examined in greater detail in Section III.

Supply-side Constraints on Growth

Supply-side constraints on India's growth potential at the macro level are best examined using the traditional growth accounting framework which explains growth of GDP in terms of growth of capital and labour inputs and the growth of total factor productivity. There are good reasons to be optimistic on all three counts.

Growth of Capital

The growth of capital inputs depends on the rate of investment, which in turn depends on the investment climate and the scope for financing the investment from domestic savings and foreign capital inflows. Although a great deal of attention is rightly focussed on the financing constraint, we need to keep in mind that in a dominantly private sector-led development process, a favourable investment climate is an essential precondition for potential investors to undertake new investment or expand capacity. One can envisage a situation in which resources to finance investment are available, but investment does not take place simply because entrepreneurs do not find investment opportunities attractive, i.e., 'animal spirits' are missing.

Private investment in India was very buoyant prior to the crisis. As shown in Table 8.8, private corporate fixed capital formation increased from 9.1 per cent of GDP in 2004-05 to a peak of 14.3 per cent in 2007-08 just before the crisis. Thereafter, it declined to 10.4 per cent in 2008-09, and was only slightly higher at 10.8 per cent in 2009-10. Data for 2010-11 are not yet available, but this percentage is likely to have increased further, though not back to the previous peak. The decline in private corporate fixed investment after 2008-09 has been partly offset by higher investment by the household sector and by the public sector. As a result, gross fixed capital formation (GFCF) in the household, private corporate and public sector combined increased from 28.7 per cent of GDP in 2004-05 to a peak of 33 per cent in 2007-08 after which it fell to 32 per cent in 2008-09 and declined further to 30.8 per cent in 2009-10.

It is difficult to predict what will happen to private investment in the short run. However, allowing for a continuing recovery in fixed investment from the post-crisis trough, we could end the Eleventh Plan with GFCF somewhere around 33 per cent of GDP. Allowing for some further increase in the Twelfth Plan period, including especially a return of private corporate investment to the peak level observed in 2007-08 and some improvement beyond that level, the average rate of GFCF in the Twelfth Five-Year Plan could be around 36 per cent, which should suffice to generate sustained GDP growth of 9 per cent per year. The gross domestic capital formation rate consistent with this projection is around 40 per cent of GDP.

Table 8.8

Savings and Investment

	2004-05	2005-06	2006-07	2007-08	2008-09	2009-10
1. Gross domestic saving (% GDP) of which:	32.4	33.5	34.6	36.9	32.2	33.7
Household sector	10.1	11.9	11.3	11.7	10.8	11.8
Private corporate sector	6.6	7.5	7.9	9.4	7.9	8.1
Government administration	-2.3	-2.1	-1.0	0.5	-3.3	-1.2
Public enterprises	4.6	4.5	4.6	4.5	4.0	3.4
2. Gross domestic capital formation (% GDP)	32.5	34.3	35.9	38	35.4	35.8
3. Gross fixed capital formation (% GDP) of which:	28.7	30.3	31.3	32.9	32.0	30.8
Household sector	12.7	11.2	10.9	10.6	13.1	11.5
Private corporate sector	9.1	11.8	12.5	14.3	10.4	10.8
Public sector	6.9	7.4	7.9	8.1	8.6	8.4

Source: Central Statistical Organisation, Ministry of Statistics and Programme Implementation.

The ability to finance this level of capital formation depends largely on what happens to domestic savings and foreign capital inflows. Prospects on both fronts are positive. As shown in Table 8.8, the average gross domestic savings rate increased to a peak of 36.9 per cent in 2007-08, declining thereafter to 32.2 per cent in the crisis year 2008-09. The deterioration of 4.7 percentage points of GDP is very largely accounted for by the deterioration of as much as 3.8 percentage points in government savings, reflecting the fact that the contra-cyclical expansion in India was largely on account of an increase in subsidies because petroleum and fertiliser prices were not adjusted.[9]

The savings rate recovered to 33.7 per cent in 2009-10 reflecting an improvement in all categories, including government administration, though the public sector enterprises savings rate continued to be low. With

9. This brings out the fact that the fiscal stimulus in India was primarily a stimulus to consumption and not investment. Had petroleum prices been adjusted but the fiscal deficit allowed to widen because of higher levels of investment in say infrastructure, it would have contributed more to medium-term economic performance. The choice between a consumption-based stimulus and an investment-based stimulus is a key aspect of the design of fiscal stimulus.

further improvement expected in 2010-11, and hopefully also in 2011-12, as fiscal consolidation takes hold we could end the Eleventh Plan with a gross domestic savings rate of around 35 per cent. Allowing for some further improvement during the Twelfth Plan, particularly in government savings, we can reasonably plan for an average saving rate in the Twelfth Plan period of around 37 per cent. This together with a current account deficit of around 3 per cent of GDP should be able to finance a gross capital formation rate of around 40 per cent.

The macroeconomic parameters presented above are tentative at this stage, and their internal consistency will be more rigorously tested through various models used by the Planning Commission in the formulation of the Twelfth Five-Year Plan. However, they do suggest that with some effort, there is scope for increasing both domestic savings and investment to levels broadly consistent with 9 per cent growth, or even a little more.

Labour Inputs

Labour supply prospects are also favourable for high growth. It is well known that the working-age population in India is expected to increase over the next 20 years, whereas in the industrialised countries, and also in China, it will be going down. While this is sometimes presented as a potential demographic dividend, it is worth cautioning that a growing workforce is an advantage only if: (a) sufficient investment is taking place to generate the GDP growth needed to absorb labour productively and (b) if the education and skill level imparted to the new entrants is consistent with employability. In the absence of these two conditions, a growing number of young entrants to the labour force could as easily be a recipe for unemployment and consequent unrest. The prospects for achieving a high level of investment are good, for the reasons outlined above. The task of ensuring that the new entrants to the labour force have employable skills is more challenging.

Table 8.9 presents data on the mean years of schooling for the population over 15 years for India and for selected comparator countries. Mean years of schooling in India increased from 3.45 in 1990 to 4.20 in 2000 and 5.12 in 2010. This compares with 5.62 in China in 1990, 7.11 in 2000 and 8.17 in 2010. India clearly lags significantly behind China in terms of the average education level of the labour force. However, India's position today is roughly comparable to China's in the 1985, and starting from that position, China achieved an average growth of GDP over 10 per cent per annum for 30 years. There is no reason why India cannot do the same, especially because efforts to expand enrollment and reduce dropout rates over the past several years will ensure that the quality of the new addition to the labour force will be much higher than the present average.

The Eleventh Plan period saw several important initiatives including near universalisation of primary education, the passage of the Right to Education Act, the initiation of a massive programme for expansion in secondary education, combined with several steps in higher education.[10] The Eleventh Plan placed considerable emphasis on quantitative expansion to improve access and this will have to continue in the Twelfth Plan. In addition, greater emphasis will have to be placed on quality. Initiatives in these areas have to be taken by the Centre and states and also by the private sector.

Skill development has been neglected in the past and needs much faster expansion. Over 90 per cent of our labour force at present has received no formal training prior to employment and skills are typically acquired only on the job. This is simply not consistent with 9 per cent growth in GDP per year in an increasingly modernising economy. The Eleventh Plan had set a target of having 500 million individuals in the labour force with some formal training by 2020. Several initiatives have been launched in pursuit of this objective, including the establishment of a National Skill Development Council under the chairmanship of the prime minister, with parallel state-level councils chaired by the chief ministers. Government financial support is now available for private skill imparting units offering courses for a wide range of skills. A Skill Development Corporation has been established with government funding to support private sector-led skill development initiative. Efforts are being made to involve private sector partners in the management of Industrial Training Institutes (ITIs) in an effort to make the curriculum more relevant. Involving the private sector in skill development is extremely important as it increases the likelihood that the skills imparted are marketable.

---

10. This includes creation of 30 new central universities, 8 IITs, 20 IIITs, 7 IIMs and 3 IISERs.

Table 8.9

Mean Years of Schooling
(Population Aged 15 and over)

	Mean Years of Schooling
India	
1990	3.45
2000	4.20
2010	5.12
China	
1990	5.62
2000	7.11
2010	8.17
Indonesia	
1990	4.25
2000	5.23
2010	6.24
Thailand	
1990	5.41
2000	6.11
2010	7.50

Source: Barro and Lee (2010). "A New Data Set of Education and Attainment in the World, 1950-2010", *NBER Working Paper* No. 15902.

Factor Productivity Growth

It is well recognised that a high rate of growth of GDP requires not only rapid growth of primary inputs such as capital and labour, but also high rates of total factor productivity growth (TFPG). TFPG itself is a combination of pure technical progress and the ability to utilise factors more efficiently, the latter often being made possible by economic and institutional reforms which enhance productivity. Much of the rationale of the reform agenda pursued since 1991 was that it will enable realisation of higher TFPG.

Studies of TFPG focussing on the manufacturing sector alone have yielded mixed results. Early studies focussing on the 1990s found a slowdown in TFPG compared to the previous decade, e.g., Das (2004), Balakrishnan *et al.* (2000), or near constancy in TFPG, as reported by Goldar (2004). In a more recent paper, Hashim and Virmani (2011) have asserted a J curve phenomenon, in which TFPG first declines but then rises, with a considerable further potential for high TFPG growth, conditional on additional reforms being implemented. Studies of TFPG at the aggregative level of the economy as a whole have been generally more positive. Virmani (2006) estimates that whereas TFPG contributed only 0.1 percentage points to the annual growth rate in the period 1965-66 to 1979-1980, this increased to 2.9 per cent in the period 1980-81 to 1991-92 and finally to 3.6 per cent in the period 1992-93 to 2003-04. Bhalla (2011) has estimated TFP growth for the period 1985-2003 to be at 3 per cent, increasing to 3.7 per cent for the period 2003-2010.

These results are subject to all the usual caveats associated with estimations of TFP growth—and there are many—reflecting concerns about data and also model specification. However, the studies, especially at the aggregate economy level, do suggest that the economic reforms initiated in 1991 have increased the growth potential of the economy by increasing the level of TFPG. The critical issue, looking ahead, is whether we can count on continuing high rate of TFPG. In this context it is worth noting that high TFPG rates in the early stages of economic reform reflect not only pure productivity growth but also the fact that the economy is moving from a position well inside the production possibility frontier to a position closer to the frontier. The contribution of the latter is obviously large initially but moderation in TFPG should be expected over time as the economy moves closer to the frontier. However, India is still at an early stage of the transition, with considerable scope for exploiting potential total factor productivity gains, provided economic reforms are systematically pursued and deepened. The scope for such deepening of reforms is discussed in Section III. It does suggest that there is a large agenda of reforms which if systematically implemented could produce significant gains.

Some Critical Policy Challenges

Favourable macro factors of the type discussed in Section II are important, but they can at best create an enabling environment that needs to be supported by specific policy initiatives in a number of areas. A comprehensive analysis of these issues is beyond the scope of this paper although it will be part of the process for formulating the Twelfth Plan. What is attempted in this section is the identification of some of the critical sectoral and policy issues that will need to be addressed if growth is to be pushed to 9 per cent or a little more in the Twelfth Plan, and also made more inclusive and sustainable. Some of the items in the agenda involve completion of what is in the pipeline, but there are several areas where new initiatives are needed.

Financing the Plan with Macroeconomic Balance

As pointed out earlier, the combined fiscal deficit of the Centre and the states had expanded because of the stimulus, and has to be brought back to sustainable levels. This process has begun, and the Centre's fiscal deficit is projected to fall from 5.1 per cent of GDP in 2010-11 to 4.6 per cent in 2011-12 followed by further reduction of 0.5 percentage point, per year in the next three years, to reach 3 per cent by 2014-15. Adding a fiscal deficit of around 2.5 per cent for the states, the combined deficit of the Centre and the states is therefore projected at about 5.5 per cent by 2014-15.

The proposed reduction in the combined deficit from 7.7 per cent in 2010-11 to 5.5 per cent in 2014-15 involves an improvement of 2.2 percentage points of GDP over four years. This is not too onerous. In fact, the proposed deficit for 2014-15 would still be higher than the 4.8 per cent achieved in 2007-08, eight years earlier. However, the real challenge is that the reduction in the fiscal deficit has to be achieved while also achieving an increase of at least around 1.5 percentage points of GDP in Plan expenditure of the Centre and states combined. This order of increase is the minimum necessary if we are to provide adequately for the essential requirements of education, health and public financing of critical infrastructure, including especially in rural and other backward areas.

Plan expenditure on education and health taken together may have to be increased by about 2 percentage points of GDP and expenditure on critical infrastructure, by at least 0.5 per cent of GDP taking the total increase on these accounts to 2.5 percentage points. If total Plan expenditure is increased by only 1.5 percentage points, it implies a considerable moderation in the demands of other Plan schemes.

Reducing the fiscal deficit by 2.2 percentage points, while also increasing Plan expenditure as a ratio of GDP to around 1.5 percentage points, requires an improvement of around 3.7 percentage points of GDP which has to be achieved through some combination of increased revenues and reduced non-Plan expenditure, as a percentage of GDP. A reasonable expectation would be to aim for an increase in revenues as a percentage of GDP by a little over 2 percentage points and a reduction in non-Plan expenditure as a percentage of GDP by about 1.5 percentage points.

As far as revenues are concerned, the aim should be to achieve higher tax ratios without resorting to distortionary taxation. We can count on some increase in the tax ratio on account of buoyancy, but a substantial part of the targetted improvement must come from tax reforms. The most important initiative in this context is the Goods and Services Tax (GST), for which a Constitution Amendment Bill has been introduced. The GST, once implemented, will convert the present regime in which the Central and state governments levy multiple indirect taxes separately on different tax bases, into a more rational system with separate Central and state taxes, but applied on a common base, preferably with a single common rate (subject to a few exceptions). Since taxes on the input stage in each of the Central and state streams will be netted out at the next stage, the GST would be a true value added tax, contributing hugely to both economic efficiency and revenue collection. Because implementation of the GST involves a constitutional amendment, a successful outcome may take time, but once achieved, it will be a major achievement. Progress of this legislation in Parliament will be closely watched by analysts and potential investors and credible signs of progress will be widely welcomed.

Some reduction in non-Plan expenditure as a ratio of GDP will happen automatically if there is high growth, because government employment is not expected to increase significantly, and no new pay commission impact is expected in the Twelfth Plan period. However, progress in this area will also depend on whether subsidies, which have grown in scale in both the Central government and the states, can be curtailed. The major subsidies in the Centre are on food, fertilisers and on petroleum products, which together account for around 2 per cent of GDP. State budgets also have subsidy elements, but the major 'subsidy' is the very large losses of the state power utilities, which has now touched almost 1 per cent of GDP.

Food subsidies, which amount to about 0.7 per cent of GDP, will be difficult to contain in view of the commitments on National Food Security. The focus of attention for subsidy control by the Centre should therefore be on the subsidy on fuel and fertilisers. In the case of the states, the principal focus must be on the large losses in the power sector. The latter reflects a combination of very substantial underpricing of electricity to farmers (with free electricity in some cases) combined with inefficiency and competition in billing and collection.

Reducing subsidies will not be easy and a conscious effort is needed to build public and political support for a significant reduction in inefficient and non-targetted subsidies as a percentage of GDP, in order to finance the much needed additional Plan expenditure in health, education and agriculture related infrastructure.

Policies for Better Agricultural Performance

The 4 per cent target for growth in agriculture, which will be missed in the Eleventh Plan, must be achieved in the Twelfth Plan as it is critical for inclusiveness. Fortunately, this is technically feasible as there is ample evidence that productivity per hectare can be increased by 80 per cent to 100 per cent for many crops in large areas by applying modern agronomic practices based on existing technology. However, achieving these increases in productivity requires action on several fronts, most of which lie in the domain of state governments.

Water is a key input, and better systems of water management, including especially the ability to control timing and quantity of water application, are critical. We return to this issue in a later part of this section. This must be combined with availability of better quality seeds, and adoption by farmers of optimal levels of seed replacement. Much greater attention also needs to be paid to soil health, focussing particularly on micronutrients and carbon content. Since micronutrient deficiencies are area-specific, a system of soil health cards issued to farmers, with periodic soil testing, must be put in place. Carbon content can be increased by shifting from the traditional practice of burning crop residue to leaving it in the field. Shifting to more efficient use of water requires new practices such as land levelling, use of drip irrigation, zero till cultivation, raised seedbed planting, and in the case of rice, adoption of the System of Rice Intensification (SRI), etc.

State governments must act on several fronts to present a package of interventions tailored to the requirements of particular agro-climatic zones. Delivering only a few elements of the package will not produce optimal results. The farmer has to be persuaded of the importance of the complete package, and both physical and knowledge inputs needed to implement the package, have to be made available. The extension system, has more or less collapsed in most states, yet a strong system of extension is crucial for knowledge delivery. At present, the principal source of information for the farmer is the retailer of inputs, who is not free of conflicts of interest.

Since most of the growth in agriculture in future will come not from food grains, but from sectors such as horticulture, dairying and fisheries, where the produce is perishable, much greater attention needs to be paid to the logistics of transporting produce from the farm to the consumer, with minimum spoilage. This requires active involvement of the private sector. To facilitate such involvement, state governments must amend the Agricultural Produce Marketing Committee (APMC) Acts which at present prevent private sector buyers from dealing directly with producers. Some states have amended their APMC Acts, but the rules are either not notified, or are not designed to encourage entry of private players. For example, giving licences to operate outside the *mandi* only for a year at a time, as is the case in some states, discourages any serious long-term private sector investment. There is an overwhelming case for exempting horticultural produce entirely from the APMC Act. Much of the reluctance to make these changes reflect the operation of vested interests who control the *mandis*. Establishing better road connectivity in rural areas helps market access and the Pradhan Mantri Gram Sadak Yojana is an important intervention in this regard.

Another area for policy intervention by state governments is the reform of laws relating to leasing of land. As holdings are subdivided and become uneconomic, very small and marginal farmers may be better off leasing out their land to more viable farmers, while seeking paid employment themselves. They would be more willing to do this if they felt that they could lease out their land and get it back when they want. Yet, leasing is not legal in some states. Where it is allowed, the law is biased towards the tenant, whereas the need of the hour is to protect the interest of the small farmers leasing out land.

Unfortunately, despite the importance of agriculture for rural prosperity very few state governments have taken up the challenge of bringing about the multifaceted transformation that is needed. There is too much focus on delivering a variety of subsidies in power, seeds and credit, and not enough on bringing about a change in farming practices and adoption of new technology that would actually raise land productivity and enable farmers to become less dependent on subsidies in the long run.

Employment Generation

A key challenge in the Twelfth Plan is how to ensure creation of a sufficient number of productive jobs in the non-agricultural sector to absorb the expected increase in the labour force and also absorb surplus labour that must be shifted out of agriculture. The need to shift labour out of agriculture follows from the fact that productivity in agriculture is relatively low and if agriculture is not expected to grow at more than 4 per cent, the only way labour productivity in agriculture can rise at a rate higher than 4 per cent is for employment in agriculture to shrink. This is actually necessary to reduce the present underemployment in agriculture and a steady improvement in real wages in this sector. Needless to say, the proposed shift out of agriculture should occur not as distress migration, but as a natural movement to higher paid employment in non-agricultural activity, some of which could be in rural areas itself. Agricultural development will itself give rise to new demands for non-agricultural services and generate employment in agriculture related sectors such as modernised marketing and agro-processing activity.

A large part of the job opportunities we need must come from a more rapid expansion in manufacturing. The industrial sector was targetted to grow at an average rate 10 per cent to 11 per cent per year in the Eleventh Plan, but the actual achievement is unlikely to exceed 8 per cent. Most economic simulations suggest that if the economy is to grow at 9 per cent in the Twelfth Plan, and agriculture, which now accounts for only 15 per cent of GDP, is constrained to grow at 4 per cent, then services should grow at around 10 per cent and industry at 11 per cent. Industry must not only grow faster than it has thus far, it must also be more able to absorb labour with relatively simple skills of the type which migrants from rural areas can acquire.

Micro, small and medium enterprises, are generally more labour absorbing, and are also potential seedbeds for innovation and entrepreneurship. The policy environment must encourage the growth of these industries and this does not mean sops and subsidies. Rather, the main effort should be to provide these smaller industrial units with first class infrastructure which includes both reliable power supply at reasonable cost, good transport connectivity, a pool of skilled labour to draw upon and a financial sector capable of making resources available to potentially successful entrepreneurs.

Expansion of industrial activity must also be regionally balanced since demographic projections suggest that the growth of labour supply in future will be much greater in the northern states that are industrially backward at present. Migration will take care of some of the regional mismatch but there is a strong case for doing more to ensure that employment opportunities expand in states that are expected to generate larger growth of labour. This is best achieved by state governments paying much greater attention to the infrastructure needs and skilled labour requirements of industry that could locate in those states. Adequate availability of power and good connectivity are crucial. State governments must also be more active in reducing the transactions cost of doing business and this means making regulatory bodies, tax authorities, and utilities more business-friendly.

Finally, some consideration has to be given to the long-standing issue of the need to rationalise our labour laws to give employers more flexibility to shed labour when faced with a downturn. This is not to advocate policies of hire and fire, but only to say that more flexibility needs to be built into the labour laws than exist at present. Flexibility to lay off labour when faced with a downturn could be accompanied by steps to enhance other aspects of labour protection, including especially safety and larger compensation for lay offs. This is obviously a politically sensitive issue and the position taken by the government thus far is that we need to build a consensus with representatives of labour. This effort must be pushed to some positive conclusion.

Infrastructure Development

The Eleventh Plan recognised the importance of investing more in infrastructure sectors such as power, roads, ports, airports and railways, and sought to raise investment in these sectors from about 5.6 per cent of GDP in the base year of the Eleventh Plan 2006-07 to around 9 per cent by the last year, i.e., 2011-12. The actual achievement is likely to be around 8.5 per cent, with some sectors, e.g., telecommunications, achieving higher levels of investment than projected, while others achieved significantly less. The task begun in the Eleventh Plan has to continue in the Twelfth Plan, which should aim at increasing the rate of investment in infrastructure to around 10.5 per cent by 2017-18. This implies that investment in infrastructure, which was targetted at $500 billion in the Eleventh Plan period, would have to increase to about $1 trillion over the Twelfth Plan period 2012-13 to 2017-18. This poses two major challenges. One is how to finance the investment needed, and the second is how to overcome implementation hurdles, which currently delay project completion.

As far as financing is concerned, it is clear that public sector resources will be scarce and, as noted above, the first priority for these resources must be education and health, which are crucial for inclusiveness and are currently underfunded. Critical infrastructure in rural areas and backward areas is another priority. Both the Central and state governments must therefore follow an infrastructure strategy which consists of a combination of public investment and public-private partnership (PPP). Public investment would have to be directed to areas where the private sector is unlikely to come, with the rest of infrastructure being developed as far as possible through PPP. Valuable experience has been gained in this area and many of the teething problems related to procedures for structuring PPP projects have been overcome. We need to build on this experience and launch a renewed effort in which the role of PPP in infrastructure investment may have to increase from around 30 per cent in the Eleventh Plan to as much as 50 per cent in the Twelfth Plan.

The second major challenge in infrastructure development relates to implementation. Infrastructure projects are often delayed due to difficulties in land acquisition, and where land has been acquired, due to other difficulties such as dealing with encroachments and lack of coordination with other utilities. Projects are also held back by difficulties in obtaining forest and environmental clearances. Protecting forests and the environment is obviously an extremely important objective, but the current processes are often not sufficiently transparent and predictable. However, project developers are not without blame. They have got used to laxity in application of environmental regulations and there is a tendency to ignore environmental regulations or act in anticipation of clearances in the belief that such actions can be regularised later. We need to move to a system with much greater transparency, predictability and also tighter enforcement in future. In the process we may need to find ways of dealing with the problems of ongoing projects in a reasonable manner while establishing better systems for the future. Both the Central government and the state governments have to give serious attention to resolving these problems in the years ahead.

Reforms in the Financial Sector

Rapid growth needs to be supported by an efficient financial system capable of mobilising the savings in the system and using them to support economically efficient units. By financial system in this context we mean the whole range of institutions such as banks, non-bank finance companies, microfinance institutions, efficient and well-regulated capital markets, mutual funds, insurance companies, pension funds and venture capital funds, each of which has an important role to play.

In one sense, India's financial sector can be said to be in a strong position having benefitted from a process of carefully calibrated liberalisation, combined with steps to strengthen the regulatory framework. The system certainly proved resilient during the global financial crisis, and this was a very strong positive factor in maintaining growth. However, while the financial system scores high on stability, there is room for improving the efficiency of financial intermediation and increasing innovation, both of which are necessary. This calls for a continuation of the process of calibrated financial reform. Stopping the process of liberalisation because it was excessive liberalisation with weak regulation which produced the financial crisis in industrialised countries would be a serious misreading of the situation.

Several important initiatives related to financial sector reform are already in the pipeline. These include: (a) announcement of the roadmap for new private sector banks and foreign investment in banks, (b) deregulation of the savings rate offered by banks which remains regulated, though it was recently raised from 3.5 per cent to 4 per cent, (c) legislation increasing the limit on FDI in insurance from 26 per cent to 49 per cent, (d) passage of the Pension Fund Regulatory and Development Bill, (e) passage of the legislation allowing shareholders to vote their equity share in banks instead of being limited to 10 per cent as at present and (f) passage of the Company Laws Amendment which will modernise bankruptcy proceedings. Completion of these steps, some of which depend on parliamentary approval, will represent very substantial forward movement in an important area.

The creation of a vibrant and liquid corporate bond market should have particularly high priority, especially in view of the need to finance large private investments in infrastructure. Several of the regulatory changes recommended by various expert committees to help develop bond markets have been implemented, but the response thus far remains limited. One reason is the very high fiscal deficit, which effectively crowds out corporate borrowing and the fiscal consolidation programme discussed above will clearly help. Reform of the government securities market in terms of building institutions, introduction of technology, etc., of the kind that was seen in the equity markets, is also necessary for the establishment of a G-sec yield curve for all maturities against which corporate bond yields can be priced. The creation of the Public Debt Management Office outside the RBI, which has been announced and is in the process of being established, will be another important step as it would free the RBI from having to perform the role of debt manager. Improved access to liquidity for primary dealers in the bond market is another important step.

Investment policies of LIC, EPFO, etc., are very conservative at present, leading these institutions to prefer lower yielding government debt to higher yielding corporate debt, except of the very highest investment grade. A possible reason could be the absence of efficient mechanisms for debt recovery in the event of default. Unlike banks, which benefit from SARFAESI, bond holders can only have recourse to liquidation and bankruptcy procedures which are hopelessly time consuming. The passage of the Company Law Amendment Bill mentioned above, which contains provisions to modernise bankruptcy proceedings, is an important step in this context.

Proposals for establishing infrastructure debt funds based on investors abroad investing in long-term debt issued by infrastructure project companies are currently being examined by the finance ministry. The establishment of such funds would help infrastructure companies to refinance shorter-term bank debt with longer-term debt while freeing banks to finance new projects. A positive decision on this proposal would be an important signal to investors.

The size of Indian banks is another important issue. Even the largest Indian bank, the State Bank of India, is actually quite small by global or even Asian standards. Since banks will continue to be the source of medium-term capital in India for some time, until the capital market becomes a credible source for corporate long-term debt, the capital of the banks has to be increased greatly to allow larger exposures to individual projects and also to sectors. Public sector banks must therefore have a larger capital base. This could be done by allowing them to issue additional capital in the market and reducing government equity below 51 per cent to some lower level which would in no way reduce effective government control. If this is not politically feasible at present, then government must be willing to increase its capital contribution *pari passu* with fresh issue of capital, so that the government share of equity in these institutions remains at 51 per cent.

A more flexible policy for allowing existing private sector banks to grow more rapidly is also urgently needed. While branch expansion is now more freely allowed, it remains linked to opening rural branches. With the growing scope for bringing banking to the rural areas through the system of banking correspondents, insistence on opening rural branches may not be as necessary as it once was.

Managing the Energy Challenge

The global supply of fossil fuels is expected to become much tighter in the years ahead, and prices of these fuels are therefore likely to remain high, with a possible upward trend. Achieving high growth in this situation requires reducing the energy intensity of GDP while simultaneously taking steps to limit dependence on imports by increasing the domestic supply of energy from both conventional and non-conventional resources.

Reducing Energy Intensity

Reducing the energy intensity of GDP calls for rationalising energy prices and adopting non-price measures to improve energy efficiency. Action is necessary on both fronts and the agenda is large.

As far as rationalisation of energy prices is concerned, our energy prices at present are significantly below world prices and unless this is corrected, it is difficult to believe that energy efficiency can be sufficiently incentivised. The Integrated Energy Policy, adopted by the government in 2009, endorsed the principle that prices of imported energy inputs must be aligned with world prices, but this policy has yet to be fully implemented. Prices of motor spirit have been successfully decontrolled. However, diesel, which is four times larger than motor spirit, has only been decontrolled in principle. The decision is yet to be implemented. LPG and kerosene prices remain under administrative control and are currently set well below global levels. It is necessary to implement diesel decontrol as quickly as possible and to bring about a phased alignment of kerosene and LPG prices with world prices, while at the same time protecting the poor.

There is an understandable reluctance to raise kerosene and LPG prices because of the impact on vulnerable groups, but it must be recognised that the subsidy implicit in the present low prices of kerosene and LPG is completely untargetted. In the case of kerosene, it also leads to large-scale black marketing, adulteration and criminalisation. The best way of helping the poor to cope with higher prices of kerosene and LPG would be to shift to a targetted direct subsidy delivered to deserving groups linked to the implementation of a unique identification number. This option is being explored.

Coal is technically not under price control, but the nationalised coal companies have set domestic coal prices well below world prices, even after adjusting for the lower quality of Indian coal. The discrepancy between domestic coal prices and much higher import prices leads to an unwillingness on the part of power producers to import coal and keep lobbying for domestic coal linkages. This problem would not arise if domestic coal prices are equated with import prices. If that is not immediately feasible, the second best option is for Coal India to import coal to meet demands from the power sector, while also introducing a system of pooled pricing whereby the higher cost of the coal it imports is absorbed in a higher price charged by Coal India for coal supplied to all power plants based on the overall mix of domestic and imported coal. Over time, domestic coal prices must be adjusted in time with global coal prices reducing the need for price pooling.

Electricity prices are set by supposedly independent state regulators, but there is strong political pressure on regulators in many states to hold back price increases, even when these are justified by economic costs. This only leads to financial unviability of distribution system, which is under strain in any case. The system must be allowed to function properly so that electricity prices are not artificially depressed, especially as coal prices are expected to rise.

Rationalising energy pricing along the lines spelt out above will encourage energy efficiency, but prices alone will not suffice to promote efficiency. Action on prices needs to be supported by a proactive use of non-price mechanisms. Regulation can be used to push major energy using industries to achieve internationally benchmarked levels of energy efficiency. We should also resort to standard setting and labelling for appliances, equipments, transport vehicles and buildings to encourage energy efficiency. Standards for buildings are particularly important because India has a leapfrogging advantage in this area since most of the commercial buildings likely to be in place by 2030 are yet to be built!

Finally, energy efficiency for the economy as a whole would be greatly helped by intra-sectoral shifts in the transport sector that would economise on energy. The most notable shift in this context is shifting freight from road to rail, and shifting from private to public transport in urban areas. These shifts can be facilitated by appropriate tax and tariff policies.

In the case of the Railways, it requires a shift away from the current practice of overcharging freight to subsidise passenger traffic. India's passenger fare to freight tariff ratio is 20 per cent of what it is in China suggesting that freight tariffs should be lowered and passenger fares raised. These price changes need to be supported by action to build necessary freight carrying capacity in the Railways. The capacity has to be created urgently, in anticipation of increased financial strength from tariff reforms. A more proactive stance is also needed to promote PPP in railways, especially in container traffic movement.

Increasing Domestic Energy Supply

Steps to reduce energy demand have to be accompanied by strong action on the supply side to expand domestic production of petroleum, natural gas and also coal to avoid excessive import dependence. There are a number of policy gaps that need to be addressed.

Both petroleum and natural gas are open for investment by the private sector, including foreign investment, and private sector investors have a good record in discovery of new sources. However, the public sector oil companies currently bear a large part of the burden of keeping domestic petroleum prices low, because they are not given the full benefit of high oil prices. This reduces the potential surpluses available for investment by these companies. Rationalisation of energy price as discussed above will help the domestic effort to enhance energy supply.

Coal production is constrained by the fact that the industry is nationalised, although private investment is allowed in captive coal mines (i.e., coal mines linked to power plants or steel and cement plants). This window for private investment provides some flexibility and there is significant investor interest in this area. However, looking ahead, the policy for the coal industry should be liberalised—allowing private investment in non-captive mining subject to appropriate regulation for safety and environment standards. There are obvious political sensitivities here, but it has to be kept in mind that what is being proposed is not privatisation of Coal India but only allowing private sector mining. On present projections of likely domestic production, we will need to import about 250 million tonnes of coal by 2016-17. Considering that the total world trade in coal at present is around one trillion tonnes, we should do everything possible to remove domestic impediments to production. There cannot be any rationale for allowing private investment in petroleum and natural gas, as we do, but not in coal.

We must also take steps to exploit the full potential of other energy sources notably nuclear, solar and wind power. The share of these sectors is small and will remain modest in the medium term but in the longer term they could become substantial. Expansion of nuclear power is an important element of India's long-term strategy and this has been facilitated by the recent agreement with the Nuclear Suppliers Group which gives India access to imported uranium, and also opens windows for other cooperation in this area. Plans for nuclear power all over the world are being reviewed in light of the recent Japanese experience at Fukushima, and lessons learnt will have to be incorporated in our own strategy. We should avoid knee-jerk reactions that might derail the nuclear power programme though we must clearly recognise the need to undertake a thorough review of our safety standards and benchmark them against evolving best practice.

India is also engaged in developing solar-based generation using both photovoltaic and thermal solar technology and a programme has been initiated to install 20,000 MW of solar power by 2020. This programme needs to be nurtured and supported in the hope of building a substantial domestic industry in this area. India has the potential to be a significant supplier of equipment to other countries.

Both nuclear and solar power are more expensive than conventional thermal generation and this means that while increased reliance on these sources will contribute to energy security, and also mitigation of climate change, it does imply higher energy costs. Costs can be expected to come down as technology develops further, but in the next decade at least all indications are that unit cost of energy will rise.

The energy challenge in the Twelfth Plan is how to deal with a situation in which global energy prices will be high and the cost of alternative energy sources will also be high. Our ability to grow rapidly in this environment depends critically on our ability to transmit the high energy prices to energy users in the economy, rather than keep the prices artificially low. Only then will users be incentivised to reduce energy intensity and energy producers will have the resources they need to expand investment in these sectors. Making this transition is not easy. It will be argued that energy prices should not be raised in a situation where inflationary pressure is high, but the need to control inflation is not a valid reason for holding back relative price changes which contribute to efficiency. In fact, raising energy prices will reduce the pressure of demand for other products and thus help moderate price pressures elsewhere. The poor certainly need help to handle the impact of higher energy prices, but it is better to do this through an income transfer rather than keeping energy prices artificially low.

Managing Water Resources

Managing water scarcity in the Twelfth Plan period is in some ways even more daunting than the challenge posed by energy. India's available supply of fresh water is the same as it was 5,000 years ago, and the population has grown and so has the GDP, with a concomitant increase in demand for water. Until recently, official estimates showed the available supply of water to be well above total demand, *albeit* with areas of regional scarcity. More recent studies indicate that the demand for water at present is roughly equal to supply for the country as a whole and this near balance at a national level hides wide regional variations with acute shortages in many parts. Since growth in GDP implies expanded water use, the water situation can be expected to worsen rapidly. Already, there is evidence of excessive drawal of groundwater in many parts of the country leading to lowering of the water table and increasing salinity, which makes the water less usable for agriculture and harmful for health.

If things are left to business as usual, the situation will worsen steadily. The Twelfth Plan must signal the need for a radically new approach. Since water is largely a state subject, success depends critically on the state governments. They need to act on both the supply and the demand side.

Supply Side

On the supply side, action is necessary on several fronts including building storage dams, investing in watershed management to improve surface water retention and groundwater recharge, and forcing industry to treat waste water for reuse. Each of these involves costs and we need to prioritise between alternative investments keeping relative costs in mind. Traditionally, most of our resources have been absorbed by large irrigation projects. These are indeed important and need to be pursued to optimise storage, though their implementation needs to be greatly improved. In terms of prioritisation we need to do much more on watershed management projects, which involve one-tenth of the cost per hectare as compared to large irrigation projects, have fewer environmental problems, and generally provide a much higher return on investment. The Central government should perhaps restructure its financial assistance to incentivise more action in watershed development.

Demand Side

Efforts at expanding supply are important but they will not suffice and they will have to be accompanied by efforts on the demand side to improve efficiency of water use. About 80 per cent of India's water use is for agriculture and it is technically feasible with better agricultural practices, to reduce water use in agriculture by 40 per cent to 50 per cent. For example, the System of Rice Intensification (SRI) enables rice to be grown with much less water than in traditional flood irrigation. However, while it requires less water, SRI requires water to be given at the right time which calls for complementary investments in land levelling drip irrigation, etc. Additional costs have to be allowed to pass through into the system in the form of higher food prices. Over the longer term, agricultural research will have to factor in the need to achieve greater water efficiency by evolving crop varieties capable of dealing with water stress. This is particularly important given the likely impact of climate change.

One reason why managing the water crisis is more difficult than the energy crisis is that whereas most people recognise that energy has to be paid for, there is much less acceptance, or even understanding, of the need to price water. Policies are often enunciated on the principle that water is scarce and we must 'conserve every drop', but if water is underpriced, there is no incentive to achieve efficiency. Pricing of canal water in large irrigation projects is supposed to be based on the principle of covering operation and maintenance (O&M) costs, but in most places it is priced at levels which cover only about 15 per cent of O&M costs. This eliminates any incentive to adopt less water-intensive cropping patterns in the command area, especially among upper end users. It also leads to poor maintenance of the canal system, which in effect means that although water is severely underpriced, farmers have no assurance that they will get the water they need at a predictable time. Farmers would be much better off paying higher prices for water, if this is accompanied by greater predictability of supply of a certain quantity at a particular time.

The first step in evolving a rational water policy is to make a scientific assessment of the available water resources in each basin in the country and then define basin-specific strategies for water management. This mapping exercise should be undertaken on a priority basis, with the involvement of the science departments, and should be completed in the Twelfth Plan.

Rational water pricing is important and must be pursued but pricing by itself may not solve the problem since prices would have to be set at unacceptably high levels to get anywhere close to optimal water use. State governments would therefore be well advised to combine price rationalisation with establishment of statutory water regulators to determine water allocation for different uses such as household needs, agriculture and industrial use. The regulator must also have a transparent method of varying entitlements for different uses to reflect variation in water availability. Water regulators must be combined with the establishment of effective water user associations which genuinely participate in the management of this key common pool resource. A start has been made in some states, e.g., Maharashtra and Andhra Pradesh using somewhat different approaches, but we have a long way to go and we must learn from different experiments. One way of incentivising the process is to link Central assistance for capital-intensive irrigation projects to the implementation of critical regulatory reforms in this area and to undertake parallel work on completing command area development.

A controversial issue that needs to be faced is whether a system of rational management of the country's water resources can be achieved without bringing in legislation that would empower the Central government to act in this area. The Constitution provides that the Central government can determine rational use of water in interstate rivers, provided Parliament passes a law for this purpose. This has never been attempted, and thus far, we have worked on the basis of consensus among states, subject to reference of differences to judicial tribunals. It is relevant to ask whether we can continue to operate in this fashion given the difficulties being faced in many interstate water disputes.

Regulating Groundwater

There is also a case for revisiting the various laws in place to regulate the use of groundwater. The present laws only provide for banning new tubewells in areas where the water table has fallen too far. This only confers a monopoly on existing tubewell owners who can pump as much water as they wish and sell it to other farmers. Free power or very cheap power for agriculture provides a wholly unjustified incentive for such activity. At the very least, state governments should consider imposing a cess on electricity for agricultural use in all areas where the water level has sunk too low, and earmark the proceeds for groundwater recharge.

Managing the Urban Transition

Managing the urban transition will pose special challenges in the years ahead. India has been slow to urbanise, but this is expected to change with faster growth. The urban percentage of the population is currently around 30 per cent, and is expected to reach 40 per cent by 2030, implying an increase in numbers from 350 million today, to around 600 million. This will require a massive expansion in urban infrastructure, especially since only about half of those currently in urban areas are adequately served even by the current very low standards.

The resources needed to achieve this expansion in urban infrastructure are much larger than what the cities or local urban bodies can mobilise on their own.[11] Most of the revenue generated from economic activity in the country occurs in urban areas, but the revenue generated from this activity accrues to the Central or state governments, and there is much less devolution to city governments than there should be. Cities and urban local bodies in India also have limited capacity to raise their own resources. It is possible to generate revenue through user charges for some services such as water, sewerage and urban transport, but a long tradition of fixing low user charges has limited the flow of revenues from these sources. High land values in urban areas could be used to leverage resources to finance urban infrastructure, particularly through PPP projects, but this opportunity has not been adequately exploited although the recent decision of the Andhra Pradesh government to adopt the PPP route for a metro in Hyderabad may provide a model for the future.

Even in the industrialised world, cities have rarely financed all the infrastructure they need themselves and national governments have contributed in various ways. The Jawaharlal Nehru National Urban Renewal Mission (JNNURM) introduced in the Eleventh Plan is a

11. For an assessment of the investment requirements in the urban sector over a 22-year period see the *Report of the High Powered Expert Group Estimating the Investment Requirements of Urban Infrastructure*, Ministry of Urban Development, 2011.

mechanism for channelling resources from the Centre to the states linked to specific reforms in urban governance and finances. The results thus far are mixed, partly because of inadequate implementation capacity at the city level and also because of reluctance to pursue reforms. The JNNURM initiative will have to be expanded in the Twelfth Plan but it is also true that the cities and the states have to take on a much larger share of the burden than they do today the former through user charges and the latter through stronger devolution of resources.

Steps to close the financing gap for urban infrastructure have to be accompanied by improved governance structures at the city level. The system of city government at present is such that city governments are not effectively empowered to plan for infrastructure development. Critical decisions on the infrastructure needs of the metropolitan cities are typically made by the state governments, which necessarily respond to the electorate in the state as a whole. This has to change so that city government is in the hands of elected representatives responsible to their local electorate.

Environment Protection and Sustainability

A difficult issue which has to be addressed in the Twelfth Plan is how to achieve the transition to higher growth without inflicting unacceptable damage to the environment. The qualification 'unacceptable' is important since some stakeholders take an extreme position in which no damage must be done. That would rule out an enormous range of developmental activity, since all such activity alters the environment in some way. There is merit in taking an uncompromising approach in certain cases, e.g., tiger reserves and very select biospheres, but the general approach must be one of balancing conflicting objectives. This means trying to ensure that first the damage is minimised and second that well designed remedial steps are taken to ensure the people affected are suitably compensated and the environmental impact is suitably repaired and or compensated. In this context, stakeholder views must be ascertained but environmental prescriptions must be drawn by technical and scientific considerations and not perceptions or prejudices. Much of the present concern about the environment arises because our environmental protection mechanisms have failed to deliver on one or more these counts.

The threat to the environment posed by high growth arises from many different sources. These include: (a) the need to meet the energy requirements of growth and the consequent demand for coal and hydropower, both of which could run into forest clearance problems even if we ignore for the present the longer-term effect of carbon emissions, (b) the impact of industrialisation upon industrial effluents which leads to water pollution and of gaseous and particulate emissions which lead to air pollution, (c) the effect of expanding urbanisation and the consequent need to treat 100 per cent of the sewage generated instead of only 30 per cent, as at present, in order to avoid damage to our rivers and water bodies and (d) the challenge of managing the large quantities of solid waste generated in cities in a manner that is environmentally benign. In addition to these endogeneous sources of environmental stress, we also have to deal with external threats to the environment arising from climate change. This will require proactive steps to increase afforestation and to harness and manage our water resources better.

Some of what needs to be done is part of the agenda for managing the energy and water related challenges discussed earlier in this paper. The measures related to price rationalisation in energy and water, and the various non-price initiatives in these areas, designed to increase energy efficiency and water use efficiency are critical for economic efficiency and will also help to moderate the environmental stress. These measures need to be supplemented by transparent and scientifically-based environmental regulations which are strictly enforced. The Approach to the Twelfth Plan, which will be discussed in the National Development Council later in the year, provides an opportunity to start building a degree of understanding and consensus on these difficult issues.

It must be emphasised that environmental protection is not cost less. The problem arises because economic agents do not take into account the external costs of their actions, some of which fall on future generations. Such actions must be discouraged as far as possible and the residual damage must be repaired or compensated. This is best done by enforcing the 'polluter pays principle'. However, though often asserted in theory, this principle is largely ignored in practice. Tax policies often fail to reflect this principle—the total tax burden on commercial vehicles for example is higher than on private vehicles. The regulatory mechanisms for enforcing pollution controls in the states are also extremely weak. We need a comprehensive review of tax policies (including state taxes) and also our pollution control mechanisms to ensure that the total impact is environmentally benign.

A new initiative introduced in the Budget for 2010-11 is the imposition of a cess of 5 per cent on coal (both domestic and imported), the proceeds of which are earmarked to a separate fund to promote green energy. Mechanisms of this sort can be used to meet the cost of environment protection and are justified by the principle that the polluter must pay. Another environmentally supportive measure is the imposition of a cess on electricity for agricultural use to be imposed in areas where the groundwater has sunk too low, with the proceeds being earmarked for use in groundwater recharge in the same area. Because the benefits from the use of the proceeds are localised, it should be politically easier to justify the action.

Market Manipulation, Crony Capitalism and Corruption

Greater reliance upon market forces was a key element of the economic reforms and it has yielded tangible benefits in terms of higher growth and efficiency. However, it is also seen to have produced an increase in manipulative crony capitalism, and the corruption it brings in its wake. Corruption and corporate wrongdoing is obviously not a problem unique to India. In recent years there has been a great deal of attention internationally on corporate corruption and various types of illegality as exemplified by high profile cases such as Enron, Worldcom, Parmalat and Bernie Madhof. The financial crisis has also drawn attention to various instances of conflicts of interest and regulatory capture which call into question the notion that markets always promote efficiency.

Rajan (2010) has drawn special attention to two areas in India which are especially vulnerable to the charge of crony capitalism. These are land related development and those areas where other scarce resources such as minerals or spectrum are to be allocated by the government through licensing. Non-transparency in land related issues has become a major problem which needs urgent attention. The problem surfaces in two different types of situations. First, land values in the major cities are hugely inflated because of highly non-transparent controls on land and there are large rents to be enjoyed by those who can obtain the relevant permissions to develop land. Non-transparent mechanisms for grant of such permissions inevitably lead to suspicion of corruption and cronyism. These areas of discretionary policy need to be comprehensively reviewed and more transparent mechanisms put in place. Second, acquisition of agricultural land for industrial development and for creating infrastructure presents many problems. The present Land Acquisition Act is hopelessly outdated and provides for highly inadequate levels of compensation often well below true market prices. Modernisation of this piece of legislation is urgently needed. This is currently under consideration and should be expedited.

Non-transparency in methods of allocating scarce resources such as minerals and spectrum has also given rise to criticism from many quarters. Allegations of corruption and cronyism have surfaced in both these areas, and they call for a thorough review of existing procedures. As a general rule, competitive bidding among qualified bidders provides the most transparent way of allocating scarce resources such as mining rights in known mineral bearing areas or spectrum. The absence of competitive bidding in the allocation of 2G licences has evoked intense criticism. In sharp contrast, the 3G auction, conducted in 2010, evoked no criticism at all, and is in fact a model which deserves careful study. There are circumstances where competitive bidding may not be the best method but the alternatives require very complex methods of evaluating the choices that have to be made, that invariably bring in discretionary decision-making, which can always become a matter of controversy *ex-post*. Similar problems arise in allocating mining rights. A new Mines and Minerals Development Bill is currently under consideration in the government which must address those issue satisfactorily.

Government procurement procedures also need to be thoroughly modernised and made much more transparent as a means of reducing the probability of corruption and cronyism. OECD reports show that introducing such changes cuts costs by up to 25 per cent in industrialised countries. Many countries have a public procurement law whereas in India government procurement is governed by rules. The government has appointed a committee to make recommendations in this area. Early action to modernise government procurement and make the procedures transparent, including through the adoption of e-procurement, would be a major step forward. It needs to be kept in mind that under the Right to Information Act, all these issues are available to the public *ex-post*. There is no reason why the transparency should not be introduced *ex-ante*.

Implementation of Government Programmes

In addition to influencing the pace and pattern of growth, and including especially its employment generating capacity, the strategy of inclusiveness also relies heavily on government programmes designed to promote inclusiveness. Programmes for health and education are particularly important in this context, and have been discussed earlier. In addition, there are a number of programmes which together constitute a structure of social security and provision of direct benefit for the poor.

The most important of the other programmes relevant for inclusiveness are: (i) the supply of subsidised food grains through the PDS, (ii) the Mid-Day Meal Scheme for school children, (iii) the Integrated Child Development Services (ICDS) which provide nutrition and pre-school education for the 0 to 6 year age group and also for adolescent girls, (iv) the National Social Assistance Programme (NSAP) which provides an old age pension, plus a pension for widows and disabled persons, (v) the Mahatma Gandhi National Rural Employment Guarantee (MGNREG), which provides assured employment for 100 days at the notified minimum wage, (vi) the National Rural Drinking Water Programme (NRDWP) which aims at covering villages which do not have an assured supply of potable water, (vii) the Rajiv Gandhi Grameen Vidyutikaran Yojana (RGGVY) which extends electricity to all uncovered villages and provides free connection to all BPL families, and (viii) the Indira Awas Yojana (IAY) which provides assistance to the rural poor to build *pucca* homes. The total provision for these programmes in 2010-11 was Rs 1,55,000 crore or about 1.9 per cent of GDP.

There is broad agreement that these programmes are aimed at desirable objective but there is a great deal of scepticism about whether these programmes are being implemented in a manner that will ensure that these objective are actually realised. Complaints of leakages, inefficiency and corruption are widespread and while these are sometimes advanced by those who do not sympathise with the welfare objectives of the programmes, there is no doubt that there is also a genuine problem of implementation.

It is important to note that the Central government only finances these programmes, and actual implementation is carried out by state government agencies.

As one would expect, the effectiveness of implementation varies greatly from state to state, with many examples of good implementation but also examples of abject failures. These failures can be traced to one or all of three problems: poor design *ab initio*, underfunding and poor implementation. In practice all three are probably present to some degree.

Problems of poor design and inadequate funding can and should be addressed by the Central government. Central government guidelines are often inflexible and not tailored to the requirement in particular states. Furthermore, many areas involve cooperation between different arms of government, e.g., of agriculture, irrigation and rural development or the departments of health, education and women and child development. Unfortunately, government typically works in silos which makes effective interdepartmental cooperation very difficult. As far as adequacy of funding is concerned, scarcity of resources is a genuine problem. The solution lies in better prioritisation. It is much better to fully fund schemes that are working well and squeeze other rather than spread resources thinly. However, this is easier said than done and enforcing prioritisation in this way will be a major challenge in the Twelfth Plan.

Improving implementation on the ground has to be a major objective in the Twelfth Plan. Opinions vary on how this can be achieved. A committed political leadership at the state level, working with an effective administration, can obviously make a big difference. Devolution of decision-making and accountability to Panchayati Raj Institutions (PRIs) is also a potential instrument improving accountability. This is in line with the 74th Amendment which provided for devolution of functions, finances and functionaries from the state government to the PRIs. Some progress has been made in devolution, but most state governments have devolved functions with very little devolution of either funds or functionaries. The Central government can perhaps help in this area by structuring its schemes of assistance in a way which increases the role of the PRIs. For this to work, it will also be necessary to build capacity at the PRI level. Earmarking some portion of Central funds for capacity building may be necessary.

Greater participation by civil society organisations promoting greater involvement of the community, with a greater awareness of its rights, will also help. The Right to Information Act is an important new initiative which empowers civil society and individual stakeholders to hold government at all levels accountable.

Conclusions

As stated at the outset, the purpose of this paper was not to present firm conclusions, but rather to pose the issues we need to address in preparing the Twelfth Plan, in the hope of provoking a wider debate. However, some broad conclusions can be drawn.

The economy will enter the Twelfth Plan period in an environment of great promise but also one that presents major challenges. We have done well on the growth front, but not so well on inclusion, though it is possible that when the data for the entire period become available, we may find that the situation is better than currently envisaged.

Much of what needs to be done to accelerate GDP growth to 9 per cent or so will be done by the private sector, but the Central and state governments have a crucial role to play in providing a policy environment that is seen as investor-friendly and is supportive of inclusive growth. A credible time path for bringing the fiscal deficit under firmer control must have top priority. This must be accompanied by continued progress on reforms that are in the pipeline in many areas, especially those that are likely to generate an early investment response. A financial sector capable of mobilising and deploying resources efficiently is extremely important and there are many steps that can be taken in this area that are entirely in the domain of the Central government.

The government's own resources have to be deployed with a clear sense of priority. In this context, health and education and critical infrastructure development, especially in water management and rural infrastructure, and infrastructure development in backward areas must have top priority. For other infrastructure areas the maximum use must be made of PPPs both by the Central government and by the states. Impediments in the implementation of large projects should be speedily removed.

Four critical challenges facing the economy in the Twelfth Plan, which are perhaps more serious than they were at the start of the Eleventh Plan, are the challenges of: (a) managing the energy situation, (b) managing the water economy, (c) addressing the problems posed by the urban transformation that is likely to occur and (d) ensuring protection of the environment in a manner that can facilitate rapid growth. Difficult choices have to be made in each of these areas and both the Central government and the states have an important role in bringing about a successful outcome. The prize, if we succeed, is that we will have put India in the small group of countries that have achieved the transition to sustained high growth and elimination of poverty.

Finally, the efficiency in implementation of projects on the ground needs to be greatly improved. Most of what needs to be done in this context rests with state governments but the Central government must find ways of improving project design, prioritising resources to fund well designed interventions that work, devolving resources to lower levels and helping build capacity. Evidence-based evaluation is critical for redesign and prioritisation. We need to greatly strengthen capacities in the area and the proposed Independent Evaluation Office which is expected to be set up during 2011-12, will be a major step in this direction.

References

Ahluwalia, Montek S. (2009). "Growth, Distribution and Inclusiveness—Reflections on India's Experience", in Kaushik Basu and Ravi Kanbur (ed.), *Arguments for a Better World: Essays in Honour of Amartya Sen*. Oxford University Press.

Balakrishnan, P., K. Pushpangandhan and M. Suresh Babu (2000). "Trade Liberalisation and Productivity Growth in Manufacturing: Evidence from Firm Level Panel Data", *Economic & Political Weekly*, October.

Bhalla, Surjit (2011). "Inclusive Growth in India: Some Facts Some Conclusion", Paper for LSE India Observatory Research Project on *Growth and Inclusiveness in India*, 27 March.

Barro, Robert J. and Jong-Wha Lee (2010). "A New Data Set of Educational Attainment in the World, 1950-2010", *NBER Working Paper Series, Working Paper* No. 15902, National Bureau of Economic Research.

Das, Deb Kusum (2004). "Manufacturing Productivity under Varying Trade Regimes 1980-2000", *Economic & Political Weekly*, January.

Goldar, Bishwanath (2004). "Indian Manufacturing: Productivity Trade in Manufacturing in Pre- and Post-Reforms Period", *Economic & Political Weekly*, November.

Hashim, Danish A., Ajay Kumar and Arvind Virmani (2011). "J-Curve Hypothesis of Productivity and Output Growth", Forthcoming in *India Economic Review* 46(1).

Kapur Devesh, Chandrabhan Prasad, Lant Pritchet and D. Shyam Babu (2010). "Rethinking Inequalities: Dalits in Uttar Pradesh in the Market Reform Era", *Economic & Political Weekly*, August.

Rajan, Raghuram (2010). *Faultlines* (Collins Business).

Rodrik, Dani and Arvind Subramanium (2004). "From Hindu Growth to Productivity Surge: The Mystery of the Indian Growth Transition", *NBER Working Paper* No. 10376.

Sen, Abhijit (2010). "Gauging Where We Are: Some Problems with Our Statistical Measuring Rods", Presidential Address at the 52nd Annual Conference, The Indian Society of Labour Economics, Karnatak University, Dharwad.

Thorat, Sukhadeo (2010). "How Socially Inclusive Has Growth Been?", Presidential Address at the 93rd Annual Conference of the Indian Economic Association.

Virmani, Arvind (2006). "Propelling India from Socialist Stagnation to Global Power", Chapter 3. New Delhi: Academic Foundation.

9 Twelfth Five Year Plan

Some Perspectives

Manmohan Singh

The Approach Paper outlines the challenges we face in achieving our goal of rapid, inclusive and sustainable growth over the next five years.

As we chart our course for the Twelfth Five Year Plan (2012-2017), we must take note of what is happening in the world economy and in our neighbourhood, and shape our policies accordingly. The world is going through a major realignment of economic power. Industrialised countries are slowing down, emerging market economies are gaining weight and regionally, Asia is gaining weight. As an emerging market economy in Asia, we stand to gain on both counts. Our policies in the Twelfth Plan must therefore be shaped to take full advantage of these emerging possibilities.

As planners, we need to ask what government should do to achieve our social and economic objectives? Much of the growth process is now driven by actors outside the direct control of government. This includes small and big farmers, small and medium entrepreneurs and of course the private corporate sector, all of whom respond to market forces. This, however, does not mean that government has no role to play in the development process. It has a very large role and I would distinguish four areas in this context.

First, government must provide a policy environment in which the creative spirit of our farmers and entrepreneurs is given full support and encouragement. This includes an environment of macroeconomic stability, efficient functioning markets which ensure competitive discipline on private sector producers, a sound financial system for allocating financial resources, good governance with transparency and effective enforcement of the rule of law.

Second, the government has a very big role to play in developing the infrastructure needed in both rural and urban areas to support broad and inclusive growth.

Third, the government must have special programmes for livelihood support for the poor and vulnerable, aimed at directly increasing their income earning capabilities and at mainstreaming them in the overall growth process.

Fourth, government must ensure that every citizen must have access to essential public services of acceptable quality in health, education, skill development, provision of safe drinking water and sanitation. Without such services, effective inclusion is simply not possible.

As we enter the Twelfth Five Year Plan, both the Central and state governments should review what they are doing in each of these areas, and strengthen policies wherever necessary.

The Approach Paper proposes a growth target of 9 per cent per year. It is relevant to ask whether this is feasible since the economy is currently slowing down. The current slowdown is a matter of concern, but it should be seen as a short-term phenomenon, reflecting highly unsettled conditions in the global economy. Growth rates are being revised downwards in all countries for the current year.

We must guard against the mood of negativism that seems to have gripped the country. Recently a distinguished business leader said that in India 'the business is better than the mood'. Investment is, after all, a reflection of the 'animal spirits' of enterprise. As we in government seek to create the foundations for higher investment, higher employment and growth, we must be particularly mindful of the impact of our policies and politics on public and private investor sentiment.

In setting targets for the Twelfth Plan we must look at longer-term potential, assuming that the immediate short-term problems will be overcome. I have absolutely no doubt that our country's longer-term prospects are very good. Twenty years ago, in my first Budget speech as Finance Minister, borrowing a phrase from Victor Hugo, I had said, 'No power on earth can stop an idea whose time has come'. I went on to say that, 'the emergence of India as a major economic power in the world happens to be one such idea'.

In the past two decades, different political parties, ruling in different times in different states, and also in the Centre, have pushed in the same general direction to ensure that my prediction is now a widely accepted reality. In the seven years since the UPA government first came to power in 2004, the economy has grown at an average rate of 8.5 per cent. India is now regarded as one of the fastest growing emerging markets. What is particularly encouraging is that many states, including some that grew relatively slowly in earlier years, have shown an acceleration in growth performance. I congratulate the chief ministers of all these states. If each of our states adopts the 'national best practice', if not 'global best practice', our nation as a whole will benefit enormously.

Of course, growth has never been our sole objective. Our aim has always been inclusive growth, by which we mean growth which ensures a broad spread of benefits to all sections of our population, particularly the scheduled castes (SCs), the scheduled tribes (STs), the other backward castes (OBCs) and other marginalised groups and also protects the environment. A criticism often advanced is that while we have delivered high growth, we have not done nearly as well on inclusiveness. I believe there is some truth in this criticism, in the sense that we should have done better. However, it is not true to say that progress on this front has not been significant.

An important aspect of our performance which is relevant for inclusiveness is that agricultural growth, which had decelerated to an average of 2.2 per cent per year in the Tenth Plan, is likely to clock an average of 3.5 per cent in the Eleventh Plan. This distinct improvement testifies to the success of many efforts made by the Central and state governments in this area. Faster agricultural growth, combined with the implementation of Mahatma Gandhi National Rural Employment Guarantee Act (MGNREGA), has produced an impressive increase in rural wages in real terms.

Education and health have been critical focus areas in our inclusiveness strategy and there is encouraging news in these areas. The Right to Education Act is now on the statute books. Enrollment of children in primary schools is near universal. Dropout rates are high, but they are falling. There remains a gap between SCs, STs and the rest of the population, which must be eliminated, but this gap is progressively becoming narrower. The gap between girls and boys is also falling. As we strive to reduce these gaps further, we must now address the next big challenge which is to improve the quality of education, and the employability of the educated.

The National Rural Health Mission (NRHM), which took off only in 2007, has begun to address the large gaps in health infrastructure. Much remains to be done but there is evidence of progress. Institutional deliveries have increased from 54 per cent in 2006 to 73 per cent in 2009. The infant mortality rate (IMR) has fallen from 57 to 50, over the same period. A major initiative in health for the poor has been the Rashtriya Swasthya Bima Yojana (RSBY), which now provides an insurance cover for in-patient treatment to well over 100 million people. We must build on this experiment to move towards a system of universal health coverage in the Twelfth Five Year Plan.

Improving infrastructure in both rural and urban areas is critical for inclusive growth. The Bharat Nirman programme, which focussed on rural infrastructure development, has channelled substantial volumes of resources into rural roads, rural electrification, irrigation, rural drinking water and rural housing. This effort will have to continue. Special efforts will be necessary to control degradation of our land and water resources which adversely affects the livelihood of millions of small and marginal farmers who live on the edge of subsistence.

General infrastructure development of the economy is also critical. Both the public sector and the private sector can play a major role, with public investment concentrating on areas where the private sector is unlikely to go. I am happy to say that both the Central government and state governments have successfully implemented many public-private partnership (PPP) projects in infrastructure in the Eleventh Five Year Plan. A recent international report has ranked India second in the number of PPP projects taken up.

The Eleventh Plan, for the first time, presented an infrastructure plan for the northeast. It has made a good start and we must continue this thrust in the Twelfth Five Year Plan. The special requirements of Jammu & Kashmir have also to be factored in our plan calculus. The tribal dominated districts in the heartland of the country, which are the focus of left wing extremism, also need a better infrastructure, particularly roads. This is essential for their development and we must give special emphasis to this task.

In many of these areas it is the state governments that have the major implementing role. The Central government can only provide support through centrally sponsored schemes (CSSs). I am aware that there are complaints about the proliferation of these schemes and the lack of flexibility in their guidelines. The Twelfth Plan provides an opportunity to streamline and restructure CSSs to overcome these gaps. The Planning Commission had appointed the B.K. Chaturvedi Committee to look into these issues and the report of the Committee has been circulated to all the chief ministers. I look forward to hearing your views on the recommendations of the Committee.

Let me also touch on the complex issue of the interaction between politics and development policies. Managing this interaction effectively is crucial if India is to achieve her full development potential.

Our democracy, our civil society and our free press, all face a revolution of rising expectations. This is to some extent caused by the visible success achieved in some areas, which has made people realise what is possible and therefore, they demand a fair share of benefits in terms of the new opportunities created. The fact that we are a functioning democracy, in which vast numbers of our people participate and have a voice, magnifies the phenomenon.

I believe we should be proud of the way our democracy forces the government to address these problems. But it is also true that this tidal wave of rising expectations puts tremendous pressure on our institutions. Since democracy is a politically competitive process, political parties naturally give voice to the demands of the people. But development also requires time and patience for policies to have an impact. It also requires cooperation.

Elected governments can deliver only if, once elections are over and a government is formed, the political process works to allow governments to function in a manner where the needs of long-term development do not become hostage to short-term concerns. What this means is that parliamentary parties have to strike a difficult balance between maintaining adversarial political positions on many issues, while also cooperating to advance a shared longer-term national agenda. This balance is not easy to strike.

At times like these, it is of vital importance that each of our democratic institutions—the executive, the judiciary, the parliament and state legislatures, the various constitutional and regulatory authorities, understand what their due role is, and play that due role in a constructive manner.

It is our collective responsibility to reverse the mood of negativism today. The future is what we make of it. Nothing is ordained or pre-determined. India can rise, but India can also falter. We live in a world of rising and faltering economies. We can either become victims of negativism, criticising ourselves all the way, or work together to put ourselves firmly in the group of rising economies. Both optimism and pessimism have an infectious quality.

I am confident that we can overcome the challenges we confront. But, I also realise that to do so we must first understand the enormity of the change underway globally and the challenge this poses for us. I urge you, honourable chief ministers, to work together with the Central government to help accelerate the pace of growth and improve the quality of development of our people. Let us dedicate ourselves to implementing the Twelfth Plan in this spirit of nation building.

The world is watching India with great interest. I also believe it is watching us with great goodwill. The world has a stake in India's success because a peaceful prosperous democratic India is a stabilising force in the world. Let us therefore embark on the Twelfth Five Year Plan journey with ambition tempered with humility and confidence, combined with determination. Let us show the world that democratic India is capable of building a prosperous, inclusive, secular and plural nation on the path of sustainable growth. The world has a great stake in the success of this Indian model of development.

PM's inaugural address at the 56th National Development Council Meeting, October 22, 2011.

10 India in 2025

Growth and Inclusion

Bibek Debroy

'Vast and deep rivers—swelling and impetuous—charming pleasure-gardens by the river banks, putting to shame the celestial Nandana-Kânana; amidst these pleasure-gardens rise, towering to the sky, beautiful marble palaces, decorated with the most exquisite workmanship of fine art; on the sides, in front, and behind, clusters of huts, with crumbling mud-walls and dilapidated roofs, the bamboos of which, forming their skeletons, as it were, are exposed to view; moving about here and there emaciated figures of young and old in tattered rags, whose faces bear deep-cut lines of the despair and poverty of hundreds of years; cows, bullocks, buffaloes everywhere—ay, the same melancholy look in their eyes, the same feeble physique; on the wayside refuse and dirt: This is our present-day India!' These are the opening lines of a monograph written by Swami Vivekananda and subsequently translated into English as *The East and the West*.[1] Swami Vivekananda was fond of a *shloka* from the Katha Upanishad— 'Arise! Awake! Do not stop until the goal has been attained.'[2] The first part of the *shloka* is quoted quite often. However, there is a second part too. That says, the wise ones have told us that the road is a difficult one to travel along. It is as sharp as a razor's edge.

Alice's Adventures in Wonderland has a conversation between Alice and the Cheshire cat. '"Would you tell me, please, which way I ought to go from here?" "That depends a good deal on where you want to get to," said the Cat. "I don't much care where—" said Alice. "Then it doesn't matter which way you go," said the Cat. "—so long as I get *somewhere,*" Alice

1. *http://www.ramakrishnavivekananda.info/vivekananda/volume_5/vol_5_frame.htm*
2. Katha Upanishad, I.3.14. What has been given is not quite a literal translation. However, it is one of the more common translations of the first part of the *shloka*.

added as an explanation. "Oh, you're sure to do that," said the Cat, "if you only walk long enough."' Where do we want India to be in 2025? Are we clear about where we want to go? Or, as a country, are we just trundling along, as long as we get somewhere?

We gave ourselves a Constitution in 1950 and the Preamble promised us a sovereign democratic republic that would ensure, for every citizen, social, economic and political justice; liberty of thought, expression, belief, faith and worship; equality of status and opportunity; and fraternity, assuring the dignity of the individual. The Preamble was subsequently amended through the 42nd Amendment Act of 1976 to make India socialist and secular and to bring in 'the integrity of the nation'. Questions about the Preamble being an integral part of the Constitution, or being non-justiciable, are not terribly pertinent for present purposes. For present purposes, we promised India's citizens justice, liberty, equality and dignity. We haven't been able to ensure that. We have failed the Constitution and the Constitutional promise. We have introduced policies that haven't ensured justice, liberty, equality and dignity.

It is not quite the case that there have been no successes since 1947, or since 1950. Consider some random figures for 1950-51.[3] Life expectancy at birth was 32.1 years. The literacy rate was 18.3 per cent. As shares of GDP, the savings rate was 8.6 per cent and the investment rate was 8.7 per cent. During the First Plan (1951-1956), the average annual real growth in GNP was 3.7 per cent. But consider also the following quote: 'In the last four or five decades, there has been considerable industrial development in India, accompanied by urbanisation and expansion of commerce. Large towns and cities have grown and transport and communications have developed extensively. The isolation of the village has been broken and the average citizen lives in an environment significantly different from the one in which he lived and worked fifty or sixty years ago. Indian enterprise has made considerable headway, and the country has now considerable experience in the fields of modern business, industry and finance. New economic and social relations have emerged, giving rise in turn to a general desire for more rapid change. But the development that has taken place is

3. These figures are from *Economic Survey 2010-11*, Department of Economic Affairs, Ministry of Finance, Government of India.

partial and limited when judged in terms of the country's needs and potentialities. Industrialism and the use of modern techniques have affected only limited segments of the economy. Agriculture is still the mainstay...of the population, and productivity in this sector is exceedingly low. The size of agricultural holdings has progressively diminished; the old cottage and small-scale industries have been decaying, and the rural population...suffers from chronic underemployment and low incomes. Population has increased by more than fifty per cent in the last fifty years, but the growth of alternative occupations either in the rural areas or in the towns has not been on a scale which could absorb this growing population. In the limited spheres which have registered expansion, the level of productivity and the level of incomes have naturally been higher. But, for the community as a whole, the economic development of the last few decades has brought no significant improvement in standards of living and opportunities for employment, and has perhaps accentuated to some extent inequalities of income and wealth.' The Planning Commission was set up in 1950 and the First Five Year Plan was launched in 1951. The Planning Commission is now drafting the Twelfth Five Year Plan (2012-2017) document. This quote isn't from that document. This quote is from Chapter 1 of the First Five Year Plan document.[4] A sense of *déjà vu* is unavoidable. The more things change, the more they seem to remain the same. We are getting somewhere, but we don't seem to care where.

This needs to change. There is an impression that India has changed a lot, particularly after 1991. Indeed it has, and this shows up in all kinds of different indicators. The July 1991 reforms were triggered by a severe balance of payments (BoP) crisis, though there were earlier reforms too, often described as reforms by stealth.[5] When those July 1991 reforms were introduced, few observers would have predicted the kind of changes India has witnessed since 1991. It is no longer a shortage economy, at least in segments where reforms have been introduced. Several news magazines have done stories on 20 years of reforms and they document these changes. But more importantly, it has led to changes in expectations and mindsets. India is described as a young country, with a median age that is around 25

---

4. *http://planningcommission.nic.in/plans/planrel/fiveyr/index9.html*

5. See, for example, Panagariya, Arvind (2008). *India: The Emerging Giant*. Oxford University Press.

years. This is a generation born after 1991. If not born after 1991, it is a generation that has grown up after 1991. It is a generation that is no longer shackled by old mindsets. It is a generation that is impatient. In earlier generations, opportunities for betterment of lives were limited. This new generation may not have benefitted entirely from these new opportunities, but it knows these opportunities exist. Thanks to the spread of information, expectations have changed. Policies have to cater to this new generation and the expectations of this new generation. Policies have to cater to the likes of Aastha Arora. Most of us have forgotten who Aastha Arora is. Aastha Arora is the billionth Indian, born on 11th May 2000. She will be 25 in 2025. When she is 25, she is entitled to an India that she is proud of. It should be an India that all Indians are proud of. India is a country that has negative net migration. Net migration is defined as the number of people who leave the country, subtracted from the number of people who enter the country. That is, more people leave India, compared to the number of people who migrate to India. Since all of us left Africa 100,000 years ago, human beings have always migrated in search of better economic opportunities, to better their lives. If relatively more people leave India, that is because they perceive better economic opportunities abroad. If we can bring about a prosperous India in 2025, there will be longer queues at Indian missions abroad and shorter queues at OECD missions in India. That's a good outcome, not something that is undesirable.

We are getting there, the question is the speed. When the rupee was devalued in two stages in July 1991, a code was used and that was 'hop, skip and jump'. The devaluation was in two stages, so as to test the waters. That is irrelevant now and is only of historical interest. What is relevant is the phrase 'hop, skip and jump', better known as the triple jump. In a triple jump, each of the three phases is stronger and longer than the preceding one. The hop provides the momentum for the skip and the hop and the skip provide the momentum for the jump. In our reforms, we have hopped. On rare occasions, we have skipped. But we have still not jumped. If this sounds like a strong statement, we should go back and read an official government document that everyone has forgotten about now. It was published in July 1993, two years after the reforms.[6] Among other things,

6. Ministry of Finance (1993). "Economic Reforms: Two Years After and the Task Ahead", *Discussion Paper*, Department of Economic Affairs, July.

this set out an agenda for future reforms. If we revisit that paper, we will find that many of the reforms that were talked about in July 1993 have still not been implemented. A snide comment is made in comparisons about India and East Asia. 'What is the difference between India and East Asia? In East Asia, they do what Indians talk about. And in India, they talk about what East Asia does.' We have talked about reforms ad nauseam, but we haven't implemented them. Earlier, pre-1991, Indian economic policy was supposed to have been influenced by Fabian socialism, though it was actually influenced much more by Soviet socialism. The reference to Fabian socialism is a reference to the Fabian Society, established in London in 1884. That kind of socialism was meant to be incremental and creeping, not revolutionary. Hence, the Society consciously adopted the name of Fabius Maximus, the Roman dictator and general during the Second Punic War (218-202 BCE) against Hannibal of Carthage. Fabius didn't take decisive action. He used delaying tactics and was thus named 'Cunctator', the delayer. One need not get into a detailed discussion of Roman history. The point is that our economic policymaking lacks decisive action. There is continual resort to delaying tactics.

There are several books on the Indian economy, more so since 1991. In terms of scope and breadth of coverage, one of the better ones is the book by Arvind Panagariya.[7] This is what Arvind Panagariya has to say. 'The UPA leadership attributed the ouster of the NDA in the May 2004 elections to the public sentiment that the NDA reforms had bypassed the rural poor. The adherence to this interpretation had the effect of weakening the resolve of the UPA government to introduce major new reforms. It did not matter that the available scientific evidence pointed to a steady decline in poverty in rural as well as urban areas following the reforms. Once the UPA publicly embraced the view that the reforms had not helped the poor, its ability to push the same reforms was greatly undercut.' This is a reference to UPA-I. However, UPA-II has been worse. At least, during UPA-I, one could blame the bogey of the Left being part of the coalition and the National Common Minimum Programme (NCMP). There is no such fig-leaf during UPA-II, no scapegoat to blame. The fact is that the Congress

7. Panagariya (2008); See Footnote 5.

has always been a reluctant reformer, even during the period 1991-1993.[8] It is a party of the status quo and almost tautologically, all reforms hurt the status quo and the interests of those who benefit from the status quo. With the relative decline of the Leftist parties, especially under UPA-II, the Congress has brought in those with Leftist sentiments within its fold. It has swung even more to the Left.

Complacency has set in. This is fuelled by external reports that are bullish about India. The first BRIC (Brazil, Russia, India, China) paper by Goldman Sachs was partly responsible for popularising the idea of India's explosive income and consumption growth potential.[9] But there have been several others since then.[10] Table 10.1 shows some of these.

What do these reports generally argue? First, the savings rate, as a share of GDP, has increased and will increase further. Second, the investment rate has also increased. Third, the efficiency in the use of capital, measured, say by the incremental capital/output ratio (ICOR), has improved because of competition. Fourth, the share of agriculture and allied activities in GDP is declining, while that of services is increasing. What is pertinent is that the services sector tends to have a lower ICOR, though not invariably. That apart, if agriculture is growing relatively slowly and services is growing relatively fast, the sectoral shift from agriculture to services itself jacks up GDP growth as a statistical inevitability. Fifth, there is the effect of export growth on GDP, though that it is contingent on a global recovery. Sixth, there is the demographic dividend and increase in labour input. Seventh, there is total factor productivity (TFP) growth, after

8. Though this government lasted till 1996, there were almost no reforms after 1993.

9. Wilson, Dominic and Roopa Purushothaman (2003). "Dreaming with BRICs: The Path to 2050", *Global Economics Paper* No.99, Goldman Sachs, 1 October.

10. For example, there have been two other BRIC reports: O'Neill, Jim, Dominic Wilson, Roopa Purushothaman and Anna Stupnytska (2005). "How Solid are the BRICS?", *Global Economics Paper* No.134, Goldman Sachs, 1st December and O'Neill, Jim (2007). "BRICs and Beyond", Goldman Sachs, 23rd November. That apart, there is Hawsworth, John (2006). "The World in 2050: How Big will the Major Emerging Market Economies get and How can the OECD Compete?", March. PriceWatehouse Coopers; Asuncion-Mund, Jennifer (2005). *India Rising: A Medium-Term Perspective*. Deutsche Bank Research, May; HSBC (2011). *The World in 2050, Quantifying the Shift in the Global Economy*. HSBC Global Research, January; McKinsey (2007). *The Bird of Gold: The Rise of India's Consumer Market*, McKinsey Global Institute, May and ADB (2009). *India 2039, An Affluent Society in One Generation*. ADB and Emerging Markets Forum.

Table 10.1

Some Existing Projections till 2025

	Real GDP Growth (%)	*GDP Constant (trillion $) 2015*	*GDP Constant (trillion $) 2025*	*Per Capita GDP ($) 2015*	*Per Capita GDP ($) 2025*
First BRIC paper[11]	5.7[12]	1.4	3.2	1,149	2,331
Second BRIC paper[13]	5.5[14]	1.7	3.6	1,369	2,656
Third BRIC paper[15]	5.95[16]	1.9	4.4	1,502	3,005
First PWC projections[17]	5.2[18]				
DB Research[19]	6[20]				5,000[21]
HSBC Global Research[22]	5.65[23]				
McKinsey[24]	5.9				
ADB[25]	9.5				6,050[26]
Arvind Virmani[27]	7				

11. See Wilson and Purushothaman (2003). For BRIC countries as a whole, an annual exchange rate appreciation of 2.5 per cent is assumed.
12. 5.9 per cent for 2010-2015 and 5.7 per cent for 2015-2025.
13. O'Neill *et al.* (2005).
14. 5.7 per cent for 2010-2015, 5.5 per cent for 2015-2020 and 5.4 per cent for 2020-2025.
15. O'Neill (2007).
16. 6.0 per cent for 2015-2020 and 5.9 per cent for 2020-2025.
17. Hawsworth (2006). This has projections for 2050, but not for the intervening years of 2015 and 2025. There were subsequent revisions to this in March 2008 and January 2011. But we are ignoring those, because they continue to relate to 2011. However, the 7.6 per cent growth (with exchange rate appreciation) was increased to 8.1 per cent in January 2011.
18. 7.6 per cent with exchange rate appreciation.
19. Asuncion-Mund (2005).
20. 7.5 per cent with substantial reforms.
21. This is a purchasing power parity (PPP) figure and is for 2020, not 2025.
22. HSBC (2011). This also has projections for 2050, but not for the intervening years of 2015 and 2025.
23. 5.7 per cent between 2010 and 2020 and 5.6 per cent between 2020 and 2030.
24. McKinsey (2007).
25. ADB (2009).
26. 2024, not 2025.
27. Virmani, Arvind (2005). "A Tripolar Century: USA, China and India", *ICRIER Working Paper* No. 160, March.

netting out increases in labour and capital inputs. Not every report or study tries to quantify and estimate this, but nevertheless, this is a factor. Eighth, the young population does things to entrepreneurship that is difficult to pin down and make tangible. Ninth and finally, projections are typically in US dollars and if the rupee appreciates against the dollar, there is the impact of exchange rate appreciation.

These reasons are all true. But one should not get carried away. With the exception of the ADB report, all the others have real rates of GDP growth that are 6 per cent and below. Consider the Third BRIC paper[28] and its projection of the largest economies in the world in 2025. In constant US dollars, the largest economies in the world are projected to be the United States ($ 20.1 trillion), China ($ 18.4 trillion), Japan ($ 5.6 trillion) and India ($ 4.3 trillion). Before we are delighted at this prospect, notice the continued gap between United States and China on the one hand and India on the other. When we get carried away by projections, we should realise that most of the explosion in consumption and growth occurs after 2025, beyond 2040. With 6 per cent growth, India will change by 2025, but not by as much as we think. Consider the per capita GDP figures, and not the total GDP. After all, India has, and will continue to have, a large population. An overall GDP figure is spread over many more people. While the precise figure varies across studies, most of them project an Indian per capita GDP of between $ 2,500 and $ 3,000 in 2025. This is per capita GDP in today's dollars and is GDP estimated with official exchange rates, the so-called Atlas method. It is not purchasing power parity (PPP) per capita GDP. One can also cite PPP figures, which will increase India's per capita GDP. PPP corrections are based on the idea that goods, and more importantly, services, do not cost the same in developing countries as they do in developed countries. Such items, which cannot be traded, do not necessarily equalise across countries. Because they are relatively lower in developing countries, PPP corrections increase per capita GDP in developing countries and decrease them in developed countries. But that is neither here nor there, since the thrust of the argument remains, whether one is using the Atlas method or PPP. $2,500 to $3,000 will take us to roughly where countries like Ukraine, Congo, Guatemala, Syria, Egypt,

28 O'Neill (2007).

Georgia, Iraq and Sri Lanka are today. More than one decade down the line, we will be as prosperous as these countries are today. That's not India Shining by any criterion. But it seems that this is the limit of our ambition. Even if we get 6 per cent growth, that's wonderful. How many countries in the world will get that?

We were a bit more ambitious once. At the time of the 2004 general elections, the NDA manifesto stated, 'The NDA believes that GDP growth, at an annual rate of 8 to 10 per cent on a sustainable basis, is achievable. This will realise our strategic vision of making India a Developed Nation.'[29] That ambition seems to have died out. At least, no one talks about the developed nation bit. There is no formal definition of a developed country though. The World Bank uses no such term. Instead, it has expressions like high income, upper middle income, lower middle income and low income. The UN has a definition of least developed countries (LDCs). By and large, the Organisation for Economic Co-operation and Development (OECD) economies are regarded as developed countries. And whatever else is left, after taking away the OECD and LDC groups, is loosely called a developing country. Today, the OECD members have an average per capita income of US $35,000. That is a long, long way off. The lower middle income economies have an average per capita income of US $2,300 today. The upper middle income economies have an average per capita income of US $7,500. Many years ago, developing economies were regarded as those that had per capita incomes that were 25 per cent or lower than that of the United States. Today, the United States has a per capita income of around US $48,000. In other words, to cross the developing country status in that loose sense, we need to have a per capita income of US $12,000 and more. The NDA manifesto of 2004 didn't set a timeframe for developed country status. But let's think of that timeline of 2025. $12,275 and more takes us to high income status in 2025, as per the World Bank and we can call ourselves developed.[30] $3,976 and more takes us to upper middle income status in 2025. We have just moved from low income to lower middle income status. In 2025, will we remain in that lower middle income status? Or will we move to upper middle income status? Or can we be

29. *http://www.indian-elections.com/partymanifestoes/nda.html*

30. *http://data.worldbank.org/about/country-classifications*

more ambitious and move to high income status and attain the status of a developed economy, the latter expression being used in a loose sense? This is one way to pose the question.

It is good to be ambitious. But one shouldn't be widely off the mark. All kinds of things in the world are possible. However, they aren't probable. High income or developed economy status by 2025 has a very low degree of probability. But crossing over to the upper middle income status is eminently doable. If we can get real growth of 9.5 per cent going, even if this does not accelerate to 10 per cent and more, we will cross over to the upper middle income status comfortably. We will have a per capita income of US $6,000 and more.

One kind of response is inevitable. When has the UPA ever given up this aspiration? Here is a quote from the Planning Commission on the Twelfth Five Year Plan and the issues the country faces.[31] 'GDP growth for the 11th Plan is likely to be 8.2 per cent, which is less than the target of 9 per cent...The target of 10 per cent is being mentioned, but our internal assessment is that even 9 per cent will be difficult given the constraints we face.' Even 9 per cent will be difficult for the Twelfth Plan. This is a departure from the days when the government glibly talked about double digit growth in a couple of years. And for the next couple of years or so, we seem to be settling down on a growth trajectory of between 6 and 6.5 per cent. The period since 2003-04 is important, since before that, growth rate of 9 per cent and more wasn't regarded as feasible. Real rates of GDP growth were 8.5 per cent in 2003-04, 7.5 per cent in 2004-05, 9.5 per cent in 2005-06, 9.5 per cent in 2006-07, 9.8 per cent in 2007-08, 6.7 per cent in 2008-09, 7.4 per cent in 2009-10 and 8.5 per cent in 2010-11. Till 2008-09, we could contemplate growth of 9.5 per cent and more. Since 2008-09, we have been struggling to get 7.5 per cent. *Atmanam Viddhi* or 'know thyself' is a good adage to follow. Why have we slowed from 9.5 per cent to 7 per cent and below? It is an unfortunate human tendency not to look inwards and follow the adage. Don't look within. Don't blame yourself. There is always a scapegoat, a red herring. Hence, instead of identifying the problems within, blame the global financial crisis. It is not the case that the global financial crisis had no impact. It certainly did. But

31. *http://planningcommission.gov.in/plans/planrel/12appdrft/issues_pc.pdf*

had reforms been introduced, this impact could have been neutralised and we would still have been on a growth trajectory of 9.5 per cent and more. In other words, the 'constraints' the Planning Commission mentions are internal, not external. The reason we are stuck on a 6-6.5 per cent trajectory is because the government is unable and unwilling to introduce reforms. What kind of reforms? These are instances of both government inaction and action.

What will it take to achieve annual real rates of GDP growth of 9 and more per cent? At one level, per capita GDP is nothing but the average productivity of India's inhabitants.[33] World Economic Forum's Global Competitiveness Index (GCI) analyses competitiveness on the basis of 12 pillars—(1) institutions; (2) infrastructure; (3) macroeconomic environment; (4) health and primary education; (5) higher education and training; (6) goods market efficiency; (7) labour market efficiency; (8) financial market development; (9) technological readiness; (10) market size; (11) business sophistication and (12) innovation.[33] As one moves up the development ladder, successive pillars become increasingly important. At India's levels of development, capital and labour inputs are key drivers behind high GDP growth. If question marks are raised about this growth reaching a plateau, that's because one assumes this input-based growth reaches a frontier and therefore, begins to slow down.

But before talking about this, a digression on reforms is useful. India's present cycle of economic reforms were triggered in 1991 by an external sector BoP crisis as mentioned earlier in the text. There was an earlier cycle of reforms that has been described as reforms by stealth.[34] This dates to the second half of the 1970s and involved trade liberalisation, as well as elements of industrial deregulation. However, this first cycle was more piece-meal and ad hoc and wasn't comprehensive as the second cycle, introduced in 1991. One should begin by asking what one means by economic reforms. Sometimes expressions like first generation and second

32. Since per capita GDP is GDP divided by population (and not just the working-age population), per capita GDP is more accurately the average productivity of India's working-age population.

33. *http://gcr.weforum.org/gcr2010/*

34. See, for example, Panagariya (2008).

generation are also used, suggesting that first generation reforms were introduced in the first post-1991 flush and that the second generation is what awaits us now. Unfortunately, the expressions first generation and second generation are never very precisely defined. However, two overlapping interpretations are possible. First, first generation refers to reforms that concern the external sector—elimination of quantitative restrictions (QRs) on exports, rationalisation and elimination of export subsidies and their replacement by a system of export incentives,[35] reduction in import duties, a market-determined exchange rate with a convertible rupee, a liberal policy on foreign institutional investments and opening up to foreign direct investments (FDI). On each of these, reforms have already been introduced, or there is a timeframe for their further introduction, although external sector reforms are also linked to negotiations, multilateral, regional or bilateral. They cannot always be introduced unilaterally. In contrast, second generation reforms concern the domestic economy, although a neat watertight compartmentalisation between the domestic and the external isn't always possible. Understandably, political economy considerations and vested interests are stronger in domestic economic reforms, compared to the external. Second, one can also interpret the first generation as reforms that concerned and were under the purview primarily of the Centre, or the Union government. In contrast, in a federal setup, second generation concerns reforms that have to be introduced at the state government level.[36] Thanks to the first generation having been implemented, the focus of policy change has thus shifted from the Centre to the states. The cutting, and the blunting edge, of reforms thus lies at the level of the states and different states have reacted differently to liberalisation. What is also of note is that most product market policies are with the Centre, while most factor market (labour, land) policies are with the states. Having said this, the major reform issues are the following.

The demographic dividend or deficit: When one contrasts the Indian growth story with that of China, attention is often drawn to China's

35. Export incentives are WTO-compatible. Even when WTO-compatible, trading partners can subject export subsidies to countervailing duties.
36. The Seventh Schedule to the Indian Constitution sets out a Union List, a State List and a Concurrent List.

success in manufacturing. The etymology of the word 'manufacture' isn't certain. But it seems to have a link with the Latin *manu factum*, meaning 'made by hand'. Irrespective of ingredients of technology, capital (plant and machinery), entrepreneurship, and perhaps even land, entering as inputs or factors into production processes, labour remains a core input. And there is no denying that India possesses, or should possess, a comparative advantage in labour. As with every other developing country, that has always been the case. Labour is relatively more abundant than capital. In a completely integrated and globalised world, national boundaries should make no difference. But that ideal never happens. Even if cross-border movements of technology and capital are relatively free, there will be restrictions on cross-border movements of labour. Integration of labour markets will only happen in niches, in selected segments. Therefore, India should be in a position to exploit its cost advantage in labour, and in natural resources, to push manufacturing growth. Nor should one forget India's strengths in science and technology and in education. These reinforce the labour cost advantage. To this traditional labour cost advantage has been added what is called the demographic dividend. With ageing populations in developed countries, and even in countries like Russia and China, there has been talk of India's demographic dividend.[37] That the demographic dividend argument works, is known. For East Asia, several studies suggest that between 25 to 40 per cent of the East Asian miracle was due to the demographic dividend.[38] Other than East Asia, it has worked in Japan in the 1950s, China in the 1980s and Ireland in the 1980s and the 1990s. Several factors explain the demographic dividend.[39] First, there is the obvious increase in working-age populations, with a

37. Kelkar, Vijay (2004). "India: On the Growth Turnpike", *K.R. Narayanan Oration*, Australian National University, reprinted in Jha, Raghbendra (2006) (ed.), *The First Ten K.R. Narayanan Orations*. ANU Press; Acharya, Shankar (2007). *Can India Grow without Bharata?*, Academic Foundation; Das, Gurcharan (2006). "The India Model", *Foreign Affairs*, July/August; Asuncion-Mund (2005); Eberstadt, Nicholas (2006). "Growing Old the Hard Way: China, Russia, India", *Policy Review*, Hoover Institution, April/May; Wilson and Purushothaman (2003) are some instances.

38. See, Bloom, David E., David Canning and Jaypee Sevilla (2001). "Economic Growth and the Demographic Transition", *NBER Working Paper* 8685, December.

39. The empirical and theoretical literature is reviewed in IMF (2004). *World Economic Outlook: The Global Demographic Transition*, September.

reduction in dependency ratios, and the direct impact of a larger quantity of labour input. To take but one dramatic number, between 2001 and 2026, India's total population is estimated to increase by 371 million and 83 per cent of the increase will occur in the age group of 15-59 years.[40] Second, the quality of the labour input can increase and this is reflected in what economists call TFP growth, measured after netting out the contribution of increased labour and capital inputs.[41] Third, when dependency ratios decline, savings rates increase, leading to increases in investment rates and higher rates of GDP growth. Fourth, if the decline in dependency ratios is at the lower end of the age spectrum as a result of fertility declines, female work participation rates increase.

The present population projections till 2026 do not yet factor in the results of the 2011 Census. In the aggregate, the preliminary figures available for Census 2011 do not suggest any dramatic changes in these projections. The key points in the present projections are the following. The population will increase to 1.4 billion in 2026, an annual increase of 1.2 per cent between 2001 and 2026. Between 2001 and 2026, because of declining fertility, the proportion of under-15 population will decline from 35.4 per cent to 23.4 per cent. The proportion of population in the working age group of 15-59 years will increase from 57.7 per cent to 64.3 per cent in 2026 and the share of old people will increase from 6.9 per cent to 12.4 per cent. The average age will increase from 23 years in 2001 to 31 in 2026, suggesting that beyond 2035, the effects of the demographic dividend will begin to wear off. The urban population will be 38 per cent in 2026 and urban growth will account for 67 per cent of the population increase. States with low rates of population growth will be Tamil Nadu and Kerala. Out of the 371 million increase in population between 2001 and 2026, 187 million will be in the states of Bihar, Chhattisgarh, Jharkhand, Madhya Pradesh, Rajasthan, Uttar Pradesh and Uttarakhand. Table 10.2 indicates

40. "Population Projections for India and States 2001-2026", *Report of the Technical Group on Population Projections*. Constituted by the National Commission on Population, Office of the Registrar General and Census Commissioner, May 2006.

41. Some scepticism of TFP estimation is warranted. However, one study that contrasted India and China in two sub-periods, 1989-1995 and 1995-2003, is worth mentioning, since it found that the labour contribution to India's growth was driven more by quantity than quality. See, Jorgenson, Dale and Vu Khunog (2005). "Information Technology and the World Economy", *Scandinavian Journal of Economics* 107(4).

these interstate variations in population growth within the working age-groups, illustrating geographical areas where the burden of employment generation will be concentrated.[42]

Table 10.2

Annualised Growth in 20-60 Working-Age Groups, 2001 to 2020

State	*2001 Population (million)*	*2020 Population (million)*	*Annualised Growth Rate (%)*
Andhra Pradesh	38.1	56.4	2.1
Assam	11.4	19.4	2.8
Bihar	30.2	53.8	3.1
Delhi	5.0	9.0	3.1
Goa	0.7	1.0	1.7
Gujarat	22.8	34.4	2.2
Haryana	8.9	15.4	2.9
Himachal Pradesh	3.2	4.5	1.8
Jammu & Kashmir	4.4	6.2	1.8
Karnataka	25.0	37.3	2.1
Kerala	14.4	19.6	1.6
Madhya Pradesh	27.3	45.4	2.7
Maharashtra	44.0	67.4	2.3
Orissa	16.4	24.5	2.1
Punjab	10.2	15.7	2.3
Rajasthan	25.0	44.6	3.1
Tamil Nadu	31.8	42.1	1.5
Uttar Pradesh	59.1	104.2	3.0
West Bengal	37.8	58.5	2.3
India	447.4	715.9	2.5

The point is the following. There is nothing automatic about a demographic dividend materialising. Among other things, that is a function of health and education outcomes. More specifically, there is question of skills. The overall skills deficit has often been flagged. For instance, in 2002, the S.P. Gupta Special Group[43] constituted by the Planning Commission stated, 'It should be noted, however, that on the average the

42. Adapted from *India Labour Report 2008*, TeamLease and Indicus Analytics.

43. *Report of the Special Group on Targeting Ten Million Employment Opportunities per Year Over the Tenth Plan Period*, Planning Commission, May 2002, *http://planningcommission.nic.in/aboutus/committee/tsk_sg10m.pdf*

skilled labour force at present is hardly around 6-8 per cent of the total, compared to more than 60 per cent in most of the developed and emerging developing countries.' In 2001, the Montek Singh Ahluwalia Task Force,[44] again constituted by the Planning Commission, stated, 'Only 5 per cent of the Indian labour force in this age category[45] has vocational skills.' While the numbers are marginally different, the Eleventh Five Year Plan document adds the following.[46] 'The NSS 61st Round results show that among persons of age 15-29 years, only about 2 per cent are reported to have received formal vocational training and another 8 per cent reported to have received non-formal vocational training indicating that very few young persons actually enter the world of work with any kind of formal vocational training.' If more numbers are needed, the following drive home the point.[47] Eighty per cent of new entrants into the workforce have no opportunities for development of skills. While there are 12.8 million new entrants into the workforce every year, the existing training capacity is 3.1 million per year. In both rural and urban India, and for both males and females, attendance rates in educational institutions drop by around 50 per cent in the age group of 15-19 years.[48] Simultaneously, labour force participation rates begin to increase in the age group of 15-19 years and by the time it comes to the age group of 25-29 years, it is 95.0 per cent for rural males and 94.4 per cent for urban males. The figures for females are lower at 36.5 per cent in rural India and 22.1 per cent in urban India. The 15-29 age group can be used as an illustration. Since post-educational institution training opportunities are limited, 87.8 per cent of the population in this bracket has had no vocational training.[49] Of the 11.3 per cent who received vocational training, only 1.3 per cent received formal vocational training.[50] 'The said results also reflect that 38.8 per cent of the Indian labour force is illiterate, 24.9 per cent of the labour force has had

44. *Report of the Task Force on Employment Opportunities*, Planning Commission, July 2001, *http://planningcommission.nic.in/aboutus/taskforce/tk_empopp.pdf*

45. 20-24 age group.

46. Eleventh Five Year Plan, 2007-2012, Vol. I, Ibid.

47. Ibid. These numbers are based on the 61st Round (2004-05) of the NSS.

48. The drop is sharper for rural females and is higher in rural than in urban India.

49. 85.5 per cent for males and 90.2 per cent for females. Understandably, the numbers without training are higher in rural areas.

50. The number is higher for males and higher in urban than in rural areas.

schooling up to the primary level and the balance 36.3 per cent has had schooling up to the middle and higher level. They also reveal that about 80 per cent of the workforce in rural and urban areas do not possess any identifiable marketable skills.'[51] Among the youth, most of those with formal training are in Kerala, Maharashtra, Tamil Nadu, Himachal Pradesh and Gujarat.[52] Not surprisingly, Bihar's share is the lowest. A better indicator of the state's performance is the share of the young population that has some variety of formal training. In this, Maharashtra, Kerala, Tamil Nadu, Gujarat and Andhra Pradesh perform well. Is this because there is better training capacity and infrastructure? Is it because industrial activity exists in these states? Is it because there is a positive correlation between some minimum level of educational attainment and acquisition of formal training? The answer is probably a combination of various factors.

Interstate differences in human development: Since interstate differences in skills have been mentioned in the context of the demographic dividend, it is worth flagging the broader issue of divergences across states. Specifically on human development, one can either use poverty ratios or broader Millennium Development Goal (MDG) indicators. Until recently, the internationally accepted poverty line used to be US $1 per day, at constant PPP prices. PPP transformations typically increase incomes in developing countries and lower them in developed countries, since prices are lower in the former. Recently, the World Bank has recalibrated the poverty line to US $1.25 per day, because prices were being underestimated in several developing countries. This is different from India's own indigeneous poverty line, but that is irrelevant for present purposes. Irrespective of which indicator is used, headcount or poverty ratios are very high in parts of rural India. However, this is expenditure or income poverty and poverty has broader dimensions too, such as access to health and education. These are captured in the MDGs. There is also a multidimensional poverty index (MDPI), devised by the Oxford Poverty and Human Development Initiative.[53]

51. Ibid.

52. NCEUS (2008). *Skill Formation and Employment Assurance in the Unorganised Sector*. August.

53. *www.ophi.org.uk*

There are different ways to look at the economic geography of a country, depending on the administrative division one has in mind. State administrative boundaries are natural dividing lines to use. Academic work and popular impression have often used the BIMARU (Bihar, Madhya Pradesh, Rajasthan, Uttar Pradesh) nomenclature, with a pun on the word *bimar*, meaning ill or sick. While this is still useful as a starting-off point, the states of Bihar, Madhya Pradesh and Uttar Pradesh have now been sub-divided and Orissa is often worse than some of these four traditional BIMARU states. BIMARU thus becomes BIMAROU, not to speak of deprivation, according to some indicators, in Jammu & Kashmir and the northeast. Although undivided Madhya Pradesh and Rajasthan are no longer as deprived and backward as Bihar and the eastern parts of Uttar Pradesh, and Uttarakhand is better off than Uttar Pradesh, many of these traditionally backward areas tend to be concentrated in the north. In understanding India's development, especially after the 1991 reforms, one thus tends to often use a north-south framework. Two simple explanations are often used to explain this phenomenon. First, in the pre-1991 era, when licensing and proximity to the Centre that granted licences was important, the north performed relatively better. With licensing having disappeared, at least for manufacturing, this relative advantage has vanished and the south has come into its own. Second, given the inadequacy of internal transport infrastructure, coastal regions, where this inadequacy is less manifest, tend to flourish. While both these arguments have a grain of truth, and property rights that govern land are also important, this north-south dichotomy is a trifle too simplistic, as is the east-west dichotomy, with a dividing line vertically drawn between Kanpur and Chennai, regions to the West of this line performing better than regions to the right. Indeed, the use of state boundaries to facilitate our understanding is itself somewhat flawed, since development and deprivation do not follow such administrative distinctions. However, there is an in-built bias in favour of using states, since data problems are easier to handle then. Data problems become more difficult to overcome if one thinks of India's regions, or even districts and villages. Having said this, whether one uses poverty ratios, MDG-type indicators or MDPI, the human development issues are especially concentrated in some states and within specific regions in these states. For instance, 99 per cent of households in Punjab have electricity connections, while the figure for Bihar is 22 per cent. 39.9 per cent of Orissa's population is below the poverty line, while the figure is 4.2 per cent in Jammu and Kashmir. 72.6 per cent of Himachal Pradesh's households possess television sets, while the figure is 18.2 per cent in Bihar. And so on. Most backward districts, identified by any criterion, are geographically contiguous and are also associated with violent movements. If one considers these backward districts, one notices that these are generally concentrated in Central India, extending eastwards, and going all the way up to the northeast, thus reinforcing the earlier impression. India cannot prosper if significant sections of India continue to be bypassed and marginalised. The Institute for Conflict Management has a map of conflict in South Asia, through its South Asia Terrorism Portal.[54] This map shows an obvious correlation between deprived districts and intensity of terrorism or violence, at least at the all-India level. Apart from Jammu and Kashmir, which belongs to a special category, this correlation is obvious for the central parts of India, extending eastwards.

The policy issue can be stated in the following way. For those who are able-bodied, there can be institutional constraints in accessing market-based opportunities. These can be in the form of inadequate access to health, education, skills, technology, information, financial products, land, physical infrastructure (roads, electricity, water) and law and order. Are all these necessarily public goods, in the classic sense? Beyond law and order, it is not obvious that these are public goods. They are often collective private goods. As a follow-up question, are there demonstrated instances of market failure in these segments? One must remember that thanks to possibilities of unbundling and advent of technology, what used to be regarded as an example of market failure in the 1950s is no longer pertinent. Therefore, there are possibilities of private sector provisioning, even if this is backed by public sector financing. Hence, have entry regulations been sufficiently relaxed for private sector entry? To the extent that there are market failures and public sector provisioning is important, how does one improve the efficiency of public expenditure? Other than this, there is the question of direct anti-poverty measures through

54. *http://www.satp.org/satporgtp/icm/index.html*

subsidies. Food, petroleum products, fertilisers, roads and power are instances. However, poverty is an individual characteristic. By equating it with collective categories like gender, caste, religion and ethnicity, one makes a double mistake. There is an error of commission, through including non-poor, simply because they are members of that particular category. There is also an error of omission, through non-including poor, simply because they are not members of that particular collective category. It is because this problem hasn't been addressed head on that there continue to be controversies about identification of below the poverty line (BPL) households, though since the Ninth Plan, and more so since the Tenth Plan, the Planning Commission has been advocating decentralised and household-based identification of BPL. The unique national identity numbers (Aadhaar) may make it easier to eliminate multiplicity. But *per se*, they don't solve the policy question.

Unorganised *versus* organised—The Indian labour market is segmented. In a recent study, the World Bank stated, 'Of the 413 million prime-aged persons in the Indian labour force in 2004-05, the overwhelming majority, about 90 per cent, are employed in low productivity informal sector jobs.'[55] The reference is to 2004-05, the 61st round of National Sample Survey (NSS), because NSS large samples are held at infrequent intervals, with an average gap of five years in between. The results of the next large sample (66th Round, 2009-10) have not been completely released. Consequently, most data-based work is still based on 2004-05 numbers. The National Commission for Enterprises in the Unorganised Sector (NCEUS) was set up in 2004 and one of its reports had a very good discussion of definitional and statistical issues in analysing India's informal economy.[56] For our purposes, let us use the terms organised and formal synonymously, just as the terms unorganised and informal are used synonymously. In contrast with developed economies, and also in contrast with several developing economies, a large chunk of employment occurs in the rural sector. In 2004-05, India's labour force was

55. World Bank (2010). *India's Employment Challenge, Creating Jobs, Helping Workers*. The World Bank and Oxford University Press.

56. NCEUS (2007). *Report on Conditions of Work and Promotion of Livelihoods in the Unorganised Sector*, *http://nceuis.nic.in/Condition_of_workers_sep_2007.pdf*

420 million. The workforce was 385 million.[57] Thirty-five million were therefore unemployed, though it is impossible to figure out whether they were unemployed voluntarily or involuntarily. Out of the labour force of 420 million, 303 million were in rural India and 116 million were in urban India.[58] Out of the workforce of 385 million, 278 million were in rural India and 107 million were in urban India. Out of the rural labour force of roughly 300 million, 72.7 per cent earned a living from agriculture.[59] But some comments are in order about such figures. First, these refer to usual principal and subsidiary status, implying that there may be a secondary occupation outside agriculture. Indeed, with the seasonal nature of the bulk of India's agriculture, that is invariably the case. Second, there are variations across states. Third, the pace of decline, as opposite to the base figures, also varies quite a lot across states. Fourth, there are gender differences. The farm to non-farm transition happens first for males and a feminisation of the agricultural workforce occurs. Fifth, out of those who are in agriculture, roughly two-thirds (64%) describe themselves as self-employed, that is, they are farmers. The remaining roughly one-third (36%) are wage workers, almost invariably on casual basis. There are labour market issues connected with transforming low productivity and subsistence-level agriculture and creating off-farm employment opportunities. We will turn to that later.

Outside of agriculture, informality can be defined in one of three different ways. First, there is a definition in terms of exemptions from paying indirect taxes. Second, there is a definition in terms of small-scale industry (SSI), which again is defined in terms of threshold levels of investment in plant and machinery. Third, there is a definition in terms of labour laws. That is, an enterprise is unorganised if it uses power and employs fewer than 10 people or does not use power and employs fewer

57. There are statistical issues we are glossing over. The working age is defined as between 15 and 59 years, though a little over one million children are also estimated to be in the labour force/workforce and the figures given include this child labour component. Employment is defined in one of three different ways: usually employed, principal and subsidiary status (UPSS), weekly status (WS) and current daily status (CDS). The first is over a 365-day period. The cited figures are for CDS. For UPSS in the same year, the labour force was 471 million and the workforce was 460 million.

58. The numbers don't add up because of rounding approximations.

59. NCEUS, Ibid.

than 20 people.[60] The last definition is the one that is used most often and according to this, in 2004-05, 92.4 per cent of employment was in the unorganised sector.[61] That 92.4 per cent of the labour force employed in the unorganised sector has no labour rights worth the name. Protective legislation is absent, be it in the form of safety, minimum wages or social security. Another important point should be flagged. Unorganised labour (wage labour without contracts) can also exist within the organised sector. The aforementioned NCEUS report estimated that there were 52.9 million wage workers in the unorganised sector (excluding agriculture). However, if one includes unorganised or informal sector workers within the organised sector, the number increases to 76.7 million.[62] This is a figure for wage employment, excluding self-employment. While the standard definition of organised/formal is in terms of labour laws, with unorganised/informal being defined as a residual category, it must be remembered that all informal non-agricultural employment isn't based on an employer-employee relationship. Other than wage employment, there is self-employment too. An ILO study found that between 50 and 75 per cent of non-agricultural employment in the developing world is informal.[63] Informal employment includes both self-employment in informal (small and unregistered) enterprises and wage employment in informal jobs (without labour contracts, worker benefits and protection). The figure is higher for India. Subject to data problems, 83 per cent of India's non-agricultural employment was estimated by ILO to be informal.[64] Self-employment constituted 52 per cent of non-agricultural informal employment.

The segmented and heterogeneous labour market thus represents a dichotomy. Labour laws create rigidities in the organised segment, while minimal labour rights are non-existent in the unorganised segment. To the extent that the labour rights exist *de jure*, they are not enforced *de facto*. Reforms should break down this segmentation and bring the two kinds of

60. Strictly speaking, this is a Factories Act definition.

61. One should also mention that more than two-thirds of the employment in the organised sector was in the public sector.

62. NCEUS, Ibid.

63. ILO (2002). *Women and Men in the Informal Economy: A Statistical Picture*. Geneva.

64. Ibid.

markets closer to one another. In the reform discourse on labour markets, one also witnesses what is a bit like a dichotomy. There is one line of argument that focusses on lack of rights in the unorganised sector, NCEUS being a case in instance. This is also true of UN documents, such as Human Development Reports (HDRs).

A digression on self-employment is necessary. In 2004-05, 56.5 per cent of the workforce reported itself as being self-employed. In the non-agricultural workforce, 62.8 per cent of workers reported themselves as self-employed.[65] There are also wide interstate variations. For instance, more than 65 per cent of non-agricultural workers reported themselves as self-employed in Andhra Pradesh (65.2%), Assam (65.6%), Bihar (80.8%), Jammu and Kashmir (73.7%), Madhya Pradesh (65.5%), Orissa (70.3%), Uttar Pradesh (68.1%), West Bengal (68.2%) and Uttarakhand (67.2%). In contrast, the figure was lower than 50 per cent in Himachal Pradesh (48.4%) and Kerala (47.9%). The higher the degree of self-employment, the lower seems to be the prosperity of the state. This suggests that self-employment is not a viable occupational category at all. It is a subsistence-level occupation because people cannot afford to remain unemployed. Outside of agriculture, the total self-employed population was 92.1 million. Some of these were in relatively high income occupations, like independent professionals (doctors, lawyers, artists, accountants), shop owners in urban areas, rice-mill owners, workshop owners, commission agents, real estate and housing brokers and owners of small hotels and restaurants. But others were in relatively low income occupations, like handloom weavers (mostly women), *chikan* workers (mostly women), street vendors, food processors, rickshaw pullers, rag-pickers, *beedi* rollers (mostly working out of home), *agarbatti* makers (mostly women), potters and bamboo product makers.[66] The self-employment category is extremely heterogeneous. But some of the self-employed workers in the relatively low income categories would be better off in wage employment, were that to be possible.

Typically, own account enterprises aren't registered. In 2004-05, 84.9 per cent of own account enterprises were not registered and this needs to be flagged, because registration also brings attendant benefits, such as access

---

66. More accurately, they reported themselves as own account workers.

66. NCEUS, Ibid.

to credit or government subsidies on marketing and technology. Why aren't own account enterprises registered? The answer isn't entirely lack of information. Opting out of registration is probably a conscious decision, because the benefits from registration are not commensurate with the costs. Not only are procedures connected with registration complicated and tiresome, registration brings with it the attendant problem of bribery and rent-seeking from the government machinery. For instance, for rickshaw pullers and street vendors, studies in many parts of urban India have documented harassment and bribery by municipal authorities and police.[67] The non-registration issue spills over into the existence of the unorganised sector in general. It is often presumed that rigid labour laws in the organised sector encourage informality. But this is a partial explanation. There are other reasons behind informality—avoidance of taxes, complicated transaction costs associated with registration, rent-seeking and few perceived benefits from formalisation. The last SSI Census was held in 2001 and found that 16.89 per cent of unregistered units were in Uttar Pradesh, with a large number of unregistered SSI units in Andhra Pradesh, West Bengal, Maharashtra, Madhya Pradesh, Tamil Nadu, Karnataka, Bihar, Rajasthan and Gujarat too. When asked about the reasons for non-registration, 53.13 per cent said that they weren't aware of the provisions, while another 39.8 per cent said that they 'were not interested'.[68]

Turning now to the organised labour market, there are several cross-country governance surveys that explicitly seek to measure and gauge the nature of the labour market and flag the Indian rigidity. This is not to deny that there are problems with such governance surveys.[69] Some of these problems are the following. First, some indicators depend on *de jure* international commitments made by countries and these may have no relation with what actually obtains *de facto*. These are indicators based on ratification of standards, codes or treaties, but monitoring implementation is close to impossible, the point made earlier. Second, measurement should be based on tangible improvements in outcomes or performance. However,

67. Manushi's work is but one example. See, Kishwar, Madhu Purnima (2005). *Deepening Democracy, Challenges of Governance and Globalisation in India*. Oxford University Press.

68. *http://dcmsme.gov.in/ssiindia/census/highlights.htm*

69. See Sudders, M. and J. Nahem (2004). *Governance Indicators: A Users' Guide*. Oslo: UNDP, for a comprehensive discussion.

governance is a process and quite apart from the problem of differing perceptions about what should be included and what should be excluded, objective data are impossible to obtain. Hence, one relies on subjective responses to questionnaires administered to respondents. Having said this, what are the various surveys that seek to rank the Indian labour market? The first one to be mentioned should be the Fraser Institute's *Economic Freedom of the World* (EFW). The structure of the EFW index involves aggregation across five heads of: (1) size of government (expenditure, taxes and enterprises); (2) legal structure and security of property rights; (3) access to sound money; (4) freedom to trade internationally and (5) regulation of credit, labour and business. Given the focus on labour market reforms, what is of interest is the fifth head, especially labour market regulations and the variables included in this sub-head encompass minimum wages, hiring and firing regulations, centralised collective bargaining, mandated costs of hiring and mandated costs of worker dismissal. In the 2010 rankings, the Indian score was 7.9.[70] What is of greater interest is the intertemporal movement. While India's labour market score has improved over time, it continues to be low for hiring and firing regulations and mandated cost of worker dismissal. Heritage Foundation and Wall Street Journal's Index of Economic Freedom is almost a parallel exercise to EFW and is based on ten broad factors of economic freedom. One of these is labour freedom, interpreted as government restrictions on wages, hours of work and so on. Under this head, in the 2011 rankings, India scored 67.2. While there has been improvement over time, 'The non-salary cost of employing a worker is moderate, but dismissing an employee is costly.'[71] There is also the World Bank's 'doing business' set of indicators, now ranked across 183 economies. One of these is on employing workers and focusses on problems associated with redundancy.[72] The simple point thus is that there is a focus on firing problems.

---

70. *http://www.freetheworld.com/2010/reports/world/EFW2010_BOOK.pdf.* The higher the number, the better, the maximum score being 10.

71. *http://www.heritage.org/Index/Country/India#labor-freedom*

72. *http://www.doingbusiness.org/data/exploreeconomies/india/employing-workers/*

The official *Economic Survey* is often interpreted as setting out the government's reform agenda. Barring one instance, *Economic Survey* has rarely been forthright about the labour market reform agenda, though it has often been mentioned in passing. Consequently, this section, from *Economic Survey, 2005-06*, deserves to be quoted at length.[73] 'Indian labour market is characterised by a sharp dichotomy. A large number of establishments in the unorganised sector remain outside any regulation, while the organised sector has been regulated fairly stringently. It can be reasonably argued that the organised sector has provided too much of job-security for too long, while the unorganised sector has provided too little to too many. Various studies indicate that Indian labour laws are highly protective of labour, and labour markets are relatively inflexible. These laws apply only to the organised sector. Consequently, these laws have restricted labour mobility, have led to capital-intensive methods in the organised sector and adversely affected the sector's long-run demand for labour. Labour being a subject in the concurrent list, State-level labour regulations are also an important determinant of industrial performance. Evidence suggests that States, which have enacted more pro-worker regulations, have lost out on industrial production in general. Perhaps there are lessons to be learnt from China in the area of labour reforms. China, with a history of extreme employment security, has drastically reformed its labour relations and created a new labour market, in which workers are highly mobile. Although there have been mass layoffs and open unemployment, high rates of industrial growth especially in the coastal regions helped their redeployment. In spite of hardship, workers in China seem to have benefited from wage growth, additional job creation and new opportunities for self employment.'

The intention is not to get into a detailed discussion of labour laws. As has been mentioned, labour laws are not the only reason behind informality. In the process of transition, India must encourage informal to become formal and self-employment to move to more productive wage employment.

The farm to non-farm transition: A comment was earlier made about labour movements from the agriculture to non-agricultural sectors. This

73. *Economic Survey 2005-06*, Department of Economic Affairs and Ministry of Finance, Chapter 10.

involves commercialisation and diversification of agriculture, as well as the creation of off-farm employment opportunities. Hence, there is an agricultural reform agenda and there is a rural reform agenda that goes beyond agriculture. Within the agriculture set, there are issues like allowing corporate sector involvement in agriculture, removal of government imposed restrictions on production, marketing and distribution,[74] refocus of public expenditure away from input subsidies to infrastructure[75] and extension services,[76] disintermediation of distribution chains, forward markets, contract farming, revamping credit and insurance, and freeing up of land markets.[77] All these are linked to encouraging commercialisation and diversification. There is also an issue of encouraging off-farm employment and this is where rural sector reforms kick in, through provision of physical and social infrastructure.

Governance: Governance has become a bit of a buzzword and there are quite a few cross-country governance surveys. As has been mentioned, there are problems with these surveys that one tends to gloss over. The point is not to denigrate the use of governance surveys. After all, one is trying to capture something that is difficult to measure. However, most governance surveys tend to gloss over these problems and suggest robustness in governance estimation that simply does not exist. Having said this, the most commonly cited governance surveys are: (1) Transparency International's[78] Corruption Perceptions Index; (2) The World Bank Institute's Governance Matters set of indicators,[79] with governance measured under six aggregate heads or clusters—voice and accountability, political stability and absence of violence, government effectiveness, regulatory quality, rule of law and corruption; (3) World Economic Forum's

74. For instance, the Agricultural Produce Marketing and Control (APMC) Acts and orders under the Essential Commodities Act.

75. Plus decentralisation in the management of rural infrastructure.

76. There is also a research and development agenda, but it is not necessarily obvious why this has to be public sector-driven. Extension services will have to be largely public sector-driven.

77. There are two distinct issues of ownership laws and tenancy laws here. The former is contentious, the latter less so.

78. *www.transparency.org/surveys*

79. *www.worldbank.org/wbi/governance*

Growth Competitiveness Index,[80] based on three components of economic growth—a technology index, a public institutions index and a macroeconomic environment index; (4) Heritage Foundation and Wall Street Journal's Index of Economic Freedom,[81] based on 10 broad factors of economic freedom—trade policy, fiscal burden of government, government intervention in the economy, monetary policy, capital flows and foreign investment, banking and finance, wages and prices, property rights, regulation and informal market activity; (5) Fraser Institute's Economic Freedom of the World,[82] based on five heads of size of government, legal structure and security of property rights, access to sound money, freedom to trade internationally and regulation of credit, labour and business and (6) The World Bank's 'doing business' indicators,[83] based on starting a business, dealing with construction permits, employing workers, registering property, getting credit, protecting investors, paying taxes, trading across borders, enforcing contracts and closing a business. This is by no means a comprehensive list of all governance surveys, but these are certainly the more important ones. There is subjectivity in each of these surveys, on responses to questionnaires, attaching weights, converting ordinal ranks into cardinal scores and methods of aggregation. Consequently, not too much weight need be attached to any particular survey. However, taken together, the surveys do show robustness and underline institutional problems in India.

If one distils out the essence of these governance surveys, one finds that one is fundamentally talking about law reform, including reform of administrative law. Quite often, the more important problem is about procedures, not about law, legislation or policy *per se*. This is the broad area of administrative law reform and if India doesn't perform well on 'doing business'-type indicators, this is because of these procedural problems, also important for labour law. Administrative law means the subordinate legislation in the form of rules, regulations, orders and instructions from ministries and government departments and these can be at state level, as well as Central. Often, constraints to efficient decision-

80. *www.weforum.org*

81. *www.heritage.org/research*

82. *www.freetheworld.com*

83. *http://www.doingbusiness.org*

making come about through administrative law, rather than through statutory law and discretion, bribery and rent-seeking are fallouts. Unfortunately, administrative law is not readily available and this is especially true at state level. Administrative law reforms are often interpreted as civil service reforms, although they should be much more than civil service reform. The broader agenda of administrative law reform involves two kinds of relationships that can overlap—dealings between the citizen and the government and dealings between an enterprise and the government. The latter can again be divided into three phases of an enterprise's existence—entry, functioning and exit. On the entrepreneurial side, countervailing pressure, highlighting constraints to efficient decision-making through discretionary subordinate legislation, have been highlighted in reports brought out by larger chambers of commerce and industry like FICCI, CII and ASSOCHAM.[84] But one should not form the impression that big business alone is the issue. Since transaction costs have economies of scale and scope, they have a distributional angle and hurt the small entrepreneur more. In 2000, the Prime Minister's Council on Trade and Industry also submitted a report on administrative and legal simplifications.[85] Understandably, this had an industry focus and listed the following as industry concerns. 'Large number of clearances/permissions required; complex regulation governing day to day functioning; multiple agencies regulating operations functioning independently; lack of co-ordination between various governing agencies; frequent changes in policies/procedures/tariff structures; unpredictability of changes; lack of clarity on issues between Centre and states; transaction oriented approach of the system instead of a corporate approach, leading to increased costs and delays; lack of openness and transparency in communication and providing information.' It is not that procedures have not improved anywhere, but the success greatly varies from state to state.

One should add to that the problem of legal reform, including dispute resolution. Within statutory law reform, there are issues of rationalisation and harmonisation across statutes that have been enacted at various points

84. Many such studies suggest that transaction costs add around 20 per cent to costs of doing business. However, these studies also tend to include infrastructure costs in transaction costs. That is, transaction costs are not procedural costs alone.

85. This was chaired by Kumar Mangalam Birla.

in time, eliminating old laws that serve no purpose, junking unnecessary state intervention in many of these statutes and even introducing new legislation where none exists. On faster dispute resolution, a new Arbitration Act has been in place since 1996, but conciliation/mediation is still not credible. Within the court system, there is an estimated backlog of 38 million cases stuck in courts, not including those that are stuck in quasi-judicial forums. There have been faster clearances in the Supreme Court, but not yet in High Courts and Lower Courts, with understandable variations across states. About two-thirds of pending cases are criminal ones. With amendments to the Civil Procedure Code in 2001 and 2002, dispute resolution should become faster for civil cases and there is some evidence of this having happened. But this is not yet true of criminal law.

Urbanisation: Globally, economic development has been correlated with urbanisation. The 2001 Census showed that 74.27 per cent of India's population lives in rural India, while 25.73 per cent lives in urban India. There are 384 urban agglomerations, 5,161 towns, 27 million-plus cities and 35 million-plus urban agglomerations. An urban agglomeration is a continuous urban spread with a city, and its adjoining urban growth. There are some areas that are classified as towns in a statutory way, in the sense that a municipality, corporation, cantonment board or notified town area committee exists. More generally, the Census defines 'urban' as an area with a minimum population of 5,000, with at least 75 per cent of the male working-age population engaged in non-agricultural pursuits and a population density of at least 400 per sq km. More to the point, there are 638,365 villages, some of which are uninhabited. More relevant is the number of inhabited villages in 2001, at 593,643. Should one plan for people to stay in rural India or should one plan for an urban India, remembering that urbanisation is slower in India than in many parts of the developing world? Not only is urbanisation lower in India than in developed countries, and even in several developing countries, it has also slowed over the decades. For instance, between 1971 and 1981, the annual average rate of urbanisation was 3.79 per cent, but declined to 3.09 per cent between 1981 and 1991 and to 2.73 per cent between 1991 and 2001.[86] There are several reasons why villages disappear. Thanks to migration and

86. There was an earlier period of decline between 1951 and 1961, but that was because some towns were declassified.

improved connectivity, some disappear. Others become mainstreamed into urban agglomerations. Still others are reclassified as urban as development proceeds. All these are desirable developments. The average population in an Indian village is 1,161 and this doesn't make the village viable, to provide physical or social infrastructure. 91,555 of India's villages have population sizes less than 200 and 12,644 of them are in Orissa, with other large numbers in Himachal Pradesh, Uttarakhand, Rajasthan, Uttar Pradesh, Jharkhand and Madhya Pradesh. Another 127,515 of villages have population sizes less than 499; 14,806 have population sizes more than 5,000 and 3,962 have population sizes more than 10,000. The idea is not to have a quota on the number of villages. Instead, the argument is that if urban planning is properly undertaken, more than 200,000 of India's villages will disappear, as they should, and there will be larger villages or towns with populations upwards of 10,000 and approaching and even crossing 100,000.

There are three kinds of resistance articulated against this rural to urban transition. The first is a sentimental kind of association with some notion of a rural Arcadia. It is also worth mentioning that several studies have documented the pro-urban bias in subsidy delivery systems. The second kind of argument is based on the premise that with this transition, India will no longer be able to feed its increasing population. This fails to appreciate the low productivity levels Indian agriculture possesses, not only in comparisons with the rest of the world, but also in comparisons between India's irrigated and non-irrigated areas, with irrigation having so far benefitted only 45 per cent of the cultivated area. If required agricultural reforms are introduced, India will have no problems in feeding double its present population. The third argument is directed against the kind of urban life that is delivered, with pressures on urban infrastructure like water supply, sewage clearance and drainage, waste disposal, transportation, power, housing, law and order and environmental pollution issues. After all, the slum population in 2001 was estimated to be 61.82 million, with 640 towns reporting slum populations.[87] This is less an argument against urbanisation and is more of an argument against the kind of urbanisation that has taken place. 68.9 per cent of the urban

87. Census 2001 figures.

population is in Category I cities and 37 per cent of the urban population lives in the 35 million-plus cities. Indeed, urbanisation has been occurring in these mega cities.[88] The point is that both push and pull factors are distorted. They are distorted in terms of preventing urbanisation and creating disincentives against rural to urban migration. And they are also distorted in terms of creating the wrong kind of urbanisation.

If these policy-induced distortions are removed, the right kind of rural to urban transition will occur. For instance, state government policies prevent creation of rural land markets and work against acquisition of agricultural land and its conversion to non-agricultural usage. Understandably, this is linked to issues of compensation, resettlement and rehabilitation and devising alternative rural or urban livelihoods, a controversy witnessed in recent SEZ (special economic zone) and non-SEZ debates. States are reluctant to notify rural settlements as towns, because many subsidies and grants from the Centre are geared towards retaining rural status. Urban land markets are also distorted through state intervention. Most land is publicly owned and does not come on to the market. This creates artificial shortages and housing and real estate shortages are compounded by dysfunctional building (and tenancy) laws. For instance, even for the slums, it is possible to unbundle ownership and create rights for the poor, so that incentives are created for improvement, including loans and the offering of collateral. Urbanisation should also lead to formalisation and employment in the organised sector.

Infrastructure: Infrastructure means several different things and there can be no quarrel with the proposition that inadequate infrastructure holds up Indian GDP growth. As a generalisation, the infrastructure area where there have been visible improvements is telecom, with roads perhaps following as a somewhat distant second. The contours of unbundling, user charges and regulatory agencies are known. The issue is simply one of getting infrastructure reforms implemented and some areas of physical infrastructure are state subjects. The issues are twofold. First, given scarce government resources, where are these best deployed? Second, again given

88. One should recognise that there is a reclassification effect here too. But this only explains part of the phenomenon. Indian censuses classify urban areas by size class of towns: I (more than 100,000), II (50,000 to 100,000), III (20,000 to 50,000), IV (10,000 to 20,000), V (5,000 to 10,000) and VI (less than 5,000).

scarce government resources, what is the scope for private sector involvement? The Eleventh Plan document states, 'Good quality infrastructure is the most critical physical requirement for attaining faster growth in a competitive world and also for ensuring investment in backward regions. This includes all-weather roads; round-the clock availability of power at a stable voltage and frequency; water for irrigation; railways that are not overcrowded, which run on time and do not overcharge for freight; ports with low turnaround time to reduce costs of imports and exports; airports to handle the growing traffic; air services that provide connectivity to all parts of the country; and telecommunications and broadband connectivity to provide the benefits of the Internet to people all over the country.'[89] It is impossible to disagree with this objective, or with the intention of increasing investment on infrastructure from 5.43 per cent of GDP in 2006-07 to 9.34 per cent in 2011-12, a target that is certain to be missed.

In 1994, the World Bank's *World Development Report* (WDR) had the theme of infrastructure for development.[90] Later WDRs have also tangentially touched upon the subject. A few pointers from the 1994 WDR are useful. First, economic infrastructure includes public utilities (power, telecommunications, piped water supply, sanitation, sewerage, solid waste collection and disposal, piped gas), public works (roads, dams, canals) and other transport (urban transport, railways, ports, waterways, airports), what economists often refer to as social overhead capital. Economic infrastructure and social overhead capital are both umbrella terms and share technical features (like economies of scale) and externalities (spillovers from users to non-users). Second, because of natural monopolies and market failures, one has often tended to assume that infrastructure is a public good and must be provided by the public sector. That's no longer necessarily true and there are opportunities for unbundling, facilitated by advances in technology. Second, using cross-country estimates, a one per cent increase in the stock of infrastructure is associated with a one per cent increase in GDP. Third, 'Major investments have been made in infrastructure stocks, but in too many developing countries these assets are

89. Vol. I, Ibid.

90. *World Development Report 1994*, Infrastructure for Development, World Bank and Oxford University Press, 1994.

not generating the quantity or the quality of services demanded...The causes of past poor performance, and the source of improved performance, lies in the incentives facing producers. Fourth, even among the poor, there is a willingness to pay higher user charges, provided that quality of service is ensured. Fifth, efficiency can increase through private sector involvement in management, financing and ownership. 'Competition can be introduced directly, by liberalising entry into activities that have no technological barriers, and indirectly, through competitive bidding for the right to provide exclusive service where natural monopoly conditions exist and by liberalising the supply of service substitutes.' In addition, though WDR did not mention it directly, there are competition policy instruments, such as through the Competition Commission of India (CCI). Sixth, even when there are privatisation options, the government will have a role in financing and regulation.

The *World Development Report* suggests that one per cent increase in infrastructure stock can increase GDP by one per cent. The Indian figures that float around are higher. For instance, the National Manufacturing Competitiveness Council formulated a National Strategy for Manufacturing, where it argued that adequate infrastructure can improve GDP growth by a factor of 1.5 per cent, with 1 per cent accounted for by the power sector alone. That National Strategy said the following: 'Among infrastructure sub-sectors there has been visible improvement in telecom, with roads sector following as a somewhat distant second. The contours of unbundling, user charges and regulatory agencies are known and the issue is simply one of getting infrastructure reforms implemented to stimulate private sector investments and public sector viability. From the manufacturing perspective, perhaps the most important infrastructure areas where reforms are to be speeded up are power, ports and railways, followed by roads...It is estimated that power shortage alone contributed to a production loss of at least one per cent of GDP.'[91] In some recent speeches, the Finance Minister has jacked up incremental GDP estimates from 1.5 per cent to 2 per cent. That thus, is the opportunity cost of lost GDP growth.

---

91. National Strategy for Manufacturing, National Manufacturing Competitiveness Council, March 2006.

Other than telecom, why has infrastructure development flagged? The Planning Commission identifies part of the problem as the following. 'In a federal country like India, participation and support of the State Governments is essential for development of world class infrastructure. The State Governments' support in maintenance of law and order, land acquisition, rehabilitation and settlement of displaced persons, shifting of utilities and obtaining environmental clearances is necessary for the projects undertaken by the Central Government or the private sector.'[92] Land and environment are major issues and there are several other issues that have often been discussed in detail.[93] But let us also mention a few other points that are often not talked about. 'However, structural and regulatory barriers that impede the flow of domestic capital into infrastructure—asset liability mismatch and exposure limit issues for banks; the high pre-emption of funds from the banking system; investment restrictions on long-term savings mobilisers, namely insurance, pension and provident funds; the shallowness of the bond market; and constrained supply of External Commercial Borrowings (ECB)—will hamper funding to the sector. Further, the global economic slowdown and rising interest rates make project funding for infrastructure more expensive and financial closure more difficult.'[94] 'India does not compare favourably with other countries in executing projects. Data from government and industry suggest that on average, each project suffers from 20 to 25 per cent time and cost over-runs, while in some sectors this is as high as over 50 per cent...Indian providers (engineering, procurement and construction or EP&C companies) often fail to tap significant opportunities to reduce time and cost.'[95] This report flags items that are often not recognised. Quality of planning and engineering design is poor. It is common to tender unviable

---

92. Ibid.

93. See, for example, *India Infrastructure Report 2008*, Business Models of the Future, Infrastructure Development Finance Company, Indian Institute of Management (Ahmedabad), Indian Institute of Technology (Kanpur) and Oxford University Press, 2008.

94. *Building India, Financing and Investing in Infrastructure*, McKinsey and Company, *http://www.mckinsey.com/locations/india/mckinseyonindia/pdf/Building_India_Executive_Summary_web.pdf*

95. *Building India, Accelerating Infrastructure Projects*, McKinsey and Company, *http://www.mckinsey.com/locations/india/mckinseyonindia/pdf/Building_India_Executive_Summary_Media_120809.pdf*

PPP projects. Inappropriate contracts are used. The pre-tendering approval process is centralised and slow. Dispute resolution processes are ineffective. Performance management is weak. There is insufficient availability of skilled and semi-skilled manpower. There are weak risk management skills. Design and engineering skills are below par. Procurement practices are not the best. Lean construction practices are not used.

One should also recognise that India is a large and heterogeneous country and there are considerable differences among states and even within states. There have been attempts to compute infrastructure indices for states. For example, Finance Commissions have been concerned with vertical equity (Centre *versus* state issues) and also horizontal equity (allocations among states). Horizontal equity and horizontal transfers have been made a function of a state's backwardness and physical infrastructure is one of the indicators used in determining backwardness. Whenever such an infrastructure index is constructed, the values depend on the variables included, the weights attached to them and the aggregation formula. Consequently, different indices can show differing results. The Twelfth Finance Commission grouped states into five categories, on the basis of an infrastructure index constructed by IDFC.[96] Goa, Maharashtra and Punjab were 'high'; Gujarat, Haryana, Kerala and Tamil Nadu were 'high middle'; Andhra Pradesh and Karnataka were 'middle'; Himachal Pradesh, Madhya Pradesh, Orissa, Uttar Pradesh, Uttarakhand and West Bengal were 'lower middle' and Arunachal Pradesh, Manipur, Meghalaya, Jharkhand, Mizoram, Nagaland, Assam, Chhattisgarh, Sikkim, Tripura, Jammu & Kashmir, Bihar and Rajasthan were 'low'.

Taxation: This has both a direct and an indirect tax angle and the directions for reform are known, involving standardisation, harmonisation and removal of exemptions, with reduction in compliance costs.[97] There are still several exemptions, leading to distortions in resource allocation and varying the incidence across sectors. Without elimination of discretionary exemptions, it is also difficult to reduce collection,

96. *Report of the Twelfth Finance Commission (2005-2010)*, Ministry of Finance, November 2004.

97. Implementation of the Fiscal Responsibility and Budget Management Act, 2003, Report of the Task Force, July 2004, summarises both direct and indirect tax reform intentions succinctly.

enforcement and compliance costs. The broad shape of indirect tax reform is also clear. There should be a combined Goods and Services Tax (GST), with service sector taxation integrated into the VAT framework instead of being a tax on turnover. This will be accompanied by a withdrawal of all other taxes like central excise, Central sales tax, octroi, state-level sales tax, entry tax, stamp duties, transportation taxes and so on. The problems with the earlier indirect tax structure are known. First, the tax base is fragmented between Centre and states. Second, services are not taxed properly and not integrated into a VAT framework. Third, there are cascading effects and multi-point and multiple (tax on tax) taxation exist. Fourth, discretion and exemption lead to distortions in resource allocation and tax revenue is disproportionately dependent on a few items. Fifth, tax administration is also complicated and there is no harmonisation of classification and valuation. Sixth, tax rates varied from one state to another, leading to tax arbitrage and rate wars among states. A VAT, with unification of state-level sales tax, was introduced between 2003 and 2006, with most states coming on board from April 2005. Uttar Pradesh was the last state to switch in January 2008. But this was never a complete VAT. It was no more than unification of state-level sales tax and there were problems there too, since the rates varied from state to state. It is by no means obvious that the proposed unified GST will remove exemptions or whether it will lead to the elimination of all other indirect taxes. In similar vein, it is by no means obvious that the proposed Direct Taxes Code (DTC) will remove all exemptions. If one includes state-level taxes, the present tax/GDP ratio is 17 per cent. With the removal of all exemptions, direct as well as indirect, the tax/GDP ratio can increase to 23 per cent.

Efficiency in public expenditure: The question of efficiency in public expenditure has already been touched upon. Therefore, only a few minor points will suffice. This has a Centre, state and even local body aspect. Although the importance of each element is a function of the level of government that one has in mind, a substantial chunk of public expenditure is on interest payments, wages and salaries and pensions. In the short run, this expenditure is inflexible, although in the long run, one can borrow less, employ fewer people and enter into new pension arrangements with new entrants into the civil service. On reforming civil services in India, several recommendations have been made. The issues of downsizing, identifying surplus manpower, retraining, voluntary retirement schemes (VRS), contractual appointments, lateral entry and evaluation and vertical mobility keep recurring and the reform agenda is also known. However, they haven't been implemented. In addition to borrowing and expenditure on the administrative machinery of the government, public expenditure also includes public services. Such expenditure is never linked to tangible improvement in outcomes and administrative costs of delivery are extremely high. Other than changes in budgetary and accounting procedures, there are issues of transfers to states and devolution within states, scrapping discretionary transfers through the Planning Commission.

A few back-of-the-envelope kind of numbers should be flagged. Whatever be the baseline trend of GDP growth, adequate infrastructure services will provide an increment of 1.5 per cent to GDP, of which, 1 per cent is on account of the power sector alone. Legal reform can add another increment of 1 per cent. Improved morbidity, mortality, skills and higher work participation rates can add another 1.5 per cent. Satisfactory delivery of public services can add another increment of 1 per cent. This is in the realm of the potential.

Why do we want growth? That's a good question to ask. Growth of 9.5 per cent and more is not an end in itself. It is a means to an end. First, growth provides additional resources for public expenditure, be it for items that are public or collective private goods, or through direct anti-poverty programmes. If a government doesn't have the resources, how will it spend on such agenda items? Second, growth is correlated with improvements in human development outcomes. As examples, as per capita income increases, so do life expectancy and literacy and assorted other indicators. Infant mortality, gender disparities in access and assorted other indicators show improvements. There is no need to debate the causation right now. It is sufficient to know that there is correlation. So if per capita income goes up, Indians lead better lives. That is precisely what we want for India in 2025. That's precisely what we want the government to do, provide the enabling environment for growth and human development. Indians have plenty of enterprise. They exhibit it when they migrate to other countries. That is not the best solution. They should be able to exhibit enterprise and improve their lives within India.

This is a quote that the 9th Report of the Second Administrative Reforms Commission quoted approvingly, though it didn't include the last part.[98] 'Government control gives rise to fraud, suppression of Truth, intensification of the black market and artificial scarcity. Above all, it unmans the people and deprives them of initiative, it undoes the teaching of self-help...I look upon an increase in the power of the State with the greatest fear because, although while apparently doing good by minimising exploitation, it does the greatest harm to mankind by destroying individuality which lies at the heart of all progress.'[99] This was written by Mahatma Gandhi. The reforms were meant to reduce government control and scarcity and increase human initiative.

Let us now turn to the issue of poverty and inequality. Since 2004, there has been complete confusion about inequality and poverty and what should be done about either. If there is lack of conceptual clarity, is it at all surprising that there should be confusion about policies to address either?

Let us take poverty first. Poverty is a multidimensional concept. It is no one's case that a minimum level of income or consumption expenditure is the sole criterion for identifying someone as BPL or above the poverty line (APL). However, the use of income or consumption expenditure is customary, because it is easier to get data on income or consumption expenditure. It is not just in India, but also in other countries, that such concepts of a poverty line based on income or expenditure are used. India was one of the earliest countries in the world to formulate and adopt the concept of a poverty line, way back in the 1950s. The methodology has evolved over time, through the Planning Commission. But since the Alagh Committee of 1979, the methodology has been something like the following, and this was also endorsed by the Lakdawala Committee of 1993. Let us fix a per capita daily calorie requirement of 2,400 calories for rural India and a per capita daily calorie requirement of 2,100 calories for urban India. This immediately suggests that the poverty line was primarily dependent on food, though a little bit was thrown in for clothing. In the late 1950s, this made eminent sense, because it was expected that items like education and health were public goods and would be provided by the

98. *http://arc.gov.in/9threport/ARC_9thReport_preface_contents.pdf*

99. *http://www.gandhiserve.org/cwmg/VOL097.PDF*

government. Therefore, they need not figure in private consumption expenditure baskets. We now ask, what is the optimal consumption basket that will guarantee people 2,400 calories per capita per day in rural India and 2,100 calories in urban India? It is a different matter that people, including poor people, need not be 'rational' quite in that sense.[100] Having determined the optimal consumption basket, we next try to figure out how much that consumption basket is going to cost in different states, using state-level prices generated through assorted consumer price indices (CPI), separately for rural and urban India. This converts a calorie-based poverty line into an expenditure-based poverty line. But prices change over time. Therefore, those price indices are again used to adjust the expenditure-based poverty line over time.

Having done all that, one needs data. Data surface through surveys. And that means the NSSO. NSS doesn't collect data on incomes, because data on incomes are felt to be unreliable. NSS collects data on consumption expenditure. Unfortunately, NSS doesn't collect such data every year. More accurately, the larger a sample, the more accurate are the data. And NSS large samples surface roughly once every five years. We had such large surveys in 1983-84, 1987-88, 1993-94, 1999-2000, 2004-05 and 2009-10. In between, there are thin or small samples and these can't be relied on. The preliminary results of NSS 66th round of 2009-10 have begun to just trickle in, after having been held up for an inordinately long period of time. However, we still don't have poverty numbers based on that. The latest poverty numbers are still based on 2004-05. Two minor issues should be mentioned. First, as with any household survey, there is underestimation. That is, the aggregate of consumption expenditure collected through a survey like NSS falls short of aggregate consumption expenditure collected through national accounts, Central Statistical Organisation (CSO) in the Indian context. This is not a problem that is typical to India. It happens in every country where surveys are conducted. Second, there is a technical issue of the recall period connected with NSS surveys, namely, the period over which respondents are asked details about their expenditure. Figures are sensitive to the recall period used. However, let us gloss over that.

100. See Banerjee, Abhijit V. and Esther Duflo (2011). *Poor Economics, Rethinking Poverty and the Ways to End it*. Random House India. 'Most people living with less than 99 cents a day do not seem to act as if they are starving. If they were, surely they would put every available penny into buying more calories. But they do not.'

In 2004-05, the percentage of BPL in major states, using the old Planning Commission methodology, was like the first few columns in Table 10.3. The northeastern states and Puducherry have been excluded from the table, because they are quantitatively not that important. There can be immediate shock and outrage. 27.5 per cent of India's population is poor? Census 2011 shows an Indian population of 1.2 billion and 27.5 per cent of that is 330 million. 330 million Indians are poor? More than 60 years after Independence? That is more than the populations of most countries in the world. True, and the shock and outrage are legitimate. But consider this. There were NSS surveys in 1950-51 and 1977-78. In both those years, the BPL percentage, that is the poverty ratio, was roughly 50 per cent. Therefore, three decades of Fabian cum Soviet policy couldn't make much dent on poverty. Indian growth picked up from the late 1970s, picked up again in the 1990s and then picked up again from 2003. In each of these instances, shackles were eased through reforms and unleashed the growth potential and poverty ratios declined. Thus, the much-maligned trickle-down effect of growth on poverty does work. In general, though not always, rural poverty is higher than urban poverty. Therefore, poverty is fundamentally, though not invariably, a rural phenomenon. We can also see that poverty is concentrated in states like Bihar, Chhattisgarh, Jharkhand, Madhya Pradesh, Orissa, Uttar Pradesh and Uttarakhand. Therefore, policies need to address deprivation in these states. Clearly, they haven't been that successful yet.

The Planning Commission faced criticism because of these calorie-based norms. Apart from anything else, lifestyles have changed, even in rural India, and even among the poor. You no longer need 2,100 calories per capita per day in urban India and 2,400 calories per capita per day in rural India. For instance, with a switch to LPG for cooking, women no longer have to walk 10 kilometres to fetch firewood. Therefore, a Tendulkar Committee was appointed. If one sticks to the essentials and does not get into complicated details, this suggested moving away from calorie-based norms. That would ensure that one wasn't bogged down by food items alone. Instead, separately for rural and urban India, let us work out monetary figures on the amount of expenditure required, per person per day and let us recalculate poverty ratios. These numbers are shown in the last few columns of Table 10.3, labelled as new. Strictly speaking, the old and the new are not comparable. With some exceptions for individual states, the new increases the poverty ratios. We have learnt that India is poorer than we used to think. Beyond that, the numbers don't help us in determining policy.

Table 10.3

Percentage of BPL, 2004-05

	Rural (Old)	*Urban (Old)*	*Total (Old)*	*Rural (New)*	*Urban (New)*	*Total (New)*
Andhra Pradesh	11.2	28.0	15.8	32.3	23.4	29.9
Assam	22.3	3.3	17.6	36.4	21.8	34.4
Bihar	42.1	34.6	41.4	55.7	43.7	54.4
Chhattisgarh	40.8	41.2	40.9	55.1	28.4	49.4
Delhi	6.9	15.2	14.7	15.6	12.9	13.1
Goa	5.4	21.3	13.8	28.1	22.2	25.0
Gujarat	19.1	13.0	16.8	39.1	20.1	31.8
Haryana	13.6	15.1	14.0	24.8	22.4	24.1
Himachal Pradesh	10.7	3.4	10.0	25.0	4.6	22.9
Jammu & Kashmir	4.6	7.9	5.4	14.1	10.4	13.2
Jharkhand	46.3	20.2	40.3	51.6	23.8	45.3
Karnataka	20.8	32.6	25.0	37.5	25.9	33.4
Kerala	13.2	20.2	15.0	20.2	18.4	19.7
Madhya Pradesh	36.9	42.1	38.3	53.6	35.1	48.6
Maharashtra	29.6	32.2	30.7	47.9	25.6	33.4
Orissa	46.8	44.3	46.4	60.8	37.6	57.2
Punjab	9.1	7.1	8.4	22.1	18.7	20.9
Rajasthan	18.7	32.9	22.1	35.8	29.7	34.4
Tamil Nadu	22.8	22.2	22.5	37.5	19.7	28.9
Uttar Pradesh	33.4	30.6	32.8	42.7	34.1	40.9
Uttarakhand	40.8	36.5	39.6	35.1	26.2	32.7
West Bengal	28.6	14.8	24.7	38.2	24.4	34.3
India	28.3	25.7	27.5	41.8	25.7	37.2

To muddy waters further, UPA-I set up a National Commission for Enterprises in the Unorganised and Informal Sector (NCEUIS) in 2005 and produced a report in 2007.[101] This created a new poverty line of Rs 20 per

101. NCEUIS (2007). *Report on Conditions of Work and Promotion of Livelihoods in the Unorganised Sector*, *http://nceuis.nic.in/Condition_of_workers_sep_2007.pdf*

person per day and using the same data for 2004-05, estimated that 77 per cent of India's population was BPL and was poor and vulnerable.[102] This is yet another number and we are still unsure about policy.

As if the waters weren't sufficiently muddied already, internationally, poverty lines of US $1.25 per day and US $2.00 per day are used. These are at constant, 2005, prices. Until recently, the accepted poverty line used to be US $1 per day. As was mentioned earlier, all PPP transformations increase incomes in developing countries and reduce them in developed countries, in relative terms. That poverty line of US $1 per day was recalibrated to US $1.25 per day, on the argument that prices in countries like India and China used to be underestimated earlier, and these are relevant for PPP conversions. Accordingly, a survey was done and based on these new prices, the poverty line was increased upwards.[103] Perfectly understandably, poverty ratios in India and China increased as a result. The World Bank is normally quite forthcoming in parting with information. It is curious that no details are available about this survey. Apparently, the survey was undertaken by the Asian Development Bank (ADB). ADB is also normally quite forthcoming in parting with this information. But no details are available through ADB sources either. Such new poverty numbers didn't only mean that poverty ratios in India and China became higher. It also meant that when PPP conversions are used, India's (and China's) overall GDP became less. Was there an ulterior motive in reducing the PPP GDPs of these two countries? But let's leave that thought aside. Thirty-seven per cent of India's population lives on less than US $1.25 per day and 75.6 per cent of India's population lives on less than US $2.00 per day.[104]

Poverty isn't only about income or expenditure poverty. Nor is development only about this. That was part of the reason why the MDG

---

102. Rs 20 per person per day was higher than the then official poverty line of around Rs 12 per person per day. If the poverty line is jacked up, it shouldn't be very surprising that the number of poor also increase. Rs 20 per person per day corresponded to US $2 per person per day in PPP terms.

103. *http://iresearch.worldbank.org/PovcalNet/povDuplic.html*. Data are for 2005. Also see, Chen, Shaohua and Martin Ravallion (2008). "The Developing World is Poorer than We Thought, But No Less Successful in the Fight against Poverty", *Policy Research Working Paper*, World Bank, *http://econ.worldbank.org/docsearch*

104. *http://data.worldbank.org/indicator/SI.POV.DDAY/countries*

system evolved, with separate targets and indicators. In September 2000, the UN General Assembly agreed to a Millennium Declaration. What was interesting about this declaration, as opposed to several other UN declarations, was that some specific timelines were set out in a section on 'Development and Poverty Eradication'. In December 2000, the General Assembly asked the Secretary General to prepare a roadmap for implementing this declaration and by September 2001, such a roadmap was available. This not only involved the UN Secretariat and the UN system, but also the IMF, the World Bank and the OECD. Effectively, it is this document[105] that first set out what came to be accepted as the eight MDGs: (1) eradicate extreme poverty and hunger; (2) achieve universal primary education; (3) promote gender equality and empower women: (4) reduce child mortality: (5) improve maternal health; (6) combat HIV/AIDS, malaria, and other diseases; (7) ensure environmental sustainability and (8) develop a global partnership for development. At that stage, there were 18 targets and 48 indicators, with specific timelines for all but goal 8. However, three additional targets were added in 2005.[106] Nor have the indicators been cast in stone. As of now, there are 21 targets and 59 indicators. The MDG system thus means the 8 goals, plus the 21 targets, plus the 60 indicators. It is important to make this point because MDGs are usually thought of in terms of the goals, which are necessarily too general. 'Success' or 'failure' in attaining the MDGs is a function of the target or indicator used, more often the latter. There is an emphasis on the social sector in the MDG framework, understandable because the evolution of the MDG system drew on some earlier UN-sponsored conferences.[107] There is an emphasis both on pro-poor development and donor support. However, because Goal 8 focussed only on the donor side and not on the recipient side, there has been some resistance on the part of donors to accept Goal 8. Consequently, international resolutions usually use the

105. General Assembly document, A/56/326.

106. On reproductive health, access to HIV/AIDS treatment and loss of biodiversity. The target on employment was also redone at the same time.

107. Such as the 1990 Jomtien Conference on Education and the 1995 Copenhagen World Summit on Social Development.

expression 'the internationally agreed development goals, including the Millennium Development Goals', rather than MDGs alone.[108]

Having said this, what is relevant for present purposes is Goal (1), on eradicating extreme poverty and hunger. This has three targets: Target 1: halve, between 1990 and 2015, the proportion of people whose income is less than one dollar a day; Target 2: achieve full and productive employment and decent work for all, including women and young people; Target 3: halve, between 1990 and 2015, the proportion of people who suffer from hunger. And there are nine indicators: Indicator 1: proportion of population below $1 (PPP) per day; Indicator 2: poverty gap ratio; Indicator 3: share of poorest quintile in national consumption; Indicator 4: growth rate of GDP per person employed; Indicator 5: employment-to-population ratio; Indicator 6: proportion of employed people living below $1 (PPP) per day; Indicator 7: proportion of own account and contributing family workers in total employment; Indicator 8: prevalence of underweight children under five years of age; Indicator 9: proportion of population below minimum level of dietary energy consumption. Let us not digress too much on MDGs. However, a recent MDG report has been published.[109] This states, 'India has also[110] contributed to the large reduction in global poverty. In that country, poverty rates are projected to fall from 51 per cent in 1990 to about 22 per cent in 2015.' That is, on the poverty reduction target, India is on track. Why has this happened? We will come back to that question. Let's talk about the UNDP first.

Every year, United Nations Development Programme (UNDP) brings out a Human Development Report (HDR). Among other things, this has a Human Development Index (HDI). HDI is based on three indicators: education (literacy, gross enrollment ratio), health (life expectancy) and PPP per capita income. The higher the value of HDI, the better it is. In 1985, India had a HDI value of 0.320, placing it in the low human development category. In 2010, India has a HDI value of 0.519, placing it in the medium

108. See the discussion in Manning, Richard (2009). "Using Indicators to Encourage Development: Lessons from the Millennium Development Goals", Danish Institute for International Studies, Report No.1.

109. *The Millennium Development Goals Report 2011*, United Nations, 2011.

110. China being the other country.

human development category.[111] By 2025, India should cross the HDI threshold value of 0.670 and move into the high human development category. India's improvements have been driven fundamentally by income growth.[112] Several states have also brought out HDRs and these not only compute HDIs for the individual states, they enable us to pinpoint backward districts and intra-state divergences. A National Human Development Report (NHDR) was also brought out by the Planning Commission in 2001. Though it hasn't been updated since then, many state HDRs have computed HDIs for other states.[113] From these, based on the HDI scores, we know that the backward states are Bihar, Uttar Pradesh, Madhya Pradesh, Orissa, Rajasthan, Chhattisgarh and Rajasthan. In recent times, HDRs have also introduced a multidimensional poverty index (MPI), conceptualised by the Oxford Poverty and Human Development Initiative (OPHDI).

In addition to standard income or consumption poverty measures, this includes deprivation measured in terms of education, health and other assets.[114] Thus, 'We see that 81 per cent of people are multi-dimensionally poor in Bihar—more than any other state. Also, poverty in Bihar and Jharkand is most intense—poor people are deprived in 60 per cent of the MPI's weighted indicators. Uttar Pradesh is the home of largest number of poor people—21 per cent of India's poor people live there. West Bengal is home to the third largest number of poor people.' There are other large numbers of poor in Maharashtra and Madhya Pradesh. One can refine this further and go down to the level of the districts. After all, state boundaries are administratively determined. Development and deprivation do not follow these administrative boundaries. There are differences within states too. For example, a MPI kind of exercise has been undertaken for 379 of

111. A HDI value of 0.500 is the threshold for crossing over to medium human development.

112. UNDP (2010). *Human Development Report 2010, The Real Wealth of Nations: Pathways to Human Development*. UNDP and Palgrave Macmillan.

113. Such as *Delhi Human Development Report 2006*. Delhi: Oxford University Press. 2006.

114. *http://www.ophi.org.uk/wp-content/uploads/Country-Brief-India.pdf*

India's districts and the deprived districts are in Assam, Bihar, Madhya Pradesh, Orissa, Rajasthan and Uttar Pradesh.[115]

This is the right moment to pause and ask several questions. First, are people willingly poor? Do they not wish to better their lives and improve their standards of living? Assuming otherwise is tantamount to a very patronising attitude towards poor people. At best, there can be a qualification for the old and the disabled and households where the head of the household happens to be a woman. These apart, people in working-age groups do not wish to be poor. Income growth and liberalisation will ensure that such people are no longer poor. As a minor statistical point, income and expenditure distributions aren't symmetric. They are log normal, with a thick part towards the left. As soon as this thick part of the distribution passes above the poverty line, however that happens to be defined, there will be sharp drops in poverty. This has already begun to happen for India and will continue, assuming we can ensure that the growth continues. In states that have grown, there have been such sharp drops in poverty—Punjab, Haryana, Kerala, Tamil Nadu, Gujarat, Andhra Pradesh and Assam. Second, even if people do not wish to be poor, they may be stuck because they do not have access to education and skills, health services, market information, technology, financial products, roads, electricity, water, sewage and sanitation. But then, the answer is to efficiently provide these public goods or collective private goods. If such people continue to be poor, that is because in more than 60 years, these goods and services haven't been efficiently provided, notwithstanding colossal amounts of public expenditure. People may also be poor because they are stuck in subsistence-level agriculture and have no other employment opportunities. If such people are poor, that is because in more than 60 years, we haven't been able to reform agriculture and the rural sector.

'People can be trapped in poverty, when poverty itself becomes a constraint to growth. This occurs in regions that display characteristics of high conflict, low savings or investment rates, dismal education or health outcomes, poor access to credit or property rights, and incomplete

115. See, Kapur Mehta, Aasha and Shashanka Bhide (2011). "Poverty: Estimates, Measurement and Profiles," in Aasha Kapur Mehta, Andrew Shepherd, Shashanka Bhide, Amita Shah and Anand Kumar, *India Chronic Poverty Report, Towards Solutions and New Compacts in a Dynamic Context*. Indian Institute of Public Administration.

insurance markets which increase the risks of crop failures, floods, and droughts.'[116] Hence, poverty results from lack of integration. Third, we should therefore ask an important question. Are there sections in the Indian Constitution that prevent such integration? For instance, Articles 370 and 371 of the Constitution ensure that certain parts of India will never be integrated and mainstreamed. If that is the case, how can we ensure that people who live in these regions will ever be mainstreamed and become part of the growth process? Fourth, this kind of mindset also ensures that we look at the problem of poverty with a distorted lens. In any table of poverty, there will be categories of SCs, STs OBCs and Muslims. But are they deprived because they belong to these collective categories? Or are they deprived because they lack access to the public or collective private goods we have mentioned? 'Indeed, if anything, the data in this volume provide pretty good evidence that the scheduled castes (SCs) and scheduled tribes (STs) are still particularly disadvantaged in many extraordinary ways. What the numbers do seem to imply are: first, there is a good deal of truth in the old-fashioned story that economic and educational opportunities, more than caste identities, are determinants of access to various goods of poverty.'[117] Poverty is an individual household characteristic. By equating it with a collective category like SC, ST or Muslim, we commit a double kind of mistake. We assume that everyone inside this collective category is poor, by virtue of being a member of a collective category. And we also assume that everyone outside this collective category is rich, by virtue of not being a member of this collective category. Neither of these propositions is true.

Fifth, it is plausible to argue that these public or collective private goods aren't going to be efficiently delivered in a hurry. Nor is the rural sector going to be reformed in a hurry. Therefore, in the intervening period, we need to subsidise the poor. And we have been going round and round in circles on this one. There is this business of Unique Identification Authority of India and Aadhaar, which is supposed to solve every problem in sight. We have of course rushed headlong into Aadhaar without the

---

116. This quote is in the context of all of South Asia. See Ghani, Ejaz (2010). "The Poor Half Billion in South Asia: An Overview", in *The Poor Half Billion in South Asia, What is Holding Back Lagging Regions*?. Oxford University Press.

117. Mehta, Pratap Bhanu (2010). "Introduction: Caste, Class and Consumption", in R. Shukla, S. Jain and P. Kakkar, *Caste in a Different Mould, Understanding the Discrimination*. New Delhi: NCAER and Business Standard Banks.

necessary legislation having been passed by Parliament and without clarity on safeguards.[118] That apart, Aadhaar numbers aren't being issued to Indian citizens, they are being issued to Indian residents. Ajmal Kasab was one of the first to be enumerated in the Census of 2011. And he must have been one of the first to receive an Aadhaar card. If Aadhaar is going to be the backbone for delivering subsidies, will non-Indians who reside in India also receive these subsidies? In similar vein, there is a great deal of talk about switching from the present system of subsidies (food, fertiliser, petroleum products at the level of the Union) to direct cash transfers. There is no question that this is more efficient. This does not distort resource allocation. It also offers poor consumers the choice. However, technology doesn't solve the problem of identifying BPL. Until the problem of BPL identification is solved, we will continue to go round and round in circles. Why is the Planning Commission engaged in this business of crunching numbers and producing poverty ratios? The Planning Commission and the Ministry of Rural Development are involved because food subsidies and subsidies in other rural development programmes are routed through the Union and amounts granted to states are contingent on poverty numbers at the level of the states. In a later chapter, we will talk about a complete revamping of this system. The simple point is that poverty is a household-level characteristic. It has nothing to do with the collective categories that were earlier mentioned, apart from the old and the disabled and women-headed households. Not only do NSS data surface with a time-lag and are available only at intervals of five years, there are always question marks about the data, because NSS conducts a survey, not a Census. Poverty has to be based on decentralised and individual household-based identification, an idea that has been floating around since the Ninth Plan (1997-2002). However, this has never properly been implemented. We have been playing around with assorted parameters and centrally-determined templates for surveys.[119] Once we streamline financial flows for development to states and also decentralise within states, why should *gram sabhas* determine who is BPL and who is not? Not only does this make better economic sense. It will help dispel the subsidy culture that

118. It has only been introduced in Rajya Sabha, *http://uidai.gov.in/index.php?option=com_content&view=article&id=173&Itemid=212*

119. See for example, *http://www.pbplanning.gov.in/pdf/BPL16-3-07.pdf*

is rampant. Increasingly with the UPA, one has come to expect doles and handouts from the government. Private entrepreneurship is at a discount. This cannot be described as a healthy state of affairs.

We now turn to the more controversial question of inequality. Poverty is an absolute concept, while inequality is relative. There is an impression that increases in inequality, real or perceived, are bad. In a paper by Suresh Tendulkar, there is an interesting anecdote about a conference in Bangkok when Manmohan Singh was the Deputy Chairman of the Planning Commission. 'After other delegations presented their experiences in managing a market economy, the Chinese vice minister presented an outline of the Chinese reform program. At the end of the presentation, Manmohan Singh, in his usual gentle but forceful tone, asked, "Would not what you are trying to do result in greater inequality in China? To that the minister replied, with great conviction, "We would certainly hope so!"'[120] There is a difference between inequality in access to inputs (physical and social infrastructure, financial products and so on) and inequality in outcomes (income). Everyone would like India to be equitable. But equity should be interpreted in terms of access to inputs and we should be legitimately upset if there is inequity in that. However, why should there be equality in outcomes? This is a hangover of the socialism introduced in the Preamble to the Constitution, as a result of which, a political party cannot be registered in India unless it abides by the principles of socialism.[121] Socialism is a delightfully vague phrase, which can never be pinned down. As a result of this damage that was done to the Constitution, we have begun to take Article 38 of the Directive Principles too literally. This states, 'The state shall, in particular, strive to minimise the inequalities in income, and endeavour to eliminate inequalities in status, facilities and opportunities, not only amongst individuals but also amongst groups of people residing in different areas or engaged in different vocations.' The second part is fine. But minimising inequalities in income is disastrous. There is a difference between saying that every student should have access to a good school and saying that every student should obtain the same

120. Tendulkar, Suresh (2010). "Inequality and Equity during Rapid Growth Process", in Shankar Acharya and Rakesh Mohan (ed.), *India's Economy, Performance and Challenges, Essays in Honour of Montek Singh Ahluwalia*. Oxford University Press.

121. The Representation of the People Act was amended in 1989.

marks. Any period of rapid economic growth results in increased income inequalities. Simon Kuznets argued this out a long time ago.[122] This should be welcome, not denigrated, while taking care of inequity in access to inputs. For the record, one standard measure of inequality in the distribution of incomes is the Gini coefficient. The higher this value, the more unequal society is. India's Gini coefficient in the distribution of incomes is 36.8. This is high, but not that high.[123]

Both on poverty and inequality, we need to be less sanctimonious and hypocritical. We should listen to our brains and not our bleeding hearts. If there is conceptual clarity, we will move forward on both growth and inclusion.

122. Kuznets, Simon (1955). "Economic Growth and Income Inequality", *American Economic Review*.

123. *Human Development Report 2010*, Ibid.

11 Inclusive Growth

Role of Sociopolitical Factors: Comparative Experience of India and China

C.H. Hanumantha Rao

Introduction

Sociopolitical factors play a decisive role in determining the rate of growth of an economy, regional disparities in growth, and how the benefits from growth are distributed between different social and income groups. This works through their impact on the mobilisation of resources and their allocation to different sectors and schemes as well as on the effectiveness with which the schemes formulated are implemented. India opted for parliamentary democracy with a multi-party system after independence but its multi-class and multi-caste social structure, inherited from the pre-independence period, remained largely intact except for the abolition of princely states and the intermediaries like the *jagirdars* and the *zamindars*. Its social structure has, however, been undergoing gradual change through the working of political democracy over the last 60 years. In China, on the other hand, the social structure underwent a radical transformation following the revolution in the late 1940s, the effective implementation of land reforms, which, unlike in India, was intertwined with its national liberation struggle, and nationalisation and public ownership of the major means of production. China adopted 'democratic centralism' as its political system which conferred pre-eminent status to the ruling Communist Party.

The avowed objective of economic planning, started in the early 1950s in both the countries, has been to step up growth in GDP and achieve equitable distribution of benefits from growth. It would be interesting to know the experience in achieving equitable or inclusive growth under these two contrasting sociopolitical systems during their plan periods spanning over half a century covering phases before and after they embraced globalisation by launching economic reforms. This paper is a modest attempt in this direction.

Growth, Poverty and Inequality

Even though China was better placed in agriculture than India, its per capita income in terms of parity dollars was substantially lower than in India in 1952 due to retarded manufacturing and service sectors. The rate of growth of national income for the period 1952-1965 was about the same in the two countries: 3 per cent for China and 3.6 per cent for India. Even in 1986, that is, eight years after launching economic reforms, per capita income in China ($315) was only slightly higher than in India ($ 298)—five years before it was to launch economic reforms (Swamy, 1989). But by 2004, i.e., a quarter century after reforms in China and a little over a decade of reforms in India, per capita income in China rose sharply to $4,660, which was almost twice the level of per capita income in India at $2,460 (World Bank, 2008).

Both India and China have been able to reduce poverty as a result of steady growth in their per capita incomes. China's achievement in this respect has been far more impressive, much of the poverty reduction taking place in the early years of economic reform by the mid-1980s, when there was an exceptionally high growth in agriculture and equality in land-holdings brought about by radical land reforms (Rao, 2005a). The remaining poverty in China is now concentrated mostly in the fast growing developed coastal regions owing to the high rate of in-migration from the poorer regions (Ghani, 2010), whereas in India it is concentrated in the slow growing less developed central and eastern states. Apparently, the pull factors have been far more effective in inducing greater human mobility in China.

The pattern is the same concerning income inequality as in respect of growth: lower in China when compared to India in the pre-reform period but rising sharply and becoming significantly higher than in India well after the introduction of reforms. Inequality in the size distribution of income in China in the late 1970s was less than in India. It was in the urban sector that China exhibited impressive equality in incomes in the pre-reform period. In terms of poverty levels, illiteracy and health, China has done decisively better than India (Swamy, 1989). However, by 2004, income inequality in China, measured by the Gini Index, rose to 0.47 as against 0.37 in India (World Bank, 2008). China has thus crossed the Gini Index of 0.40, a figure above which is usually considered 'dangerous' because of its potential for giving rise to social discontent and unrest (Weil, 2008).

It is interesting to see how India and China are placed on the world map in respect of income inequality. In the late 1990s, Denmark, Czech Republic, Japan, Norway, Slovak Republic and Sweden showed the lowest income inequality in the world with the Gini Index of around 0.25. The highest Gini Index ranging from 0.50 to 0.60 in the early years of the present decade related to the Latin American countries, e.g., Argentina, Bolivia, Brazil, Chile, Columbia and Peru. South Africa is also in the same group with the Gini Index of 0.58. The inequality in the United States of America was well below this level with the Gini Index of 0.41 (World Bank, 2008). Income inequality in India is thus well above that in the group of countries showing the lowest inequality and seems to be fast approaching the level in the United States—'the land of capitalism'; whereas China—'the land of socialism'—already shows greater income inequality than the United States and is nearer the levels in some Latin American countries.

Sociopolitical Compulsions for Course Correction

In China, the dismantling of communes and absence of secure private ownership rights over land prevented farmers from benefitting from the rising economic value of land when the demand for land for non-agricultural purposes rose phenomenally under the impact of high overall economic growth as well as rapidly rising income inequality. With the farmers becoming vulnerable to dispossession, there was a massive land grabbing, especially in fast developing coastal areas, for the development of villas, golf courses and race tracks (Riskin, 2008). As many as 40 million farmers lost their land within a decade and the incidence of slave labour, including children, surfaced in a big way (Chandra, 2009). Besides, throughout the 1990s, most of the state and collectively owned enterprises were privatised which led to the millions of workers being laid off. Further, dismantling of rural collective economy and basic public services forced millions of peasants to migrate into cities as workers (Li, 2008). Despite such massive migration into cities, regional as well as rural-urban disparities in incomes became greater. Widening social polarisation led to strikes, protests, confrontation over corruption, land takeovers and environmental damage (Lotta, 2009). The number of such collective disturbances rose 10 times from 8,700 in 1993 to 87,000 in 2005 (Lee and Selden, 2008).

In India, the rate of growth of agriculture GDP which was a little over 3 per cent per annum when the green revolution was in full swing in the 1980s decelerated during the Ninth and Tenth Plan periods, with the growth in food grains output falling below the population growth rate. The difference in per capita income between agriculture and non-agriculture widened sharply. The regional divide became similarly sharp with the per capita gross state domestic product (GSDP) of Bihar—the poorest state in the country—dropping to 20 per cent of that in the richest state in 2004-05 (Planning Commission, 2008a).

Since the less developed states in India account for over 60 per cent of the population below the poverty line in the country, the pace of poverty reduction slowed down in the post-reform period, despite the rise in average national per capita GDP at a faster rate. The population belonging to the socially and economically disadvantaged sections like scheduled castes, scheduled tribes, backward classes, large majority of minorities, and women and children benefitted the least from growth and rising prosperity (Radhakrishna and Ray, 2005; Dev, 2008; Government of India, 2006; Kannan, 2009).The popular discontent arising from this economic polarisation reached its climax seven years ago when the GDP growth rate was at its peak and 'India Shining' campaign, then in full swing, coexisted with widespread rural distress and suicides by a large number of farmers (Rao, 2009).

Despite lower per capita income, higher poverty and democratic institutions providing outlets for ventilating grievances, the social unrest manifest in India appeared less serious than in China at the time of the formulation of their respective Eleventh Five Year Plans. This could well be attributed to the fact that China was ahead of India by at least a decade in implementing market-oriented reforms and experienced a much higher growth rate in GDP than India for a quarter century with sharply rising income inequalities accompanied by large-scale dispossession and displacement of vulnerable groups. This experience shows that high inequalities are no less a source of social discontent than high incidence of poverty. Even so, the mass discontent in India did appear to cross the 'tolerance limits' within a parliamentary democracy, as is evident from the change of government following the general elections in 2004.

Rising income inequalities, dispossession, loss of traditional livelihoods, inadequate measures for compensation, rehabilitation and resettlement, and emerging social tensions forced both India and China to attempt a course correction in their policies, surprisingly around the same period, in the formulation of their respective Eleventh Five Year Plans. India's Eleventh Plan (2007-2012) promised 'Faster and Inclusive Growth' through 'reforms with human face', and China's Eleventh Plan (2006-2010) came out with the objective of 'Building Harmonious Society' by 'putting people first'. Unlike in India where the multi-party system with a parliamentary democracy can force a change in the policy framework relatively quickly in response to the emerging unrest, the delayed response to the discontent in China could well be attributed to its political system which assigns a pre-eminent place to a single party.

Structural Bottlenecks to Inclusive Growth

Notwithstanding the recent attempts at course correction in both the countries towards 'inclusive growth' and 'harmonious development' through their Eleventh Five Year Plans, it would be naïve to expect that the change would be quick and smooth. The recent official pronouncements in both the countries represent, at best, the avowed intentions of the ruling elite made in response to the prevailing discontent. The roadblocks to achieving inclusive growth are formidable as they are structural in nature—having to do with political system in China and social structure in India.

Political System in China

China embarked upon economic planning in the early 1950s with favourable initial conditions in respect of its social structure that emerged as an aftermath of the revolution. When it launched economic reforms in the late 1970s, it had the additional advantage of adequate physical and social infrastructure built over a period of three decades of economic planning. Its authoritarian political system and mobilising power deriving from the highly organised and centralised party apparatus right from the grassroots enabled the authorities to take quick decisions and implement the development schemes effectively (Rao, 2005b). This is amply borne out by the unprecedented high rate of growth in GDP achieved by China over the three decades of reform. But the equally unprecedented rise in income inequality in this period is something not quite anticipated by Marxist ideologues. At the time of launching economic reforms, 'egalitarianism' practiced earlier was openly derided officially and a call was given to the people to become rich: 'Let some people get rich, so that others can follow' (Rao, 2005c). This is surprising because with all the variants of 'revisionism', one never found such a slogan in communist literature. Evidently, they became sick of the extreme form of 'egalitarianism' practiced earlier and the resultant slow growth in productivity. They admit that economic disparities would rise under the new policy, but believe that these can be corrected in course of time.

If income inequalities in China rose sharply to the Latin American levels within a short period of 2-3 decades despite an equitable social structure prevailing at the onset of planning and the development of relatively broad-based physical and social infrastructure before launching economic reforms, a plausible explanation is the prevalence of a political system which confers pre-eminent status to the ruling party with hardly any statutory and organised political opposition. This could be the source for the emergence of high inequalities in the wake of globalisation and market-oriented reforms.

The emergence of inequalities is often a consequence of high growth owing to the differential comparative advantages experienced by different regions arising from geographical and other locational factors, and to the interpersonal differences in access to education, skills and resources. An analysis of income inequalities in China concludes that the 'most important factors explaining overall inequality are differential returns to schooling and sector of employment...investing in people, in particular improving education service in lagging areas to poor people are important for sustainable growth and equitable distribution in the long-run' (Luo and Zhu, 2008). Neglect of the development of education and skills in the lagging regions and sectors and among the poor is traceable to the biases in decision-making regarding the allocation of resources and other measures. The sensitivity and resilience of the prevailing political system to take timely corrective measures could make a big difference to the degree of inequalities and mass deprivation.

The observations of Milovan Djilas, made decades before a country like China under 'communism' embraced globalisation and market reforms, are prophetic, especially in respect of the consequences of an authoritarian and closed polity for income distribution:

> The new class obtains its powers, privileges, ideology, and its customs from one form of ownership—collective ownership—which the class administers and distributes in the name of the nation and society...the so-called socialist ownership is a disguise for the real ownership by the political bureaucracy (Djilas, 1957).

The collective or socialist ownership is no longer a predominant feature of Chinese economy. In fact, the state economic sector accounts for only 35 per cent of economy, which, nevertheless, serves as an economic base of power of the leading Chinese bourgeoisie (Lotta, 2009). It is a 'state-led' market economy where, contrary to conventional wisdom, state plays a pre-eminent role in influencing the growth rate as well as the distribution of income. In the post-liberalisation period, the patronage extended by the state in awarding contracts, choice of location for private sector projects and technical institutions, decisions about the number, type and location of special economic zones, land acquisition and compensation policies, and various kinds of patronage extended to different enterprises and activities, could together make a greater impact, when compared to the pre-liberalisation period, on the growth of economy as well as on how the benefits from growth are distributed. If collective ownership of means of production was the source of power and privileges for the ruling political leadership and bureaucracy in the socialist countries half a century ago, it is basically the continued exclusiveness in access to state power conferred by the prevailing political system that enables the ruling political and bureaucratic class to distribute patronage to the privileged groups of people for operating in a market economy. This could well have become a source of high inequalities—interregional as well as interpersonal—in endowments of infrastructure, skills and resources.

The Chinese leadership has seen growing 'inequality as a central political threat to political stability, that is, to communist party rule...and in 2005 re-emphasised the primacy of social justice...to construct "harmonious society"' (Lee and Selden, 2009). This is evident from the use of redistributive instruments like fiscal transfers to reduce regional disparities. Although regional disparities continued to increase, they levelled off after 2000 (Wang, 2008). However, the change required is really basic, *viz.*, reforms in the political system that 'engages broad democratic forces in the business of policy making' (Riskin, 2008). But, 'the general yearning for greater democracy and transparency is almost entirely blocked' and there is 'growing frustration at the inflexibility of the current system' (Weil, 2008).

The prevailing authoritarian and closed political system appears to be a stumbling block to inclusive and ecologically sustainable development. Despite periodic attempts at course correction, prospects for inclusive development look gloomy without systemic political reforms towards an open and competitive polity.

Social Structure in India

Unlike China, India started its economic planning within a highly inequitable social structure in the early 1950s. The level of infrastructure—physical as well as social—has been way below that in China, as the saving and investment rates have been much lower than in China. Even now, social structure in rural India is more inequitable than in China. The Gini Index of land distribution in rural India was 0.74 in 2003, as against 0.49 in China in 2002—which, however, was zero after the revolution. The Gini Index of the distribution of adult schooling years in the population in the year 2000 in India (0.56) was higher than in China (0.37). It was higher than even in most Latin American countries (World Bank, 2006). The pace of poverty reduction in India is slower than in China, 'not just because growth has been much faster in China, but also because the same 1 per cent growth rate reduces poverty in India much less, largely on account of inequalities in wealth—particularly land and education' (Bardhan, 2007).

Like China, Indian economy is also a 'state-led' market economy and, contrary to common belief, the role of the state has become critical in determining the course of development even in the post-reform period. As in China, its direct role in the allocation of investment resources has declined, but its indirect role as facilitator of private investment and economic activity has vastly increased, with greater impact on growth and distribution of benefits than in the pre-liberalisation period. If the change is not as rapid as in post-reform China, it is because of various in-built pressures, checks and balances in the decision-making process, and the hierarchical social structure which has a debilitating influence on the delivery systems, resulting in much lower outcomes than expected.

Unlike in mature western democracies where democratic institutions evolved in the course of radical social transformation over a long period, in India the institutions of democracy had to be virtually transplanted on the traditional and iniquitous social structure. In the event, the working of democratic institutions has been twisted and moulded by the socio-economically dominant groups by dint of their wealth, status and power. This explains why the social change has been slow.

Although India's traditional inequitable social structure has been undergoing gradual transformation through the working of political democracy, the impact of entrenched economic interests represented by the big landed sections, business groups and growing middle class on economic policymaking as well as on changes in government has been significant. Being a mixed economy, private sector has had a strong presence in India since the beginning of economic planning. Its role has considerably increased with the opening up of the economy following economic reforms. These entrenched interests have a dominating influence in policymaking even when the governments come to power with popular mandate to address the concerns of the poor like employment guarantee, food security and other measures for social protection.

The recent experience demonstrates how the Eleventh Plan's agenda of inclusive growth is being undermined in practice by the pulls and pressures from such interests. For example, an avowed objective of the Eleventh Plan is to reduce regional disparities in development. But, whereas the fiscal transfers recommended by the statutory body like the Finance Commission are significantly higher in per capita terms for the poorer states, the discretionary schemes of the Central government show higher per capita expenditures in the richer states. Similarly, subsidy on fertiliser benefits richer regions much more than the poorer regions (Ghani, 2010). There is no increase in central assistance in the Eleventh Plan for infrastructure development of the backward regions. Such assistance constitutes less than 1 per cent of the total Eleventh Plan outlay for all states.

Land alienation continues to be a serious problem in tribal areas. The enactment of Scheduled Tribes and Other Traditional Forest Dwellers (Recognition of Forest Rights) Act, 2006, held a great promise as a major step towards protecting the rights of scheduled tribes and other traditional forest dwellers. However, a prerequisite for its effective implementation is the necessary 'political will' to ensure adequate say for the tribal population in the implementation process by countering the pressures from the vested interests. But the efforts on the ground so far do not seem to match the challenges involved (Planning Commission, 2008b; Government of India, 2009). Unless the laws that focus on exploiting the natural resources at the expense of human beings are changed and the feeling of alienation among tribal population is removed through pro-people steps, we may end up waging a war against our own people (Singh, 2009). If the Left-wing extremism has emerged as the foremost threat to the internal security of the country, it is due to the decades of exploitation and neglect of the poorest and the most backward regions of the country, especially the tribal belt.

The traditional norms for compensation and rehabilitation and resettlement of displaced persons are unsatisfactory. Government and industry are not yet willing to supplement the principle of fixed 'compensation' with measures for assuring original landowners or the displaced persons adequate stake, on a secure footing, in the new projects and enterprises including those in special economic zones (SEZs).

There is a renewed effort recently to expand institutional credit to rural areas, but there is no evidence of an improvement in the share of small-scale industries in total bank credit; and the small and marginal farmers account for only about one-third of institutional credit for agriculture, the remaining two-thirds going to the farmers above two hectares (Shetty, 2009).

Thanks to the 73rd and 74th amendments to the Constitution, elected *panchayats* have been in place. But they are deprived of necessary functions, finances and functionaries. No serious effort has been made so far to devolve such powers, not to speak of any effort to build up local capabilities by training the elected functionaries. This is explained solely by the resistance from the entrenched interests to part with their powers. Therefore, the change in attitudes has necessarily to be driven by the political process.

It is naïve to expect a genuinely inclusive governance without inclusive politics or empowerment of social groups hitherto not having access to political power at different levels. While the recent decision of the Central government to enhance reservation for women in local bodies to 50 per cent is a step in the right direction, the efforts to provide 33 per cent reservation for women in parliament and state legislative bodies have not met with success so far because of the absence of gender sensitivity and the fear of losing power and privileges among a significant section of legislators.

At the moment the disadvantaged sections are basically made to serve as 'vote banks' through the dispensation of patronage by the privileged groups who, being effective decision-makers, are the dominant players. Mere electoral participation by the underprivileged can not be equated with participatory democracy. In the ultimate analysis, empowerment of the disadvantaged sections means their ability to actively participate in decision-making and implementation by becoming the dominant players.

This can not be left to the forces that are random and chaotic. There needs to be a clear agenda for speedy social change.

The basic goal has to be the political and economic empowerment of the disadvantaged sections whether by caste, religion, gender or regions. A two-pronged strategy to address the problem is called for: first, 'social and economic empowerment' of the excluded groups by improving ownership of capital assets like land and business, and education and skills; and second, providing 'equal opportunity' for them through legal safeguards, reservations and similar measures in public as well as private sectors, and by ensuring adequate participation in governance at various levels through broadening and deepening of the working of our democracy by effectively extending it to the grassroots. Achieving equity through such measures will not only restore self-esteem and confidence among the socio-economically disadvantaged sections, but also improve the overall efficiency of the economic system and ensure the sustainability of growth momentum by tapping the vast underutilised human potential (Thorat and Newman, 2009).

Conclusion

In China, there are indications that 'activism informed by notions of rights and citizenship, as well as class inequality, has the potential to heighten pressure for change in the social order' (lee and Selden, 2008). How soon the change will occur in the political system in China and how smooth the transition would be is uncertain. But the change seems inevitable because individual freedom in economic decision-making within a market setting is incompatible, in the long-run, with the denial of individual freedom in the political sphere (Chakravarty, 1993).

India's open and democratic polity provides opportunities for public dissent, protests and periodic change of governments. Of late, a large number of 'development projects' in different parts of the country which displace the poor and destroy their livelihoods and harm the ecology have been stalled because of the protests and organised resistance by the affected people. Therefore, despite its shortcomings, India's democratic framework constitutes the greatest asset as an instrument for achieving inclusive and sustainable development. In the present Indian situation, democracy and state power have to become catalysts for social transformation.

The social change underway in India is faster than before—thanks to the rise in awareness of the common people, their improved staying power, and growing civil society activism. But it is bound to be gradual because of resistance from the vested interests. It is also bound to be, by and large, peaceful because of the visible prospects for change through the democratic process and pro-poor measures, even in areas presently affected by extremist violence. There is already an air of optimism about such a change.

References

Bardhan, Pranab (2007). "Inequality in India and China: Is Globalisation to Blame?", *Yaleglobal*, 15 October.

Chakravarty, Sukhamoy (1993). *Selected Economic Writings.* Delhi: Oxord University Press.

Chandra, Nirmal Kumar (2009). "China and India: Convergence in Economic Growth and Social Tensions?", *Economic & Political Weekly,* January 24-30.

Dev, Mahendra S. (2008). *Inclusive Growth in India—Agriculture, Poverty, and Human Development.* New Delhi: Oxford University Press.

Djilas, Milovan (1957). *The New Class*. London: Thames and Hudson.

Ghani, Ejaz (2010). *The Poor Half Billion in South Asia*. Oxford University Press.

Government of India (2006): *Report of the High-Level Committee on the Social, Economic and Educational Status of the Muslim Community of India.* New Delhi.

———. (2009). *Report of the Committee on State Agrarian Relations and the Unfinished Task in Land Reforms.* New Delhi: Department of Land Resources, Ministry of Rural Development.

Kannan, K.P. (2009). "Dualism, Informality and Social Inequality: An Informal Economy Perspective of the Challenge of Inclusive Development in India", *The Indian Journal of Labour Economics* 52(1):1-32, January-March.

Lee, Ching Kwan and Mark Selden (2008). "Inequality and Its Enemies in Revolutionary and Reform China", *Economic & Political Weekly,* December 27.

Li, Minqi (2008). "Socialism, Capitalism, and Class Struggle: The Political Economy of Modern China", *Economic & Political Weekly,* December 27.

Lotta, Raymond (2009). "China's Rise in the World Economy", *Economic & Political Weekly,* February 21-27.

Luo, Xubei and Nong Zhu (2008). *Rising Income Inequality in China: A Race to the Top.* The World Bank, East Asia and Pacific Region, Poverty Reduction and Economic Management Department, August.

Planning Commission (2008a). *Eleventh Five Year Plan (2007-12),* Vols I & III. New Delhi.

———. (2008b). *Development Challenges in Extremist Affected Areas—Report of an Expert Group to Planning Commission,* Vols. 1 & 2. New Delhi: Government of India.

Radhakrishna, R. and Shovan Ray (ed.) (2005): *Handbook of Poverty in India—Perspectives, Policies, and Programmes.* New Delhi: Oxford University Press.

Rao, C.H.H. (2005a). *Agriculture, Food Security, Poverty, and Environment—Essays in Post-Reform India.* New Delhi: Oxford University Press.

———. (2005b). "Rural Transformation in China and India: Comparative Experience in the Post-Reform Period", *Economic and Political Weekly,* August 13-19.

———. (2005c). *Agricultural Growth, Farm Size and Rural Poverty Alleviation in India,* New Delhi: Academic Foundation.

———. (2009). "Inclusive Growth: Recent Experience and Challenges Ahead", *Economic & Political Weekly,* March 28-April 3.

Riskin, Carl (2008). "Property Rights and Social Costs of Transition and Development in China", *Economic and Political Weekly,* December 27.

Shetty, S.L. (2009). *Growing Inequality: A Serious Challenge to the Indian Society and Polity.* Dr. V.K.R.V. Rao Memorial Lecture-6, Bangalore: Institute for Social and Economic Change.

Singh, Digvijay (2009). "How to Combat the Maoists", *The Economic Times,* New Delhi, October 23.

Swamy, S.(1989). *Economic Growth in China and India 1952-1970.* Vikas.

Thorat, Sukhadeo and Katherine Newman (eds.) (2009). *Blocked by Caste: Economic Discrimination in Modern India.* New Delhi: Oxford University Press.

Wang, Shaoguang (2008). "Double Movement in China", *Economic & Political Weekly,* December 27.

Weil, Robert (2008). "A House Divided: China after 30 years of 'Reforms'", *Economic & Political Weekly,* December 27.

World Bank (2008). *World Development Indicators.*

———. (2006): *World Development Report.*

This paper is based on the Silver Jubilee Lecture delivered by the author at the 27th Annual Conference of the Andhra Pradesh Economic Association held at the National Institute of Technology (NIT), Warangal, 14-15 March, 2009, published in the Economic and Political Weekly, April 16-22, 2011.

12 Why for a Class of Bribes the Act of Giving a Bribe should be Treated as Legal

KAUSHIK BASU

Preamble

This paper I wrote a few months ago, as a discussion paper, on a very different subject—the control of corruption. The paper had generated a huge amount of controversy with serious comments in *The Indian Express, The Telegraph, Le Monde, The Economist,*[1] and several other newspapers, web chat groups and television channels.[2] This paper puts forward a new idea for the control of one kind of corruption, namely, bribery, in India. In describing this as 'new', I am aware that as a research idea it is sufficiently obvious not to be thought of as novel. It constitutes a standard exercise of backward-induction reasoning in two-period games. Yet, in the world of policymaking this kind of analysis is new—this became more evident by the angry reaction to the original version that I made available on the web—and I am convinced that this kind of 'law and economics' analysis needs to be used in conjunction with civil society activism, if we really want to control corruption and do so in ways that are morally acceptable.

Bribery is rampant in India. It is a scourge that deserves to be banished. Tackling this is a problem, that has to be a joint effort of all wings of the government and also of all political parties and even civil society. While it is not possible for a single person or even a single ministry to cure this malaise, one can think of small steps which, taken together, can add up to something substantial. It is in this spirit that this paper is

1. Dreze (2011); Mitra (2011); Seabright (2011); The Economist (2011).
2. The reader may also like to see the comment by Narayana Murthy on this proposal for controlling corruption, as reported in *The Economic Times: http://economictimes.indiatimes.com/tech/software/infosys-chairman-narayana-murthy-backs-kaushik-basus-proposal-to-make-bribe-giving-legal/articleshow/9299479.cms*

being written. Though in the domain of policymaking in India the proposal in this paper is novel, related ideas, which rely on creating divergent incentives among partners in crime, have been discussed in the past by economists and academic lawyers (see, for instance, Schroth and Bostan, 2004; Spagnolo, 2006; Buccirossi and Spagnolo, 2006; Apesteguia *et al.*, 2011; Bigoni *et al.*, 2011; Rose-Ackerman, 2011).

What the paper puts forward is a small but fairly radical idea of how we can take one step towards cutting down the incidence of bribery. There are different kinds of bribes and what I am concerned with in this paper are bribes that people often have to give to get what they are legally entitled to. I shall call these 'harassment bribes'. Suppose an income tax refund is held back from a taxpayer till he pays some cash to the officer. Consider a case where to buy a regular train ticket you are told that you have to pay some money under the table. Suppose government allots subsidised land to a person but when the person goes to get her/his paperwork done and receive documents for this land, she/he is asked to pay a hefty bribe. Consider the case of an exporter who has fulfilled all formalities but is asked to make an illegal payment before getting a customs clearance. These are all illustrations of harassment bribes. Harassment bribery is widespread in India and it plays a large role in breeding inefficiency and has a corrosive effect on civil society.[3]

The central message of this paper is that we should declare the act of giving a bribe in all such cases as legitimate activity. In other words, the giver of a harassment bribe should have full immunity from any punitive action by the state.

It should be clarified that the act of bribery is still being considered illegal, and the total punishment meted out for bribery may still be the same. That is, if under the old system, the bribe giver and the bribe taker are fined Rs x each, what I am suggesting is that we fine the bribe taker 2x and the bribe giver 0. In other words, what is being argued is that this entire punishment should be heaped on the bribe taker and the bribe giver should not be penalised at all, at least not for the act of offering or giving the bribe. It is recommended that we in fact go further and say that, in the

3. For surveys of bribery and corruption, especially in the context of developing countries and in particular India, see Bardhan (1997) and Dasgupta (2011).

event of a case of bribery being established in the court of law, the bribe taker is required to give the bribe, to the extent that its size can be uncovered, back to the giver.

The main argument of this paper is that such a change in the law will cause a dramatic drop in the incidence of bribery. The reasoning is simple. Under the current law, discussed in some detail in the next section, once a bribe is given, the bribe giver and the bribe taker become partners in crime. It is in their joint interest to keep this fact hidden from the authorities and to be fugitives from the law, because, if caught, both expect to be punished. Under the kind of revised law that I am proposing here, once a bribe is given and the bribe giver collects whatever she/he is trying to acquire by giving the money, the interests of the bribe taker and bribe giver become completely orthogonal to each other. If the act is revealed, the bribe giver will go scot free and will be able to collect his bribe money back. The bribe taker, on the other hand, loses the booty of bribe and faces a hefty punishment.

Hence, in the post-bribe situation it is in the interest of the bribe giver to have the bribe taker caught. Since the bribe giver will cooperate with the law, the chances are much higher of the bribe taker getting caught and that way the bribe giver can get back the money she/he gave as bribe. Since the bribe taker knows this, he will be much less inclined to take the bribe in the first place. This establishes that there will be a drop in the incidence of bribery.

Indeed, under the new law, when a person gives a bribe, she/he will try to keep evidence of the act of bribery—a secret photo or jotting of the numbers on the currency notes handed over and so on—so that immediately after the bribery, she/he can turn informer and get the bribe taker caught. The upshot of this is not that the bribe taker will get caught but, more often, he will not take the bribe in the first place in anticipation of getting caught.[4]

4. This use of rationality calculus as in Becker (1968) may be questioned by some. I myself believe that trying to understand crime by assuming relentless self-interested behaviour on the part of all individuals is inappropriate. There are moral individuals and their existence makes a large difference to how behaviour in society at large plays out (see Guha and Guha, 2011). However, once one is analysing the behaviour of those who have chosen to be engaged in an act of corruption or bribery, it seems reasonable to analyse the outcome by utilising standard rationality calculus.

Since the argument is being made here for harassment bribes, it can reasonably be expected that, if a change in the legislation is made in the manner suggested in this paper, there will be a sharp drop in the incidence of harassment bribery.

Institutional Details

In India, the main law concerning bribery is a 1988 legislation called the Prevention of Corruption Act, 1988. According to this law, bribe taking by a public servant and bribe giving are equally wrong and, in the event of conviction, both are punishable by anywhere between six months and five years' imprisonment and they shall also be liable to fines. For the most part, the act of giving and taking a bribe are treated on par under this law. As Section 12 states, 'Whoever abets any offence [pertaining to bribery], whether or not that offence is committed in consequence of the abetment, shall be punishable with imprisonment for a term which shall be not less than 6 months but which may extend up to five years and shall also be liable to fine.' It may be added here that the giving of a bribe is treated by lawyers as abetment to the crime of bribery, and so bribe giving is covered under this section.

There is, however, an exception to the bribe giving or abetment law in the form of Section 24 of the Prevention of Corruption Act, 1988. I reproduce this section in full here:

> Notwithstanding anything contained in any law for the time being in force, a statement made by a person in any proceeding against a public servant for an offence under sections 7 to 11 or under section 13 or section 15, that he offered or agreed to offer any gratification (other than legal remuneration) or any valuable thing to the public servant, shall not subject such person to a prosecution under section 12.

However, this section has a lot of ambiguity. In a case, three years ago, *Bhupinder Singh Patel vs. CBI*, 2008 (3) CCR 247 at p. 261 (Del): 2008 Cri LJ 4396, it was ruled that this exemption would apply only if the bribe giver could establish that the bribe was given unwillingly and in order to get the public servant trapped. But the word 'unwillingly' is itself so ambiguous that the use of this judgement as precedence is not easy either.

As a consequence, Section 24 is increasingly becoming a clause meant for those wanting to carry out a sting operation to trap a public servant in the act of bribe taking and seeking protection from the law. This was clear from a ruling of the Delhi High Court in *Bharadwaj Media Private Limited vs. State*, 2008 146 DLT 108 (Del): 2008 (1) CCR 11: 2008 (2) Crimes 244.

What this paper argues for is a much clearer statement concerning the legality of the bribe giver's action in the context of harassment bribes. In other words, this would amount to a revocation of Section 12 in the case of harassment bribes. In addition the law should say that once the fact of bribery is established in court, the amount of the bribe has to be returned to the person who gave the bribe.

One problem with the new law is the following. Once it is completely clear that a bribe giver has immunity from our bribery law, it is true that many more people will be willing to give bribes. However, since, every time a person gives a bribe, after that it will be in the interest of the bribe giver to expose this act of corruption (since by that not only will she/he not be punished but she/he will be getting back the money that she/he gave as a bribe), the bribe taker will not want to take the bribe. Since the crime of bribery cannot occur without both sides, the giver and the taker agreeing to undertake this act, the fact of greater desire on the part of the bribe giver to give a bribe under the new law will be of little consequence. This paper predicts that the end result will be a sharp decline in the incidence of bribery.

For the sake of clarity, let me emphasise what to the careful reader will be obvious anyway. It is not being argued here that the (harassment) bribe giver be pardoned in retrospect. A retrospective pardon is like an amnesty; and barring rare exceptions, amnesties are not worth it. They encourage corrupt behaviour by raising hopes of future pardon and corrodes society's morals.

What is being argued is that the law should be changed, so that, at the time of committing harassment bribery, both parties know that the giver has immunity and that the taker not only has a heftier penalty but also has to return the bribe. If we simply grant clemency to the bribe giver *after* the crime has been committed, none of the benefits being talked about here will be achieved.

One can today get a snapshot view of harassment bribery across the nation thanks to the innovative work by the not-for-profit organisation, Janaagraha, and its remarkable website, *ipaidabribe.com*. It illustrates well how citizens are often compelled to give a bribe; and by bringing such practices out of the closet, the idea is not to take away the guilt from such actions but the reverse, to discourage the very act of bribery. The legal change that this paper suggests will simply strengthen this kind of action, by strengthening the voice of the harassed bribe giver and increasing the penalty on the bribe taker.

The argument in this paper is founded in both strategic and moral precepts. The strategic element consists of breaking the bond between the bribe giver and the bribe taker in the post-bribe scenario.[5] This is reminiscent of the old 'Sati' laws in India. In their eagerness to put an end to the practice, the British had declared illegal not only abetment but also the witnessing of 'Sati'. This was all fine, except that, when the charge of 'Sati' came up and the courts looked around for witnesses, they invariably did not find any. The only way to change this was to distinguish between the abettor and the innocent bystander.

The moral precept lies in the recognition that even if a particular action involving two parties is considered a crime, we must be prepared to distinguish between the victim and the perpetrator of the crime. In cases of dowry, for instance, not to distinguish between the taker and the giver, seems not only to be foolish (from the point of view of strategic economic theory, as argued above) because that makes both parties partners in crime and for that reason harder to uncover proof of the crime, but also morally unjustified. Surely, we must separate out the roles of the dowry giver and the dowry taker and not hold the former culpable. To me this is not just good economics but morally the right way to go.

5. This amounts to creating incentives for the whistle blower (see Apesteguia *et al*., 2011).

Non-Harassment Bribes

I have confined the above analysis to harassment bribes.[6] The question that naturally arises is about other kinds of bribe, for instance, the kinds of bribery that are believed to occur when government gives out big development contracts. Should the bribe giver be given full immunity in such cases? The simple answer to this is a 'no'.

But what should be the optimal policy be in such cases? We need to give this much greater thought and subject it to formal law and economic analysis before we have an answer. The main problem arises from the fact that in such cases the bribe giver is likely to have got something by giving a bribe that she does not deserve to get. Hence, in the event of bribery being established in a law court, the issue remains about the bribe giver being in possession of an object that is not supposed to be in her/his possession.

A full answer to how the law should treat such cases will have to await further analysis. But I am inclined to believe that even in such bribery cases there ought to be an asymmetric treatment of the bribe taker and the giver. In particular, the punishment meted out to the bribe taker should be substantially greater than on the giver. This will mean that the collusive bond between the bribe taker and the giver will be weakened and the bribe giver will be more likely to cooperate with the judiciary in exposing the crime than under the current circumstances.

Further, it may well be argued that the public servant who takes the bribe is the gate keeper who violates his responsibility and sells off the property that she/he is supposed to protect. Since bribery is not a case of theft but of collaboration between two agents, the primary moral responsibility for the same rests on the shoulder of the bribe taker. Of course, if the bribe giver uses threats to induce the public servant to take a bribe that becomes a criminal act in itself.

---

6. Also, we ignore here the fact that in a society with widespread corruption there is the problem of 'bribe hierarchy', that is, the possibility that even after one gets caught taking a bribe one may be able to escape by bribing the very person or agency that caught you taking a bribe. This immediately opens up another layer of the same problem. What these 'towers of bribery' do to a society is discussed in Basu *et al.* (1992). In a fuller analysis of policy change, it is critical to pay attention to these towers of bribery and how we can strategise to break them down.

Caveats

It is worth being clear that giving immunity to the bribe giver, even when this is restricted to harassment bribes, will not cause bribery to vanish altogether. This is because of the interests of the serial bribe giver, that is, a person who regularly meets with government officials and is asked or offers to pay a bribe or the agent who acts as go between in crimes of bribery. For such a bribe giver, reputation is a matter of great importance, as game theory emphasises and people with common sense know. In other words, a serial bribe giver, planning to aid the judiciary in trapping a bribe taker, will have to weigh the cost of his loss of credibility among the officials with whom he interacts repeatedly and give bribes against the gain of getting her/his bribe money back.

What is being argued here is that the legal amendments being suggested in this paper will not remove all incentives to bribery. But to the extent that it does create mistrust between the bribe giver and the taker in the post-bribery situation, it means that the comfort zone within which bribery occurs in today's world will cease to exist and the upshot will be a decline in the incidence of bribery. However, the fact that the changes in the law suggested in this paper will diminish the incidence of bribery should not lull us into the sense that there are no other actions needed to tackle this ubiquitous phenomenon. Among these is the effort to use e-technology to make procedures rule-based and to minimise the interface between ordinary citizens and the public servant. Fortunately, important steps along these lines have been initiated in recent times.

If we want to put a virtual end to bribery and corruption, what we really have to rely on are individual values and character traits. As I had argued in a paper many years ago (Basu, 1983), human ingenuity is so great that no matter how many plugs we put in to stop corruption, people will almost invariably find a way around it.[7] One of the most acute observations

7. It may be pointed out here that the game theorist's ingenuity is also so remarkable that we can technically create models whereby we can create complex models of good compliant behaviour which do not rely on individual moral commitments. For a very skillful model of this see Myerson (2004). Importantly, Myerson manages to illustrate the powerful role of institutions in these kinds of situations. It shows, that trying to understand human behaviour without recognising the important role of institutions and collective beliefs, can easily lead us to erroneous conclusions.

on this go back by two millennia—Kautilya's *Arthashastra* (p.281), where we find this wonderful but cynical observation: 'Just as it is impossible to know when a fish moving in water is drinking it, so it is impossible to find out when government servants in charge of undertakings misappropriate money.'

In the scheme I am suggesting, one problem that will open up is that public servants may be vulnerable to blackmail and false charges of bribe-taking. We could try to plug this loophole by increasing the punishment for blackmail and false accusation. What all this underlines is the fact that there is nothing fool-proof in economic policy design.

If we want to really get at corruption, what we need to build up are values of honesty and integrity in society. In the language of the *Arthashastra,* we have to wean fish off water. This has received so little attention and even to make such an argument sounds like moral claptrap because mainstream economics has taught us that human beings are endlessly self-seeking. In truth, they are not. Honesty, pro-social preferences and a sense of right and wrong constitute a part of the human psyche (Hauser, 2006), even though we can create societies where such traits are barely visible.

It is possible to go further and argue that we cannot have an efficient market economy unless human beings are endowed with a minimal amount of integrity and pro-sociality (Basu, 2011). Because of the propensity of economics to ignore these traits, these are under-researched areas. But if we want to substantially cut down the incidence of corruption, such as bribery, and want an efficient and vibrant economy, alongside getting our laws and economic policies right, we need to work on building up appropriate social and cultural traits, which provide the foundations for such an economy.

References

Apesteguia, Jose, Martin Dufwenberg and Reinhart Selten (2011). "Blowing the Whistle", *Economic Theory* 48(1).

Bardhan, Pranab (1997). "Corruption and Development: A Review of Issues", *Journal of Economic Literature* 112.

Basu, Kaushik (1983). "On Why We Do Not Try to Walk Off Without Paying After a Taxi Ride", *Economic and Political Weekly* 18 (November).

————. (2011). *Beyond the Invisible Hand: Groundwork for a New Economics.* Princeton: Princeton University Press and New Delhi: Penguin Books.

Basu, Kaushik, Sudipto Bhattacharya and Ajit Mishra (1992). "*Notes on Bribery and the Control of Corruption*", *Journal of Public Economics* 48.

Becker, Gary (1968). "Crime and Punishment", *Journal of Political Economy* 76.

Bigoni, Maria, Sven Olof Fridolfsson, Chloe Le Coq and Giancarlo Spagnolo (2011). "Trust, Salience and Deterrence: Evidence from an Antitrust Experiment". University of Bologna. (*mimeo*)

Buccirossi, Paolo and Giancarlo Spagnolo (2006). "Leniency Policies and Illegal Transactions", *Journal of Public Economics* 90: 1281-97.

Dasgupta, Arindam (2011). "Corruption", in K. Basu and A. Maertens (eds.), *New Oxford Companion to Economics in India.* New Delhi: Oxford University Press.

Dreze, Jean (2011). "The Bribing Game", *The Indian Express*, April 23.

Guha, Ashok and Brishti Guha (2011). "The Persistence of Goodness", *Journal of Institutional and Theoretical Economics* (forthcoming).

Hauser, Marc (2006). *Moral Minds: How Nature Designed Our Universal Sense of Right and Wrong.* New York: Harper Collins.

Kautilya (1992 edition). *Arthashastra.* Edited by L.N. Rangarajan. New Delhi: Penguin Books.

Mitra, Ashok (2011). "The Unquiet Grave", *The Telegraph*, April 22.

Myerson, Roger (2004). "Justice, Institutions and Multiple Equilibria", *Chicago Journal of International Law* 5.

Rose-Ackerman, Susan (2011). "The Law and Economics of Bribery and Corruption", *Annual Review of Law and Social Science* (forthcoming).

Schroth, Peter and Daniela Bostan (2004). "International Constitutional Law and Anti-Corruption Measures in the European Union's Accession Negotiations: Romania in Comparative Perspective", *American Journal of Comparative Law* 52.

Seabright, Paul (2011). "Should Corruption be Legalized?" (my translation from the French), *Le Monde*, 24 May.

Spagnolo, Giancarlo (2006). "Divide et Impera: Optimal Leniency Programmes", *Discussion Paper* No. 4840. London: Centre for Economic Policy Research.

The Economist (2011). "Novel Way to Combat Corruption: Who to Punish", *The Economist*, 5 May.

Acknowledgements and Disclaimer: I briefly spoke about the main idea behind this paper in my inaugural remarks at a conference organised by the National Institute of Public Finance and Policy in New Delhi on 15 March; and, subsequently, put it up as a working paper on the web. What is presented here is a marginally revised version of that paper. I am grateful for comments and criticisms received from Merijn Bosnan, Supriyo De, Sean Dougherty, Arun Duggal, K.P. Krishnan, H.A.C. Prasad, Ramesh Ramanathan, Ajay Shah, Shekhar Shah, Giancarlo Spagnolo, T.C.A. Srinivasa-Raghavan and Yang Yen Thaw. I am also grateful to Sayali Phatak and Jyoti Sagar for drawing my attention to some of the relevant legal literature. The ideas presented in this paper are personal and do not necessarily reflect the views of the Ministry of Finance, Government of India.

13 Global Cooperation on Sustainable Growth and Development

Views from G-20 Countries

Pranab Mukherjee

The G-20 demonstrated its relevance to international policymaking with the success of its coordinated response on the fallout of the global financial crisis. The economic downturn was moderated and growth resumed in the second half of 2009 in most economies, although the pace of recovery remained uneven. Advanced economies grew more slowly than before, while emerging economies like China and India led the way, with Latin America and Africa following closely. It appeared that policymakers had learnt theirs lessons from history by honing and harmonising the use of macroeconomic policy and keeping markets open. At the same time, countries in the developed and the developing world adopted revival strategies in keeping with the needs of their respective contexts.

Developments in recent months have been less encouraging. There is widespread apprehension that even the tepid global economic recovery that we have seen so far is stalling. Growth in most advanced economies has declined in the second quarter of 2011 and emerging markets are witnessing a combination of moderation in growth and rising inflation.

Advanced economies, the Euro zone and the US, are seized with sovereign debt problems. This is making financial markets nervous. Elevated fiscal deficits and public debt have always followed deep recessions in the past, which could be overcome with stronger recovery in output. In the present instance, the nominal output is yet to reach the pre-crisis levels. There are structural constraints coming in the way of advanced economies returning to their trend growth path. As a result, their fiscal position looks increasingly unsustainable. Despite the aggressive fiscal and monetary policy, unemployment continues to be at its highest in many advanced countries. The question is what more can policy makers do to improve growth or to avoid another downturn. While Europe has started fiscal tightening in response to an adverse market response, the United States has recently announced another big fiscal stimulus, perhaps in the belief that there cannot be fiscal consolidation without growth.

Emerging markets recovered quickly from global slowdown, but are facing elevated commodity prices, inflation, moderating growth and volatile capital flows all at once. Central banks have been forced to raise policy rates repeatedly, potentially compromising growth in the short term. They are also confronted with the impossible trinity. While raising rates may help stabilise growth, it may also invite more capital inflows. It is true that emerging economies are relatively better placed with regard to their public debt and fiscal deficit due to their stronger growth momentum and relatively robust banking systems. Their downside risks are on account of high oil and commodity prices and volatility in capital flows, partly due to the easy money policies in advanced countries.

Unlike at the outset of the global financial crisis, when G-20-led policy coordination across economies could be achieved rapidly, it may be more difficult now. The advanced and developing countries are at different stages of the business cycle. It is important, therefore, to pause and think about what the G-20 agenda has been thus far and how it needs to evolve in future.

One of the central objectives of the G-20 has been to address the root causes of the global financial crisis, prevent a recurrence and, going forward, to take measures to achieve strong sustainable and balanced growth. Dealing effectively with the interrelated issues of global imbalances, financial regulation and the international monetary system are central to this agenda.

Most observers believe that the proximate cause of the recent crisis lay in a small, sub-prime segment of the US housing market. The ultimate reasons included the growing weaknesses in financial regulation and the buildup of global imbalances. Since the international monetary system does not have an effective mechanism for preventing the build up of global imbalances, the G-20 took up the issue of its reform on a priority basis.

There is an understanding that the G-20 Framework for Strong, Sustainable and Balanced Growth may be the mechanism for adjusting these imbalances. This workstream, in which India plays an important role as co-chair of the Framework Working Group, is vital for the success of the G-20.

Strengthening domestic drivers of growth in developing and emerging economies is necessary for rebalancing of the global economy. As a result, the development agenda has become a central theme for the G-20 since the Seoul Summit. Moreover, as financial markets were seen to be destabilising commodity markets, commodity price volatility and food security were also added to this agenda.

While welcoming these initiatives, we need to be cautious regarding the danger of working with a 'one-size-fit-all' approach. Basel III is a good case in point. It is quite demanding on developing country banks. Different stages of economic development require different levels and quality of support from the financial sector. If capital adequacy standards become too high, there is a danger of inefficient disintermediation in markets. Emerging markets should use prudential regulation and close supervision rather than merely high capital standards.

Global macroeconomic imbalances are at the heart of destabilising sustainable economic growth at the international level. We know that all imbalances are not bad as some of them reflect multi-paced growth, different savings-investment behaviour and productivity levels across economies. Such differences may not be destabilising *per se*. At the same time, some imbalances reflect structural inefficiencies usually created by policy distortions relating to the external sector, trade, capital flows and exchange rate policies, financial markets, tax and subsidy regimes, which have to be addressed.

The reform of the international monetary system is high on the agenda of the G-20 and various issues including capital flows management, financial safety nets, measuring global liquidity, composition of the SDR basket are currently under discussion.

Let me take this opportunity to emphasise a few specific issues. An issue of immediate concern for emerging economies is managing large capital flows. Large and volatile capital flows to emerging markets can be destabilising as they lead to high exchange rate volatility and in some cases make it incumbent to maintain high levels of foreign exchange reserves as an insurance against sudden or large-scale flight of international capital. Large and volatile inflows are also associated with asset price booms and encourage excessive risk-taking by traders and investors and therefore threaten financial stability.

Secondly, recent commodity and food price rise and their volatility have induced considerable threat to economic growth and food security in energy dependent emerging, as well as, developing economies. Factors behind recent price hikes are yet to be pin pointed. Even the G-20 is undecided on the role of speculation and global excessive liquidity on the international commodity prices. Though it does seem odd that commodity prices should be so buoyant even as the outlook for global growth is weak. We need more research and debate on whether speculation in currency and commodity markets has been playing a role in recent price rises. If yes, how do we check it in the future without stifling the functioning of markets?

Thirdly, G-20 development agenda is understandably very vast. It covers areas that are also being handled by a number of developmental agencies. While we are committed to concerns of 'development' and of sharing the fruits of economic growth, it is imperative to prioritise among various development needs. One development issue that deserves priority is the recycling of global savings for infrastructure investment. Enhancing infrastructure investment in emerging economies and developing countries would have positive spin-off for rebalancing global demand. It would result in real investments with tangible growth. The G-20 is well placed to coordinate various stakeholders including governments, especially the ones that have large surpluses, the private sector, and multilateral development banks, for investment in developing economies. I hope the conference can suggest innovative ways to recycle global savings and identify viable strategies to overcome the presumed hurdle of 'lack of enabling environment' for infrastructure investment in emerging and developing countries.

Even though there are no simple answers or magic solutions to some of these issues, I for one do not see any reason for despair. I am hopeful that our deliberations will help in addressing global challenges at the current conjuncture and also the structural problems that confront us all, in an innovative and cooperative framework. The need of the hour is global reforms with an eye on medium- to long-term sustainability of economic growth.

Finance Minister's Speech, September 13, 2011.

14 Challenge of Transforming Indian Agriculture

V.S. Vyas

Increased agricultural production in last two-three years cannot hide the fact that Indian agriculture is facing a serious crisis. The crisis is clearly evident in falling share of agriculture in GDP with little decline in the workforce depending on agriculture; progressive diminution of agricultural holdings and impoverishment of the large majority of the farmers who cannot make two ends meet from their agriculture income. With 17 per cent share in GDP, agriculture is supporting nearly 52 per cent of country's workforce. Very large numbers of farmers, nearly 83 per cent, are having holdings of less than two hectares, and their number is increasing. Except in some special circumstances, e.g. the holdings growing vegetables or other high value crops, these holdings are economically non-viable. As the farmers' situation analysis revealed, most of the farmers are having negative, or at best a meagre income from agriculture. The challenge facing agriculture, and in way for the economy as a whole is to increase production on vast number of small agricultural holdings and enable a sizeable number of workers to shift from agriculture to non-agricultural sectors. In most of the circumstances, increase in productivity in agriculture is a precondition for the growth in the non-farm employment, particularly in rural area. Hence I am concentrating on the factors that inhibit growth in productivity, and measures to overcome these inhibiting factors.

There is stagnation, if not decline, in yields of major crops. Even in ancillary sectors such as dairying and horticulture, rate of growth is decelerating in the recent years. Need for major improvement in agricultural productivity is clearly indicated. With rising input costs and declining productivity, farmers' income is declining, resulting in acute distress. Near stagnation in agriculture is also affecting the consumers.

While the demand for basic food as well as other agricultural products is increasing, especially after income generating programmes for the poor such as MNREGA, the supplies are falling short, be it food grains, vegetables and fruits or animal husbandry products, thereby fuelling inflation.

Option of large-scale imports of food grains and other agricultural products is not realistic for our country. International prices of agricultural commodities are rising, and are likely to continue the upward swing in next few years. An additional and complicating fact is that bulk of tradable surplus in important agricultural commodities such as rice and wheat is concentrated in two or three countries, making the price of these commodities largely dependent on the production in these countries, hence more volatile. More importantly, the income of a large section of workforce depending on agriculture can be sustained only if domestic production increases, and terms of trade remain favourable. It should be recognised that in our situation possibility of extending the area under crops does not exist. There is a clear need for a substantial breakthrough in agricultural productivity.

Vision of Dynamic Agriculture

It is important to be clear about the future of agriculture one is contemplating. We are envisaging a sector where increase in production is sustained by a class of economically viable small and medium farmers. This would necessitate transfer of a sizeable number of farmers with miniscule holdings from agriculture to non-agricultural sectors. But this transformation will be predicated on a labour-intensive rural industrialisation to meet the demand generated by a productive farm sector. In other words, we are rejecting a scenario where small farms are amalgamated in large holdings supposedly to avail the economies of scale. We believe that that model is socially disruptive and economically inefficient. It is possible, as I will argue, to transform present agrarian structure from a stagnant and impoverishing one to a dynamic and just system.

Green Revolution: An Earlier Period of Growth in Productivity

We had gone through more or less similar period of stagnation in agriculture especially in food grains production, in the mid-1960s, when we were faced with a 'ship-to-mouth' situation, which threatened to compromise our political sovereignty. The country was saved due to green revolution, which was characterised with significant enhancement in productivity. From the late sixties to the middle of the eighties, agricultural production, especially food grains production increased in a sizeable way. The remarkable feature of agricultural growth in that period was doubling of agricultural output on virtually the same land area.

This was made possible, among other factors, because of a well-defined goal, namely food self-sufficiency. Political support, bureaucratic skills and scientific talents converged to achieve this goal. A variety of complementary measures were taken, such as development and extension of high yielding varieties of seeds, continued expansion of irrigation and farmer-friendly price policies. Institutional support for research, extension, credit and marketing, was provided to implement the yield augmenting strategy. Land reform legislation of the earlier period though failed to achieve redistribution of land to any remarkable extent, did succeed in breaking the hegemony of the large farmers and created conditions, which led to the emergence of a middle peasantry who spearheaded the green revolution. All this was achieved not due to a grand strategy, but by pragmatic steps in tune with the prevailing economic and political environment.

The strategy which made the green revolution a success had also inbuilt lacunae which became manifest over the period of time. Resting mainly on irrigated or well-watered land, it led to the neglect of rainfed area, and thus widened regional inequalities. Excessive use of chemical inputs resulted in deterioration of the quality of land and water. Heavy reliance on so-called superior cereals, i.e., wheat and rice, resulted in the neglect of more nutritious coarse grains. Price policy, which was designed to ensure the adopters of the new technology that their cost of production would be recouped, at the same time ensured that gains of productivity would be shared between producers and consumers, became an ad hoc exercise to placate one or the other section. In any case the input-intensive technology could not be sustained without huge food and input subsidies.

The Changed Circumstances

For forging a strategy with the objective of imparting dynamism to agriculture and ensuring improvements in the living standard of the households depending on agriculture, we have to appreciate the changes that have taken place in the sector and the country during the quarter of a century since the mid-1980s, i.e., in the post-green revolution period. Agriculture today has become basically a small farm sector. Its production base, land and water, is weakening; cropping mix as well as the demand pattern for agricultural produce is changing; it is much more integrated with other sectors of the country's economy as well as with the external economies; there is 'technological fatigue' especially in the crops grown in the rainfed areas and there is a general decay in the self-help institutions. None of these can be ignored.

It is not that all the developments impinging on agriculture have been unfavourable. We have, for example greater resources to invest in agriculture; developments of infrastructure in general and IT in particular has helped not only in terms of better communication, but also greater awareness. Private sector, which was always dominant in marketing has now a significant presence in certain regions and for certain commodities in production processes with contract farming and through input delivery. Economic reforms in key sectors have resulted in improvement in terms of trade for agriculture, which has helped certain sections of cultivators easier access to key inputs such as credit, and expanded the domestic as well as international markets for agricultural products. I have discussed these changes elsewhere but a few words on major development may be appropriate.

Indian agriculture is progressively becoming small farm agriculture. Dominance of small farmers was a factor recorded since we started counting holdings under the Census of Agricultural Holdings and the National Sample Surveys. However, the phenomenon of larger areas cultivated in the small and marginal holdings, now approaching more than 40 per cent of the total cultivated area in the country, has gone relatively unnoticed. Salient features of the existing agrarian structure can be briefly noted.

- For the country as a whole, small (including marginal) farmers constitute largest segment of agricultural holdings with major concentration in Uttar Pradesh, Bihar and Andhra Pradesh.
- Practically in all states of the country, small holdings account for overwhelming majority of total holdings in the state. For the country as a whole, they account for 83.5 per cent of agricultural holdings.
- Share of land cultivated under these holdings in most of the states is one-third or more, of the total cultivated area of the respective state, only exceptions are Maharashtra (31.7%), Punjab, (29.9%) and Rajasthan (22.6%). For the country as a whole, nearly 46 per cent of area is cultivated in the small holdings.
- Small farmers supply 62 per cent of paddy, 54 per cent of coarse cereals and 52 per cent of wheat.
- In most of the states, and in the country as a whole, number of marginal cultivators and the area cultivated by them is progressively increasing.
- Only in a limited number of states, most notably in Punjab, both the number of small holdings and the area operated by them has decreased.

Above data pertains to the year 2003. As this process of diminution of the size of holdings is continuing, it should be factored in as an important element in the strategy for agricultural growth.

Another disturbing feature of agricultural growth in recent years is the stickiness of labour force. GDP from agriculture is progressively declining but there is no corresponding reduction in the workers depending on agriculture. In this context, another significant change is the progressive feminisation of agricultural labour force.

An equally important, and worrisome fact is deterioration of the land resources. Though the estimates vary but it is generally agreed that one-third of the agricultural land is suffering from one or the other debilitating factor. Besides, the net area under cultivation, which has stagnated around 140 million hectares is likely to further diminish, as increasing pace of urbanisation and industrialisation will divert land from agriculture to non-agricultural purposes. Same is true as regards water. Claims of non-agricultural sectors on water are increasing, and efficiency in the use of water in agriculture is not improving. This is indicated by the fact that even with the expansion of irrigation share of double-cropped area is not increasing.

There is a significant change in the composition of agricultural produce. Now more than half of the value of agricultural produce is accounted by ancillary sectors such as horticulture, dairy and animal husbandry and fishery. Within the crop sector also major changes have taken place in the crop composition. Cereals are losing ground to so-called commercial crops. Within the cereal sector, superior cereals are gaining more land at the cost of coarse cereals, especially, millets and pulses. Changing consumer preferences have triggered this change. With increase in income, importance of cereals, especially coarse cereals, is declining in consumers' food budget and share of expenditure on milk, fruits, vegetables, eggs and meat is increasing. Producers are responding to these signals. Public distribution of food by emphasising wheat and rice in PDS has accelerated this change.

Finally, agriculture is much more integrated with the rest of the economy than was the case during the mid-1980s. There is integration both at the input end and at the produce end. Share of purchased inputs in the input structure has gone up in a remarkable way. With the importance of the horticulture, dairying and fishery sectors, more and more is being produced for the market. In the crop sector also there is a marked preference for high value crops. Changes in expenditure pattern—more expenditure on education and health thus necessitating cash income—have hastened this process of market orientation. As the number of marginal holdings is increasing and with that option of self-provisioning is weakening, this section also has to rely more on purchased food. With the opening of the economy, foreign trade in agriculture as ratio of imports and exports to the gross value of agricultural produce has risen. All these factors have made agriculture more market oriented and also highly sensitive to macroeconomic trends.

Indian agriculture is in a flux. We have seen that significant changes are taking place in its internal organisation as well as in the external environment. The policies and programmes should be designed while taking note of changes taking place in this sector, which are affecting lives of a large number of our people. Agricultural transformation should aim, first and foremost, at improving income of the producers with improvement in productivity.

Strategic Interventions

As mentioned above, one of the major handicaps faced by a large number of farmers is palpably small size of their holding. Even with gains in productivity many of the miniscule-sized holdings will remain economically non-viable. In order to raise income of the bulk of agricultural producers they should be enabled to have economies of scale in procuring inputs and selling their output. At the same time, providing opportunities to the small and marginal farmers for expansion of their holdings should be explored seriously. Let me touch upon the latter possibilities first.

Enlarging Small Holdings

Option of enlarging marginal holdings should not be ruled out. There are principally three ways in which the marginal farmers can be enabled to enlarge holdings: by stricter enforcement of existing ceiling legislation, by encouraging and legalising leasing–in of land and by facilitating purchase of land by small farmers. None of these are impractical suggestions. These have been successfully tried out in different locations in the country. There is a need to scale up such initiatives.

Leasing land: A large number of marginal and small farmers lease in land to expand their meagre holdings. As most of the states have made tenancy illegal, hence bulk of these transactions are not recorded. NSS (2003) has recorded 7 per cent of the operated as leased in area and 11.5 per cent of rural households as those leasing in land. Micro studies all over the country have shown that 15 to 35 per cent land is leased in. Among the tenants, large majority are the marginal and small farmers. Only in highly commercialised areas, phenomenon of 'reverse tenancy' exists. If tenancy can be made legal within the provisions of ceiling and registered, more land, and on better terms, can be made available to the marginal and small farmers. It has been rightly suggested, 'land lease markets are more flexible than land sales market and involve low transaction costs'.

Redistribution of surplus land under Ceiling Legislation: The other major initiative for expanding the holdings i.e., redistributive land reforms was tried in the past. The legislation provided for declaring ceiling on land-holding and distributing 'surplus' land among landless, marginal and small farmers. This was a bold initiative, but proved to be totally flawed when it came to implementation. There were serious leakages at all stages: less land was declared surplus than what should have been declared, (land declared surplus was hardly 2 per cent of the cultivated area); less land was taken possession than the declared surplus; less land was allocated to the beneficiaries than was acquired and, less land was actually given possession than what was allocated. Even then, as several micro level studies have shown where redistributive land reform could be implemented properly those who got land did benefit.The Committee on State Agrarian Relations and the Unfinished Tasks in Land Reforms has suggested that substantial area of land can be acquired for redistribution, even if the existing laws on ceiling are properly implemented. One must agree, however, that in the given environment redistributive land reforms are like 'an idea whose days have gone'.

Enlarging of holdings through the operation land market: Resorting to market led operations to enlarge holdings is not taken seriously in our country. This needs to be revisited.

True, number of individuals who wanted to purchase land, as suggested by the bank credit advanced for land purchase, was negligible. At the same time, where ever the state took interest in acquiring land, large chunks of land could be obtained. The cases of state acquiring land for establishment of special economic zone (SEZ) are fairly common. What is less known is the several initiatives of the states to acquire land for establishing homestead for landless rural households were relatively successful. This route of expansion of marginal holdings should not be overlooked.

National Bank for Agriculture and Rural Development (NABARD) has a scheme to refinance amount advanced by the banks for land purchase, which was started towards the end of the year 2002. Hardly any state took advantage of the scheme, only Haryana showed some interest. There too, less than 8,000 persons availed of the scheme in the last five years. In no other state even 1,000 persons have availed of the scheme during this period.

Reasons given for virtual failure of the scheme include:

- Information is not disseminated by the banks, or by the state governments in SLBC.
- Land records have not been updated, hence banks find it difficult to advance loan.
- There is wide gap between district land ceiling rates (DLC) and the market rates. As the banks tend to finance at the DLC rates, small/marginal farmers are not in a position to fill the resource gap.
- Generally, the owners do not sell irrigated land, and there is little interest in purchasing small fragmented pieces of dryland.
- Large farmers are not interested in selling land as the land values are increasing rapidly.

All these hurdles can be removed, and an active land market can be brought to existence with small farmers benefitting from it. But it will need active support of the state governments and the banks.

At least three states, Karnataka, Andhra Pradesh and West Bengal, acquired large areas of land for giving sites for home construction to the home less people. The procedures evolved, especially in case of Karnataka, are fair blend of market forces and state initiative, and active role given to *panchayats*. It should be possible to enlarge this programme to get land for the marginal farmers.

Improving Productivity on Small Farms

Other prong of the strategy is to improve productivity on farms, especially in the small farm sector. There was a good deal of research in the 1960s and 1970s on the size productivity relationship in agricultural sector. The overwhelming evidence suggested that the relationship was adverse and the small farms were more productive. The explanation given was that small farmers use their owned resources more intensively resulting in higher productivity. This conclusion was challenged in the recent years as purchased inputs claimed larger share in the input structure and the small farmers were constrained as far as own cash resources or credit are concerned. But more recent evidence at the all-India level has suggested that per hectare value of output on the small farms is even today higher than that on the medium and large farms. It was Rs 14,754 on the marginal farm and Rs 13,001 on the small farms, as against Rs 12,335 as average for all farms.

However, because of the small area, income generated by these households from agriculture is not adequate. Disadvantage of the small size is not compensated by higher per hectare output. It should be remembered that most of the southeastern and eastern countries, including China, have smaller holdings than ours, yet mainly because of higher productivity, they are able to earn much larger income.

There is large scope to improve productivity and earn higher income from the traditional crops on the small holdings. Yields of these crops (i.e., rice, wheat, millets etc.) are much lower than those obtained in other major producing countries. They are lower than the yields obtained by the progressive farmers in the same regions. Possibilities of a remarkable increase in yield on all types of holdings are illustrated by the growth in area, and income from dynamic crops, such as Bt cotton, maize and soyabean on all types of holdings. The main features determining the growth of these crops are:

- Size neutral, high yielding varieties,
- Economy in input use,
- Better quality,
- Active participation of the private sector in input supplies, principally seeds, and
- Growing market.

Such prospects exist in other major crops also, (e.g. hybrid rice).

Shift to High Value Crops

Another option for the small farmers is to shift from low value subsistence crops to high value crops. As it is, typically a small farmer devotes some land and resources to high value crops to generate cash income. The share of the high value crops, such as spices, fruits and vegetables is slowly increasing. However, the problems arise if the share of these crops were to grow significantly.

Logic for expansion of high value crops on small holdings is based on following premises: increasing demand due to income growth and urbanisation; higher and regular income flow; labour-intensive production.

With all these advantages, small farms find it difficult to make a major shift from grain-based cropping pattern to high value crops due to:

- Overarching requirement for self-provisioning,
- High capital requirement,
- Difficulties in marketing and
- High risks entailed in raising high value crops.

Of these handicaps, requirement for self-provisioning can be taken care of by an efficient public distribution system (PDS). Last three are more important.

Availability of credit: There has been phenomenal growth in credit to agriculture from the organised banking sector in recent years. Yet the credit available to the small farmers is not increasing. Difficulties in availing credit are more severe for tenant farmers and those small farmers who are not able to offer collaterals. They have to depend on the informal sources to obtain credit on onerous terms. Innovations favouring small borrowers such as self-help groups (SHGs) have largely bypassed the small farmers, as the main thrust is on consumption loans, or loans to small artisans. Disintegration of cooperative credit system has further worsened their plight. A more focussed attention is needed to provide credit to the small farmers, if they have to introduce high value crops on their holdings.

Marketing: Because of the small lot to sale, lack of holding capacity and immediate need for cash, small farmers are always at a disadvantage in dealing with the middlemen. These handicaps are aggravated in case of perishables like vegetable and fruits. For providing appropriate marketing facilities, along with transfer of superior technology and assured supply of inputs, contract farming is advocated. Contract farming is not a new innovation in Indian agriculture; it was introduced decades back by sugar factories both in the private and cooperative sectors, and later by milk unions. These arrangements were successful to the extent farmers had decisive voice in these institutions. Recent interest in contract farming by private sector should be encouraged. However, fair terms for contracting parties have to be ensured and an effective adjudication mechanism has to be established.

Risk mitigation: Propagation of high value agriculture in Indian agricultural setting is predicated on the access to reliable instruments of crop and income insurance. Existing instruments such as agricultural crop insurance to mitigate weather induced risks, and minimum support prices to ensure minimum prices for the staple crops, are not functioning properly. Defects in these devises are now well known and need to be corrected so that small farmers may take advantages of these protective measures.

Without proper and effective instruments of risk mitigation to ask the small farmers to go for high input intensive, high-risk prone, high value crops is to compound their difficulties. In the present circumstances the better alternative will be to propagate mixed farming with emphasis on self-provisioning, and 'commercial crops', or agriculture related enterprises such as dairying, playing a supplementary role. This is the model which bulk of the farmers in risk prone areas are adopting on their own.

With the existing institutional arrangements for risk mitigation and marketing, it will be advisable to emphasise strengthening of enterprises such as dairying, which ensure fuller use of small farmers resources; for which marketing facilities are reasonably well developed; which are well accepted by this category of farmers. (In 2003, small farmers accounted for 69 per cent of the total milk production.)

The small farmers on the fringe of towns who are growing fruits and vegetables should be supported to develop farm horticulture in more efficient way. (Although with increase in demand for land in the periphery of towns and cities for housing and industrial use, comparative advantages enjoyed by the small farmers in say, vegetable growing in the peri-urban areas is being threatened.) As a rule, for this highly vulnerable group, the strategy for diversification should be guided by the norm of 'from familiar to less familiar'.

Improvements in Delivery Systems

There are technologies available to raise productivity on the existing crops as well as to expand the share of high value crops. Policy environment at the macro level is by and large favourable. The major difficulty is the inefficiencies in the delivery systems.

Whatever strategy is adopted, the success hinges on the efficiency of the delivery systems. Bulk of the small farms are potentially viable in most of the ecological regions in our country provided institutional support is provided to them in terms of extension, credit and marketing and risk mitigation. An important ingredient of agricultural strategy should be to strengthen institutional structure to support the small farm agriculture. We have an extensive network of institutions, but they are of little avail to the small farmers.

Making Institutions Relevant to Existing Agrarian Structure

Strategy should be to adapt large delivery institutions in credit, input supply etc., to the reality of the small-scale agriculture by reducing transaction costs and protecting against high risk. This can be done as illustrated in the credit delivery by organisational innovations such as business correspondent (BC) model, and by use of IT and other technologies as practiced by several private sector firms dealing in the agricultural input supply or marketing of agricultural produce.

For risk mitigation, there is a need for strengthening and improving existing crop insurance system, increasing the reach of the 'minimum support prices' regime, popularising warehousing receipts as negotiable instrument, aggregating farmers to operate in the future markets and encouraging value chain financing by the financial institutions.

Reforming delivery systems in order to make them congruent to small farm agriculture is extremely important. State policies in this as in other respects should be consciously designed to support the small farm sector.

Aggregating Different Functions on Small holdings

Policies for strengthening delivery system have to grapple with the main problem of higher transaction costs to deal with the small farmers, perceived higher risk in dealing with the small farmers, limited capacity of the small farmers in absorbing high value inputs, and credit. Solution to all these problems is some form of collective action.

We have tried with different forms of cooperative societies, from collective farming to different variants of joint farming societies, but these have not succeeded. But there are examples of successful cooperatives particularly in dairy and sugar sectors. Newer forms of aggregation for availing of inputs and marketing of produce, such as producers companies also have better record. For other types of collective actions, examples of several initiatives in Andhra Pradesh (Velugu), Gujarat (SEWA) and Kerala (Kudumbashree), as well as of SHG federations in different parts of the country can be cited in this context.

There are certain features of successful group efforts, which need to be emphasised. The basic units in these structures are small homogeneous groups of farmers; there is a dedicated 'agency' to initiate and support them for a length of time; there are distinct gains in productivity and or realisation of higher value for their products; there is sufficient stress on capacity building. We will like to emphasise that in present circumstances, homogeneous groups of agricultural producers, with joint efforts to cater multiple needs of farming, can provide effective foundation for an efficient and equitable agrarian structure.

Integrating various functions such as input supply, extension and quality control, and more importantly, the marketing and processing with larger organisations in a vertical manner is another possible route. Even such arrangements will be more effective if farmers' group rather than individual farmer is a contracting party. We have now sufficient experience of working with different models of vertical linkages, and should be able to adapt them to the given circumstances.

We have successful examples of innovations supported by research and extension establishments, farmers organisations safeguarding and furthering members interests, innovative credit supply and marketing institutions, innovative risk-sharing arrangements, successful interface with spot and forward markets by the farmers groups. But such examples are few and far between. India's vast small farm sector can be a strong feature of the economy rather than a drag on it if such institutions and practices can be scaled up, and become the rule rather than exception.

Non-Farm Employment

Main focus of my lecture today is the growth in productivity, particularly on the small farms. However, it is equally true that a large number of small farmers will have to shift from agriculture to non-agricultural sectors. If that has to occur due to the 'pull' factor of better opportunities rather than the 'push' factor of lack of opportunities in agriculture, it will be important to understand what type of non-farm employment can be created and by whom. Such opportunities will be more sustainable if they meet the growing demands of a productive and prosperous agriculture. Since growth in the modern industries is virtually a 'jobless growth', two principal avenues for non-farm employment will be wage-paid employment in programmes such as MNREGA, and employment generated by rural industrialisation. There is enough written on employment schemes such as MNREGA, let me say a few words on rural industrialisation.

It is instructive to refer to China's experience in this regard. Agricultural prosperity in the earlier phase of reforms in China led to a spurt in household and prefecture level industries, in our terminology, tiny and small industries. There were three main factors accounting for remarkable growth of rural industries in China in the initial phase of reforms. Firstly, these industries were geared to meet the requirements of small farms (machinery for small farms) and demand from prospering rural households (furniture, building materials). Secondly, rural entrepreneurs started them. Thirdly, they had excellent technical support by government programmes such as SPARK programme.

These conditions can be fulfilled in our context too. Thanks to the reach of media and easy communication 'Revolution of Rising Aspiration' has also spread in the rural areas. With increased income a vast majority of rural households will provide an expanding market for consumption and production related goods. The large farmers in the country-side provide a pool of potential entrepreneurs who have investible resources, right contacts and capacity to bear risk, factors that are necessary to start and run a small enterprise. There is a network of institutions capable of transferring relevant technologies and imparting needed skills. We need a positive approach to rural industrialisation and give it an important place in plans and programmes.

Shift in Policy Stance

For ushering in a just and productive agriculture sector, we will also have to take a careful look at the economic policies. One of the causalities of the 'economic reforms' is the neglect of agriculture in the policy domain. While formulating macro policies, agriculture is totally neglected. This is despite the fact that even with the declining share in GDP, agriculture remains the largest industry in terms of gross output. Of course, it is the largest employer in the economy. The major policy initiatives, be it in monetary policy, fiscal policy or trade policy, should be examined in reference to their impact on this large sector. This has become necessary as agriculture is getting more and more integrated not only with the domestic economy but with global economies as well. Now it is deeply affected by macro policies.

Apart from macro policies, there is need to examine sector-specific policies also. Despite substantial reforms, there are still some kinks in the credit, marketing and trade policies. Price policies and trade policies are not properly aligned. Policy of 'cheap inputs–cheap output' implying huge subsidies needs to be reviewed. Greater attention has to be paid to the rural infrastructure in allocation of resources. Similarly, greater allocation has to be made for rejuvenating land and water resources, and on skill formation. Role of the private sector and of the public sector should be clearly defined in agricultural development. Above all, policies should recognise the reality of growing small farm sector.

We have to relate policies, programmes and delivery systems to the reality of a small farm dominated agrarian structure on the one hand, and changing demand pattern for agricultural produce on the other. Then alone we will be able to face the challenge of transforming a stagnant and impoverishing agriculture to a just, efficient and dynamic sector.

First green revolution was initiated and sustained by medium and large farmers. With appropriate supportive actions, the next revolution can be ushered in by the small farmers. And that will be the just and sustainable transformation.

6th Tarlok Singh Memorial Lecture, 11th October 2011.

15 Reforming Agriculture

Ashok Gulati

By now, it is almost certain that the agri-GDP growth for this ongoing Eleventh Five Year Plan (2007-2012) will remain around 3.2 per cent, way below the targetted growth rate of 4 per cent per annum. This is not the first time that the achievement will be short of the target by a full 20 per cent; in the last five year plan (2002-2007), the situation was even worse when the actual agri-GDP growth was only 2.4 per cent against a target of 4 per cent, and almost similar to the performance (2.5%) in the plan even before that (1997-2002). This repeated failure to achieve a modest target of 4 per cent, plan after plan, speaks volumes of the hollowness in our policy-making process, which either does not understand what drives growth in agriculture, or does not know how to design policies that can work towards attaining that target, or does not have the political will to do so.

But one thing needs to be made clear to our policymakers: unless the agri-sector takes off to a 4 per cent plus growth trajectory, the chances of reducing poverty in any significant manner and within a short timeframe will remain dim, no matter how many freebies are doled out. The approach paper to the coming Twelfth Five Year Plan (2012-2017) itself recognises that a one per cent growth emanating from the agriculture sector would be at least two to three times more effective in reducing poverty than the same growth coming from non-agriculture sectors. In the case of China, it was 3.5 times more effective and in the case of Latin American countries, especially Brazil, it was 2.7 time more effective.[1] Remember that China started off its reforms with agriculture in 1978, and during 1978-1984, agri-GDP increased by more than 7 per cent per annum and farm incomes by more than 14 per cent per annum (due to liberating of agri-prices), halving poverty in just six years!

1. *World Development Report 2008.*

It should not be difficult for a country like India to recognise the importance of agriculture, where 52 per cent of the labour force is still engaged, a large mass of the poverty stricken are to be found in the rural areas and whose main occupation remains agriculture, and where an average Indian spends about half of the household expenditure on food (the bottom 30 per cent population spends 60 per cent). If this is the reality, why can't our policymakers put agriculture on the highest agenda for the Twelfth Five Year Plan, if they are in fact committed to alleviating poverty from this land?

Assuming there is a 'political will' to banish poverty on a sustainable basis, and not temporarily through doles (and this is a big assumption), what could be the agenda for reforms that can give us at least four per cent growth in agriculture for the next 10 years and make a significant dent on poverty?

An outline of an agenda for reforming agriculture is presented below.[2] There are basically three elements (troika or trinity) needed to propel agriculture, call it the magic of three 'I's, namely investments, incentives and institutions. Let us discuss each of them in some detail to get a better handle on why things are not moving in agriculture at a pace they need to.

Investments and Subsidies in Agriculture

Elementary growth theory tells us that the growth of a sector depends upon the investments made in that sector, its capital-output ratio, and the efficiency of capital in that sector. The Planning Commission assumes that the capital-output ratio in agriculture is around 4:1, i.e., to get one per cent growth in agriculture GDP, we need to invest about four per cent of agri-GDP. That means to get four per cent growth in agriculture, investment should be around 16 per cent of agri-GDP. During much of the period from 1980-81 onwards till 2007-08, investment in agriculture (gross capital formation) from both the public and private sectors was always below this threshold mark of 16 per cent (Figure 15.1). One wonders then why our

2. Some of these points have been discussed in several papers written by this author, most notably in "Accelerating Agriculture Growth: Moving from Farming to Value Chains", in *India's Economy: Performance and Challenges* (Essays in Honour of Montek Singh Ahluwalia), edited by Shankar Acharya and Rakesh Mohan, Oxford University Press, 2010.

policy planners even expect a four per cent growth in agriculture when they are neither putting in enough resources from the government kitty nor incentivising the private sector to do so. It is only in recent years that capital formation has crossed the 16 per cent mark, and one hopes that it will stay there for us to see some positive results on the agri-growth front.

Figure 15.1

Gross Capital Formation (GCF) in Agriculture as Per cent of Agri-GDP

GCF (Agri) as a % of GDP (Agri)

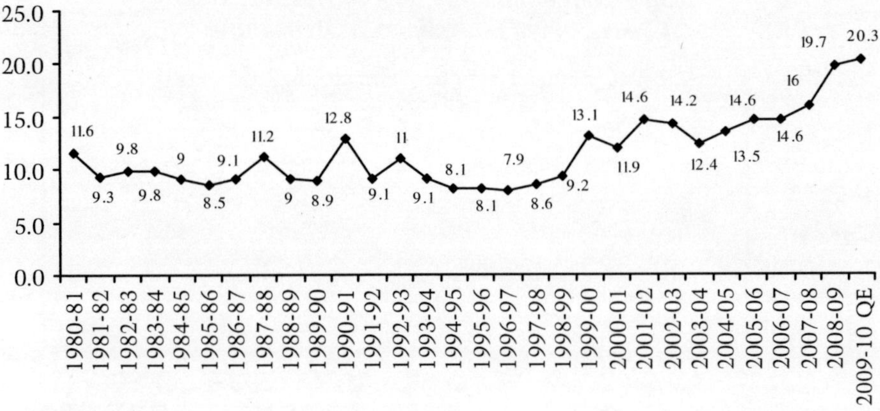

Source: CSO.

The only consoling factor in Figure 15.1 is that somewhere in the middle of the 1990s, the falling trend of investment in agriculture was arrested and reversed, and this trend has continued, with some occasional hiccups. Was it the impact of overall reforms in the economy that has attracted more private investment, or was it the government's policy choice to allocate more public resources to agriculture? The answer can perhaps be gauged from Figure 15.2, which gives a breakup of public and private investments in agriculture since 1980-81.

It is interesting to note that in the early 1980s, the share of public and private investment in agriculture was almost equal, but subsequently the share of public investment fell drastically. There was an attempt in the early 1990s to escalate the share of public investment, but the impetus soon petered out. It did marginally improve during 2003-2007, only to fall again. By the end of the 2000 decade, the share of public investment in agriculture amounted to only about a quarter of the total investment, a drop of 50 per cent from its position in the early 1980s. So, primarily, it was the investment by the private sector, by the farming community itself, that drove growth. If one were to conjecture that the efficiency of private investment is higher than the efficiency of public investments, this result, that growth in agriculture is primarily driven by the private sector, will become even more pronounced.

Figure 15.2

Share of Public and Private Investments (Gross Capital Formation) in Agriculture

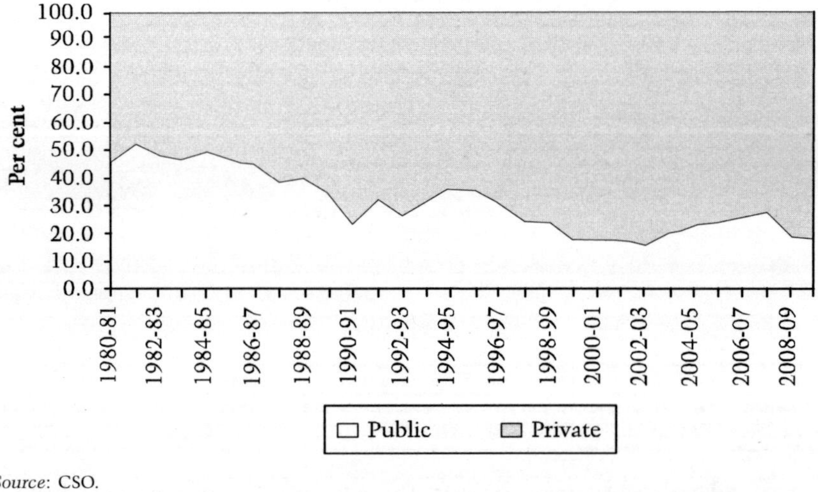

Source: CSO.

This in turn raises two questions: (a) what happened during the 1990s and 2000s that helped propel private investments in relation to public investments in agriculture and (b) did the government deliberately withhold investments in agriculture and divert them elsewhere? The first question relates to the issue of incentives in agriculture during the period of economic reforms, which I will take up later in the paper, but at present let us respond to the issue of public resources in agriculture. It is incorrect to say that the government deliberately withdrew resources from this sector, but if we look at the overall public resources going to agriculture through investments and subsidies, the picture becomes clearer. And it is here that the political economy of agriculture policymaking rests. The overall public resources going to agriculture in the form of investments and subsidies on inputs like fertilisers, power, irrigation and credit is shown in Figure 15.3. The trend demonstrated in the figure is very clear: that resources going through the input subsidy route are increasing at a rate that is almost three times faster than the rate at which public investment has increased. Overall, it appears that there are sufficient public resources going to agriculture. Also, it may be noted that even public investment in agriculture has improved, especially after the drought of 2002-03. And this was a conscious policy decision. However, the fact remains that the public resources in the form of subsidies are overwhelming greater (five and half times more) than those going through public investments.

Figure 15.3

Public Investments and Input Subsidies in Indian Agriculture (at Constant 2004-05 Prices)

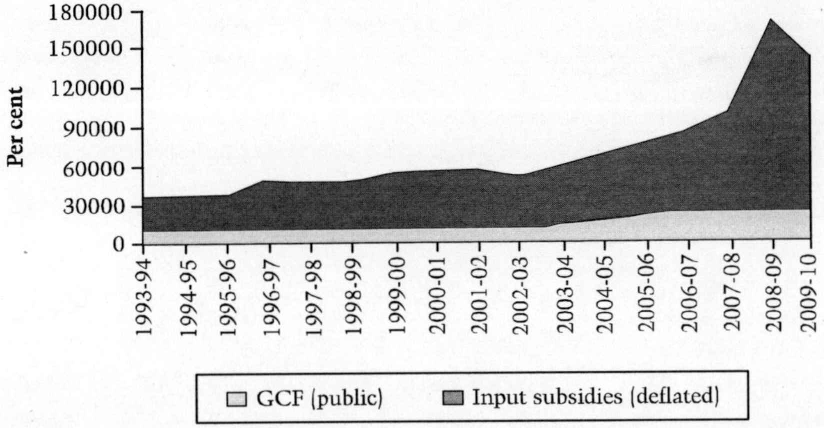

Source: CSO.

What is the problem with this type of approach where input subsidies outweigh public investments by almost five and a half times? It reflects an inherent policy preference in favour of subsidies, which seems to give quick political returns. But public investments are dominated (more than 80 per cent) by major and medium irrigation schemes which have long gestation lags, and it is difficult to associate them with any political party, particularly when parties lose power quickly. So that is as far as the political economy works, which looks to quick political returns.

But how about the economics of investments and subsidies? An earlier study by Fan *et al.*[3] suggests that the marginal returns to public investments are at least 5 to 10 times higher than through subsidies such as on fertilisers, power, and so on, insofar as the objective function is either agricultural growth or poverty alleviation. The key results of this comprehensive study are presented in Table 15.1.

Table 15.1

Returns in Growth and Poverty Reduction to Investments and Subsidies

	1970s	*1980s*	*1990s*
	Returns in agricultural GDP (Rs per Rs spending)		
Roads	19.99	8.89	7.66
Education	14.66	7.58	5.46
Irrigation investment	8.00	4.71	4.37
Irrigation subsidies	5.22	2.25	2.47
Fertiliser subsidies	1.79	1.94	0.85
Power subsidies	12.06	2.25	1.19
Credit subsidies	18.77	3.00	4.26
Agricultural R&D	8.65	7.93	9.50
	Returns in rural poverty reduction (number of poor reduced per million Rs spending)		
Roads	4124.15	1311.64	881.49
Education	1955.56	651.40	335.86
Irrigation investment	630.37	267.01	193.21
Irrigation subsidies	393.70	116.05	113.47
Fertiliser subsidies	90.07	109.99	37.41
Power subsidies	998.42	125.50	59.15
Credit subsidies	1448.51	154.59	195.66
Agricultural R&D	642.69	409.00	436.12

Source: Fan *et al.* (2008).

The interpretation of just a few results from this table suggests that if the public exchequer had an extra billion dollars to spend on say roads, education, irrigation investments, irrigation subsidies, power subsidies, fertiliser subsidies, credit subsidies and on agriculture R&D, and if the

3. Fan, Shenggen, Ashok Gulati and Sukhadeo Thorat (2008). "Investments, Subsidies and Pro-Poor Growth in Rural India", *Agricultural Economics* 39.

objective was to maximise returns in terms of agri-GDP, public expenditure on agri-R&D would have yielded returns equal to 9.5 times the expenditure, while if the same money was spent through fertiliser subsidies, the returns would have been only 0.85 times the expenditure incurred during the 1990s. This shows that investment expenditure on agri-R&D is the most powerful driver of agri-growth, followed by rural roads, education and irrigation investments during the 1990s. The returns from subsidies, particularly from fertiliser and power, are pitiably low.

If, however, the objective was to reduce the number of poor, then the returns during the 1990s were highest from investments in rural roads followed by agri-R&D, education and credit subsidies and irrigation investments (public), and lowest from fertiliser and power subsidies. It is also interesting to note the rate of returns changed over the three decades.

The policy message for reforming agriculture is very clear: we need to rationalise and prune input subsidies and channelise those savings towards investments in agri-R&D, rural roads, rural education and irrigation. That is the way to go if we wish to put agriculture on a four per cent plus growth trajectory, and also solve the problem of poverty in rural areas. Investments may have to be doubled, even trebled and quadrupled, and this would be feasible (given the size of subsidies) provided the policymakers are bold enough to bite the bullet and prune input subsidies.

One way to contain the subsidy bill and to make it much more productive than is the case today, is to give subsidies directly to the farmers. For example, the fertiliser subsidy can be directly transferred to farmers' accounts on a per hectare basis, thereby freeing the fertiliser sector. In this way one can avoid paying for the inflated and gold plated costs of fertiliser plants. An earlier analysis had revealed that almost half of the fertiliser subsidy shown in the budget actually goes to maintain high cost fertiliser plants, and only half reaches the farmer.[4] The problem with power subsidies, which also incorporate high costs of SEBs, as well as thefts by non-agricultural sectors, is also similar. There is need for major reform in this area.

---

4. Ashok Gulati and Sudha Narayanan (2003). *Subsidy Syndrome in Indian Agriculture*. Delhi: Oxford University Press.

Incentives

As noted earlier, private investment in agriculture is the prime mover behind growth of agriculture, and its share has almost doubled between the early 1980s and the late 2000s. And private investment responds to incentives, both at macro level as well as at micro level. The macro-incentive environment, which earlier discriminated against agriculture through an overvalued exchange rate and high industrial tariffs, was substantially corrected and then almost eliminated during the economic liberalisation process which actually started in the mid-1980s, and then got a shot in the arm in the early 1990s. This made Indian agriculture competitive in global markets, and with the opening of agri-exports in the early 1990s, agriculture got a positive response with the growth rate registering 4.8 per cent per annum during the five year plan period: 1992-1997.

But just as agri-exports were on the upswing, and domestic prices for farmers started improving, the government put a ban on exports of several agri-products in 1996 and began following restrictive domestic agrimarketing policies with a view to containing food prices at home. This objective of protecting poor consumers through the tools of trade and pricing policies adversely affects incentives to the producers. This conflict needs to be resolved. The global experience in this regard is to increasingly use income policy to protect the poor, while continuing with a liberal trade and price policy as far as the producers are concerned. But India has yet to make this transition, and in the interim, the policy of restrictive trade and prices does not help either.

An argument is often made that India has a large number of small landholders, and an even larger number of poor consumers; therefore, reaching each one through an income support route is practically impossible. This may have been the case in yesteryears, but now, given that India prides itself in IT, one can use this high technology to reach each one through the UID route. This would help protect the poor in case domestic prices of agri-products go up, but will not interfere with incentives to farmers.

However, pending the above switch in the use of policy instruments—from trade and pricing to income policy—many other things can be done to improve incentives for farmers and enhance their productivity and income levels. Much of the adverse impact on incentives comes from strangulating domestic markets under the Essential Commodities Act, 1955. This law allows the states to restrict movement of agri-products across state boundaries, impose levies on processors, impose stocking limits on traders, suspend futures markets, and so on. States like Punjab also impose heavy fees and taxes, often as high as 14.5 per cent, on basic staples like wheat and rice.

The Agricultural Produce Marketing Committee Act (APMC) is another lethal instrument that goes against the interests of farmers and favours commission agents at the cost of farmers and consumers alike. For a five minute auction, e.g., in the Azadpur market in Delhi or the Vashi market in Mumbai, the commission agents charge as high as a 6-15 per cent commission on the value of output sold. This is utterly disproportionate to the services rendered. No wonder they have prospered at the cost of farmers and consumers. What is needed as a first step is a clean sweep of both the ECA and APMC Acts that can ensure the free movement of goods across India, without multiple taxes, and direct buying by organised retailers and processors from the farmer groups. With these two policy changes, India can usher in a revolution in marketing of agri-produce, improving incentives and incomes of the farmers.

Institutions

Structurally, Indian agriculture is dominated by smallholdings. About 83 per cent of holdings are less than two hectares in size and together they account for a little more than 40 per cent of the cultivated area, contributing roughly half of the value of agricultural output. So in terms of productivity they are not far behind; in fact they are, and can stay ahead of large farms if only they have access to modern inputs. Where they lose out is in marketing, as the top end of the value chain (organised retailing and processing) is consolidating and scaling up, while farm holdings are still fragmenting. This poses a challenge of matching the scale. In order to scale up at the bottom end, two major institutional reforms are needed. One, small farmers need to be organised in clusters, call them cooperatives or farmer producer organisations (FPOs), and they need to link up with processors and organised retailers. This was achieved under the Amul model in case of milk and needs to be replicated for most other high value perishable commodities such as fruits and vegetables, poultry and meat products. Second, the land lease markets need to be freed so that there can be a vibrant market for land lease without fear of anyone losing his/her land. This would involve changes in tenancy laws that at present favour the tiller and would go a long way in enabling an economically viable holding size in India.

Another critical institutional reform required is in the area of agri-R&D. We have already mentioned the need to increase investments in agri-R&D as it gives high returns in terms of agri-growth as well as poverty alleviation. But this would be even more effective if the R&D setup undergoes a major institutional reform, where scientists are hired, say on three to five years of renewable contracts, depending upon their performance in terms of delivery. Similarly, in extension of agri-R&D, we need to create a hybrid with the private sector under a PPP model where government extension workers work with the private sector on deputation and the private sector pays them, say 25 per cent on top of their government salary. This would incentivise the whole agri-R&D system and research can move from lab to land quickly, giving high returns to the society at large.

These are some of the critical policy changes required to put Indian agriculture on a higher growth trajectory. There are many others in the area of insurance, credit, and the like that one can elucidate, which would contribute to India's growth story in agriculture.

Seminar 629, January 2012.

16 On Strategies for Disinvestment and Privatisation

Vijay Kelkar

The conceptual foundation of India's industrialisation strategy was laid by the Bombay Plan, which envisaged a strategic role to the public sector enterprises. Over the years, the size of the public sector has increased and currently, there are 473 Central PSUs including banks and insurance companies. Out of these, 104 are listed and 369 unlisted; while at the state level there are 1,160 PSUs. It is estimated by informed financial analysts that the valuation of the Central PSUs on P/E basis for the listed companies and P/B basis for the unlisted companies is now placed at $450-$500 billion or 40-45 per cent of the country's GDP.

However, according to the latest Centre for Monitoring Indian Economy (CMIE) data, the net profits of the Central PSUs work out to be only 2.2 per cent of their total assets. It is true that this ratio is higher for the oil companies such as ONGC and Oil India, but in general, the net return on the capital employed in PSUs seems to be lower than for the India's private corporate sector. If one includes the state-level PSUs, then the private corporate sector would show significantly higher returns on the capital employed. While the public sector or the state-led entrepreneurship played an important role in triggering India's industrialisation, our evolving development needs, comparatively less than satisfactory performance of the public sector enterprises, the maturing of our private sector, a much larger social base now available for expanding entrepreneurship and the growing institutional capabilities to enforce competition policies would suggest that the time has come to review the role of public sector, particularly the structural composition of the portfolio of public sector or in other words, of the country's 'public capital assets'.

What should the composition of state assets be? The answer to this critical question can provide an important perspective on the issue of disinvestment and privatisation. Very often, this question is not seen in the correct light. Many people in the policy discourse advocate state ownership of one more enterprise. Each of these proposals might appear to make sense in the small. But budget constraints are a harsh reality of life. Ultimately, there is a budget constraint in terms of the overall assets of the state. When the state chooses to own Re 1 of something, this comes at the cost of owning Re 1 of something else.

Public *versus* Private Ownership

The interesting and important question that we should all be asking ourselves is: what should the portfolio composition of the Government be? What assets should be held by the state? We need to think about this question, and once we have a consensus and clarity about what the portfolio composition ought to be, we should embark on a set of adjustments that take us to a different, and hopefully better, asset composition.

The portfolio composition of the state is not something that should remain static at all times. A few decades ago, India was in a very different setting. After Independence, the Bombay Plan was drafted by the business community. It envisaged government investment in capital-intensive and technologically-complex problems of the time, such as production of steel or electricity. In the 1970s, the argument was made that if the Government did not run an airline, then the private sector could not.

Some of the choices made in this period reflected the needs of the developmental state and this was a useful part of the early growth trajectory of a country. But those compulsions are no longer with us. The private sector is now fully able to muster the capital and technology required to produce steel or electricity. The landscape has changed and our thinking must change too.

So what assets should the government own and control? Most of us would agree that the airline industry works quite well as a purely private affair. All over the world, governments have got out of airlines. The decades of losses and poor performance of Alitalia airline is commonly held up as an example of what goes wrong when a firm is brought under public ownership. At the opposite end, most of us would agree that rural roads have to be on the balance sheet of the state. These roads typically do not have adequate traffic, and tolling would not generate adequate revenues. If the government did not own rural roads, these roads would not exist. Similarly, the public health capital in our towns and cities will need to come from the public sector. Equally, the preservation and improvement of forest cover will have to be a new priority for the public sector assets.

So there is a spectrum of assets, ranging from airlines to rural roads, where government ownership is inadvisable for airlines but required for rural roads or public health infrastructure. How should we think about where each problem falls? I would like to describe two broad categories where I think the story is quite clear.

The first area where we have a good understanding is goods and services in ordinary competitive markets. An example is steel. Now that India has near-zero tariffs on steel, it is a globally competitive market. Many private companies produce steel. The old argument—about capital and technology required for steel companies being out of reach for the private sector—is no longer convincing. We are now seeing Indian firms exporting steel into the global market—which demonstrates that there is no gap in technology. And, we are also seeing Indian companies turning into multinationals and buying up global steel companies—which demonstrates that there is no gap in capital availability for Indian companies.

Under these conditions, private ownership works best. This should be seen at different levels. First, under ordinary circumstances, private ownership generates the best incentives for cost-minimisation, innovation, and dynamic adjustment of corporate strategy. This is not an ideological position. An extensive research literature has examined privatisation experiences from all across the world, and the findings suggest big gains in productivity from private ownership.

The second aspect of public *versus* private ownership concerns the issues that arise when a company approaches bankruptcy. In the private sector, bankruptcy is taken seriously. The fear of bankruptcy generates drastic responses in terms of selling off parts of the company, modifying business strategy, etc. These are healthy responses from the viewpoint of the economy. When an unhealthy company sells off a factory to a strong company, the control of assets of the economy moves into the best hands.

Output and employment are optimised through these adjustments. In contrast, in the public sector, managers have a tendency to be relatively relaxed about the prospect of bankruptcy. Drastic adjustments when faced with extinction do not take place, because the managers know that there is no real danger of extinction. Public sector companies are always able to access capital from the taxpayer. So, there are two problems. Adjustments do not take place because of the lack of fear of extinction, and the taxpayer suffers from periodic claims on resources every time the company gets into trouble. There is also a deeper problem here. If in the market place, one of the participants like a PSU is operating under a 'soft budget constraint' and that too with deep pockets, then it can adversely affect the performance and fortunes of even efficient private sector companies operating in that sector and such a market structure will systematically misallocate resources.

The second area where private ownership is clearly desirable is in regulated industries. In India, we are now seeing numerous regulated industries, ranging from finance to infrastructure, where a government agency performs the function of regulation and multiple competing firms are located in the private sector. Here, the simple and clean solution—government as the umpire and the private sector as the players—is what works best. This configuration is used in every advanced country, and we in India also face the challenge of setting up this architecture of government as regulator with massive investment coming in from the private sector which builds multiple competing firms.

In many of these industries, we have a legacy of government ownership either directly by government departments or in the form of PSUs. The problems described above are very much there: productivity tends to be lower in public sector companies, the fear of bankruptcy is absent, and the risk of asking for money from the taxpayer is ever present. There is an additional issue. This is the conflict of interest between government as an owner and government as the regulator. For instance, the formulation and implementation of competition policy will be much vigorous and fair if government companies are not out of action. Look at the recent example of government's various policy measures to support Air India. Many of these can be construed as anti-competitive as these vitiate the playing field for our private airlines.

India's future lies in building a new institutional architecture with government as regulator and with the private sector doing investment. There is a problem when the government is conflicted. If the private sector feels that the regulator will not be an unbiased umpire in the competitive process, because a ward of the government is one of the players, then this makes the private sector feel uncomfortable. In the eyes of the private sector, this is a political risk. To pay for higher risk, the private sector demands a higher return. Fewer projects are implemented; the magnitude of investment goes down. With a higher rate of return on capital demanded by the private sector, user charges go up.

If we think of the next 25 years, a very substantial portion of the investment in all regulated industries in India is going to come from the private sector. It would be myopic for the government to have a regulator who is conflicted, which reduces the quantum of investment and drive up user charges. It makes more sense for the government to reorganise itself, shifting into the role of the umpire and away from the role of the player. We must move towards a simple and clean solution: government as an umpire and the private sector as players.

There are other areas where there are shades of grey or complexities. For instance, natural resource-based industries such as upstream hydrocarbons sector. Here, there is a strategic issue as well as the issue of optimal appropriation of the underlying vast resources rent. Similarly, the role of government *vis-à-vis* universities is also complex. Barring such a few but key areas, we can confidently set about reformulating the activities of the state in the following two key areas. Firstly, the state should not be producing things which can be produced in competitive markets—this covers areas like steel or aluminium or cars. And secondly, the state should not be a player in regulated industries—this covers areas like airlines, railways, shipping, telecom, banking or insurance.

A useful way to visualise this is essentially as a balance sheet adjustment. Suppose the government undertakes a portfolio adjustment, where Rs 10,000 crore of shares of Air India is sold and used to build 2,000 kilometres of highway. Let us trace through the full implications of this. Even if Rs 10,000 crore of shares of Air India constitute a minority sale (i.e., 'disinvestment' in the Indian jargon), then also certain efficiency gains are obtained. We now have our own empirical evidence which show that the mere act of listing induces improved productivity. Four channels seem to be at work: listing induces increased transparency, the stock market brings pressure on senior managers by doing daily performance evaluation, corporate governance is typically improved after listing, and to the extent that employees are given some shares, they become more aligned towards the growth and success of the organisation.

If Rs 10,000 crore of shares of Air India constitutes a majority sale (i.e., 'privatisation'), then even bigger efficiency gains are obtained. Extensive international evidence shows that productivity goes up strongly after privatisation. The increase in India's GDP because of a better-run Air India is the first gain from the proposed portfolio adjustment. The second gain from the proposed portfolio adjustment lies in obtaining an additional 2,000 kilometres of highway. The benefits for India of this public asset are simply enormous. The 2,000 kilometres of highway that we do not have is the opportunity cost that we suffer every year owing to an investment of Rs 10,000 crore in Air India.

In short, it makes a lot of sense for India to undertake this portfolio adjustment of public sector assets to switch from owning Air India to owning highways or public health infrastructure or augmenting 'environmental capital'. The motivation for disinvestment or privatisation should not be narrowly seen as being only about maximising the proceeds from the sale of assets. The real big gains come from the full picture. We gain when the private sector obtains higher productivity (and this happens even with mere disinvestment, but it happens much more strongly with privatisation). We gain when the private sector becomes more comfortable bringing capital into investing in India in regulated industries. And, we gain when the government is able to build highways and canals, metro systems and railroad, which are crucial for India's growth and legitimately belong on the government's balance sheet.

Privatisation

We may embark on disinvestment today, but we have to think about the end-game which is privatisation, where the government fully gets out of the picture. How do we want to approach the ownership and governance of PSUs? The two broad approaches that can be adopted for privatisation are 'strategic sales' (where a controlling stake is sold to one buyer) or 'open market sales' (where shares are sold to the public at large).

There are three arguments which favour strategic sales:

a. In some situations, the buyer brings in essential new technology or expertise.
b. The buyer can exert sound governance inputs into the firm, and has incentives to do so owing to the large stake and
c. The buyer can decisively displace government as the controller of the firm.

Other arguments in favour of strategic sales are somewhat suspect. For example, the argument that strategic sales fetch higher prices raises concerns. If the valuation of the buyer is solely driven by expectations of improved dividends from the firm, then there is no difference between his valuation of shares as compared with those of the broad public. If a buyer is willing to pay much more than the wide public, this would generally mean that the buyer plans to extract private benefits (i.e., steal) from the company, at the expense of minority shareholders. Such a transaction needs to be questioned.

Strategic sales of large public sector companies such as Vizag Steel or Hindustan Petroleum Corporation Limited (HPCL) are more likely to encounter operational and political difficulties. They yield reduced competition when existing incumbents take over such large PSUs. Most importantly, strategic sales serve to increase the concentration of power and wealth in the hands of a few hundred families of the country.

Strategic sales are often attractive owing to the perception that they yield higher proceeds. Perhaps, in the case of smaller public sector companies operating in competitive markets, strategic sales may be an easier option. However, as emphasised earlier, the full impact of privatisation lies in its impact on GDP growth and not just on maximisation of proceeds. There are other dimensions of the privatisation process in which strategic sales fare poorly.

Apart from strategic sales, open-market sales are an important instruments for disinvestment, and should not be overlooked in our policy efforts. Open-market sales are the path to obtaining dispersed share ownership, widely-held, professionally managed companies, and creation of widespread shareholder wealth. A disinvestment strategy based on open-market sales would strengthen institutions and corporate governance in the country.

At the simplest, in cases where a strategic sale has been completed, and a new management team is clearly in the saddle, government can eliminate the residual shareholding by selling in the open market. For firms where no strategic sale has taken place, government can privatise through open-market sales designed to deliberately disperse share ownership over a very large number of households, and create professionally-managed, widely-held companies.

India has now a growing experience of good corporate governance by professional management teams with widely dispersed shareholding, where no one family has a controlling stake in the company. Some of the best-run and most-respected companies in India, such as HDFC, Infosys and L&T, lead by an example.

According to CMIE data, there are 300 companies in India today where the 'promoters' control below 10 per cent. In each of these companies, the managing director and the rest of the top management team do not own a controlling stake in the company, yet these companies continue to function without being captured by other firms or individuals. This suggests that we do have significant skills and institutions in the country in the creation and operation of professionally-managed, widely-held firms.

The disinvestment or privatisation programme could explicitly target conversion of the larger PSUs into widely-held, professionally-managed companies, as an alternative to strategic sales which explicitly give over control of the company to a narrowly defined buyer. There could be provisions in the disinvestment mechanism that creeping acquisitions—which are currently regulated by SEBI—would not be permitted for a few years. For instance, there could be a rule requiring that no one individual or firm could own more than 5 per cent of the firm for a period greater than five years. This would give time for the professional management team to develop modern corporate governance mechanisms. Such an approach can be also applied to disinvestment in our banking sector.

India already knows quite a bit about having well-run widely-held and professionally-managed companies. PSUs which turn into private, widely-held, professionally managed companies could perform a valuable role in economic policy by strengthening this crucial part of the economy.

There is another dimension in which dispersed shareholding makes a lot of sense, and that is the political economy. If the disinvestment process is designed appropriately, it can lead to dispersed share ownership amongst millions of households. This could have enormous economic and political consequences. It would help in sharing the benefits of disinvestment with the people of India; it would improve support for the reforms process, and improve the stake in the functioning of the country as seen by households. The significance of dispersed ownership is not limited to the economy. Dispersed ownership would also have beneficial impact upon democracy. An exclusive reliance on strategic sales would greatly increase the wealth and power of a few hundred families in the country. Dispersed ownership, spread across millions of households, would spread wealth across a much larger slice of the country.

As an example of an international experience, it has been argued that the exclusive use of strategic sales in the privatisation process of some large Latin American countries was detrimental to obtaining dispersion of wealth and income in the country. We should seek to avoid such an outcome in India.

In the international experience, open-market sales have been widely used in all major countries which have strong capital markets and democratic institutions. Among OECD countries as a whole, in the decade of the 1990s, two-thirds of privatisation proceeds were obtained using public offerings of shares in the stock market. The stock market in India has made enormous progress in technology, whereby millions of investors now access the market using tens of thousands of satellite terminals and internet trading. Mutual funds, banks and foreign institutional investors

(FIIs) also exclusively trade through these computer screens. In the future, we could see foreign investments brought into India for FDI purposes become indirectly deployed into purchasing shares in the disinvestment process also.

Thus, selling shares through these screens is a powerful tool for accessing a very large investor base, which includes Indian retail households, Indian institutional investors such as banks, insurance companies and mutual funds, and FIIs. This is in contrast with the narrow group of buyers who interact with government on strategic sales. When shares are sold in India, they are accessible to foreign buyers of shares through the FII route. This channel can be strengthened by further liberalisation of the entry rules into FII status, and increasing the fraction of shares which can be held by FIIs. In contrast, when shares are sold in London or New York through the Global Depository Receipt (GDR) or American Depository Receipt (ADR) route, they are not accessible to domestic buyers. Hence, disinvestment within India is the channel through which the largest possible investor base can be accessed.

The primary market in India is a large conduit for selling shares and bonds. The disinvestment process could creatively exploit the sale of convertible bonds, exchangeable bonds, or exchange-traded warrants, thus better catering to the needs of retail investors, and current market conditions. From an international perspective, strategic sales have been heavily used in countries which lack domestic capital markets, such as the erstwhile communist countries. This is not a constraint that India suffers from. The National Stock Exchange (NSE) and the Bombay Stock Exchange (BSE) are now amongst the largest exchanges in the world, measured by the number of trades per year where they occupy ranks 3rd and 7th respectively. The stock market mechanism in India today—using electronic trading, clearing corporation, depository, and T+3 settlement coupled with vibrant equity derivatives markets—is now up to the best international standards.

The incentives of employees of PSUs could be influenced by sale of shares, and employee stock option plans (ESOPs), whereby every employee in the company would end up having a stake in obtaining a higher stock price. This would serve to align the interests of employees with the interests of owners, and encourage support for the disinvestment process on the part of employees. This is another attractive feature of the strategy of selling shares widely, instead of doing strategic sales to a few.

One of the important areas where the disinvestment process should seek to make continued progress lies in the domain of companies where the first listing has been achieved, and a clear secondary market benchmark pricc exists. For these companies, there is no impediment to establishing a steady and ongoing mechanism for government to gradually reach zero per cent shareholding.

There are concerns about the impact upon prices when government sells shares of (say) CMC (Computer Maintenance Corporation Pvt. Ltd.), which is listed on the stock market today. However, it is important to see that the valuation of CMC is fundamentally driven by the growth prospects of dividends paid by CMC. When the ownership of shares changes from government to some other hands, it does not (in itself) alter the number of shares, and it does not alter the prospects for dividend growth. Hence, sales by government are fundamentally different from fresh equity issuance, which dilutes the cash flows of the company and diminishes share prices.

A transaction where government sells shares could have a temporary impact upon market prices. This can be contained using two tools: the call auction and a sequence of preannounced small transactions.

Call Auction

The call auction is a computerised market mechanism through which buyers and sellers discover a single price which clears demand and supply. It is used, for instance, to discover the New York Stock Exchange (NYSE) opening price. The call auction is very effective at clearing large blocks of supply and demand, while giving all transactions a single price (i.e., zero 'impact cost').

It is possible for the NSE to build software which runs the call auction. Once that is done, the NSE opening and closing prices would come out of call auctions. This would offer government a mechanism to steadily sell shares using the routine processes of the secondary market, using a market mechanism specially designed to absorb large transactions without incurring market impact cost.

Preannouncement

A key element which should play a role here is a preannounced schedule of sales. Government can make a public announcement about a programme of future sales using the call auction. For example, government could announce that on the 1st of every month, 100,000 shares of VSNL would be sold on the NSE pre-opening call auction. This would serve as advance notice for myriad prospective buyers of Videsh Sanchar Nigam Ltd. (VSNL) shares to flock to the NSE trading screens on the 1st, thus generating demand for those shares. These sales would realise a value which is close to prevailing market prices.

Through such a programme of preannounced sales, government can engage in a steady selling of shares in simple, depoliticised way. Markets become volatile when they are surprised; by doing full preannouncement of all future transactions, there would be minimal disruptive effects upon the market.

There is yet another instrumentality, particularly for partial disinvestment and this relates to the sale of underperforming or underutilised assets of the PSUs. A prominent example of such assets is 'land'. Many of our PSUs have large tracts of land which have become very valuable with creeping urbanisation and with growing reluctance to make land available to new industrial units. One Central PSU alone in Bangalore has as much as 2,000 acres of such underutilised land. In cooperation with the state governments, such land assets can be leveraged by the PSUs by making them available to new units. This will remove one of the new constraints faced by Indian industries. When one includes such land assets of the departmental enterprises such as Railways and Port Trusts, a mind-boggling amount of resources will be available for the government for restructuring its balance sheet and for further industrialisation and alleviating housing constraints. This is also true for the state-level public sector enterprises.

There is one additional point, and this relates to the policy for deployment of resources generated through disinvestment/privatisation. According to current policy, this is to be channelised through the National Investment Fund (NIF). It may be argued that this is a restrictive policy and we should liberalise this fully by allowing the government to use these resources as a part of the budgetary resources to create new public capital assets—whether in the form of better urban infrastructure by providing capital grants to our cities or for revamping the country's energy base through an ambitious solar energy programme or the expansion of rural road network or for recharging the country's depleting water bodies and cleaning of rivers. This would require the Union government sharing the proceeds from disinvestment or privatisation with the state governments on a systematic basis on the lines of the Finance Commission's devolution formula for the sharing of union taxes with the states.

For coming decades, water, environment and urban infrastructure are going to be the key binding constraints on India's growth ambition. To remove these binding constraints, we will require large investments to accelerate the country's march towards high quality growth. Disinvestment and privatisation policy has now assumed strategic importance in our country.

We should recognise that disinvestment is an area of economic policy with multiple objectives. The most important objective should be that of increasing the efficiency with which the labour and capital, that is in existing PSUs, is converted into GDP. In addition, other auxiliary goals include enhancing investment in the country, creating new traditions of corporate governance, catering to consumer interests by maximising competition in product markets, and reducing the stock of public debt. An important positive impact of disinvestment upon our fiscal problems would flow through a higher GDP growth.

Policies on disinvestment must be particularly mindful of its ramifications to the political economy. The disinvestment process can lead to dispersed share ownership amongst millions of households. This would disperse wealth in the country. It would help create a middle-class constituency which has a stake in the profits of PSUs and (more generally) in the economic well-being of the country. This could have larger ramifications for the reforms programme. The design of disinvestment policy needs to cater to these multiple goals. In particular, a narrow focus upon maximising proceeds is unlikely to yield sound policies on disinvestment.

In terms of implementation, the recent successes with strategic sales have been a very important achievement of the disinvestment programme. At the same time, open-market sales are also a useful instrument in pursuing disinvestment. Strategic sales are attractive in decisively displacing government from the driver's seat, but suffer from many other important weaknesses which I have already outlined. Dispersed public ownership of PSUs particularly of our large PSUs is attractive in many ways, but requires obtaining sound governance. Towards this, we need to guard against a risk of PSUs being captured by managers, which can happen if control is not contestable and governance is weak.

There is a strong role for utilising asset management companies (AMCs) for managing the disinvestment process, and for performing corporate governance functions for PSUs pending complete disinvestment. There is also a need for building a consensus around extending the domain of disinvestment to PSUs in the financial sector. In a recent thoughtful paper, Dr Ajit Ranade has persuasively argued for such a strategy as there is a dire need to capitalise our banking sector. Undoubtedly, a relatively undercapitalised banking sector will considerably slow down the Indian economy.

To sum up, we need a bold and imaginative programme for disinvestment and privatisation calling for restructuring of the portfolio of the country's 'public capital assets'. It does not mean a retreat of the state but essentially a re-engineering of its portfolio of public capital assets. This will help our country meet the challenges of the first half of the 21st century just like our PSUs helped the country in the second half of the 20th century to overcome our industrial backwardness.

26th Sir Purshotamdas Thakurdas Memorial Lecture, Mumbai, January 29, 2010.

17

Empowering MSMEs for Financial Inclusion and Growth

Issues and Strategies

K.C. Chakrabarty

Importance of the MSME Sector

In a developing economy, the micro, small and medium enterprises (MSMEs) play a vital role and if India were to have a growth rate of 8-10 per cent for the next couple of decades, it needs a strong micro, small and medium sector and for that micro entrepreneurs need to be nurtured. As per available statistics (4th Census of MSME Sector), this sector employs an estimated 59.7 million persons spread over 26.1 million enterprises. It is estimated that in terms of value, MSME sector accounts for about 45 per cent of the manufacturing output and around 40 per cent of the total export of the country. The MSMEs are the best vehicle for inclusive growth, to create local demand and consumption and also to fight with the global meltdown. Public policy has rightly accorded high priority to this sector in order to achieve balanced, sustainable, more equitable and inclusive growth in the country. A microenterprise of today will be a big enterprise of tomorrow, and might well become a multinational enterprise eventually, if given the support in finance and capacity building. It is also an opportune time for putting more emphasis on MSMEs due to recession in many countries of the globe and rupee depreciation. The recession, while slowing down the global demand for goods and services, should not impact the sector, so adversely, as there is a huge demand in the local markets which could be tapped and the depreciation of the rupee has improved their price competitiveness of exporting firms in the sector.

Assistance provided by Smt L. Vadera in preparation of this paper is gratefully acknowledged.

Sizeable Growth in Credit: Yet MSMEs Feel not Enough is being Done

The MSMEs primarily rely on bank finance for their operations and as such ensuring timely and adequate flow of credit to the sector has been an overriding public policy objective. Advances extended to the micro and small enterprises sector are treated as priority sector advances. Over the years there has been a significant increase in credit extended to this sector by the banks. As at the end of March 2011, the total outstanding credit provided by all scheduled commercial banks (SCBs) to the MSE sector stood at Rs 4,575 billion as against Rs 3,622 billion in March 2010 registering an increase of 26.3 per cent. Despite the increase in credit outstanding to the sector, the MSME borrowers feel that the lenders are not doing enough for the MSMEs and are catering more to the needs of the large corporate. Let me now focus on the major problems/challenges/issues faced by the MSMEs and, more specifically, the micro and small sector.

Major Problems/Challenges/Issues Faced by the Sector

Access to Credit

Notwithstanding the increase in credit outstanding to the sector, access to adequate and timely credit at a reasonable cost is a critical problem faced by this sector. The statistics compiled in the Fourth Census of MSME sector (September 2009), revealed that only 5.18 per cent of the units (both registered and unregistered) had availed of finance through institutional sources, 2.05 per cent had finance from non-institutional sources; the majority of units i.e., 92.77 per cent had no finance or depended on self-finance. Thus, the extent of financial exclusion in the sector is very high. But, this is not entirely unexpected because if one looks at the financial exclusion in our country in general, then MSMEs cannot remain unaffected by it. But there is a need to bridge this gap through enabling policies and the Government of India (GoI) needs to play a catalytic role to cater to the needs of this sector.

First Time Entrepreneurs

The MSE borrowers, especially new generation entrepreneurs, do not have collaterals to offer to avail of bank finance. It is generally observed that collateral security provides comfort to the lenders as it ensures commitment of the borrower to the project and is also available to them for recovery in thc cvcnt of failure of the enterprise.

Infrastructure

In the present global environment, the MSMEs and more specifically the micro and small enterprises (MSEs) have to be competitive to survive and thrive. To ensure competitiveness of the MSEs, it is essential that the availability of infrastructure, technology and skilled manpower are in tune with the global trends. MSEs are either located in industrial estates set up many decades ago, or have come up in an unorganised manner in rural areas. The state of infrastructure including power, water, roads, etc., in such areas is inadequate and unreliable. Further, the MSE sector in India, with some exceptions, is characterised by low technology levels, which acts as a handicap in the emerging global market. Although India has the advantage of a large pool of human resources, the industry continues to face deficit in manpower with the right skill sets for specific areas like, manufacturing, service, marketing, etc. The HR problem is further exacerbated by the low retention rate.

Access to Alternate Sources of Capital

The ability of MSMEs (especially those involving innovations and new technologies) to access alternative sources of capital like angel funds/risk capital needs to be enhanced considerably. For this purpose, removing fiscal/regulatory impediments to use such funds by the MSMEs should be considered on priority. Access to equity capital is a genuine problem. At present, there is almost negligible flow of equity capital into this sector. Absence of equity capital may pose a serious challenge to development of knowledge-based industries, particularly those that are sought to be promoted by the first-generation entrepreneurs with the requisite expertise and knowledge. There is a demand for a dedicated Exchange for MSMEs.

Delayed Realisation of Receivables

Considerable delay in settlement of dues/payment of bills by the large-scale buyers to the MSMEs units adversely affected the recycling of funds and business operation of MSME units. Though the Government has enacted the Delayed Payments Act, 1998, many of the MSME units are reluctant to pursue cases against major buyers. After the enactment of the Micro, Small and Medium Enterprises Development (MSMED) Act, 2006, the existing provisions of the Interest on Delayed Payment Act, 1998 to Small Scale and Ancillary Industrial Undertakings, have been strengthened. The banks have been advised to sanction separate sub-limits within the overall limits sanctioned to the corporate borrowers for meeting payment obligations in respect of purchases from MSME sector. Necessary instructions have been issued by banks to their branches to monitor the position of payment by corporates to MSME and wherever found necessary, persuade the corporate to release the same on priority basis.

Sickness of Units

Growing incidence of sickness of the sector is yet another area of concern. When the sickness prolongs, it leads to the closure of units and unemployment. The mortality of the MSE units is high. This has wider implications including locking of funds of the lending institutions, loss of scarce material resources and loss of employment. As on March 2011, the number of units identified as potentially viable as a percentage to total sick MSE units is around eight. The units placed under nursing as a proportion to the total number of sick units stood at 5.22 per cent. The causes of sickness are both internal and external. The major causes are limited financial resources, lack of organisational, financial and management skills and expertise, non-availability of power supply shortage of raw materials, marketing difficulties, delayed and inadequate credit, obsolete technology, inadequate infrastructure, etc.

Exit Policy for MSMEs

An exit route for non-viable units is necessary to manage sickness. Worldwide, MSMEs are credited with high level of innovation and creativity, which also leads to higher level of failures. Keeping this in view, most of the countries have put in place mechanisms to handle insolvencies and bankruptcies. The present mechanism available in India for MSMEs is archaic. Business failure in India is viewed as a stigma, which adversely impacts individual creativity and development in the country. The existing legislations may have to be toned up so as to provide for efficient liquidation of non-viable businesses.

Initiatives by Government of India/Reserve Bank of India

Recognising the important role played by MSMEs in economic development and its sizeable contribution to employment and GDP, and realising that financial access is critical for MSMEs' growth and development, Government and Reserve Bank of India are taking the lead in supporting initiatives that improve access to finance. While at the broader level, financial inclusion makes growth broad-based and sustainable by progressively encompassing the hitherto excluded population, and has become a national priority at the more narrower level. Since the level of financial exclusion is very high in this sector, drive to universal financial access, including SME finance, is no longer a policy choice but a compulsion. The Reserve Bank of India has intensified a number of measures and endorsed quantitative access targets over the last year to further financial inclusion. Let me very briefly touch upon a few of them.

With an objective of ensuring uniform progress in provision of banking services in all parts of the country, banks were advised to draw up a roadmap to provide banking services through a banking outlet in every unbanked village having a population of over 2,000 by March 2012. The Reserve Bank advised banks that such banking services need not necessarily be extended through a brick and mortar branch but could be provided also through any of the various forms of information and communication technology (ICT)-based models, including business correspondents (BCs). A total of about 74,000 such unbanked villages have been identified and allotted to various banks through State Level Bankers Committees (SLBCs). As at the end of September 2011, as reported by the State Level Bankers' Committees of various states/union territories, banking outlets have been opened in 42,079 villages across the various states in the country. This comprises 1,127 branches, 39,998 BCs and 954 other modes like rural ATMs, mobile vans etc.

To ensure enhanced credit flow to the sector, in terms of the recommendations of the Prime Minister's Task Force on Micro, Small and Medium Enterprises (MSMEs) (Chairman: T.K.A. Nair, Principal Secretary, Government of India) constituted by the Government of India, banks were advised to achieve a 20 per cent year-on-year growth in credit to MSEs; the allocation of 60 per cent of the MSE advances to the microenterprises is to be achieved in stages *viz.*, 50 per cent in the year 2010-11, 55 per cent in the year 2011-12 and 60 per cent in the year 2012-13 and achieve a 10 per cent annual growth in number of microenterprise accounts. The Reserve Bank is closely monitoring the achievement of targets by banks on a quarterly basis. The matter is followed up with the laggard banks to know their constraints and impress upon them the need to devise strategies to gear up the credit mechanism for the sector.

Further, based on the recommendations of the Working Group (Chairman: V.K. Sharma, Executive Director, RBI) constituted by the Reserve Bank of India to review the Credit Guarantee Scheme (CGS) of the Credit Guarantee Fund Trust for Micro and Small Enterprises (CGTMSE), the limit for collateral free loans to the MSE has been increased from the present level of Rs 5 lakh to Rs 10 lakh and it has been made mandatory for banks. The Working Group has also made recommendations regarding increase in the extent of guarantee cover, absorption of guarantee fees for the collateral-free loans by CGTMSE subject to certain conditions, simplification of procedure for filing claims with CGTMSE and increasing awareness about the scheme. CGTMSE, which is implementing agency for CGS, has been advised to expedite implementation of the recommendations. The implementation of the Recommendations of the Working Group should result in enhanced usage of the guarantee scheme and facilitate increase in quality and quantity of credit to the presently included, as well as excluded, MSEs, leading eventually to sustainable inclusive growth

All SCBs have also been advised on May 4, 2009, to review and put in place MSE loan policy, restructuring/rehabilitation policy and non-discretionary One Time Settlement scheme for recovery of non-performing loans duly approved by their Board of Directors. Banks were advised in December 2009 to give wide publicity to the non-discretionary One Time Settlement scheme for recovery of non-performing loans for the MSE sector by placing it on their bank's website and through other possible modes of dissemination.

On the issue of alternate sources of credit, dedicated Exchange for MSMEs, marketing, technology upgradation and infrastructure, the PM's Task Force has examined the issues and has made several recommendations to address the bottlenecks. The implementation of the recommendations in a time-bound manner are being monitored by the GoI.

Role of Banks and Industry Associations in Empowering MSMEs

Role of Banks

There has been a burst of entrepreneurship across the country, spanning rural, semi-urban and urban areas. This has to be nurtured and financed. It is only through growth of enterprises across all sizes that competition will be fostered. As I mentioned in the beginning, a micro entrepreneur of today will become a small entrepreneur and then a big entrepreneur of tomorrow, and might eventually well become a multinational enterprise if given the comfort of financial support and capacity building. There will be failures and successes. Despite the risk, financing of first time entrepreneurs is a must for financial inclusion and growth. Banks will therefore, have to tone up their risk assessment and risk management capacities and provide for these failures as part of their risk management.

Banks have to recognise the vast potential that exists in responsible lending to the MSE segment. The banks must deliver on their voluntary commitments enshrined in their Code of Commitment to their MSE borrowers. Banks have, no doubt, through the Code of Bank's Commitment to MSEs, voluntarily committed to their MSE customers to provide easy, speedy and transparent access to banking services in their day-to-day operation. In the last Standing Advisory Committee meeting held on July 5, 2011, it was decided that the SCBs should understand the problem of the sector and devise strategies to gear up their credit mechanism structure so as to achieve the prescribed target of lending to the sector by the PM's Task Force. Sensitivity on the issue to be developed at various hierarchical levels, such as, discussion of the issue in the Board meetings, management level meetings once in three months. Branch manager's conference on financing to the micro sector to be held and the local NGOs, Khadi and Village Industries Commission (KVIC) could be involved so as to appreciate the problems of the sector and flagging major issues to remove constraints/bottlenecks in financing. The performance of branch managers in dealing with the sector should be made a criterion in their performance appraisal.

With increasing competition, introduction of new products and stringent regulatory environment, the role of banks needs to change from mere lenders to partners in business. There is a need for greater participation of banks in the affairs of their constituents by convergence of credit services and non-credit services. The bank's staff should be trained and sensitised through customised training programmes to meet the diverse needs of MSEs such as knowledge of markets, both domestic and global, use of technology, etc. Banks should be actively providing advisory and planning services and in fact hand-holding their clients through the setting-up stage and such services should be extended to all regardless of the size of their turnover. The banks should not only provide differentiated products for MSMEs, but also provide counselling & guidance to new and established businesses, marketing support etc. In short, all banks, in fact, may develop innovative mechanism to provide not only finance and banking services to their MSME customers but also non-credit related services to them under one roof at reasonable charges.

For creating transparency and wider dissemination of services provided by banks for their MSME clients, it was decided in the 12th Standing Advisory Committee on MSMEs that all SCBs should set up a SME portal on their website, where they could put in all information/ products of their bank for their MSE clients, as well as information on awareness programmes etc., organised by them. I am sure Central Bank of India and other banks would have taken a step in that direction.

In order to expedite sanction and disbursement of loan to MSMEs, a single window concept could be provided by Central Bank of India, if not already done. Loan facility to small units, say microenterprises, should be sanctioned at the level of the branch. A centralised Credit Processing Cell

(CPC) for MSMEs could be introduced. These cells may be utilised for single point appraisal, sanction, documentation, renewal and enhancement. The arrangement is expected to help in reduction in delay and multiple queries, utilisation of the available talent in an optimal fashion besides building reliable Management Information System (MIS), developing fair practices and easier tracking. Initially, the CPCs may be set up at each regional office of the banks and subsequently in the recognised clusters. In case of MSEs, simplified procedure of loan/application/sanction should be followed, score-based lending be done up to Rs 2 crore, working capital limits be given by projected turnover method, and term loans be sanctioned as recommended above to prevent the burden of data collection, project report/projections preparation for MSMEs. The disposal of applications should be done in a time-bound manner, which should be within the overall time limit prescribed by RBI. All banks should tap the available technology and setup Central Registration of Loan Applications. The same setup can be used by the borrower for tracking of the status of application on the internet on the basis of the receipt issued to him. The borrower may also be provided option of tracking his application over telephone on the toll-free helpline. The same technological setup may also be used for making online applications. Online applications may be popularised and publicised by all branches.

Lack of adequate capacity is the key feature, as regards MSMEs are concerned. In order to equip the MSMEs with the capacity to manage their businesses effectively and efficiently, comprehensive guidance and training on setting up new units as well as providing continuous education on different aspects of successful management of existing business enterprises must be provided. While the Rural Self Employment Training Institutes (RSETIs) are working in this direction, there is a need to examine the impact of RSETIs. A scheme for utilising NGOs to provide training services to tiny microenterprises could be encouraged. Entrepreneurship development is important in view of its visible impact on wealth creation and employment generation. To facilitate and encourage this, skill building has been impressed upon by the Prime Minister's Task Force for MSMEs. Enterprise development centres (EDCs) should be set up by the Central/state governments with incubators to provide training not just for setting up of new units but also to provide continuing education on different aspects like product design, packaging, technology upgradation, financial management and marketing.

Role of Associations

All SLBC Convenor banks have been to review their institutional arrangements for delivering credit to the MSME sector, especially in 388 clusters identified by United Nations Industrial Development Organisation (UNIDO) spread over 21 states in various parts of the country. The Central Bank of India has presence in 47 clusters identified by UNIDO and these branches have been designated as 'specialised MSME branch'. The MSME associations/chambers may bring to the notice of SLBC Convenor banks about the clusters where banking facilities are not available, so that the same could be addressed. Specific issues concerning the sector where banks could play a role should also be brought to the notice of the SLBC Convenor banks and the Empowered Committee on MSMEs by the industry associations for appropriate measures to be taken to solve the issues.

As any other sickness, the need for timely treatment after identification of sickness cannot be overemphasised in MSMEs. For viable units, timely and effective rehabilitation by way of renegotiations of terms of loans, induction of fresh dose of funds, business restructuring, change of management etc., may become necessary. The process should not only be quick, efficient, cheap and fair to all stakeholders but also acceptable to and implementable by all, with necessary monitoring arrangements for implementation of the same. In case the unit is not found viable, recovery of the dues of lenders through a fair, efficient and swift legal mechanism should be the focus. The senior-level representatives of MSME associations in each state are members of the Empowered Committee set up by the RBI at each of its regional offices, of which the SLBC convenor, representatives of banks having predominant share in SME financing in the state, SIDBI, Director of Industries of the state government etc., are also members. MSME associations need to use this forum not only for removing bottlenecks in the smooth flow of credit to the sector but also for reviewing the accessibility of bank finance to more and more MSMEs but also highlight gaps if any in the attitude and skills at the bank branch level. As it is observed that rehabilitation of sick MSMEs could not be taken up due to non-availability of promoters' contribution in a large number of cases, we have recommended to the GoI to set up a Rehabilitation Fund for rehabilitation of sick MSME enterprises.

The industry associations have often been representing on the delayed payments from large corporates. While banks have been advised to allocate a sub-limit in respect of large borrower accounts, for making payments to the MSE units against purchases from them but it is not possible for banks to force the large buyers to utilise the limit for making payments. This problem could be institutionally tackled by factoring. In the recent meeting of the Standing Advisory Committee to review credit flow to this sector, it was urged upon the industry associations to bring forward exemplary cases where big corporates have defaulted in making payments to MSE suppliers so that appropriate action, under the Act, could be taken by the Government of India.

The MSME associations and Chambers of Commerce have an important role to play in stepping up credit to this segment. Asymmetry of information and lack of transparency and reliability of data has been a major concern for organisations dealing with MSMEs world over. The association need to therefore, proactively engage themselves in organising workshops and training programmes for their members to enlighten them about cash flow cycles, various financial products, accounting practices, etc. In this regard, I would urge upon the other MSME associations, Chambers of Commerce etc., to collaborate, in the same manner with banks, National Institute of Bank Management (NIBM, Pune) or any other training institute in the area of banking and finance, basic accountancy and information technology for MSMEs.

Role of MSMEs

MSMEs too, on their part, should understand that banks are responsible to their depositors and shareholders and, therefore, they, i.e., the MSMEs, as customers of bank credit, have certain obligations to fulfill by way of repaying bank loans, maintaining proper books of accounts, submitting information correctly and more importantly sharing information about financial problems when these arise so that they can work together with the bank in resolving these. On the cost of credit, while interest rates have been deregulated by Reserve Bank of India, my message to the MSME sector is that: as interest costs are a very small fraction of their operating costs, only approximately 4 per cent, do not ask for low interest rates from the banking sector, and instead ask for credit at competitive rates. Credit has to be self-liquidating on a viable project and has a cost.

In fact, what the small entrepreneurs need to focus on are four typical mistakes entrepreneurs make as rightly pointed out by Peter F. Drucker in his book *Managing in the Next Society*. Many new businesses start out with high promise but suddenly run into trouble after a year or two. There are typical mistakes entrepreneurs make and all are foreseeable and avoidable. Firstly, majority of successful new inventions or products do not succeed in the market for which they were originally designed. So one has to keep options open and not be dogmatic about pushing a product in a market for which initially designed or targetted. Success may lie elsewhere. Secondly, entrepreneurs believe that profit is what matters most in a new enterprise. But profit is secondary. It is the cash flow that matters. A business that grows fast devours cash. Constant investments have to be made to just keep even. Thirdly, when a business grows, it is necessary to create a management team. Young entrepreneurs often cannot afford to bring in an external management team. So, it is necessary to identify the core competencies of the people working with you. This planning should take place well in advance. Lastly, when the business is a success, the entrepreneur needs to ask what the business needs at this stage and whether he is concentrating on the right things. As successful entrepreneurs, they have gained experience and wisdom from their mistakes and going forward, it is necessary to ensure that the same mistakes are not repeated.

Need for Financial Infrastructure

Establishing a solid financial infrastructure (credit registries/bureaus, collateral and insolvency regimes) should be a priority in the financial development agenda, as it can lower the costs and risks to financial institutions of serving MSMEs. Bankruptcy regimes regulate the efficient exiting of the market, and make the resolution of multiple creditors' conflicting claims more orderly, resulting in more extensive opportunities for recovery by both the bankrupt entity and its creditors. Stronger creditor rights improve access to finance. Stronger creditor rights tend to have a higher number of loan accounts per adult population and also higher rates of private credit to GDP.

There is a need for adequate and reliable credit information mechanism, such as an MSME credit bureau, that serves the needs of both the MSMEs and the potential lenders. Transparency shall facilitate them in obtaining finances, getting favourable contracts and improving their business prospects. A World Bank report stated that a good credit information infrastructure can contribute significantly towards assisting MSMEs' access to capital. The report further highlighted that small firms with access to credit bureaus have a 40 per cent chance of obtaining a loan, whereas firms without access to credit bureaus have only a 28 per cent chance of receiving a loan. Therefore, significant opportunities exist to increase lending activities to MSMEs with the establishment of MSME credit bureaus. A sound financial information infrastructure should improve transparency and disclosure for MSMEs in a cost-effective way, and help MSMEs build a credit history, which is critical in helping to address both challenges of information asymmetry and cost to serve. Setting of credit information companies has already been approved by Reserve Bank of India.

Conclusion

The recent past has been a challenging time for the banking sector in India. While the banking sector has responded well so far, there are several challenges that lie ahead. Our banking system needs to equip itself to deal with emerging challenges and be prepared to cash in on the opportunities unleashed by higher growth. In dealing with the needs of small and medium enterprises, banks have to look for new delivery mechanisms.

Keynote address at the Central Bank of India SME Conclave, December 20, 2011, Mumbai.

18 Monetary Policy Dilemmas

Some RBI Perspectives

Duvvuri Subbarao

Over the last decade, the profile of central banks has gone up. First, we had the Great Moderation—a period of extraordinary benign macroeconomic environment globally, characterised by steady growth in advanced economies and accelerated growth in emerging economies, and low and stable inflation all around. Central banks took credit for this, believed they had discovered the Holy Grail and declared victory.

That sense of triumph was dented by the crisis as central banks came to be blamed for policies and actions that got the world into the crisis. Even so, central banks battled the crisis from the frontlines and regained some of the lost reputation by acting quickly, decisively, and where required in concert, to stabilise the global economy which was hurtling towards collapse. Over the last few months, fears of a double-dip recession have resurfaced, and governments in advanced countries are locked in a policy logjam over the balance between short-term fiscal stimulus and long-term fiscal consolidation. This has willy-nilly pushed central banks to the fore once again as monetary stimulus is having to bear the burden of being the first, and in some cases, possibly the only line of defence against recession.

The crisis has been an intellectual challenge in many ways. It has tested the armoury of instruments available to central banks and the limits of their policy force. It has also reopened questions that we thought had been answered and renewed debates that we thought had been settled. My own experience has been that real world problems are too complex to fit template solution of textbooks. I want to use this opportunity that you have provided me to communicate to you some of the complexities and dilemmas in real world policymaking, and I will do so from the perspective of the Reserve Bank of India (RBI).

What is the Appropriate Monetary Policy Response to Complex Growth-Inflation Dynamics?

India recovered from the crisis sooner than even other emerging economies, but inflation too caught up with us sooner than elsewhere. Inflation, as measured by the wholesale price index (WPI), which actually went into negative territory for a brief period in mid-2009, started rising in late 2009, and it has remained around 9-10 per cent since January 2010 reflecting both supply and demand pressures. Supply pressures stemmed from elevated domestic food prices and rising global prices of oil and other commodities. The source of demand pressures was an economy with low per capita income which recovered sharply from the crisis. The supply pressures and demand pressures collided triggering a wider inflationary process.

In response to the inflationary pressures, the Reserve Bank began to reverse its accommodative monetary policy as early as October 2009. We have been criticised for our anti-inflationary stance, ironically from two different directions.

From one side, we have been criticised for being hawkish on inflation. The argument has been that our inflation is driven largely by supply shocks, particularly, since mid-2010, by high oil and other commodity prices, and that monetary policy should not respond to such inflation. We will only end up hurting growth. The criticism from the other side has been that the Reserve Bank has been soft on inflation, the baby step approach we followed—of increasing policy interest rates by 25 basis points (bp) each time—was not deterrent enough, and that the persistence of inflation is a result of our delayed response. Both these critiques cannot obviously be right at the same time. Let me offer a response to them and in the process explain the rationale for our anti-inflationary stance.

Monetary Policy Too Hawkish

My response to the 'doves' is as follows. Admittedly, monetary policy is best suited to contain inflationary pressures stemming from the aggregate demand side. In that case, the policy prescription is clear. If inflation is high, tighten monetary policy; and if inflation is low, loosen monetary policy. Monetary policy options in the face of supply shocks are less straight forward. Whether monetary policy is effective in dealing with supply shocks is therefore a matter of both academic debate and policy contention.

The conventional wisdom is that if inflation expectations are well anchored, monetary policy need not react to supply shocks. This premise is based on two assumptions; first that the supply shocks are purely temporary, and second that supply shocks are the only ones driving inflation. These assumptions do not always hold. In the real world, oftentimes supply shocks lead to a permanent trend upward shift in prices. Also, sometimes, demand pressures combine with supply shocks to stoke inflationary pressures.

A good illustration of the first assumption—mean reverting supply shocks—not holding comes from the world prices of oil which have trended up on a long period basis. International crude oil prices recorded an annual average increase of around 17 per cent during the 2000s as against only a modest increase of 2 per cent during the 1990s and a decline of 3 per cent during the 1980s. This obviously is the outcome of structural changes in supply and demand for oil. Monetary policy has to recognise these underlying trends and respond to them. If it looks upon these trends as pure transient supply shocks and ignores them, it runs the risk of destabilising inflation expectations.

And now about the second assumption—of supply shocks not usually acting alone to stoke inflation. The shifting drivers of inflation in India over the past year and a half offer a good illustration. The increase in global commodity prices coincided with rapidly rising demand at home. GDP grew at 8.5 per cent last year (2010/11), faster than the trend growth rate which is now estimated to be of the order of 8 per cent. In an environment of rapid growth and high capacity utilisation, corporates regained pricing power and were able to pass through the increase in input prices to higher output prices, thus, fuelling generalised inflationary pressures.

Similar dynamics were at play on the food front. Rising incomes, especially in rural areas, have resulted in a shift in dietary habits away from cereals and toward protein-based foods. This is a structural change and monetary policy will be misled if it treats this as a one-off supply shock. Given the high share of food in the various consumer price indices (46% -

70%), persistent supply pressures on the food front can fuel inflation expectations; and in the face of growing demand pressures, rising inflation expectations can trigger a wage-price spiral. Recent reports that real wages of rural labour have gone up markedly suggest that such a wage-price spiral may already be underway.

To summarise, the inflation that we have experienced over the last nearly 20 months is a result of a combination of supply shocks that had a trend impact on prices as well as demand pressures. Given the nature of the inflation drivers and their combined impact, clearly there is a significant role for monetary policy in combating inflation. Our monetary policy stance is guided by this understanding, and is aimed at restraining demand and anchoring inflation expectations. The argument of our critics that monetary policy has no role because inflation is a result of imported commodity prices would have been valid if the increase in commodity prices was a pure and transient supply shock or if there were no demand pressures. That clearly was not the case in India.

Monetary Tightening Hurts Growth

Another argument made in this line of criticism is that monetary policy tightening is hurting growth. I believe a much more nuanced evaluation of our policy stance is necessary. Evidence from empirical research suggests that the relationship between growth and inflation is non-linear. At low inflation and stable inflation expectations, there is a trade-off between growth and inflation. But above a certain threshold level of inflation, this relationship reverses, the trade-off disappears, and high inflation actually starts taking a toll on growth. Estimates by the Reserve Bank using different methodologies put the threshold level of inflation in the range of 4 per cent to 6 per cent. With WPI inflation ruling above 9 per cent, we are way past the threshold. At this high level, inflation is unambiguously inimical to growth; it saps investor confidence and erodes medium-term growth prospects. The Reserve Bank's monetary tightening is accordingly geared towards safeguarding medium-term growth even if it means some sacrifice in near-term growth.

Monetary Policy Behind the Curve

Now let me turn to the criticism from the opposite side—that the Reserve Bank was slow in closing the monetary spigots, that our 'baby step' approach was inadequate to tame the inflationary pressures, and that we are having to tighten aggressively lately to make up for lost time.

This criticism fails to appreciate the context—the nature of domestic inflation and global uncertainty—in which we were operating. The calibration of our monetary tightening was guided by the changing drivers of inflation over the course of fiscal year 2010/11. Early on in the year, inflation pressures had their origin in food prices, and accordingly our monetary policy response was aimed at containing the spillover risk to non-food inflation. Note that policy rates had gone down to historically low levels during the crisis, and an abrupt adjustment would have disrupted the market. Our judgement, therefore, was that tightening should be done gradually, in small steps, so as to allow time for the banks and the private sector to adjust to a higher interest rate environment.

The inflation scenario changed starting August 2010 when global commodity prices surged higher than anticipated. Global oil prices came under further pressure starting January 2011 because of political developments in the Middle East and North Africa. Also, as I had indicated earlier, because of the narrowing of the output gap, producers were able to pass on higher input prices to higher output prices leading to inflationary pressures getting generalised as evidenced by the increase in non-food manufactured product inflation from 5.3 per cent in August 2010 to 8.5 per cent in March 2011. We responded to these changes in underlying drivers of inflation by tightening more aggressively starting May 2011.

The second factor relevant in the 'behind the curve' debate is that we also had to contend with an uncertain global recovery. Even as there was some talk of spring shoots in April 2010, the optimism did not last; soon thereafter, the Greek sovereign debt crisis and unemployment concerns in the US revived concerns about the pace and shape of global recovery. These uncertainties increased both in nature and size as time passed with the Euro area sovereign debt problem not only spreading but proving to be intractable, the US recovery stalling and the Japanese economy assaulted by an unprecedented natural disaster. Our 'baby step' approach during 2010 was accordingly a delicate balancing act between supporting recovery at home amidst growing global uncertainty and containing inflation pressures.

If the above factors are reckoned with, the 'behind the curve' argument loses potency. Starting in March 2010, we have so far raised policy interest rates (the repo rate) by 350 bp. The effective tightening has been even more, 500 bp, as the operational policy rate shifted from reverse repo rate (absorption mode) to repo rate (infusion mode).

In offering a response to the criticism of our monetary policy stance from both sides, my endeavour has been to communicate to you that every monetary policy action involves complex judgement. The supply shocks we confront in the real world are different from pure textbook versions; oftentimes they coincide with rising demand pressures. We have to balance growth-inflation concerns. On top of that, monetary policy actions need to be forward looking even in the face of external uncertainty. This in essence is the dilemma of monetary policy decisions.

How do you Justify Liquidity Injection in the Midst of a Tightening Cycle?

The conventional tools of monetary policy are controls over the volume of money (liquidity) and the price of money (policy interest rate). Typically an expansionary stance would involve easing both the rate and volume, and conversely, a contractionary stance would involve tightening both of them. Occasionally, there arise situations when the price and volume instruments are deployed in opposite directions—for example, injecting liquidity amidst a rate tightening cycle—that call for both cautious judgement and extra effort at communication.

In understanding the motive force for liquidity adjustment by a central bank, it must be noted that a growing economy requires the central bank to inject primary liquidity to meet the requirement for currency and credit. This injection can come about only through an expansion of the reserve (base) money. In the first instance, liquidity injection happens through overnight borrowing by banks under the liquidity adjustment facility (LAF). If the liquidity shortage is of a durable nature, the central bank needs to meet that need through outright open market operations (OMOs) by buying government securities.

As we progressed with monetary tightening through 2010, the LAF window shifted from a surplus (absorption) mode to a deficit (injection) mode. This was consistent with our anti-inflationary stance since a deficit liquidity situation would improve monetary transmission. We had also indicated clearly that it would be the endeavour of the Reserve Bank to maintain the absorption or injection through the LAF window at about ± 1 per cent of the net demand and time liabilities (NDTL) of banks. However, towards the second half of 2010, systemic liquidity tightened further pushing the injection through the LAF window beyond 1 per cent of NDTL. This was owing to a combination of structural and one-off factors. Recognising that the deficit in systemic liquidity was of a durable nature, the Reserve Bank conducted outright OMOs to inject liquidity of a durable nature.

This liquidity injection through OMOs happened at a time when we were tightening policy rates to combat inflation. These were seemingly contrarian actions, and many observers may have seen them as being conflicting and incoherent. We realised that there was a communication challenge here—to explain to the market that we remained committed to bringing inflation down, that our action in injecting liquidity was not inconsistent with our anti-inflation stance, that we continued to hold that liquidity should be in a deficit mode in a monetary tightening cycle, but that we were injecting liquidity only to ease the 'excessive deficit' in order to ensure that flow of credit for productive purposes was not choked.

Informed market participants did of course understand the rationale for our actions. But we recognised the importance of communicating the rationale to the larger public. If people got confused policy signals and believed thereby that the central bank's commitment to inflation control was not credible, inflation expectations would get unhinged and that would erode the effectiveness of our anti-inflation strategy. We, therefore, went the extra mile to communicate the rationale at a non-technical level.

Forward Guidance: How Transparent can/should a Central Bank Be?

Received wisdom today is that successful monetary policy is not just a matter of effective calibration of overnight interest rates, but also of shaping market expectations of the way in which interest rates, inflation and income are likely to evolve on the way forward. Among the important instruments used by central banks for this purpose is the 'forward guidance' they give in their monetary policy statements.

The practice of giving forward guidance varies across central banks. By far the most explicit has been the Bank of Canada which, given the uncertainty during the crisis, gave a definite timeframe until which it would keep overnight rate at the 'current' level, subject of course to the outlook for inflation. The European Central Bank (ECB) has traditionally been less explicit on the ground that policy commitment is not possible in an uncertain macro environment. The US Fed has a more credible record of using forward guidance to shape and manage expectations. For over two years since the crisis, the Fed had guided the markets by saying that 'economic conditions are likely to warrant exceptionally low levels for the federal funds rate for an extended period'. In its most recent statement of August 9, 2011, the Fed quantified 'extended period' as 'at least upto mid-2013', thereby giving a more definitive timeframe for market participants to plan. The Fed evidently expects that by reducing uncertainty, at least in one dimension (time dimension), the forward guidance will help stimulate demand.

Giving forward guidance is not always necessarily a positive sum game. Central banks face several dilemmas. The first is how exactly is the conditionality surrounding the guidance to be worded. It cannot be so vague as to lose all content value; on the other hand, it cannot be so precise that the central bank becomes a prisoner of its words and loses any flexibility to deviate from the guidance should the underlying circumstances change. A second, and related, dilemma is how to ensure that the market correctly appreciates the conditionality and does not interpret the guidance as an irrevocable commitment.

Starting early 2010, in keeping with the best practice, the Reserve Bank too has begun giving forward guidance. And as expected, we too have confronted the classic communication dilemma. Let me illustrate. In the *First Quarter Review* of July 2011, we said:

> Going forward, the monetary policy stance will depend on the evolving inflation trajectory, which in turn, will be determined by trends in domestic growth and global commodity prices. A change in stance will be motivated by signs of a sustainable downturn in inflation.

Simultaneously, we also noted that the stance of monetary policy will be to 'manage the risk of growth falling significantly below trend'.

Reading the two statements together, some analysts have criticised the guidance for its lack of precision; more specifically, there were questions like, 'what is the trend growth rate' and 'how much deviation from trend would the RBI tolerate'. This was valid criticism and these questions were relevant. With our trend growth rate, post-crisis, estimated at 8 per cent, the balance of policy stance would shift if growth fell consistently and substantially below that rate. But a shift in stance will also be a function of the behaviour of the external and internal drivers of inflation. What we said in response to the criticism therefore was that defining precisely 'what significantly below trend' *ex-ante* was difficult, and that the ambiguity in the guidance was deliberate because it was unavoidable.

Central to this whole issue of forward guidance is that a central bank is handicapped by external uncertainty over which it has no control. The crisis has brought this dilemma into sharp focus. On the one hand, central banks want to use the instrumentality of forward guidance to manage expectations, and even outcomes; on the other hand, they cannot be precise enough because of external uncertainty. How to communicate monetary policy so that the benefit-cost balance is positive is yet another dilemma for central banks.

Should Monetary Policy Respond to Asset Prices?

Among the many questions thrown up by the crisis is one about the role of central banks in dealing with asset price bubbles. The broadly accepted theology before the crisis—although not the only view—was the Greenspan orthodoxy which can be summarised as follows. First, asset price bubbles are hard to identify in real time, and the fundamental factors that drive asset prices are not directly observable. A central bank should not therefore second guess the market. Second, monetary policy is too blunt an instrument to counteract asset price booms. And third, central banks can 'clean up the mess' after the bubble bursts. The surmise therefore was that the cost-benefit calculus of a more activist monetary stance of 'leaning against the wind' was clearly negative. In other words, it is not the job of central bankers to remove the punch bowl, no matter that the party is getting wild.

The crisis has dented the credibility of the Greenspan orthodoxy. The emerging view post-crisis is that central banks cannot remain indifferent to asset price bubbles. However, it has thrown up a debate over what should be the role of the central bank and how that role might affect its other responsibilities, and indeed its autonomy. The debate is still fluid and there are no conclusive answers. Nevertheless, it has helped in crystallising some views to guide the way forward. Let me discuss some of them.

As much as the pre-crisis orthodoxy about not deploying monetary policy in aid of asset price management has now lost its potency, reservations persist about its efficacy. The essence of the argument is that the typical monetary policy action of raising policy interest rate in small steps of 25-50 basis points will not help contain the surge in asset prices. On the other hand, monetary policy action aggressive enough to deter asset price buildup will take a heavy toll on the real economy. A consensus is building around the view that the most appropriate way of addressing asset prices is through macroprudential instruments, either independently or in conjunction with monetary policy. Indeed, macroprudential instruments are at the heart of the Basel III package which was agreed upon last year.

Macroprudential policies are neat in concept but throw up a host of problems in operation. The tools of macroprudential policy such as capital norms, countercyclical buffers and risk weights fall within the domain of regulation. But there also has to be consistency between the monetary stance and macroprudential policy. Does this then mean that the central bank should also have responsibility for bank regulation? If on the other hand, the responsibilities are distributed across different agencies, what should be the platform and protocol for coordination? What should be the role of the government?

Indeed, the post-crisis trend has been to entrust macroprudential supervision to central banks, and where central banks already have this responsibility, to define it more explicitly. While there could be some synergies in that, there are also questions about potential conflicts of interest such as when, for example, the macroeconomic situation may require a tight monetary policy, but the central bank may demur because such tightening may raise concerns about the stability of the banking system. Some people argue though that potential conflicts between monetary policy and macroprudential policy are being exaggerated. In entrusting responsibility for macroprudential supervision, and more broadly for financial stability, to central banks, there are concerns also about how this responsibility might impact the prized autonomy of central banks. This apprehension arises because macroprudential decisions entail a greater element of subjective judgement than do monetary policy decisions, and if that be the case, it opens up scope for interference from the outside.

My attempt as above has been only to give you a flavour of the many complex questions thrown up by this issue of central bank responsibility for asset price management, indeed more broadly for financial stability. The scope of this lecture does not permit a detailed assessment of the debate. But let me give you the Reserve Bank perspective on this.

The Reserve Bank has traditionally had a much broader mandate, including responsibility for some development functions, than is typical of advanced economy central banks. Our experience in regard to simultaneously managing both monetary policy and macroprudential policy has been positive, indeed synergistic. Asset price trends are one of the many variables we take into account in monetary policy calibration. We have used conventional monetary policy instruments such as policy interest rates if demand pressures are across board. On the other hand, if demand pressures are confined to specific sectors, we have found it more efficient to use macroprudential instruments such as risk weights and provisioning norms so as to put sand in the wheels of credit flowing to those sectors. We have also used macroprudential instruments symmetrically—tightening in times of excess demand as, for example, in the years before the crisis, and easing in times of slackening demand, for example, as part of the crisis response.

Even as macroprudential policies have become the talk of the town post-crisis, deploying them requires careful judgement. In order to make a judgement, a central bank has to ascertain if the asset price buildup is driven by 'excessive leverage' and if the price buildup is across board or confined to specific sectors. By far the most important thing to remember in deploying macroprudential policies is that, with the benefit of hindsight, all conservative policies look safe. But excessive conservatism in order to be prepared to ride out a potential crisis could thwart financial innovation and progress. It is this balance between preventing instability and promoting innovation that central banks have to learn to manage. And this is especially important in an emerging market economy like India where the responsibility of the central bank for market development, though not explicit, is nonetheless quite important.

How should Monetary Policy Manage the Interface with Fiscal Policy?

The 70 odd years since the Great Depression saw a famous rivalry between fiscal and monetary policies for influence. For much of this period, almost across the developed world, Keynesian theology ruled, fiscal policy dominated and monetary policy remained subservient to that. The stagflation of the 1970s, the influential monetarist views of Friedman *et al.* and the apparent success of supply-side policies to tame inflation prompted a shift in thinking away from full bodied Keynesianism. Also important were the theoretical analysis of discretion *versus* rules in setting monetary policy. Together, the theoretical advances and empirical evidence allowed monetary policy to wean itself away from fiscal dominance and central banks started asserting their autonomy.

Even as the advantages of having an apolitical monetary authority as an effective counterpoise to politically-driven fiscal policies were becoming evident, democratic compulsions made fiscal discipline increasingly difficult. To get around this, starting 1990s, several countries voluntarily enacted fiscal responsibility laws. The laws imposed limits on fiscal deficits/public debt on the one hand and prohibited primary financing of the fiscal deficit by the central bank on the other. This institutional framework allowed operational independence to the central bank in its conduct of monetary policy within a rule-based regime and was successful in keeping inflation low.

The rule-based fiscal regimes unravelled during the crisis as both governments and central banks implemented expansionary policies in close coordination. While such coordination during the crisis was not questioned except by extreme purists, now in the recovery period, several fundamental concerns are resurfacing. At the heart of these concerns is whether monetary policy is once again becoming hostage to fiscal compulsions? The specifics of the debate vary but the basic issues are similar. In the US, the debate is over the trade-off between short-term fiscal stimulus and long-term fiscal consolidation. In the Euro area, the question is about the shared benefits of a monetary union without the shared responsibilities of a fiscal union. The questions all around are: Are central banks being forced beyond their comfort zone to maintain expansionary monetary stances to compensate for fiscal laxity? Aren't the so called unconventional monetary actions thinly veiled fiscal measures? Aren't central banks, in the process, compromising their basic commitment to price stability? Are central banks becoming vulnerable to political pressures? Is their autonomy at risk? The answers to these questions will be shaped by how the current big issues are settled.

As in many economies, in India too, monetary policy was dominated by fiscal considerations during the 1970s and the 1980s. Large and growing fiscal deficits ended up being financed by the Reserve Bank. This led to more than desired growth in base money and money supply which ultimately reflected in high inflation. Like other economies, we too put in place a fiscal responsibility legislation—the Fiscal Responsibility and Budget Management (FRBM) Act, 2003—with ceilings on deficit and debt ratios and provisions prohibiting primary financing of government debt by the central bank. These provisions facilitated fiscal consolidation during 2003-2008 and afforded the Reserve Bank the necessary flexibility to implement monetary policy aimed at low and stable inflation.

Like elsewhere in the world, both monetary and fiscal policies were eased in India too in response to the crisis. In particular, this meant interrupting the fiscal consolidation process enjoined by the FRBM Act. As India emerged from the crisis, the Government adopted a revised roadmap for fiscal consolidation as recommended by the Thirteenth Finance Commission. Nevertheless, meeting the roadmap targets is going to be a formidable challenge. The quantum of non-discretionary expenditure (salaries, pensions, interest payments) is large and this cannot be adjusted easily, at any rate in the short term. By far the largest component of discretionary expenditure is on subsidies—on food, fertiliser and petroleum products. In reducing these subsidies, there is inevitably a tension between democratic compulsions and economic virtue. Even as the Government pursues a quantitative target, it also has to be mindful of the quality of fiscal adjustment—that is to prune unproductive expenditure and increase productive expenditure which is necessary for raising the potential output of the economy.

As I said, the Reserve Bank has been battling inflation for the last 20 months. Monetary tightening, as is well known, works by restraining demand. In as much as the fiscal stance is supportive of demand, the monetary stance has had to be more aggressive than otherwise. For monetary policy to be more supportive of growth, it will be necessary for fiscal consolidation to take root more firmly.

The dilemma for monetary policy in India is thus somewhat different from that of the advanced economies. The dilemma for advanced economy central banks is whether monetary policy is having to be kept more accommodative than necessary to offset fiscal contraction. In contrast, the dilemma for the Reserve Bank is whether monetary policy is having to be tightened that much more because of fiscal demand.

Conclusion

I have tried to present some of the dilemmas we confront in monetary policy management. All central banks confront these, with differences in the extent and timing. I have tried to give the Reserve Bank's perspective on these. The message I tried to convey is that there are no template answers to real life policy issues. Analysis is important, but judgement is crucial. I believe a two-way communication between central practitioners and central bank scholars will help in sharpening both our analysis and judgement.

Comments at the Stern School of Business, New York University, September 26, 2011.

19 Legislative Reforms

Strengthening Banking Sector[1]

Anand Sinha

Introduction

Empirical research shows that better developed financial systems accelerate economic growth and shrink income inequality by disproportionately increasing the earnings of lower income families[2] i.e., enabling growth with equity, which is so vital for our country. A well developed financial system will require sound legislative framework because legislation is the foundation on which institutional frameworks stand. To be effective, legislation not only needs to be unambiguous and fair but also should be robust enough to address all the existing concerns while, at the same time, being flexible enough to accommodate the new needs on account of evolving environment.

Role of legislation in the context of economic development in general and the financial sector in particular, is an interesting area of study. It has been argued that strong legal systems foster development of sophisticated financial markets and intermediaries,[3] which enhances the economy's ability to manage risk and eventually lead to economic growth. Measures such as robust contract enforcement and disclosure discipline go a long way in strengthening the financial systems.

Every legislation has a time dimension and its relevance has to be seen *vis-à-vis* this dimension. With the changing environment, practices

---

1. Inputs provided by P.R. Ravi Mohan, G.S. Hegde, Subrat Das and Smt Sadhana Varma are gratefully acknowledged.

2. Levine, Ross.

3. Levine, Ross (1999). "Law, Finance and Economic Growth", *Journal of Financial Intermediation* 8.

and processes change, necessitating a review of extant legislations. This holds all the more true for an area like financial system where changes are rapid and frequent. The dynamic nature of legislation was well articulated when Aristotle said 'Even when laws have been written down, they ought not always to remain unaltered'.

India is said to be one of the most over-legislated countries. We have numerous Acts and regulations, some of which date back to decades. As times have changed quite significantly since they were enacted, there is an emphatic need to update and fine tune them so as to enhance their relevance for the rapidly changing financial landscape. It is a welcome step that Financial Sector Legislative Reforms Commission (FSLRC) has been constituted to look into and revise the existing financial legislation. In this context, the role of this Congress is very important in facilitating deliberations.

Financial sector policies comprise a set of policies, such as:

- Prudential policies to ensure safety and soundness of the financial system (financial stability).
- Regulatory and supervisory policies.
- Depositor and consumer protection policies.
- Financial inclusion policies.
- Other policies for ensuring adequate supply of credit to economically important sectors i.e., SMEs, infrastructure, etc., and
- Market structure and competition.

Prudential policies comprise macroprudential and microprudential policies aimed at ensuring the safety and soundness of the financial system. Collectively, both macro- and microprudential policies ensure the stability of the financial system which would facilitate efficient allocation of resources to the real economy. While financial stability is a necessary condition to ensure other objectives of financial sector policies as well as for growth and macroeconomic stability, it is not a sufficient condition to attain these objectives. Other financial sector policies will have to be implemented for balancing numerous considerations such as growth imperatives, flow of credit to disadvantaged and preferred sectors, consumer protection, financial inclusion and equity, etc. At times, it becomes extremely challenging to balance these considerations and, if adequate care is not taken in designing and implementing the other financial sector policies, financial stability may be adversely affected. Therefore, it is important that a set of sound financial sector policies (including prudential policies) backed by sound legislation must be adopted to deliver the various objectives—growth with equity in the backdrop of financial stability.

Recent Amendments Carried to Various Financial Sector Laws

Before I delve into some of the key issues requiring legislative review, I list some of the enactments and amendments that have been made to the various Acts during the last decade to highlight the dynamic nature of legislation.

i. Reserve Bank of India Act, 1934 was amended in 2006 to provide legality to certain over-the-counter (OTC) derivative transactions and also to give explicit regulatory powers to Reserve Bank over derivatives and money market instruments.

ii. The Banking Regulation Act, 1949 was amended in 2007 for removing the lower limit prescribed in maintenance of statutory liquidity ratio (SLR) by banks and conferring wide powers on RBI in stipulating the SLR requirements for banks and to control liquidity in the market.

iii. The State Bank of India Act, 1955 was amended in 2007 for enabling transfer of ownership from RBI to Government of India and again in 2010 to provide for enhancement of capital, issue of preference shares, raise capital by public issue or preferential allotment or private placement or rights issue; and to issue bonus shares to the existing shareholders, etc.

iv. The State Bank of India (Subsidiary Banks) Act, 1959 was amended in 2007 to facilitate enhancement of capital, raise resources from the market and raise capital through rights issue.

v. The Banking Companies (Acquisition and Transfer of Undertakings) Acts, 1970 and 1980 were amended in 2006 to enable nationalised banks to issue preference shares in accordance with the guidelines framed by the Reserve Bank and to raise capital by preferential allotment or private placement or public issue, with the approval of the Reserve Bank.

vi. The Negotiable Instruments Act, 1881 was amended in 2002 to introduce the concepts of 'electronic cheque' and 'cheque truncation' by expanding the definition of 'cheque'.

vii. The Securities Contracts (Regulation) Amendment Act, 2007 was passed with a view to providing a legal framework for enabling listing and trading of securitised debt instruments, including mortgage-backed debt.

viii. The Government Securities Act, 2006 was enacted to consolidate and amend the laws relating to Government securities and its management by the RBI. The Act simplifies the procedure for settlement of claims of legal representatives, provides for admissibility of computerised information as evidence, contains provisions for effectively dealing with misuse of subsidiary general ledger (SGL) accounts and facilitates pledging and hypothecation of Government securities.

ix. The Payment and Settlement Systems Act, 2007 was enacted empowering the Reserve Bank to regulate and supervise payment and settlement systems of the country and provides a legal basis for multilateral netting and settlement finality.

x. The Prevention of Money Laundering Act, 2002 was enacted as a follow-up to UN General Assembly resolution in 1998, calling for adoption of national anti-money laundering legislations and programmes by member states. The Act provides for preventing money laundering and connected activities, enables confiscation of proceeds of crime, setting up of agencies and mechanisms for co-ordinating measures for combating money laundering, etc.

xi. The Foreign Contribution (Regulation) Act (FCRA), 2010 was enacted by repealing the erstwhile Foreign Contribution Regulation Act, 1976 mainly to rectify several deficiencies found in the previous Act. The new Act covers the electronic media and organisations, other than political parties, apart from entities in the prohibited list in FCRA, 1976.

xii. The Credit Information Companies (Regulation) Act, 2005 empowers the Reserve Bank to regulate the Credit Information Companies (CIC) and to facilitate efficient distribution of credit and matters concerned or incidental to it.

xiii. The Factoring Regulation Act, 2011 has been enacted to provide for and regulate assignment of receivables by making provisions for registration of assignment of receivables. The said Act codifies the rights and obligations of the parties to a contract for assignment. Further, Section 35 of the said Act read with the Schedule thereto, *inter alia*, amends the Indian Stamp Act, 1899 and provides for exemption to an agreement or other document for assignment of 'receivables' from liability to duty under the stamp law.

The Road Ahead: Legislative Reforms in the Banking Sector

Multiple Acts: Need for Consolidation

Banks are regulated and supervised under the Banking Regulation Act, 1949. Public sector banks (PSBs) *viz.*, State Bank of India (SBI), SBI subsidiary banks and nationalised banks which are constituted under different statutes are governed by their respective statutes and by some of the provisions of the Banking Regulation Act. The provisions relating to the ownership and management of banking companies as contained in the Banking Regulation Act are not applicable to the PSBs. Cooperative banks are constituted by the respective State Cooperative Societies Acts or by the Multi-State Cooperative Societies Act and the provisions of Banking Regulation Act are made applicable to them with certain modifications.

Since the origins of the banks have been historically different, they continue to be governed by the respective statutes as well as other general laws. Each of the statutes was crafted in a contemporaneous setting, reflecting the needs and concerns of the time. Therefore, almost all the statutes were amended from time to time to reflect changes in circumstances and context prevailing at that time.

There is a strong case for reviewing these legislations and recasting them for a number of reasons. First, prudential regulations are ownership neutral. However, the fact that different banks are governed by different laws has resulted in an uneven playing field which needs to be addressed. For example, while amendments were carried out to enable SBI, SBI subsidiary banks and nationalised banks to issue preference shares, though at different points of time, banks in private sector cannot issue preference shares as the amendments to the BR Act is still to be carried out. Similarly, while bilateral netting in the event of liquidation is admissible for private sector banks governed by the Companies Act and the normal bankruptcy laws, the position in this regard for PSBs, SBI and its subsidiaries is not clear in law, as liquidation, if at all, of such banks would be as per the notification to be issued by the Government in this regard. Second, a single, harmonised and uniform legislation applicable to all banks will provide transparency, comprehensiveness and clarity and provide ease of regulation and supervision to the Reserve Bank. Third, there is also a need to sort out the conflicts and overlaps between the primary laws governing the banking sector and other applicable laws. For example, the Competition Act, 2002 (as amended by the Competition (Amendment) Act, 2007) is in conflict with the provisions of the Banking Regulation Act, SBI Act and other statutes dealing with the amalgamation of banks. Consolidation of banking sector laws and laying down of common regulatory framework for commercial banks are issues requiring serious consideration.

Management of Banks

Management of banking institutions by 'fit' and 'proper' persons plays an important role in securing the safety of banks. While RBI has power, under certain circumstances, to remove the managerial and other persons from the banks and appoint additional directors, etc., these powers may not be effective in handling a situation where supersession of the Board is warranted. RBI, currently, does not have the power to supersede the Board of Directors of a banking company. In the Banking Laws Amendment Bill, 2011 amendments are being proposed for conferring such a power on RBI, for being used with appropriate safeguards. With respect to public sector banks, by way of amendments, similar powers have been vested in the Central government, which has the majority shareholding in those banks.

The shareholding pattern also plays a vital role with respect to the management of banks and, therefore, it is necessary that shareholders having sizeable holding should also be fit and proper. RBI has, by way of regulatory prescriptions, implemented an acknowledgement procedure. In the 2011 Bill, statutory provisions are being proposed for obtaining prior permission of RBI for acquiring 5 per cent or more of the equity shares or voting rights in a banking company. At present, a deadlock situation arises if a group of persons acquires sizeable equity or voting rights in a bank without following the acknowledgement procedure. There is no statutory power for directing disgorgement of shares and as such, if any such acquisition takes place, it may result only in contravention in provisions of BR Act. The main object of preventing the management of a bank from being captured by persons who are not fit and proper for holding such sizeable interest will not be achieved. RBI should, therefore, have the power to direct, by order, at any time that persons who are not fit and proper to hold such equity or voting power in contravention of these provisions, shall not have voting power. The 2011 Bill proposes to confer such power on RBI. This will help prevent unscrupulous persons from exercising control over banks.

Deposit Collection Activity

Currently, collection of deposits from members/shareholders is not treated as acceptance of public deposits. This is a matter of serious concern, particularly, with respect to cooperative societies. Deposits are accepted by enrolling members on tap and by collecting nominal amounts from them, exposing such depositors to serious risks. Banking Regulation Act does not apply to such cooperative societies and they are outside the regulatory purview of the Reserve Bank. It is necessary to plug this important loophole. Unless deposits are received from members who have voting rights, the deposits have to be treated as public deposits and the exemption from the provisions of Banking Regulation Act should not be made applicable. Every entity that accepts deposits from persons having no voting rights has to be treated as deposit accepting entity and should be regulated as such by RBI. RBI should have the discretion to determine the level and intensity of regulation and supervision depending upon the risk to the system from such entities.

Financial Conglomerates

In India, banks are entitled to carry on certain financial activities under the bank subsidiary model. Some banks have formed subsidiaries to carry on securities and insurance business. The performance of the subsidiaries affects the balance sheet of the bank. On account of varied activities carried on by the entities in the group which fall within the regulatory jurisdiction of multiple regulators, the risk to the system as a whole posed by such financial conglomerates is difficult to assess. These raise systemic issues and RBI as the regulator of banks needs to be empowered to obtain information, with respect to each of the entities functioning under the umbrella of a bank. The 2011 Bill proposes to confer such powers on RBI to get information with respect to such entities. This ought to be pursued in the new legislative framework also.

Non-Operative Bank Holding Company

The traditional theories of economies of scale and scope support bigger entities. In India, we need bigger banks to finance our very large infrastructure needs and also large industrial projects. Thus, while there are advantages in growing big and handling multiple activities, nobody knows where exactly the tipping point is, when the bigness of size starts becoming a disadvantage. The crisis has highlighted the downside of having 'too-big-to-fail' entities. Very big and complex entities pose supervisory issues to the regulators and pose serious systemic risks. So we need to ensure that structures are not complex and that there are effective resolution mechanisms to ensure orderly winding up of these systemically important entities, in case of crisis.

It has been suggested that a non-operative bank holding company structure may be useful to deal with financial conglomerates as this greatly mitigates the risks spilling over from other entities in the Group. While the functional regulator of each subsidiary of the non-operative holding company may regulate and supervise the business of the subsidiary concerned, the non-operative holding company needs to be regulated on the lines of a bank and needs to be placed under the regulatory and supervisory control of RBI. Appropriate legislative measures are necessary for operationalising this model.

Apart from the regulatory issues in the above model, there are other challenges to be addressed. One of them is related to placing public sector banks under such holding companies. Another is the impact of taxation on the transfer of shares of the subsidiaries to the holding company. Unless adequate tax relief is granted, it will be difficult for existing banks to come under the holding company structure.

Stamp Duty Issues

In India, there are certain issues with respect to stamp duty on documents. One of the major hurdles facing the development of the securitisation market is the stamp duty structure. It can add up to a substantial cost as there are differentiated duty structures in different states. While some states have recognised the special nature of securitisation transactions and reduced the stamp duties, other states still operate at stamp duties as high as 5 per cent to 12 per cent for transfer of secured receivables. It is significant to note that the recently enacted Factoring Regulation Act, 2011 makes specific amendments to the Indian Stamp Act, 1899 exempting factoring agreements, i.e., agreements for assignment of receivables, from paying duty under the stamp laws. Exemptions on similar lines for securitisation transactions would be advantageous.

Concerns about stamp duties have also been raised in the context of the proposed subsidiarisation of foreign banks. The broader objective of proposed subsidiarisation of foreign banks is to promote financial stability in India and this requires harmonisation and simplification of stamp duty structure across the country.

Minimum Capital Requirements

The minimum capital prescribed in the Banking Regulation Act for banks is too low and Reserve Bank is prescribing the minimum capital requirement in case of private sector banks from time to time (currently banks should have a minimum net worth of Rs 300 crore). Minimum capital requirements prescribed under the 'Ownership and Governance' guidelines and that prescribed/being prescribed for new banks in private sector are way above the current provisions of the Act. It would, therefore, be more appropriate to empower Reserve Bank to stipulate the capital requirements and other quantitative parameters from time to time, instead of prescribing quantitative limits in the respective Acts.

Migration to IFRS

As part of the efforts to ensure convergence of the Indian Accounting Standards (IAS) with the International Financial Reporting Standards (IFRS), the formats of financial statements will undergo changes consequent to the introduction of IFRS. Further, whenever banks introduce new types of capital instruments, etc., these will have to be appropriately incorporated in the format. Therefore, Reserve Bank should be empowered to prescribe the format of the balance sheet, profit and loss account, etc., given in Third Schedule of the BR Act.

Bilateral Netting Issues

Various banks had requested the RBI to allow bilateral netting of counterparty credit exposure, in respect of interest rate and foreign exchange derivatives, and gold. The legal position regarding bilateral netting is not unambiguously clear in case of banks established by special statutes [like SBI Act, Banking Companies (Acquisition and Transfer of Undertakings) Act, etc.]. Amendments to a large number of enactments particularly in a synchronised manner may be practically difficult. Enacting a single legislation which covers all aspects of banks' functioning, while possibly providing differential legislative framework for corporate governance issues on account of ownership differences may make the legislative framework more efficient.

Bank Resolution

The significance of effective resolution mechanism for promoting financial stability as well as consumer protection cannot be underestimated. The legal framework should address the resolution mechanism from a practical point of view and must have at least the following characteristics:

- early intervention before insolvency,
- speed of intervention/resolution,
- ability to transfer or merge operations,
- effective write-down of shareholders' rights and
- protection of ongoing business.

In addition to banks, the resolution mechanism should address resolution of other systemically important financial institutions (SIFIs) also. Post-crisis, globally, there have been initiatives to strengthen the resolution framework of financial market infrastructures (FMIs) and other entities in the financial sector. The resolution mechanism should also include a framework for resolution of NBFCs and entities operating payment systems. Swift and simple procedure for quick resolution, particularly, that of systemically important entities—global and domestic, is necessary. Under the evolving international framework, it would be required of jurisdictions to have adequate resolution framework as per international standards. The key attributes of Effective Resolution Regimes were adopted by the Financial Stability Board (FSB) Plenary and endorsed by G-20 leaders at the Cannes Summit and these are an essential component of the package of policies to reduce the risks of moral hazard and the potential for systemic disruption associated with SIFIs. This will require legislative changes and administrative actions.

The powers of RBI for effective resolution of regulated entities from this perspective need enhancement.

Mergers

Voluntary mergers and transfers help consolidation in financial sector and pave the way for stronger financial institutions to rescue the weaker ones. Such voluntary measures, while saving the constituents of weaker institutions, provide business opportunity to the stronger ones to spread their presence in different geographies. The BR Act empowers RBI to sanction a scheme for voluntary amalgamation of banking companies. However, such a power is not available with respect to cooperative banks. Considering the challenges faced in quick resolution of failed cooperative banks, certain enabling provisions in the BR Act facilitating RBI to sanction a scheme for takeover of banking assets and liabilities of a cooperative bank by commercial banks would be desirable. Partial merger of certain businesses or assets and liabilities of banks also may need to be examined.

One of the issues that could complicate the resolution of banks through mergers and transfers due to the sensitivity of the process is the applicability of Competition Law. An enterprise proposing to enter into a combination via a merger or an amalgamation is required to notify the Competition Commission, and the Commission has been allowed up to 210 days to decide on it before the default clause kicks in. The 2011 Bill tries to address this issue.

Consumer Protection and Globally Compatible Secrecy Laws

For speedy redressal of consumer grievances, RBI has framed the Banking Ombudsman Scheme by statutory directions under the BR Act. The scheme is working satisfactorily.

Secrecy of customer information is a principle of common law which is practiced in India also by banks, and recognised by courts. Statutory basis for this has to be provided, by clearly setting forth the exceptions relevant to the present requirement of preventing money laundering and cross-border financing of undesirable activities. The law should strike a balance between the privacy rights of the customer and the need to share crucial information with law enforcement agencies and other regulators, both domestic and foreign. In matters of crime and proceeds of crime, the larger public interest would outweigh the private interests of individuals. Appropriate amendments may have to be carried out in the BR Act to provide a statutory backing for the banking secrecy laws and the limits on the privacy of customers should be laid down.

Protection is required in the law to the regulators with respect to the information collected from the regulated entities including its assessment and analysis made by the regulators or supervisors and the correspondence related to such information.

In larger public interest, the law should enable sharing of information with other regulators, both domestic and overseas, for mutual benefit. The recent crisis has demonstrated the need for such cooperation. The absence of specific protection to the information held by the regulators whether collected from the regulated entities or from other regulators impedes sharing of information. Our laws have to be globally compatible and specific exemption from disclosure needs to be provided in this regard. Disclosure of sensitive information could compromise the effectiveness of regulation and supervision. Further, unless the secrecy laws in our jurisdiction are compatible with global standards, it will not be possible to receive from, or share information with, overseas regulators. Appropriate provisions may have to be inserted in the RBI Act and the BR Act in this regard.

Conclusion

Financial sector is a very important segment of the economy and has direct bearing on growth and prosperity. Strong financial systems need strong legal systems which provide unambiguous and fair legislation. The financial system in India including banking, insurance, capital, taxation, etc., has many regulators, each having a separate mandate. This blend raises pertinent concerns. First, financial system is still characterised by considerable fragmentation of legislation, regulation and enforcement. Second, policy related frictions might arise from the diversity of different legislations and the overlapping of the regulatory jurisdictions. Third, there might be a risk of legal arbitrage among financial jurisdictions.

A need has been continuously felt to rewrite and streamline the financial sector laws, rules and regulations and to bring them in harmony with the requirements of India's fast growing financial sector. The current legislations were drafted in the contemporaneous setting and have had to be amended from time to time to incorporate changes in the milieu. Enacting new law or amending old law is a continuous process to remain aligned to changing circumstances. In the emerging scenario, the task of preventing financial risks has become more important and challenging. Amid global economic worries, this is an enormous task which, on completion, would immensely benefit the financial sector in India and economy at large. A sound legal framework may help deter imprudent risk-taking by financial institutions and reduce systemic risks. Revision of banking sector laws should also be motivated by the recognition that the banking sector has been and remains a critical factor not only for accelerating India's growth but also for making it inclusive. Harmonising of financial sector legislations, rules and regulations has, therefore, become imperative.

Address at Financial Planning Congress'11 organised by Financial Planning Standards Board of India, Mumbai, December 18, 2011.

20 Towards Rapid, Sustainable and Inclusive Growth

Challenge of the Future

Manmohan Singh

The year that has just ended was a very difficult year for the world. Economic crises, socioeconomic tensions, political upheavals in many developing countries and political deadlock in some of the developed countries, all cast their shadow on 2011. A 'revolution of rising expectations', fostered by the extraordinary reach of the electronic media and the connectivity provided by new social networking platforms, has kept Governments around the world on their toes.

We in India have had our share of problems.

The Indian economy slowed down and inflation edged up. Concern about corruption moved to the centre stage.

We must not be too downcast at these events. All countries and economies go through cycles. We must remember that downturns are followed by upturns. Indeed, they are often a test of our ability to respond to new challenges.

The task before us is clear. We must address the new concerns that have arisen while remaining steadfast in our commitment to put the nation on a development path which ensures rapid, inclusive and sustainable growth. I want to assure you all on this New Year's day that I personally will work to provide an honest and more efficient government, a more productive, competitive and robust economy and a more equitable and just social and political order.

I believe we have made more progress than is commonly realised. I am personally delighted that the Government was able to introduce the Food Security Bill and the Lokpal and Lokayukta Bill in parliament. The

Lokpal and Lokayukta Bill was passed by the Lok Sabha. It is unfortunate that the Bill could not be passed in the Rajya Sabha. However, our Government is committed to the enactment of an effective Lokpal Act. Taken together with the Right to Information Act, the National Rural Employment Guarantee Act and the Right to Education Act, these are legislative legacies that generations of Indians will come to value, appreciate and benefit from.

On this New Year's Day I do not wish to dwell on the year gone by. Instead, I would like to focus instead on the challenges of the future, so that we can all work together to overcome them.

Our biggest challenge today remains that of banishing poverty, ignorance and disease. Simultaneously, we must work to build an India that holds the promise of prosperity to the many millions of our people who are just beginning to emerge out of poverty. We must remain focussed on this fundamental task in the Twelfth Plan period which begins in 2012-2013.

Five Key Challenges

As I look ahead I see five key challenges facing the nation. To meet these challenges we need the concerted efforts of the Central government, the state governments, political parties and indeed all concerned citizens.

Challenge of Livelihood Security

First, there is the urgent challenge of eradicating poverty, hunger and illiteracy and providing gainful employment to all. I call this the challenge of livelihood security.

There are many steps we need to take to address this challenge and of these, the most important is to empower every citizen with the light of education. I say this with the deepest conviction because I know what education did for me.

I was born into a family of modest means, in a village without a doctor or a teacher, no hospital, no school, no electricity. I had to walk miles every day to go to school, but I persevered and was fortunate to be able to secure a high school education, and then go on to higher education.

It is this access to education that transformed my life and gave me new opportunities which others with my background could not dream of.

I firmly believe that educating our children, providing them with employable skills, while also ensuring their good health, must be our first and primary task. There is no better investment we can make in the future—the future of our children, of our families, of our communities, and of our nation.

Along with education and affordable health care, we must also generate a growth process that can provide gainful employment to all. This is the only way that we can wipe out poverty in a sustainable fashion.

However, since many elements of this strategy will take time to bear full fruit, we must in the meantime pay urgent attention to the needs of those who need immediate support. It is for this reason that the government has taken steps to provide minimum employment and access to food to those who need it most.

I believe that the initiatives we have taken to invest in education and health, provide an employment guarantee and also provide food security, constitute a robust response to the challenge of providing greater livelihood security for our people.

Challenge of Economic Security

The second challenge that demands our attention is economic security. Economic security comes from having an economy that can produce the material output required to achieve desired consumption levels for the people and one that can generate the productive jobs needed to satisfy the aspirations of the workforce. To reach this level we will have to ensure rapid growth accompanied by adequate job creation. Rapid growth is also necessary to generate the revenues we need to finance our livelihood security programmes.

The process of economic reforms was initiated in the mid-1980s and accelerated the 1990s precisely to accelerate our growth potential. Because of our democratic system, the reforms were introduced gradually to begin with, in order to garner broad-based support. That we succeeded in this objective is evident from the fact that successive governments of different political complexions at the Centre, and many governments belonging to different political parties in the states, have more or less pushed in the same direction. However, this gradualist pace also meant that the full effects of the reforms took time to have effect.

Yet the fruits of this effort have been amply evident in the past several years. The average growth rate of the economy was around 4 per cent per year before the 1980s. It increased to an average of about 8 per cent since 2004.

Although we have every reason to be satisfied with this performance, it would be wrong to conclude that India is now unshakeably set on a process of rapid growth. Our growth potential is indeed established. But there are many challenges we have to face if we want to maintain this growth in the years ahead, as indeed we must.

To achieve sustained rapid growth we need to do more than halt the current slowdown though that is certainly the first step. We need to usher in a second agricultural revolution to ensure sufficient growth in rural incomes. We also need to usher in the many reforms needed to trigger rapid industrialisation and to build the infrastructure which such industrialisation needs.

Rapid growth will also bring structural change, notably in the rate of urbanisation. Our urban population is expected to grow from 380 million at present to 600 million by 2030. We must be able to provide productive jobs in the non-agricultural sector for this expanding urban population and we must also be able to expand our urban infrastructure to deal with the expected expansion of the urban population.

In 1991 when we liberated our economy from the shackles of the Licence Permit Raj, our main objective was to liberate the creativity of everyone of our citizens from the deadweight of bureaucracy and corruption. Today's youth, born in the 1980s and later, would have no memory of the kind of corruption that the regime of controls and permits had created. To get a railway ticket or a telephone connection you had to bribe someone. To buy a scooter you had to bribe someone to jump the queue!

However, even as the creative energies of our people have been unleashed and old forms of corruption have vanished, new forms of corruption have emerged which need to be tackled. Elimination of corruption is critical to support genuine entrepreneurship. It is also the demand of the ordinary citizen who encounters corruption all too often in everyday transactions with those in authority. This is a serious problem that calls for a multidimensional response.

New institutions such as the Lokpal and the Lokayuktas are an important part of the solution and we have initiated the process for establishing them. But this is only one part of the solution. We also need reforms in systems of government which would increase transparency and minimise discretion so that the scope of misgovernance is reduced. We have taken several steps in this regard. We have introduced in Parliament a Bill on Citizen's Charters which will empower citizens to demand services at appropriate standards from government departments. We have introduced a Bill on Judicial Accountability.

These initiatives will take time to have their full effect and we must therefore be patient. But I do believe they are transformational initiatives, which will be recognised as such a few years down the line.

A critical element in ensuring economic security and prosperity is the need for fiscal stability. India has paid a heavy price in the past for fiscal profligacy. Many of us can recall the dark days of 1990-91 when we had to go around the world begging for aid. Fortunately we were able to overcome the problem fairly quickly and for most of the past two decades we have been able to hold our head high, because we have managed our fiscal resources well. We must ensure that the country does not go down that road once again.

I am concerned about fiscal stability in future because our fiscal deficit has worsened in the past three years. This is mainly because we took a conscious decision to allow a larger fiscal deficit in 2009-10 in order to counter the global slowdown. That was the right policy at the time. But like other countries that resorted to this strategy, we have run out of fiscal space and must once again begin the process of fiscal consolidation. This is important to ensure that our growth process is not jeopardised and, equally important, our national sovereignty and self-respect are not endangered.

The most important step for restoring fiscal stability in the medium term is the Goods and Services Tax. This would modernise our indirect tax system, increase economic efficiency and also increase total revenues. Another important step is the phased reduction in subsidies. Some subsidies, such as food subsidies are justifiable on social grounds and are expected to expand once the Food Security Bill becomes operational. But there are other subsidies that are not and these must be contained.

Some of the reforms needed for economic security attract controversy and cause nervousness. This is understandable, but we should learn from our past experience with reforms. Things that we take for granted today caused similar controversy 20 years ago. We should remember that change is necessary for development and while we must anticipate change, and even protect the most vulnerable from ill-effects, we should not lock ourselves into a blind refusal to contemplate change. If we have confidence in ourselves, we will be able to meet any challenge.

Challenge of Energy Security

The third challenge we face, is the challenge of energy security. Energy is an essential for development because higher levels of production inevitably involve larger energy use. Our per capita energy levels are so low that we need, and must plan for, a substantial growth in energy availability.

The energy security challenge is particularly great for India because we are trying to develop in an environment in which our domestic energy resources are limited and the world is transiting to a period when energy is likely to be scarce and energy prices are expected to be high.

As a first step, we must ensure effective utilisation of all available domestic energy resources. Unfortunately, our attempt to tap both old and new sources of energy is being threatened by a range of problems. Be it coal or hydro power, oil or nuclear power, we find new challenges that have to be overcome to develop these resources to the fullest extent possible. We must re-examine all domestic constraints on such development to see how they can be overcome.

The domestic agenda for energy security is clear. We need new investment in established sources of energy such as coal, oil, gas, hydro electricity and nuclear power. We also need investment in new sources of energy, like solar and wind. Parallel with expanding domestic supplies, we need to promote energy efficiency to contain the growth of energy associated with rapid growth.

Both goals of expanding new investment and achieving energy efficiency require a more rational pricing policy, aligning India's energy prices with global prices. This cannot be done immediately, but we need to outline a phased programme for such adjustment and then work to develop support for making the transition. I realise that this will not be easy, but unless we can achieve this transition we will not be able to promote energy efficiency as much as we should, and we will certainly not be able to attract enough investment to expand domestic energy supplies.

Energy security also has a global dimension. Even with the best domestic effort our dependence on imported energy is expected to increase. We need assured access to imported energy supplies and also access to new energy related technologies. This means we need sensible policies that can promote economic partnership with countries that have energy resources and technologies. We also need a proactive foreign policy, protecting our access to such resources and to foreign technology.

Challenge of Ecological Security

A fourth important challenge we face in the years ahead is the challenge of ecological security. Economic growth is essential for the well-being of our people, but we cannot allow growth to be pursued in a manner which damages our environment. We owe it to future generations to ensure that the environment they inherit from us is at least as capable of providing economic security for them as the one we inherited from our parents.

We cannot allow the waters of our rivers to be polluted by untreated effluent and sewage. Yet this is happening today because of weak regulation and lack of enforcement over industry and the cities. Similarly, we cannot allow air pollution to proceed unabated promoting respiratory diseases which impose a heavy burden on large numbers of our people especially the poor.

Ecological security also involves protection of our forests which play a critical role not only in absorbing carbon emissions but also in providing us with water security. Forests help reduce water run-off and siltation and increase water retention in the ground, recharging our underground acquifers. Some forest land often has to be surrendered to allow the exploitation of natural resources including energy and mineral resources and hydroelectric potential. This must be done in a manner which minimises the extent of surrender and also provides sufficient compensatory afforestation to ensure ecological security to the nation.

All these problems can be solved and have been solved in other countries. It requires stronger and more transparent regulation and it also involves extra costs. These costs must be borne by those who pollute and this principle must be well understood and strictly enforced.

Looking beyond the immediate ecological issues, there is the larger challenge of climate change. As responsible citizens of the world we must pursue a pattern of development which reduces greenhouse gas emissions per unit of our GDP by about 20-25 per cent by 2020 as our contribution to global ecological security. This objective is closely linked to the pursuit of rational energy policies mentioned earlier.

Challenge of National Security

Finally, and most importantly, our vibrant democracy faces threats to internal and external security which together can be viewed as the challenge of national security.

Despite grave provocations from extremists and terrorists, the people of India have remained united. They have not lost faith in our plural, secular and inclusive democracy. Across the world people look to India for inspiration. Our model of inclusive growth in an open society inspires those who seek freedom from tyranny.

A new wave of democracy demanding the empowerment of ordinary people is sweeping the world and India stands tall as a functioning democracy. We are a nation of over a billion people, plural, secular, democratic—with all the great religions of the world freely practiced here, with so many languages and cuisines, so many castes and communities—living together in an open society. This is an achievement for which every Indian can be proud.

The world acknowledges this achievement. I do believe that the world wants India to succeed because India offers hope.

Our democracy has its faults, but our people are aware of them and have shown their ability to correct these faults.

Often democracy can be frustrating—both to those who are in government and to those who expect it to be more efficient, effective and humane. But our democracy is our strength. It is the basis of our unity. It is also the most important guarantor of internal security.

Equally important for our national security is the modernisation of our defence forces. Indeed, India's economic and energy security also require this. Our Army, our Navy and our Air Force require modernisation and upgradation of personnel and systems. Ensuring this will remain my most important task as Prime Minister.

Today I have shared my thoughts with you to make you understand the nature of the challenges we face entering a new year.

Thus, I have identified five key challenges facing us. These will be on top of our policy agenda this year—livelihood security (education, food, health and employment), economic security, energy security, ecological security and national security.

In addressing each of these five challenges we must work together as a nation, while working with like-minded nations around the world.

I assure you that I will work with all the energy at my command to ensure that we meet each of these challenges and overcome them.

Let us stand united as a people in overcoming these challenges.

Prime Minister's New Year Message to the Nation, December 31, 2011.

Index

A

B

H

I

R

S

T